NORSE DISCOVERIES
AND EXPLORATIONS
IN AMERICA
982-1362

Leif Erikson to the Kensington Stone

by

HJALMAR R. HOLAND

DOVER PUBLICATIONS, INC.
NEW YORK

This Dover edition, first published in 1969, is an unabridged republication of the work originally published in 1940 under the title *Westward from Vinland: An Account of Norse Explorations and Discoveries in America, 982-1362*. It is reprinted by special arrangement with Duell, Sloan & Pearce (an affiliate of Meredith Publishing Company), publisher of the original edition.

Library of Congress Catalog Card Number: 68-14764

Manufactured in the United States of America
Dover Publications, Inc.
180 Varick Street
New York, N. Y. 10014

INTRODUCTION

PERHAPS the most dramatic series of events in the history of man is the discovery and settlement of the western hemisphere. Before that time for many millenniums empires and republics rose and fell, and man was very busy subduing the earth. But it was an activity which was confined to but one side of the earth—the other remained in hiding like the dark side of the moon.

To learn what lay beyond the setting sun has always appealed to men. At first they only dreamed of it as a place of perpetual bliss—the abode of the meritorious dead. But then with more indomitable energy, little by little, they pushed over the edge of the disc, through mist, storm and apprehension, until they discovered a new world. Then they found that the dreams of their ancestors were not without foundation, for there in the West lay the most bountiful region of all.

It is the purpose of this volume to record some of the earlier steps in the conquests of the West. For four centuries this continent has been known as America, but for an even longer period before that time it was known (at least in part) as Vinland (Wineland)—a name more suggestively characteristic of its good qualities. Many previous writers have told the story of the push westward to Vinland, and told it deservingly, for most of them have had the creative pleasure of adding something new to our history. Animated by a similar hope, the present writer has endeavored to present evidence that far back in pre-Columbian days there was a further exploration westward *from* Vinland—an undertaking prompted, not by greed of gold, but born of brotherly love and the hope of saving human souls.

The Norse discovery of America some centuries before

Columbus is now generally admitted to be a fact. But this early discovery is commonly looked upon as an isolated incident which was soon forgotten. Therefore, when the claim is made that Norse explorers penetrated to the very center of the North American continent one hundred and thirty years before Columbus sighted San Salvador, such an assertion will naturally be met with the greatest skepticism.

Such a documented claim has come, not out of the musty archives of foreign libraries, but out of our own wilderness, engraved in ancient characters upon a stone found wrapped in the roots of a forest tree. The question of the authenticity of this extraordinary inscription—The Kensington Stone—has been subjected to a searching inquiry by hundreds of people more or less competent to discuss it; and many able scholars—historians, runologists, linguists, and geologists—have presented arguments for or against the authenticity of the inscription. A number of old Scandinavian weapons of the late Middle Ages which challenge the attention of the antiquarian have also been unearthed in the same region where the runic stone was found.

Inasmuch as this stone was under my immediate observation for several years, I became fascinated with its inscription. Its archaic symbols and dramatic narrative have been my absorbing study for more than thirty years and have led me to make several trips abroad for research in most of the libraries and museums of northern Europe.

In 1932 the essential results of this prolonged and meticulous investigation were presented in a small volume entitled *The Kensington Stone* which was privately published. Since then so much new and confirmatory evidence has come to light, that the present volume is not merely a second edition of the former, but a new book. For this reason I have given it a new name—*Westward from Vinland*.

HJALMAR R. HOLAND.

Cedar Hill, Ephraim, Wis.

CONTENTS

PART ONE

WESTWARD TO VINLAND

PART TWO

WESTWARD FROM VINLAND

CONTENTS

PART THREE

APPENDIX

ILLUSTRATIONS

FIGURES

PART ONE
WESTWARD TO VINLAND

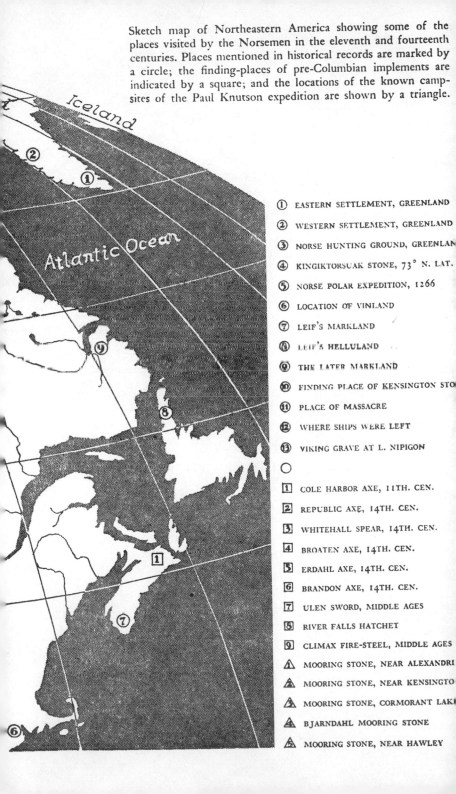

Sketch map of Northeastern America showing some of the places visited by the Norsemen in the eleventh and fourteenth centuries. Places mentioned in historical records are marked by a circle; the finding-places of pre-Columbian implements are indicated by a square; and the locations of the known camp-sites of the Paul Knutson expedition are shown by a triangle.

① EASTERN SETTLEMENT, GREENLAND

② WESTERN SETTLEMENT, GREENLAND

③ NORSE HUNTING GROUND, GREENLAN

④ KINGIKTORSUAK STONE, 73° N. LAT.

⑤ NORSE POLAR EXPEDITION, 1266

⑥ LOCATION OF VINLAND

⑦ LEIF'S MARKLAND

⑧ LEIF'S HELLULAND

⑨ THE LATER MARKLAND

⑩ FINDING PLACE OF KENSINGTON STO

⑪ PLACE OF MASSACRE

⑫ WHERE SHIPS WERE LEFT

⑬ VIKING GRAVE AT L. NIPIGON

○

1 COLE HARBOR AXE, 11TH. CEN.

2 REPUBLIC AXE, 14TH. CEN.

3 WHITEHALL SPEAR, 14TH. CEN.

4 BROATEN AXE, 14TH. CEN.

5 ERDAHL AXE, 14TH. CEN.

6 BRANDON AXE, 14TH. CEN.

7 ULEN SWORD, MIDDLE AGES

8 RIVER FALLS HATCHET

9 CLIMAX FIRE-STEEL, MIDDLE AGES

△ MOORING STONE, NEAR ALEXANDRI

△ MOORING STONE, NEAR KENSINGTO

△ MOORING STONE, CORMORANT LAK

△ BJARNDAHL MOORING STONE

△ MOORING STONE, NEAR HAWLEY

I. THE FIRST TRANSATLANTIC EXPLORER

IN one of the vessels conveying the first company of white pioneers bound for the western hemisphere, there was a Norseman from the Hebrides who in the height of a roaring tempest composed a poem that has lived to the present day. This is the first stanza:

> Almighty God, to whom alone
> The hearts of all thy saints are known,
> Sinless and just, to Thee I pray
> To guide me on my dangerous way:
> Lord of the heavens that roof the land,
> Hold o'er me Thy protecting hand.[1]

There were twenty-five vessels in the company and almost half of them perished. The rest of them proceeded warily, for this was in the year 986, when sailing vessels were small and without any nautical instruments to help in guiding the course. Still worse was the fear of the unknown dangers which unfamiliarity with this distant ocean had created: fabulous monsters of the sea who could reach up a mighty arm and drag the vessel beneath the deep; crashing tidal waves that towered like mountains over the small open boats; and—worst of all—the great, black abyss somewhere beyond into which all the waters of the sea plunged with no backward motion. A century later, Adam of Bremen, a learned scholar, wrote thus of the terrifying danger of this abyss:

This was lately tested by the most enterprising Harald, prince of the Norwegians, who, when investigating with his

[1] Translated by G. M. Gathorne-Hardy in his *Norse Discoverers of America*, Oxford, 1921, p. 25.

ships the breadth of the northern ocean, hardly escaped with safety from the awful gulf of the abyss by turning back when at length the bounds of the earth where it ends grew dark before his eyes.[2]

The leader of this first company of pioneers who charted the trail to the West was Erik Thorwaldson, also known as Erik the Red, who was the first man authentically known to have set foot on the western hemisphere. He has been described by many commentators as a troublesome fellow, a brawler who could not live in peace with his neighbors, and who was banished from his own country because of murder. To be sure, there are incidents in his life which may prompt a reader to make this judgment, but such incidents are not always good evidence. They may mean much or little. *Njal's Saga*, one of the world's great epics, deals principally with the life and character of two men who were so irreproachably peaceful and temperate in their dealings with their fellow men that their patience and gentleness stand out in strong relief against the pugnacious attitude of their age. Yet, through no volition of their own, they became involved in so many feuds that scores of men came to a violent end through them. There is, therefore, a possibility that Erik Thorwaldson has been judged too harshly.

He was born about the year 955,[3] and was descended from a prosperous family of large landowners in Jaeren, a district in the extreme southwestern part of Norway. But evil days had overtaken the family, and about 978 his father, Thorwald, emigrated to Iceland with his family. This was upwards of a hundred years after Iceland had

---

[2] *Gesta Hammaburgensis*, Ch. IV, p. 38.

[3] In *Floamanna Saga*, Chapter 15, it is recorded that Thorgils Orrabeinsfostre, its great hero, met Erik Thorwaldson at the court of Haakon Jarl who was then ruler of Norway. This was in 977 (see *Grønlands Historiske Mindesmærker*, II, 32-33). They spent the winter together at the court and became bosom friends. Thorgils was then twenty-one years old, and apparently the two young men were of approximately the same age. This indicates that Erik was born about the year 955.

been settled, and all the good land had been taken up. They were therefore compelled to settle in a desolate spot in the extreme northwestern corner of Iceland. Here old Thorwald eventually died. Dissatisfied with the loneliness and limited opportunities of his surroundings, Erik moved south to Haukedal, in a more favored part of the island. Here he was married and obtained a tract of wild land on which he built a small house and began to clear land.

But bad luck still pursued him. He had a few slaves and, by accident or in mischief, they one day caused a small landslide to hurtle down and destroy some of the buildings of a farmer in the valley below. Terror-stricken, the slaves fled, but were discovered and killed by Eyolf Saur, a relative of the farmer whose buildings were damaged. Erik felt aggrieved at the loss of his slaves and went to Eyolf to ask for compensation. A quarrel followed and Eyolf was killed. Shortly afterward Erik was challenged by a professional avenger of wrongs by the name of Ravn, probably at the instigation of Eyolf's relatives, and Erik also killed Ravn. The matter was then brought before the district court by Eyolf's relatives. As Erik was a stranger without influential friends to back him up, he had little chance to win and was outlawed. He lost his slaves, his farm, and his liberty to live in the district.

However, he still had his vessel, and he took his family and sailed out upon Broadfjord where he took possession of some desert islands which lay in another district. These islands had practically no tillable land, and for a few years Erik had only temporary habitations on different islands. In the meantime, he loaned the posts of his highseat to Thorgest, a large landowner on the mainland who was married to a daughter of Thord Gellir, one of the most important chiefs of Iceland at that time. These posts, called *setstokkar*, were ornamented pillars at the back and on each side of the highseat, and among the ancient Norsemen were considered sacred to the family's guardian spirit. For this reason we see many of the earliest land-seekers in

Iceland, as they approached their destination, bind their *setstokkar* together and throw them into the sea so that their guardian spirit would choose their place of settlement for them. Erik's pillars were probably brought from the old family hall in Norway, and were therefore a precious heirloom to him.

Eventually he found a place where he decided to build his house and went to Thorgest to get his pillars, but Thorgest refused to give them up. He had not been able to resist the temptation to build them into his house, perhaps thinking that Erik would not return, and to pull them out now would invite ridicule. Why bother to pay any attention to this penniless newcomer who moreover had been outlawed in his own district?

But this was too flagrant an act to escape censure. Many men sided with the stranger, Erik, and urged him to go to Thorgest and take his pillars by force. This was, in fact, the only course open to Erik if he did not wish to be branded a coward. Accompanied by some supporters, he therefore went to the house of Thorgest and took his pillars by force. They were pursued by a band of Thorgest's men, and a fight resulted in which Thorgest's two sons and some other men were killed. After this skirmish both parties were joined by many supporters, and it looked as if the conflict would assume serious dimensions. This was checked, however, by the case being brought before the district court. After much argument, back and forth, it was decided that Thorgest had suffered a greater loss than was his due under the circumstances, and Erik was declared an outlaw for three years.

Yielding to the decision of the court, most of the supporters of Erik sheathed their swords and went home. But not so with Thorgest. He did not have the forbearance to let his defeated enemy depart on his banishment exile, but gathered a large band of men with whom he rushed about from island to island to slay Erik. But the latter's friends did not entirely desert him. While some of them brought him to a safe hiding place and kept him guarded, others hastened to put his vessel in order and to provide him with supplies for a long cruise. After some days Erik and his family went on board and sailed away.

Up to this time Erik's stay in Iceland had been marked by misfortune and embarrassing situations which largely were brought about by circumstances that were thrust upon him. The incidents mentioned therefore throw no other light on his character or ideals than that he was a brave man not afraid to defend what he thought were his rights even against great odds. But when he left Iceland behind and sailed out on the open sea, he was freed from all these entanglements and could plan his course in life according to his own nature. To the east lay the populous countries of Europe with the sea lanes crowded with merchant vessels. This must have presented an excellent opportunity to recoup his losses and satisfy his alleged tendency toward pugnacity, for it was in the height of the Viking Age when piracy was looked upon as quite a proper occupation for gentlemen of temporary leisure, and Erik had his own vessel and nothing to detain him.

But Erik did not choose this common way of rehabilitating himself. Instead of east, he turned west into a sea that no man before him had willingly steered his vessel into. About a hundred years before this time a kinsman of Erik named Gunbjörn had been driven by storms far west from Iceland and came upon some islands which were called Gunbjörn's Skerries after him. It was to discover and explore these islands that Erik sailed west. This act of Erik is hardly in keeping with what we would expect from a man of brawl and bloodshed, brooding over real or imaginary wrongs. Rather it suggests the curiosity of the man of vision eager to extend the known boundaries of the earth.

This was no new idea in Erik's mind, for the discoverer of Iceland was also a kinsman of Erik, being a brother of one of his paternal ancestors in a direct line.[4] This man, Naddod by name, discovered Iceland about 865, and, curious to learn what he could about it, he had sailed completely around it. Circumstances prevented him from settling on the land he had found, but twenty thousand other men and women in the meantime had settled there and created a colony famous for its independence, prosperity and the excellent qualities of its people. To Erik this discovery of his ancient kinsman must have been a proud memory which prompted him to deeds in the same direction.

He sailed westward and eventually reached the stern and glaciated coast of Greenland. Here he found many islands, but they were all naked and uninhabitable. This was disappointing, but he did not turn back. Instead he followed the forbidding ramparts of Greenland toward the southwest looking for habitable land, but in vain, for there is none fit for white man's occupancy on the entire east coast. Finally, after having passed five hundred miles of the inhospitable coast, he came to Cape Farewell, the southernmost point of Greenland. Then he turned westward, and in the present district of Julianehaab he found the land deeply indented by fjords, some of which were a hundred miles long. Here he spent the winter as the sea froze up. For three years he continued his explorations, going almost a thousand miles northward to learn the extent and nature of his new land. Professor Andrew Fossum believes, with much justification, that Erik also crossed Davis Strait to Baffin Land.[5] How he managed to conquer all the many difficulties which he must have met with in these sub-arctic waters of fog, drift-ice, hidden shoals and violent storms will always remain a mystery.

But with amazing resourcefulness he pushed on in his

[4] The line is as follows: Erik was the son of Thorwald, the son of Oswald, the son of Ulf, the son of Oxen-Thore who was a brother of Naddod who discovered Iceland.

[5] *The Norse Discovery of America*, 1918, pp. 46-50.

small vessel without a deck and with no compass to guide him and explored both the eastern and western coasts of Greenland—a feat which was not repeated for more than eight hundred years afterward. He asked no king or corporation for aid, and he found his provisions in the waters that surrounded him. He was accompanied by his wife and one or two children still in babyhood and a few other men. Six hundred years later when the Danish government endeavored to rediscover Greenland, it took about a hundred years with many well-fitted expeditions before as much was discovered as Erik visited on his one journey. Frithiof Nansen, who was one of the world's greatest explorers, says that Erik on this journey proved himself to be one of the boldest and most resourceful navigators of all times.

Erik's discovery of Greenland took place in the year 982, and this is the first authentic date in American history. Like the West Indies, Greenland is a part of the western hemisphere and it lies just as close to the American mainland as do most of these islands upon the discovery of which the fame of Columbus is founded.

After Erik had made his extensive explorations up and down the coast, he found that the most promising place for settlement was at the head of the long fjords about a hundred miles northwest of Cape Farewell. Here was pasture land in abundance covered with rich grass. Plenty of fuel was also present in the form of large tracts of birch and willow of which many trees had big trunks, although the trees were seldom more than ten feet high. The rushing streams were filled with salmon, the waters of the fjord abounded in cod, bass and other fish, seals, walruses and wild ducks; while on land were reindeer, polar bears, rabbits, grouse and other game birds. To him these verdant green fields, seen against the background of the great glaciers, seemed far more green than the volcanic soil of Iceland, most of which is scarred by the eruptions of lava and gneiss. Because of this, and prompted by the loving pride of his own discovery, he called this new land Greenland. He selected a spot for his home near the inner end of a long fjord which he called Eriksfjord (now Tunugdliarfik). Here he built his home which he called *Brattahlid*, i.e., the steep slope. This *Brattahlid* became a famous place as it continued to be the home of the chief or principal official of Greenland for more than four hundred years. Here, a thousand miles of stormy seas beyond the western frontier of civilization, Erik made his home. The foundations of the buildings may still be seen.[6]

Erik's three years of banishment were now ended, and being well satisfied with the land he had discovered, he returned to Iceland to seek fellow colonists. He was received with much honor when he arrived there and reported his discoveries. But his old enemy, Thorgest, was implacable and challenged him to a duel. In this duel Erik was wounded, whereupon Thorgest felt that his honor was vindicated and they were reconciled. Erik proved to be as competent as a colonizer as he had been as an explorer, for when he departed for Greenland the next year, 986, he led a fleet of twenty-five vessels filled with colonists.[7]

In indomitable enterprise and persuasive salesmanship Erik may well be called the first American, for although he was taking them to a land they had never heard of before, over an ocean whose evil repute they knew only too well, they were eager to go. From this it appears that Erik must have had a personality that inspired confidence and respect. In view of the adverse circumstances that attended this enterprise and the limited area from which the colonists were drawn, this was an emigration of exceedingly large dimensions. Unfortunately a great storm was encountered on the voyage and many vessels foundered as mentioned in the beginning of this chapter. Only fourteen vessels survived this storm and reached Greenland. Here

[6] See Poul Nörlund and Maarten Stenberger, *Brattahlid* in *Meddelelser om Grönland*, Copenhagen, 1934, Vol. 88, 1-161.

[7] Another account says that the fleet consisted of thirty-five vessels.

they founded a colony which soon numbered approximately three thousand people and survived for four hundred and fifty years. It was divided into two parts. The principal settlement, which was in the region selected by Erik, was known as the Eastern Settlement. The other part lay about three hundred miles farther northwest in the present Godthaab District and was known as the Western Settlement.

These two districts comprised a republic of the simplest kind, a commonwealth not based on inherited prerogative, wealth or strong arm usurpation, but founded entirely on mutual respect. As such it continued for several hundred years. Of taxes there were none except the Peter's Pence that went to the Pope in faraway Rome. Disputes were usually settled by recourse to a simplified code of the laws of the fatherland. While money was recognized as a medium of exchange, it was little used as there were no salaried officials or servants, and trade was carried on by barter or the exchange of services. Erik Thorwaldson was the generous and respected chief of this primitively idyllic state and ruled it wisely, for there is no hint of dissension during the twenty years of his over-lordship. By his own industry he gained the mastery over his savage surroundings and wrung an ample living from a barren soil. He built a commodious home where he almost every winter hospitably entertained visitors from abroad. He died about the year 1005.

II. A GLIMPSE OF THE AMERICAN MAINLAND

JOHN FISKE in his admirable work, *The Discovery of America*, makes the following apt remark: "When once the Northmen had found their way to Cape Farewell, it would have been marvellous if such active sailors could long have avoided stumbling upon the continent of North America." This expectation we see fulfilled the very year (986) when Erik Thorwaldson led the first company of settlers to Greenland.

In this company of pioneers who emigrated with Erik was a man named Herjulf Bardson. He took land at Herjulfsness [1] in the southernmost part just west of Cape Farewell. He had a capable son by the name of Bjarne (Herjulfson) who since his youth had been engaged in commerce at sea in his own vessel. It was Bjarne's custom to spend every alternate winter with his father. In the late summer of the year in which Herjulf had departed for Greenland, Bjarne returned to Iceland and was much surprised to learn of the mass emigration. However, he determined to spend the winter with his father as usual, and after obtaining what sailing directions he could, he set sail for Greenland. The following translation of the saga narrative of his journey is so terse and vivid that it is better than a synopsis.

Bjarne was much concerned at the news, and would not discharge his cargo. His men thereupon asked him what he meant to do; he replied that he meant to keep to his custom of passing the winter with his parents, "And I will," said he, "take my ship on to Greenland, if you will accompany me."

---

[1] The missionary station of Frederiksdal was later located there.

They all said that they would abide by his decision; upon which Bjarne remarked, "Our voyage will be considered rash, since none of us have been in Greenland waters." Notwithstanding this they put to sea as soon as they were ready, and they sailed for three days before the land was laid; but then the fair wind ceased, and north winds and fogs came on, and they did not know where they were going, and this went on for many days. After this they saw the sun, and so were able to get their bearings, whereupon they hoisted sail, and after sailing that day they saw land, and they discussed among themselves what land this could be, but Bjarne said he fancied that it could not be Greenland. They asked him whether he would sail to this land or not. "I am for sailing in close to the land," he said, and on doing so they soon saw that the land was without mountains, well timbered, and there were small knolls on it, whereupon they left the land on the port side, and let the sheet turn towards it.

Then after sailing two days they saw another land. They asked Bjarne if he thought this was Greenland; he said that he did not think this was Greenland any more than the first place, "For it is said that there are very large glaciers in Greenland." They soon neared this land, and saw that it was a flat country and covered with timber. At this point the fair wind dropped, whereupon the crew suggested that they should land there: but Bjarne would not. They considered that they were short both of wood and water. "You are in no want of either," said Bjarne, but he got some abuse for this from his crew.

He ordered them to hoist sail, which was done, and they turned the bows from the land, and sailed out to sea for three days before a south-westerly breeze, when they saw the third land: now this land was high and mountainous, with ice upon it. So they asked if Bjarne would put in there, but he said that he would not, since—as he put it—this land appeared to him to be good for nothing. Then without lowering sail they kept on their course along the coast, and saw that it was an island. Once more they turned the bows away from the land, and held out to sea with the same breeze; but the wind increased, so that Bjarne told them to reef, and not crowd more sail than the ship and rigging could stand. They now sailed for four days, when they saw the fourth land. Then they asked Bjarne if he thought this was Greenland, or not. Bjarne replied, "This is most like what was told me of Greenland, and here we will keep our course towards the land." So they did, and that evening they came to land under a cape, which had a boat on it, and there on that cape lived Herjulf, Bjarne's father, and it is from him that the cape received its name, and has since been called Herjulfsness.

Bjarne now went to his father, and gave up voyaging, and he was with his parents as long as Herjulf was alive, and afterwards he succeeded his parents, and lived there.[2]

There are three theories concerning Bjarne's voyage. One is that the first and second lands seen by him were parts of the Labrador coast. Another is that the first land was the Cape Cod Peninsula, the second Nova Scotia, and the third Newfoundland. The third theory is that the whole narrative is a piece of fiction.

The first theory (most fully presented by A. W. Brögger)[3] has much to commend it because a comparatively short drift southward is more probable than a long one. But the description of the lands seen by Bjarne cannot be made to fit any part of the Labrador coast. The narrative states that the first land was "without mountains, well timbered and with small knolls on it." The second is described as a "flat country covered with woods." No such low-timbered shores are visible to a seafarer passing along the shore of Labrador. While there is considerable timber many miles inland along the deep fjords, the coast front has none, and the narrative states definitely that Bjarne did not linger to explore the inlets. Furthermore, it is not a low, flat country but a high, mountainous one. The following description is from *Encyclopaedia Britannica:*

As a permanent abode of civilized man, Labrador is on the whole one of the most uninviting regions on the face of the earth. The Atlantic coast is the edge of a vast solitude of rocky

[2] *Flateyjarbok*, I, 430-432, Kristiania edition of 1860.
[3] *Vinlandsferdene*, Oslo, 1937, pp. 68-80.

hills, split and blasted by frosts and beaten by the waves. . . .
Dark and yellow headlands towering over the water are ever
in sight, some grim and naked, others clad in the pale green of
mosses and dwarf shrubbery. With miles on miles of rocky
precipices alternate lengthened sea slopes, tame and monotonous, or fantastic and picturesque in form, with stony vales
winding away among the blue hills of the interior. . . . It is
only in the interior valleys, at some distance from the coast
that any extent of forest appears. . . . Though Labrador is
detached from Arctic lands, and though much of it lies between the same parallels of latitude as Great Britain, the climate is rigorous in the extreme, owing mainly to the ice-laden
Arctic current which washes its shores. Snow lies from September and October till June. In winter the whole coast is
blockaded by ice fields drifting from Baffin's Bay and other
outlets of the Arctic Ocean; while in summer icebergs,
stranded or floating, impart a stern grandeur to the frowning
shores. At Nain the mean annual temperature is 22.52° Fahr-
enheit, at Okkaak 27.86° and at Hopedale 27.82°. (This is
much too cold for forest vegetation.)

With this picture before us, it appears that Bjarne's first
two lands are not to be found in Labrador. Moreover, the
sailing directions do not fit this theory. Erik had spent a
year in Iceland while enlisting emigrants for his colonization project, and during that time had told much about
Greenland which became generally known.[4] Before de-
parting from Iceland Bjarne had gathered enough of this
information about Greenland so that he was able to recognize it when he finally came to it. Among the things
that Erik would have stressed for the guidance of his
fellow colonists in the event that the fleet became separated on the voyage, was the fact that the region selected
for the colony lay on the southwestern coast of Greenland. With this knowledge Bjarne would not be looking
for a land with a north-eastern front. We therefore read

[4] The discovery of a new land to which no less than twenty-five ship-
loads of colonists had emigrated in a body must have been such a unique
piece of news that everyone would be talking about it.

that he sailed away from the new lands (which fronted east) without landing. He "left the land on the port side, and let the sheet turn towards it." With the wind from the southwest and the sail in this position, he could not have followed the coast of Labrador which runs northwest, even if he had seen it, but would have sailed obliquely away from it in a northeasterly direction.

The principal reason why Brögger takes Bjarne up along the Labrador coast is the statement in the narrative that Bjarne saw a glacier (*jokull*) when he came to the third land. As the first glacier along the Atlantic coast is on Baffin Land, Brögger identifies this as the third land. But as Bjarne's description of the two lands which he saw previously cannot with the most generous interpretation be made applicable to the Labrador coast, we will for a few moments postpone the consideration of the glacier and consider the alternate route.

According to the narrative, Bjarne after three days' sailing from Iceland was driven far south for many days by a northerly wind. This was so far south that it took him nine days' steady sailing with a good wind to sail back to Greenland in a northeasterly direction. As Mr. Gathorne-Hardy says, "The whole point of giving the direction of the wind is to supply an indication of the course." With the standard speed of 150 nautical miles per *dægr*, this amounts to 1,350 miles.[5] This does not include the distance traveled in sailing around an island which is mentioned. Assuming that this is Newfoundland, 265 miles must be added for its length, making a total of 1,615 miles, which is the approximate distance southwest of Greenland where Bjarne sighted his first land.

A distance of 1,600 miles southwest of Greenland by

[5] The distances are given in nautical miles throughout the chapter. *Dægr* is often translated by the word *day* with which it sometimes, but not always, agrees. *Dag* (day) is masculine while *dægr* is neuter and is most often used in speaking of a unit of distance equal to 75 or 150 miles according to local usage. *Cf.* Vigfusson's *Icelandic Dictionary*.

the shortest water route brings us to the vicinity of the Cape Cod Peninsula. Here Bjarne found a land "not mountainous, well wooded, and with small knolls upon it." This is about as good a description of the Nantucket and Cape Cod vicinity including the sand dunes, before the timber was cut, as could be given in so few words.

From here Bjarne sailed for two *dægr* or 300 miles in a northeasterly direction when he came to "a flat country covered with timber." 300 miles northeastward from the Cape Cod vicinity brings us to Cape Sable, the southernmost point of Nova Scotia or a little beyond, and here again we find that Bjarne's description is very fitting.

Bjarne then sailed for three *dægr* or 450 miles until a new land opposed his course. Unlike the other lands, it was high and mountainous. He spent some time in following its shore and finally discovered it was an island. Finding that the land was desolate and uninviting, he then continued on his northeast course until he reached Greenland.

The third land was evidently Newfoundland. 450 miles from Cape Sable in Nova Scotia in a northeasterly direction brings us to Newfoundland with a few miles to spare, the distance to the Burin Peninsula being 430 miles. As Bjarne had now traveled northward for a long distance, the possibility would present itself to him that this might be Greenland. Not being interested in a coast facing east, he would sail westward around Cape Roy and then northward to Cape Norman. He would then discover that this was an island. The whole western shore of Newfoundland is flanked by a mountain chain called the Long Range, and although the island has been settled for 400 years, this western shore is still for the most part a bleak wilderness. Bjarne's description of the land that it was high and mountainous and "good for nothing" is therefore very fitting.

It was on this island—the third land—that Bjarne is said to have seen a *jokull*, or glacier. But, according to Vigfusson, *jokull* has several other meanings. It is used in the meaning of ice generally, also icicles and drift ice. It is also used in the meaning of icebergs which are called *fall-jöklar*. It is probable that Bjarne, on arriving at the Strait of Belle Isle where icebergs are so common, had seen a stranded *fall-jokull*, perhaps miles wide, and mentioned it, and that some later copyist misread the passage. With so many possible meanings and the impossibility of verifying the original reading, this reference is useless in identifying the land mentioned.

It now remains to consider briefly the objection that Bjarne's narrative is a piece of fiction.

In this narrative, written hundreds of years before there were any maps or other descriptions of the American seaboard, we find an accurate mention as far as it goes of the lay of the land, its various projecting land-forms, the almost precise distances between them, and a brief topographical description of each. There is no imaginative fiction about all this; it is a clear and concise statement of existing facts and conditions. It is not only excellent proof of the early discovery of America, but it shows that someone must have sailed this route and observed the things that are here recorded. This being granted, there is no good reason for doubting that his name was Bjarne Herjulfson.

One of the objections against the reliability of the narrative is that Bjarne is not elsewhere mentioned! This is true, but Bjarne does not stand quite as isolated as the objection implies. We find the name of his father and mother and other ancestors given in *Landnama*, the highly respected roll of honor of all the original settlers in Iceland. This was compiled by the eminent historian, Ari the Learned, born in 1067. It therefore seems entirely credible that they had a son by the name of Bjarne, a good sailor, but otherwise an ordinary person who quite involuntarily played a part in a matter of later interest and then retired from the world's stage.

Another objection is the complaint that he showed no

curiosity concerning the new lands he had seen. But there is nothing strange about this. His business was to find Greenland—a place he had never seen—and the season was getting very late. It is doubtful if he had any time for exploring. He had lost many weeks on this far-flung journey, and he was anxious to save his vessel and his crew before winter shut him out of the Greenland harbors where the ice forms early. He therefore showed good judgment in availing himself of favorable winds and refusing to be diverted from his main purpose so late in the season.

Bjarne has also been censured and even ridiculed on the alleged ground that he did not mention his discovery of new lands for fifteen years. This silence is purely hypothetical and probably not true. At this time Greenland had only few settlers. Bjarne lived far from the other settlers, close to the southern extremity of Greenland, and it was more than a hundred-mile journey to the inner end of Eriksfjord, where Erik Thorwaldson lived, which was the most thickly settled part of the colony. Bjarne therefore had little opportunity to talk with other settlers, although we may assume that he occasionally did. It is reasonable to assume that at such times he told what he knew of these unknown islands that he had seen, which was not much as he had only seen them from afar. As John Fiske says, "In the dense geographical ignorance of those times there is no reason why his discoveries should have aroused any speculation." Gathorne-Hardy aptly remarks that "the battered and storm-tossed remnant who successfully accomplished the emigration to Erik's new colony had little motive, in Bjarne's bald description . . . to induce them to tempt Providence again." [6]

A further complaint is that it would have been quite impossible for Bjarne to sail from Newfoundland to Greenland in four days.

[6] *The Norse Discoverers of America*. See his excellent comments on Bjarne's voyage on pp. 114-117, 244-251.

This objection is without any basis. The standard length of a *dægr* sail was 150 miles, or 600 for four days. The distance from Cape Norman in Newfoundland to Herjulfsness in Greenland is 580 miles and comes within that standard. Sometimes that speed was greatly exceeded, as when Thorarin Nevjolfson sailed from Möre in Norway to Eyrarbakke in Iceland in four days. The distance is more than 750 miles. Under similarly favorable circumstances it would therefore be possible to sail from any part of Newfoundland's northeastern coast to Greenland in four days.

Still another objection is that it is absurd to think that Bjarne would be able to sail straight to his father's house when he knew nothing about the country nor had any knowledge about his father's place of settlement.

If Bjarne had sailed from Baffin Land to Greenland, this criticism would be justified for he would then have skirted the entire length of the settlement, more than a hundred miles, before reaching his father's house. But to Bjarne coming from the south, the situation is quite different. Greenland has a narrow front toward the south and Bjarne's first sight of land in coming from that direction would be the high mountain, Cape Farewell, off the extreme southern point of Greenland toward which he would steer. Just a short distance west or rather northwest of Cape Farewell was his father's homestead, the southernmost of all the settlers in Greenland. Moreover, his house stood on a ness or point of land out by the sea in plain sight of the seafarers that passed outside. As Bjarne was approaching Greenland from the south looking for human habitations, it is natural that he would land at this first homestead to inquire for his father's settlement.

There remains the question of whether it is conceivable that Bjarne could have drifted as far south as the forty-second parallel. This is very far, but such a long drift is by no means unique in the voyages of those times. Just a few years later Thorstein Erikson left Greenland for Vinland with a picked company. They never caught sight of the American mainland, but were driven by storms to Iceland, then to Ireland and then over unknown wastes of water for many weeks until they, the first week in winter, found themselves up in the Western Settlement of Greenland, about 300 miles northwest of where they started from. Several well known characters in Icelandic history are reported to have had similar experiences. Among them are Ari Marson, Björn Asbrandson, and Gudleif Gudlaugson who severally drifted to even more southerly points in America. These men were all well known historical characters whose adventures are told in *Landnamabok* and *Eyrbyggjasaga*.

All in all, the picture we have of this forthright sailor and the journey, so full of sailors' idioms, are sketched in such a concise yet comprehensive manner that they are good evidence of the truth of the story, and indicate that it has suffered less garbling by later copyists than have other reports of the discovery.

III. LEIF ERIKSON DISCOVERS VINLAND

FOR the next dozen years after they arrived in Greenland, the colonists were busy in getting their homes established. As Greenland was barren of timber suitable for building purposes, it was necessary to build their houses, barns, and fences of stone and turf which with the quarrying and transportation was slow and hard work. As feed and shelter had to be provided for their stock, it is likely that few cattle were brought on their first voyage. This necessitated many voyages back and forth to Iceland. In the meantime they lived almost entirely on fish and game for cereals do not ripen in Greenland. Very few colonies have been started under more adverse conditions than this one in Greenland.

Even with all diligence in hunting and fishing, there were many things that had to be imported, particularly lumber for roofs, furniture, ship repairs and tools. The nearest known place to get lumber was Norway on the other side of the Atlantic. With walrus tusks, eider down, reindeer hides, and polar bear skins as purchasing media, considerable commerce was carried on with Norway.

In 999 Erik's son Leif made a journey to Norway by which he gained much fame. Up to this time no one had attempted to make a direct passage from Greenland to Norway. With the small open boats which were then in use and with no instruments whatever with which to guide their course, this was considered too risky, the distance being very nearly the same as from Newfoundland to Ireland. It was therefore customary to go by way of Iceland which cut the open sea journey in two. But Leif Erikson was a venturesome young man, and on this journey he chose to sail directly to Norway. He reached it safely and thereby set a new record in ocean navigation.

Leif Erikson at this time could have been only nineteen years of age. It is known from *Floamanna Saga* (see *ante*, p. 4) that his father spent the winter of 977-78 as a guest at Haakon Jarl's Court. The earliest date for Erik's emigration to Iceland is therefore 978. He spent some time, perhaps only one winter, at Hornstrandene in the extreme northwestern corner of Iceland where his father, Thorwald, died. He then moved south to Haukedal where he was married in 979 at the very earliest. Leif, his oldest son, could not therefore have been born before 980. If he seems rather young to have undertaken such a transatlantic voyage, it must be remembered that men matured much earlier a thousand years ago than they do now. Early Norwegian history mentions numerous heroic exploits achieved by boys only twelve to fifteen years old.

At that time Olaf Trygveson was king of Norway. He was a tremendously energetic and athletic man—a veritable Achilles of the Middle Ages. On hearing of this new achievement in navigation, he sent for Leif Erikson and, finding that he had a pleasing personality, he made him a *hirdmann* or member of the King's bodyguard. Leif was the guest of the King during the following winter.

King Olaf, besides being a great lover of physical sports, had another interest of even greater importance. He had been a great warrior who threatened to tear the kingdom of England to shreds, but in the midst of it he became a proselyte of Christianity. Full of ardor for the new faith, he now became an equally determined crusader who devoted all his time to forcing his Norwegian subjects to accept Christianity. During the winter Leif was baptized, and in the spring King Olaf commissioned him to return to Greenland to establish Christianity there. Leif was provided with priests, whereupon he set sail for Greenland and reached it safely.

The mandate that had been given to Leif was a difficult one to fulfill, as the King well knew. For many years King

Olaf had endeavored to introduce Christianity in Norway, and although he had had an executioner by his side and was followed by an army, he had made but poor progress. But Leif was remarkably successful in his work. He accomplished it without violence and with enduring success. So tactful and persuasive seems to have been his conduct that he everywhere made openings for the priests who accompanied him. He required neither army nor executioner. As a missionary Leif Erikson deserves a high place. His mother, Thjodhild, built the first church in the new world. It was known as Thjodhild's church.

It is likely that Leif while on one of these missionary journeys came to Herjulfsness and heard from Bjarne Herjulfson the story of the timbered lands he had seen some fifteen years earlier. To Leif with his broader vision and daring initiative this narrative must have been electrifying. Greenland was not a bad land in some respects, but it was bleak and treeless, the production base of all the icebergs in the northern seas. In contrast to this, Bjarne told of a land covered with green forests somewhere in the southwest. What great possibilities did not this vision hold? This new land must be explored. He forthwith bought Bjarne's bigger vessel and hired a crew of thirty-five men, among whom no doubt he had some of Bjarne's men. Most important of all, he would get from Bjarne as detailed a record as possible of the latter's courses and sailing directions to the unknown lands. The success of Leif's enterprise depended on his knowledge of these things.

The Saga mentions that Leif first sailed to the land that Bjarne had last seen, and there he found a land of no value. "It was like one flat rock right up to the glaciers," and he therefore called the land Helluland or Flat Rock Land.

It has been shown in the preceding chapter that Bjarne's last land was northern Newfoundland, and Leif presumably landed somewhere in the vicinity. Nevertheless many commentators have assumed that Helluland was somewhere on Baffin Land because of this mention of glaciers. This is erroneous because it is nowhere stated that Helluland lay northwest of the settled part of Greenland. On the contrary, whenever the location of Helluland is mentioned, it is always said to lie south or southwest of Greenland. In an early geographical treatise said to be the work of Abbott Nicolas of Thingeyre or Tverå who died in 1159, we read the following: "South from Greenland is Helluland; next to it is Markland; then it is not far to Vinland," etc.[1] There are several fourteenth and fifteenth century statements to the same effect.

In *Gripla*, a geographical treatise, it is stated that opposite Greenland lies Furdustrands, "where there is so hard frost that the land is not, as far as is known, inhabited." This cautious statement is quite true because Northern Labrador and Baffin Land are pre-eminently such lands of frost that they are only visited by nomadic Eskimo. Then it continues: "South of this land is Helluland which is called Skællingeland, and from there it is not far to Vinland."[2] According to this, Helluland lay southwest from Greenland.

In Örvar-Odd's Saga it is also told that Helluland lies southwest of Greenland. While this saga is a medieval work of fiction, the writer would naturally conform to the geographical conceptions of his times, just as do modern fiction writers, otherwise their readers would judge them ignorant of well known facts.

In agreement with this conception, we read in Hauksbook that Thorfin Karlsefni sailed from the Western Settlement of Greenland with a northerly wind whereupon he reached Helluland which also shows that Helluland lay southwest of Greenland.

Finally Leif's temperament and known skill as a navigator are helpful in determining the location of his Hellu-

[1] *Grönlands Historiske Mindesmærker*, III, 220; *Alfrædi Islenzk*, Copenhagen, 1908, p. 12.
[2] Björn Jonsson's *Grönlands Annaler*, in *Grönlands Historiske Mindesmærker*, III, 224.

land. Even if we assume for the sake of argument that Bjarne's third land were Baffin Land, it seems certain that Leif as an experienced navigator would not go a thousand miles out of his way to Baffin Land. The geographical area between Newfoundland, Baffin Land and Leif's home in Greenland comprises a large triangle which approaches the equilateral in form. If Leif went to Baffin Land on his way to the south, he would be going around two sides of this triangle, thus doubling the length and hazards of his journey. The man who only a couple of years before had boldly traced a new and direct course across the broad Atlantic would not be so helpless. He was not interested in seeing a glacier in Baffin Land—his objective was the timbered lands that Bjarne had seen farther south, and he would know how to cut corners. The most reasonable conclusion, therefore, is that Leif's Helluland was Newfoundland or a neighboring part of Labrador.

Following Bjarne's course in reversed order, Leif after some days reached the second land, which was "low-lying and wooded with stretches of white sand." Leif said: "This land shall be called Markland [Forestland] after its resources." His landing place was probably not far from the place seen by Bjarne near the southern end of Nova Scotia. The explorer, Henry Hudson, thus describes this part of Nova Scotia: "The land by the water side is low land, and white sandy banks rising, full of little hills."

Then they sailed away with a northeasterly wind for two days before they again sighted land. They came to an island lying north of a cape or long point. After having landed on the island they sailed south of it and westward past the cape until they came to the mouth of a river which issued out of a lake. When the tide came in they sailed up the river and into the lake and, finding the country pleasing, they erected sheds for temporary habitations. It was not long before they decided to spend the winter there, and they then built large houses.

The place they had come to seemed very pleasant. They

caught salmon in the river and lake, and it seemed to them that cattle would be able to feed themselves all winter for there was no frost and the grass did not wither much. Day and night were more equally divided than in Greenland and they found that the sun was already up at their *dagmal* (breakfast time) and had not set when they ate their *eyktmal* (afternoon meal).

We now come to the most interesting episode in their journey, and this will be told in a literal translation of the saga narrative:

But when they had completed their house building, then Leif said to his men: "Now we shall divide our company in two parts and explore the vicinity. Half of the men shall remain here [to watch over the buildings] and the other half shall explore the country, going no further than they can return by nightfall, and they must not separate." And this they did for some time, Leif sometimes going with the explorers and sometimes staying at home. Leif was big and strong and the most noble-looking of men. He was intelligent and in all respects a most capable commander.

One evening it was found that a man was missing. It was Tyrk, the southerner. Leif was much distressed to learn this as Tyrk had long been with him and his father and had been very fond of Leif as a child. Leif therefore severely reprimanded the men and made ready to go to look for him with twelve men. But they had gone only a short distance when they met Tyrk and were very glad to see him. Leif saw at once that Tyrk was in high spirits. He was a small and insignificant man but a good craftsman. He had a projecting forehead and restless eyes.

Then Leif said: "Why are you so late in coming home, foster-father, and why did you separate from the others?"

Tyrk for a long time spoke in German, rolled his eyes and made many grimaces, but they could not understand him. Then he spoke in Norse and said: "I did not go much farther than you, but I found something new to report. I found grapevines and grapes!"

"Can that be possible, foster-father?" exclaimed Leif.

"It certainly is true," answered Tyrk, "for I was born where there was no scarcity of grapevines or grapes."

They now went to bed for the night, but in the morning Leif spoke to his men: "We shall now get busy with two occupations and we shall take alternate days for each. [One shall be] to pick grapes or cut vines and [the other] to cut logs for our cargo when we return home." This plan was followed and it is said that their stern boat was filled with grapes. They also cut the logs.

And when spring came they made ready and sailed away with a favorable wind. And Leif named the land after its special product and called it Vinland.[3]

It is commonly said that Leif Erikson discovered America in the year 1000, but this is inaccurate. It is based on an incidental mention of the discovery of America, by a writer of about 1200 (later borrowed by Hauk Erlendson), in which the fact of the discovery is summarized in a sentence or two. There are several reasons why Leif did not discover Vinland on his return voyage from Norway to Greenland in the year 1000, but only one needs to be mentioned. This is the observation concerning the height of the sun on the shortest day in the year (see Chapter V, Section 3). This is considered by all commentators to be the most significant information we have about the location of Vinland, and all are agreed that Leif made it. But if so he must have been in Vinland at least as late as December 21st. In such case he could not have returned to Greenland in the fall of 1000 as is claimed by those who believe he discovered America in that year. Moreover, his return is said to have been so early in fall that a shipwrecked crew of men and women whom he rescued on the same voyage from a bare rock off the Greenland coast are said not to have suffered from the cold.[4]

<hr />

[3] *Flateyjarbok*, pp. 539-540, Christiania, 1860.

[4] The captain of this vessel was a Norwegian by the name of Thore, and his wife who accompanied him is said to be named Gudrid. This has caused much confusion among commentators because they have assumed that this Gudrid was the same as the one who shortly after-

In order to determine the date of Leif's discovery it is necessary to turn to the Flateybook where his activities at this time are mentioned with all necessary detail. He returned to Greenland in the summer of the year 1000 and immediately set to work to introduce Christianity. He could not have set out for Vinland in 1001, partly because his missionary campaign needed his presence, and partly because Bjarne, whose vessel he bought for his Vinland voyage, had that year gone to Norway. Bjarne returned in 1002, but too late for Leif to get started that year. The year 1003 is therefore the earliest possible time for Leif's expedition.

There are indications which point to the probability that Leif planned to become the first white settler of the great land he had discovered. When he departed from Vinland he did not dismantle his buildings and take the logs with him, although by so doing he could have taken a larger cargo, the logs being dry. They would moreover have been ready for erection in Greenland. The most probable reason for leaving them behind is that he planned to return and occupy them. But the winter after his return from Vinland his father died. Leif had taken five of the shipwrecked people as his guests for the winter which with

ward married Leif's brother Thorstein. In that case there would be a glaring discrepancy in the two accounts concerning one of the principal characters in the discovery. But the explanation is not difficult. We know from the detailed account in Hauksbook that Gudrid Torbjörn's daughter arrived at Herjulfsness while still unmarried and shortly afterward married Thorstein Erikson. As she became the ancestress of several bishops and other prominent men including Hauk Erlandson, the editor of the saga, this family record is no doubt reliable. But Gudrid was a very common name, and we know from Gisle Surson's Saga that another Gudrid, the daughter of one Ingjald in Iceland, went to Norway where she married and about this time came to Greenland. (See *Grönlands Historiske Mindesmærker*, I, 796; II, 585.) This is the Gudrid, married to the Norwegian Thore, whom Leif saved. But one of the Flateybook copyists, misled by the name like his later learned commentators, has aided the confusion when in mentioning Thorstein's marriage to Gudrid he added the explanatory remark: "who was previously married to the Norwegian Thore as stated above." If this intrusive "explanation" is eliminated, the discrepancy is removed.

Erik's large household made quite a congestion. A contagious disease broke out and many of them died. Leif thereupon had to take up the duties of the colony's supervision and there were many things to do. Christianity in Greenland was still in its infancy, churches had to be built, and new laws debated and adopted.

But in spite of these many new obligations, Leif appears still to have looked upon Vinland as his future home. When his brothers and other travelers came and asked him for his houses, he always replied, "No, I will not give them to you, but you can use them." In his quiet hours he no doubt often dreamed of the green, tall timber of Vinland where the climate was mild and grapes grew wild, and where the brown soil was deep and warm for planting and seeding.

There has been some question about who really discovered America—whether it was Bjarne Herjulfson who first saw it, or Leif Erikson who first landed on its shores. But this is immaterial. Neither action was of importance unless it was accompanied by the vision of new values. Herein lies the difference between these two men. To Bjarne this new land was just a body of dead matter. He had *seen* something new, but he had *discovered* nothing because he lacked the understanding of what he had seen. But to Leif the vision of Vinland meant a world in growth. In his planned discovery of the American continent as well as in his earlier non-stop voyage across the Atlantic he is the symbol of those bold sailors and intrepid pioneers from Great Britain, Holland, Normandy and the Scandinavian countries who conquered this land and impressed upon it the culture of northern Europe.

IV. THE FIRST AMERICAN HOMESTEADERS

WHEN Leif Erikson returned to Greenland in 1004 or 1005, he became a famous man for he had explored a new country, and he had also rescued the crew of a ship-wrecked vessel. Because of these accomplishments he was called Leif the Lucky, and there was much talk of visiting this "Vinland the Good," as it was called. Leif's brother Thorwald in particular thought that this new land had not been sufficiently explored. Evidently there lurked in his mind the thought that it might prove a better place for settlement than Greenland, for he obtained the loan of his brother's vessel—the vessel of Bjarne Herjulfson—and the following year set forth with a crew of thirty men. Nothing is said of his adventures until he reached Leif's log houses in Vinland.

Many commentators have heaped critical scorn upon this claim that Thorwald was able to find Leif's houses, so far away in an unknown country. But this hypercriticism is not well founded. It is customary when navigating new waters to have pilots on board if they are to be had. Thorwald's crew probably was largely made up of men who had been with Leif the preceding year, and with these men as pilots there should have been no difficulty in finding Leif's camp, unless they were carried far out of their course by storms. Thorwald and his companions seem to have arrived at Leif's camp in fall, for nothing is said of any explorations that year. The following winter they lived chiefly by fishing.

The next spring (1006) Thorwald went with some of the men in the stern-boat to explore the country westward. "It seemed to them a beautiful country, well timbered, the forest coming down close to the beach which had white sands. There were many islands and many shoals." On one of the islands toward the west they found a shed made of poles for the storage of grain. This must have been an Indian corncrib. A. C. Parker says: "Corncribs are an Indian invention and for general construction have been little improved by white men."[1] They found no other signs of human life and returned to the camp later in the summer or fall.

The following summer Thorwald and some of the men took the vessel and sailed eastward and along the more northerly part of the country. They encountered a gale near a cape (presumably Cape Cod), and the vessel was thrown ashore. The keel was broken and they stayed there a long time while replacing it with another. Then they raised the old keel on the headland which they called Keelness.

After this they "sailed east of the land" and explored the bays northward. The last direction is not expressly mentioned, but inasmuch as they were exploring new shores, and the large indentation between Markland and Vinland had not previously been visited, this conclusion follows. From Cape Cod the land north of Plymouth can be seen, and they probably crossed the sound and followed the shore northward. Eventually they came to a headland (Cape Ann?) where the water was deep enough so that they moved their vessel right up to the shore and put out a gangplank. The surroundings were so beautiful that Thorwald declared that he would build his home here.[2] On returning to the vessel they discovered three mounds on the beach inside the headland which on nearer

[1] *New York Museum Bulletin 144*, p. 36 (Albany, 1910).
[2] Professor A. W. Brögger has given distinguished emphasis to this decision of Thorwald's. He writes: "The quotation in the saga is quite monumental: '*Here it is beautiful and here I will build my home.*'" *Vinlandsferdene*, Oslo, 1937, p. 117. Edward F. Gray believes that Thorwald turned south into Cape Cod Bay, and that the site he picked for his home was Hockanom, a headland north of Yarmouth, Mass. See *Leif Eriksson, Discoverer of America* (1930), pp. 132-138.

view proved to be skin canoes under each of which three Indians were sleeping. The Norsemen surrounded them and took them all prisoners except one who escaped with his canoe. Then the text laconically adds that "they killed the eight."

Apparently something has been lost out of the narrative about this incident. To murder a group of sleeping men, evidently the first natives they had seen, would not only be brutal, it would also be amazingly imprudent. It does not conform to the Norse reputation for common sense and fair play. It is probable that the Norsemen captured these natives with the harmless motive of getting acquainted with them. This may have failed because of the terror of the Indians at the sight of these white strangers. A fight probably followed in the course of which the natives were killed.

Some commentators have thought that these natives must have been Eskimo because of the "skinboats." But the Eskimo kayak is covered all over except for a small space big enough for the lone occupant to sit in, and it is too small to shelter even one man, not to mention three, which the narrative says were sleeping under it. The Eskimo also use a large boat called a *umiak*, but this is so heavy that it takes many men to carry it, whereas the skinboat in the narrative was carried away by one man.

Nor is it likely that it was a birch bark canoe as the canoe birch does not thrive south of latitude 45°. The probability is that these were Indians who, influenced by their neighbors to the north, used a boat of the bark canoe type, but covered with skins. Many tribes in the West, such as the Sioux, the Hidatsa and the Mandans, used skinboats, and Baron La Hontan mentions that the Outagami of Wisconsin sometimes used them.

From another elevation they saw further up the bay a whole village of natives, but did not go near them. Later as they were sleeping on the vessel they were suddenly awakened and discovered a large fleet of canoes coming to attack them. Thorwald told his men to put up their shields along the sides of the ship in battle array. The Indians attacked them with bows and arrows but soon withdrew. The only one among the Norsemen who had been wounded was Thorwald, who said an arrow had found its way between a shield and the gunwale and had pierced his side. Feeling that he was about to die, he told his men to bury him on the headland which he had chosen for his home and to put up a cross at the head and foot of his grave. They did as they had been told and then returned to their headquarters. They remained there the following winter, getting ready a cargo of timber, and returned to Greenland with their evil news the next spring.

THORSTEIN'S VOYAGE

One of the men who had actively supported Erik Thorwaldson in his trouble with old Thorgest was a proud and prominent man by the name of Thorbjörn Vifilson. About fifteen years after Erik led his emigrants to Greenland, Thorbjörn found that his good fortune in Iceland was declining. He therefore emigrated to Greenland rather than retrench his mode of life in Iceland, and Erik gave him a tract of land near his own. Thorbjörn had a daughter named Gudrid who is described as having been very beautiful and gifted. She plays an important part in the saga of Thorfin Karlsefni and became the ancestress of many outstanding men in Iceland of whom Hauk Erlendson, the compiler of Hauksbook, was one. During the time when Thorwald's expedition was absent in Vinland, she was married to Thorstein, Leif's brother.

When Thorwald's men returned with the sad news of their captain's death, Thorstein, who was a very religious man, determined to go to Vinland to get his brother's body for the purpose of interring it in consecrated ground in Greenland. He borrowed Leif's vessel, selected with great care a crew of twenty-five men and, accompanied by his wife Gudrid, he set forth in the summer of 1009 or 1010. However, they were beset by storms and were driven far and wide. They came in sight of Iceland and were then driven almost to Ireland. Finally, after a most exhausting voyage of several months, without coming near any part of the American mainland, they arrived in the Western Settlement of Greenland in the first week of winter. Some time during the following winter Thorstein died.

THORFIN KARLSEFNI'S EXPEDITION

The following autumn when Gudrid had returned to Brattahlid where she became the ward of Leif, a prosperous merchant seafarer arrived in Eriksfjord with a large vessel. His name was Thorfin Karlsefni, and his descendant and biographer with reasonable pride gives his genealogy which shows that he, both on his father's and mother's side, was descended from royal stock. With him came Snorri Thorbrandson, an old friend of Leif's father. They had forty men on board. About the same time came another vessel from Iceland also carrying forty men. The men in charge of this company were Bjarne Grimolfson and Thorhall Gamlason who were from the east coast of Iceland. With the lavish hospitality of the times, Leif invited these captains and their men to be his guests for the winter. During that winter there was much festivity at Brattahlid including a great wedding, for the wealthy Thorfin had become enamored of the charms of the beautiful widow, and Gudrid became his wife after Christmas.

There was also much talk of the wonders of Vinland, and the result was that all these visitors determined to seek it. By spring 160 persons, including some women, made ready to go.[3] This included a number of Greenlanders among whom was an old retainer of Erik's called Thorhall the Hunter. He had heard so much about the wine of Vin-

---

[3] This is according to Hauksbook. The Flatey version says there were 65 persons in the expedition.

land that he was thirsty for some of it. They had different kinds of cattle with them for it was the intention of Thorfin and Gudrid and many of the others to settle in Vinland permanently.

After making a couple of stops on the way and after having passed a very long and dreary sea-coast which they called *Furdustrand* the expedition reached a place which they called *Straumsfjord* because of the currents or strong tides. Here they spent most of their time during the following three years. Unfortunately it is impossible to determine the location of this place even approximately. The account of the expedition is taken from Hauksbook because the compiler of that codex was a descendant of Thorfin Karlsefni and therefore gives a much fuller account of it than does the narrative in Flateybook. But unlike the clear and concise reports of the previous expeditions as told in Flateybook, this narrative in Hauksbook is confused and sometimes contradictory, which indicates that certain parts have been lost. The sailing directions are quite chaotic.

As illustration of this hopeless confusion may be mentioned that while Storm believes that Straumsfjord was somewhere on Cape Breton Island, Steensby thinks it was 600 miles west on the south shore of the St. Lawrence River. Hovgaard believes Sandwich Bay in Labrador answers the description, while Babcock locates it in the Bay of Fundy west of Nova Scotia. Gathorne-Hardy favors Long Island Sound near New York, while Hermannsson is positive that Chaleur Bay north of New Brunswick is the place. Brögger, the latest writer, discreetly refuses to attempt any identification.

On reaching Straumsfjord they built houses and spent their time in exploring and hunting which for a time was good. "There were mountains there and the view was beautiful." But as the severe winter slowly dragged by, the food supply became very short, and they would have perished of starvation but for the discovery of a stranded whale. When spring came conditions improved, and they continued their search for the much extolled grapes, but in vain. When a whole year had passed by without finding either grapevines or grapes, Thorhall, the old hunter, with nine men left the others to return to Greenland. Before leaving, as he was carrying water to his vessel, he recited these verses:

> They flattered my confiding ear
> With tales of drink abounding here:
> My curse upon this thirsty land!
> A warrior, trained to bear a brand,
> A pail instead I have to bring,
> And bow my back beside the spring:
> For ne'er a single draught of wine
> Has passed these parching lips of mine.
>
> Now let the vessel plough the main
> To Greenland and our friends again.
> Away, and leave the strenuous host
> Who praise this God-forsaken coast
> To linger in a desert land,
> And boil their whales in Furdustrand.[4]

Thorfin and his party now made ready and sailed southward for a long time in search of Vinland. They finally stopped at a place where a river entered the sea through a lake. Here they found a very good land. Every brook was full of fish, and they caught an abundance of halibut. In the low places they found "self-sown fields of wheat" (probably wild rice), and on the hills grapes. Finding the country to their liking they built houses in which to live.

About two weeks after their arrival they were visited by a party of Indians in nine skin-boats. The approaching Indians waved staves "with a noise like threshing" and they were waved "with the sun" (i.e., from east to west). Karlsefni had his men raise white shields as a sign of peace.

[4] Translation by Gathorne-Hardy in *The Norse Discoverers of America*, pp. 59-60.

The visitors were "swarthy men and ugly with unkempt hair on their heads." They remained for a while and then departed peacefully. The winter passed in comfort.

The next spring a large fleet of Indian canoes appeared. The staves and shields were waved as before, and the Indians landed and brought skins for trading. They also wanted to buy swords and spears, but Thorfin forbade his men to sell any weapons. In exchange for the furs the Norsemen gave a span's length of red cloth which the natives bound around their heads. "When the supply of cloth began to give out, the Norsemen cut it into pieces so small that they were not more than a finger's breadth. The savages gave as much for it as before, or more."

In the midst of this peaceful barter Thorfin's bull ran out of the woods and bellowed loudly. This apparition so terrified the natives that they dropped what they had and ran to their canoes. One of them tried to snatch a spear, but he was killed by one of Thorfin's men. The Indians then paddled southward and nothing was seen of them for three weeks.

Thorfin thought it probable that they would return to avenge the loss of their man who had been killed, and he therefore made preparations to receive them. He set some of his men to work on the point in front of the camp, but placed the larger number in the woods on one side cutting down timber so as to be in position to make a flank attack when the natives came.

Three weeks later the Indians came in vast numbers, but this time they waved their staves "against the sun" and shouted their war-cry. The Norsemen answered by raising red shields and soon the battle was on with hundreds of arrows flying through the air. Although greatly outnumbered, the Norsemen held their ground well until the Indians raised a large globe resembling a sheep's paunch on a pole and flung it against them. It made a frightful noise when it came down. Believing it to be some devilish magic and, in their consternation thinking that they were being attacked on all sides, Thorfin's men beat a hasty retreat upstream until they came to some rocks where they made a new stand.[5]

Freydis, a half sister of Leif Erikson, came out of the house and seeing the men retreating, she said: "Why are such fine fellows as you running away from these unworthy men, whom I thought you could have butchered like cattle? Now if I had a weapon it seems to me I could fight better than any of you." They paid no attention to her but continued running. She tried to follow them, but was rather slow as she was with child. Then she saw a Norseman who had been killed. It was Thorbrand, the son of Snorri Thorbrandson, one of the leaders of the expedition. His sword was lying by his side. She took it up and as the savages charged upon her, she bared her breasts and stroked them with the sword. Startled by this defiant demonstration, the Indians came to a sudden stop and then ran back to their canoes and paddled away.[6]

On looking over the field, it was found that the Indians had lost quite a number of warriors. The Norsemen had lost two, but many of the men were wounded. After considering the matter, Thorfin and his men decided that

[5] Eight hundred years later we find that the same formidable kind of weapon was known among the Indians. Schoolcraft, for many years U. S. Indian Agent at Mackinac, writes the following: "Algonquin tradition affirms that in ancient times during the fierce wars which the Indians carried on, they constructed a very formidable instrument of attack by sewing up a large boulder in a new skin. To this a long handle was tied. When the skin dried it became very tight round the stone, and after being painted with devices, assumed the appearance and character of a solid globe upon a pole. This formidable instrument, to which the name of 'balista' may be applied, is figured (Plate 15, Fig. 2) from the description of an Algonquin chief. It was borne by several warriors who acted as balisteers. Plunged upon a boat or canoe it was capable of sinking it. Brought down among a group of men suddenly it produced consternation and death." *Indian Tribes of the United States*, I, 85.

[6] The Indians must have thought that she was crazy. We know from the later experiences of the French among the Indians that the latter believed that a demented person was under the special protection of some powerful spirit and were therefore careful not to molest him.

while this was a pleasant place in which to live, it was too unsafe to be thought of as a permanent place of habitation. Some time after the skirmish they therefore returned to their camp in Straumsfjord. Here they spent the winter and then returned to Greenland. Shortly after their first arrival in Straumsfjord, a child was born to Gudrid and Thorfin who was given the name of Snorri. He was almost three years old when they returned to Greenland, and he became the ancestor of many prominent men in Greenland.[7]

This was the largest of the Norse colonization attempts on the American mainland, but, like Captain Smith's colony in Virginia 600 years later, it was not large enough. Ruminations on what might have been are ordinarily of little use in historical narrative, but it is interesting for a moment to contemplate how very different the history of America might have been if Erik Thorwaldson instead of Bjarne Herjulfson had been driven to the lands far southwestward on his first trip into the West. With his organizing ability he would probably have gathered together an even larger company of emigrants to accompany him to Vinland than went with him to Greenland. This larger group would probably have been able to hold its own against the natives and would have grown quickly as the conditions for successful colonization were more favorable here than in Iceland, Greenland, Shetland Islands, Faroe Islands and the Orkneys where the Norsemen created prosperous colonies. The result might have been that a Norwegian empire would have antedated a British.

About the year 1880 a Norse axe of eleventh century type was found near the northeastern extremity of Nova Scotia. This is the only relic of Norse visits that has yet been found along the Atlantic coast. The discovery was

[7] The following year (1015?) another expedition was made to Vinland in which the indomitable Freydis played the part of a fiendish Lady Macbeth. But as this expedition throws no new light on Vinland, it is not necessary to dwell on it here.

made by a farmer while tilling a small field bordering on Cole Harbor, an indentation on Tor Bay, just west of Cape Canso in Nova Scotia. Mrs. Grover, a granddaughter of the man who found the axe, is still living on the farm.

The axe which was covered with rust and clay was put on a shelf and no one took much interest in it until 1936. Then a prospector by the name of James P. Nolan was shown the axe. He had a shack near by and was allowed to take the axe home with him for the purpose of cleaning off the rust and clay. On returning to his home, he placed the axe in a basin of kerosene to soften the rust. While the axe was still in the bowl his shack caught fire and burned completely to the ground. Later, while searching in the ruins, Nolan found that the clay and rust adhering to the surface of the axe had become loose, revealing a number of mystic marks. These may be secret runes, but no satisfactory reading of them has yet been found. The axe is now in the possession of Mr. William B. Goodwin of Hartford, Conn. It has been examined by A. B. Greninger, Professor of Physical Metallurgy, Harvard University. In a letter to the writer, dated April 6, 1939, Professor Greninger writes as follows:

The Goodwin axe is undoubtedly of primitive manufacture; however, from the short study that I have made, it would be impossible to state whether the manufacturer was alive a hundred years ago or a thousand years ago. Additional study might supply further evidence, and I am awaiting a second visit from Mr. Goodwin before going ahead on this.

It might be interesting for you to know that the actual metallographic structure of the axe metal is about the only one it could be if the axe actually were about a thousand years old.

(Signed)   ALDEN B. GRENINGER.

V. THE LOCATION OF VINLAND

IT is impossible to determine the precise location of Leif Erikson's habitation in Vinland, but there are a number of circumstantial indications which are helpful in arriving at an approximate location.

1. *The general direction.* The first guide to the location of Vinland is its general direction from Greenland. Bjarne on his way to Greenland was driven by storms far southwest down the Atlantic for many days and eventually discovered a land "without mountains, well timbered and with small knolls on it." From this new land he sailed in a general northeasterly direction until he came to Greenland, discovering two more lands on the same voyage. Leif, after getting all possible information from Bjarne, reversed the latter's course and, sailing in a general southwesterly direction, found the lands described by Bjarne and called them Helluland, Markland and Vinland. These lands therefore lay on a roughly northeast-southwest axis. A glance at the map shows that the eastern seaboard of America conforms to this axis with projecting landforms abutting on it at the designated intervals, and here we must seek Vinland.

2. *The mild climate.* When Leif and his men arrived in Vinland, they found a number of things which were different from what they had been accustomed to in Greenland or Iceland, and they mention these things. One was the mild climate. "It seemed to them that cattle would be able to pick their own food all winter for there was no frost and the grass did not wither much." In such descriptions it is of course necessary to make allowance for the exaggerations which invariably creep into travelers' narratives. A pleasing country is always pictured a little more delightful by the enraptured visitor than an unbiased judg-

ment would warrant. When the explorers said that there
was no frost in winter, they probably meant that there was
very little frost, but even this shows that the expedition
must have spent the winter in a spot quite far south. Then,
too, it may have been quite a mild winter. John Fiske,
commenting on this passage in 1891, thus describes the
winter in his own neighborhood two years previously:

The winter of 1889-90 in Cambridge, for example, might
very naturally have been described by visitors from higher
latitudes as a winter without frost and with grass scarcely
withered. Indeed, we might have so described it ourselves. On
Narragansett and Buzzard's bays such soft winter weather is
still more common; north of Cape Ann it is much less common. The severe winter (*magna hiems*) is of course familiar
enough anywhere along the northeastern coast of America.[1]

He therefore thinks this description applies very well to
the coast south of Cape Ann.

3. *The long daylight in winter.* Another thing which
impressed the explorers was the greater length of the day
in winter time. In Iceland, which had been the home of all
these men for many years, the sun during the latter part
of December was visible for only about three hours each
day, but here, in Vinland, they saw it shining very much
longer. In order to tell how much longer the day was,
they record a rather explicit observation: *Sol hafdi par
dagmalastad ok eyktarstad um skamdegi*, that is, "The sun
was already up at *dagmalastad* and had not set at *eyktarstad*
at the time of the winter solstice."

These designations are the names of two of the eight
fixed times of the day which were used in the Scandinavian countries in the Middle Ages. Having no clocks,
they selected points on the horizon or erected cairns and
markers which in their apposition to the sun would show
the time of the day. Another way of translating the passage would therefore be to say that the sun rose before

[1] *Discovery of America*, I, 184.

dagmalastad and set after *eyktarstad* on the shortest day of the year.

The question now comes, At what point on the horizon was one or the other of these two marks?

In the old Icelandic ecclesiastical code, *eyktarstad* is thus defined: "It is *eykt* when *utsudrs-ætt* is divided into three, and the sun has passed through two divisions and has one to go." [2]

The next question is, What is the meaning of *utsudr-ætt?* Here we have two words, the first meaning *south-west* and the second referring to *eight*. The old Northmen divided the horizon into eight parts, each comprising an arc of forty-five degrees. This is illustrated in the following passages: "The sun passes through one *ætt* in three hours." [3] "The sun runs through eight *ætts*." [4]

Utsudr-ætt is therefore that octant of the horizon which has SW in the middle, that is, the arc between S 22½° W to 67½° W. This comprises 45 degrees. As *eyktarstad* is at the azimuth when the sun has passed through two-thirds of this octant and has one to go, this azimuth would be at 52½° W. On this basis the astronomer, H. Geelmuyden, determined that the latitude where the sun would set at *eyktarstad* on the shortest day of the year in the beginning of the eleventh century would be 49° 55′. [5]

Another astronomer, Professor Turner of Oxford University, on the basis of the same premises computed a lati-

---

[2] *Kristinn-rettr*, p. 92.

[3] *Konungs-Skugsjå*, Copenhagen, 1768, p. 54: *þat eru þa þrjar stundir dags er sol veltist um eina ætt.*

[4] *Ibid.: Medan sol veltist um atta ættir.*

[5] *Arkiv for Nordisk Filologi*, III, 128. Two recent commentators, Mr. Mjelde and Professor Brögger, have advanced the theory that *utsudr-ætt* means the whole southwestern quarter of ninety degrees (cf. M. M. Mjelde, *Eyktarstad-problemet og Vinlandsreiserne*, Norsk Historisk Tidskrift, 5te Rekke, VI, Oslo, 1927, p. 259; A. W. Brögger, *Vinlands-ferdene*, Oslo, 1937, pp. 99-105). On this basis they arrive at an azimuth of 60 degrees for *eyktarstad* and a latitude for Leif's observation of 36° 54′. But the evidence that *utsudr-ætt* represented an octant and not a quarter of the horizon is too strong to permit their conclusions.

tude of 48° 57′.[6] This is therefore the northernmost limit of Leif's observation if he were in a position to make it scientifically correct. As he lacked instruments necessary for such accuracy, it may be assumed that it was just a casual observation over the broken ground to illustrate his statement that "day and night were more equal than in Greenland." If the observation was made over broken ground, the sun would disappear from his view before it had actually reached its setting time. Furthermore, he says nothing about the sun disappearing, but on the contrary says that it was still shining as it reached *eyktarstad*. These two circumstances indicate that the actual setting of the sun took place several degrees beyond his *eyktarstad*. Assuming a difference of five degrees in the azimuth due to these circumstances, which seems a moderate allowance, the latitude at which the sun set would be about 42°.[7]

4. *The abundance of grapes.* Another suggestive indication is the great abundance of grapes. It is said that the explorers filled their stern boat with grapes. This abundance of a product unknown to them, and suitable for making a good wine, is given as the reason for naming the land Vinland (Wineland). The northern limit of grapes along the Atlantic seaboard is 47°. The vine is scarce along the coast of Nova Scotia, New Brunswick, Maine and New Hampshire. It is only when we reach the shores of Massachusetts that we find it growing abundantly.

Some writers, especially the botanist Professor M. L. Fernald, have endeavored to show that these *vinber* were not grapes but the mountain cranberry (vaccinium vitis idaea), known in Norwegian as *tyttebær*.[8] As an alternative he suggests some species of the currant.

This theory is based principally on an error by Professor

[6] See Gathorne-Hardy, *The Norse Discoverers of America*, p. 217.

[7] The same conclusion is reached by Gathorne-Hardy in *op. cit.*, pp. 217-219, and by Hovgaard in *The Voyages of the Norsemen to America*.

[8] M. L. Fernald, *Notes on the Plants of Wineland the Good in Rhodora* (Boston), Vol. 12, 1910. Fernald's view is refuted by A. Leroy Andrews in *Ibid.*, Vol. 15, 1913.

Gustav Storm. The latter writes: "The grapes are discovered in winter, nay, even in spring (!), the man who found them gets drunk from eating the fruit (!), the grapes are gathered too in the spring (!), and the ship's boat is filled with them (!). And again, the vines are spoken of as big trees, which are felled in order to be used as timber (!)." [9] But all this jeering is very much out of place because nothing is said about picking *vinber* in spring. As stated in the saga narrative printed above, Leif first put up some temporary sheds, then, finding the country to his liking, he built large houses for winter use. With thirty-five men this would not take long. As soon as the houses were under cover, he sent out half of his men each day to explore the vicinity. Then, shortly afterward, Tyrk discovered the grapes. All this, therefore, happened in autumn. There is nothing remarkable in this except possibly the claim that the pinnace was filled with grapes. But the fruit had to be stored somewhere until it was disposed of, either by drying or pressing. Nor are the vines spoken of as big trees which are felled to be used as timber. Leif is quoted as telling his men to "cut vines and fell trees" (*hoggua vinvid ok fella mörkina*). Nothing is said concerning the intended use of the vines, but it is probable that he planned to use them as withies for which there were many uses. We know for instance that withies played an important part in the construction of their boats.[10] After this, the narrator has nothing more to tell of their doings until spring comes. Then he says: "When spring came they made ready and sailed away."

The narrator very plainly endeavors to show that this discovery was something quite remarkable. In order to fully understand its significance the reader must, if pos-

[9] Gustav Storm, *Studier over Vinlandsreiserne* in *Aarböger for Nordisk Oldkyndighed*, Copenhagen, 1887, p. 293 ff. For other errors in Storm's presentation see P. P. Iverslie, *Gustav Storms Studier*, Minneapolis, 1912.

[10] Cf. Wm. Hovgaard, *The Voyages of the Norsemen to America*, pp. 52, 53. New York, 1914.

sible, place himself within the narrator's mental horizon.
To him and the people he wrote about, the grape was a
fruit they had never seen, but they knew that a very deli-
cious wine was derived from it. It was therefore something to arouse their interest so much that the land was
named in honor of the fruit. Not so with cranberries and
currants, for they were as common in Iceland and Norway
as corn in Iowa. Nor would these berries have sent Tyrk
into spasms of joy for he had been with Leif since the
latter's childhood, and cranberries were nothing new to
him. But with his mobile temperament (*vide* his restless
eyes) it must have been a sensational discovery to find
once more the grapes he had not seen for a quarter century. He was not drunk, as Storm seems to think, but
enraptured with the vision of his childhood home, which
this discovery so suddenly brought to him, he uncon-
sciously spoke German, which would be a most natural
thing to do in such circumstances.

The essential facts of the discovery of Vinland and
its grapes is furthermore proven by a witness far removed
from the Icelandic sagas both in space and time. Adam of
Bremen was a learned *magister* who in 1070 became rector
of the cathedral school in Bremen. Before that time he
had been engaged for some years in collecting material for
an extensive history of the archbishopric of Hamburg.
This diocese included Prussia, Northern Poland, the Baltic
States, Russia, Finland, the Scandinavian countries and all
the islands of the North Atlantic with the exception of the
British Isles. In order to give a comprehensive history of
the diocese, he traveled widely and talked with many men
supposedly well informed. Among these was King Swen
of Denmark who gave him much information. He mentions one interesting item:

He (the King of Denmark) told me of yet another island,
discovered by many in that ocean, which is called Wineland
because grapes grow wild there, producing the best of wine.

Moreover that self-sown grain abounds there we have ascertained, not from fabulous conjecture, but from the reliable report of the Danes.[11]

Here, almost within the lifetime of the explorers themselves, we have not only the statement that many persons had made voyages to Vinland, but also that even then this new country was famous for its wild grapes and self-sown grain. It is absurd to suppose that King Swen would have mentioned the discovery of wild currants or the mountain cranberry as something very remarkable. But to find grapes from which good wine was made—that was an extraordinary discovery, and for this reason Adam pauses to assure his readers that these reports were absolutely reliable.

5. *The salmon*. Another factor in determining the location of Vinland is the statement concerning the abundance of salmon. The southern limit of the salmon habitat on the Atlantic seaboard is the waters of Connecticut and Rhode Island, that is, 41°. From here northward it is found in great abundance.

6. *Leif's sailing course and distance*. We have the description of Leif's sailing course, which in fact is given twice, as he is said to have reversed Bjarne's course. The sailing distance is not given until Leif leaves Markland. Then it is said that he sailed with a northeast wind (that is, in a southwesterly direction) for two days before he saw land. According to the standard speed of vessels in those days, this would be about 300 nautical miles. It is then said that he passed westward between an island and a cape into a sound and entered a river flowing out of a lake. On the shore of this lake he built his houses. The only lands approximately 300 miles southwest from southern Nova Scotia, which project far out into the sea to permit further westward sailing to a river basin beyond, are the Cape Cod Peninsula and Nantucket. Here, a short distance

[11] Adam of Bremen, *Gesta Hammaburgensis*, Ch. IV, p. 38.

west of these two eastern land projections, Leif built his houses.

7. *The local physiographic conditions.* Finally we have the description of Vinland's littoral. The saga mentions that when or after the seafarers entered "the sound" and approached the shore where a river flowed out, they found that "it was very shallow there at low tide, so that their ship ran aground, and soon it was a long way from the ship to the sea." These extensive shallows are also mentioned in the description of the voyage of Thorwald, Leif's brother, who wintered at the same spot. The narrative reads: "It seemed to them a beautiful country, well timbered, the forest coming down close to the shore which had white sands. There were many islands and many shoals." [12] There were in fact so many shoals that Thorwald, when he the following year made an exploration trip westward, did not think it safe to take his vessel but instead took his "after-boat." The only place on the Atlantic coast from Long Island northward where there are many islands and shallow waters is the region of Nantucket Sound, Vineyard Sound and Long Island Sound.

Summarizing, we have here seven descriptive indications concerning the location of Vinland. First, the direction in which Leif sailed shows that Vinland lay far down on the Atlantic coast. Second, the mildness of the winter points to southern Massachusetts or regions farther southwest. Third, the *eyktarstad* observation points to the same region with a possible slight increase of its northern limit. Fourth, the abundance of grapes indicates Massachusetts or regions farther southwest. Fifth, the abundance of salmon shows that the southern limit of Vinland is the Cape Cod-Connecticut region. Sixth, the sailing distance and direction indicate that the camp was on or near the Cape Cod Peninsula or Nantucket. Seventh, the physiographic aspects

[12] *Flateyjarbok,* I, 541.

of the Vinland waterfront are in exact agreement with
those of Nantucket Sound.[13] As all these indications and
agreements meet in this vicinity, there seems to be little
doubt that here was Leif Erikson's Vinland.

Two other considerations are of importance in circum-
scribing the location of Leif's camp. (1) As he and his
men had made a long sea voyage, it is obvious that they
would be eager to make a speedy landing to inspect this
mysterious new land. (2) As they had now arrived in a
locality of dangerous shoals, it is equally obvious that they
would lose no time in finding a safe anchorage for their
vessel before it was wrecked on a sand bar. The first land
that they sighted after leaving Markland was probably the
hill, one hundred feet high, on Nantucket Island. To the
north they saw the low-lying Monomoy Island. From here
the mainland to the west and northwest could be seen.
They evidently entered the sound with the coming of the
tide and reached the mouth of a river, but here their vessel
was left high and dry on an extensive shoal as the tide
went out. When the tide returned they pulled it into the
river for safety.

In 1926 a runic inscription was discovered on a rock on
the island of No Man's Land, about three miles south of
the west end of Martha's Vineyard. The rock lies on the
beach on the south side of the island near the western end
and is subject to the constant pounding of the waves. Unfortunately no steps have been taken to remove the stone
so that the inscription may be preserved. Because of its
inaccessible location, it has not been inspected by any
runologist, and the readings that have been made are based
on photographs which are unsatisfactory because of the
worn surface of the stone. The inscription contains four

---

[13] *The United States Coast Pilot, Atlantic Coast, Section B*, gives detailed descriptions of these shoals, many of which extend for many miles
seaward.

lines of which the uppermost is fairly legible. It reads:

L I I F E R I K S S O N

(in runic characters). The second line shows only the two Roman letters:

M I

The third and fourth lines seem to consist only of a succession of vertical lines. The inscription has been subjected to a number of weighty, though not necessarily conclusive, objections as they are based on the photographs made of the chalked lines on the stone which may be faulty. There is a possibility that some amateur student of the Norse discovery of America carved the inscription as a memorial to Leif Erikson a few decenniums back when the stone lay on top of the fifty-foot cliff behind its present location. Recession of the cliff has been proceeding at the rate of more than a foot per year for a long time. It is highly improbable that anyone would have gone to the trouble of cutting an inscription while the stone was lying in its present exposed position.[14]

Some writers have attempted to identify Vinland with the region at the mouth of the St. Lawrence River. As this lies much nearer to Greenland and permits of a coast-wise journey for half the distance, it has its appeal to those who shrink from the thought of long voyages in the small vessels of those times. But to these old Norsemen who thought nothing of sailing across the Atlantic where they would be out of the sight of land for weeks and months, a voyage to Vinland could not have been terrifying. We read of their voyages to the Holy Land, to Spitzbergen and to the northern parts of Greenland, which were longer and more hazardous, but they are not mentioned as anything amazing.

[14] See E. F. Gray, *Leif Eriksson, Discoverer of America*, 1930; Annie M. Wood, *Noman's Land, Isle of Romance*, 1931; E. B. Delabarre, *The Runic Rock on No Man's Land*, in *The New England Quarterly*, 1935, VIII, 365-377.

It is quite possible that the Thorfin Karlsefni expedition spent most of its time in some place on the Gulf of St. Lawrence, and there is reason to believe that this region was later included in the appellation of Vinland. But when it comes to identifying Leif Erikson's Vinland, the St. Lawrence region will not do. The sailing directions and distances do not fit. The climate in winter is fully as severe as in Greenland and colder than in Iceland. While grapes may be found, they are not abundant, and the "shallow waters with many islands and shoals" are not there.

Recently a new theory has been advanced by Mr. J. W. Curran who has done some excellent work in establishing the authenticity of the Viking grave found near Lake Nipigon in northern Ontario (see pp. 64-72, *post*). In order to account for the presence of this remarkable find, he has written a number of articles, later published in book form,[15] in which he has attempted to show that Vinland was the region south of the James Bay inlet of Hudson Bay. But a comparison of the characteristics of Leif's Vinland with the desolate wilderness of northern Ontario will show that this identification is not possible.

[15] *Here Was Vinland*, Sault Ste. Marie, Ontario, 1939.

VI. THE LITERARY SOURCES CONCERN-
ING THE DISCOVERY

THE principal information that we have concerning the Norse discovery of America is contained in two collections of manuscripts, known respectively as *Hauksbok* and *Flateyjarbok*. Both of these collections in their present form date from the fourteenth century. Because of this late date the objection is sometimes heard that the accounts of the discovery are unreliable, inasmuch as the reports concerning it were not put into writing until more than three hundred years after the alleged events took place.

This conclusion shows a misconception of the facts. These two manuscript collections were the private libraries of their one-time owners, and include such sagas as they desired and could get copied by some clerk. The older copies in the course of time became dim and unreadable or were damaged and destroyed, and it was necessary for anyone who was a lover of books to have copies made for himself. The date of the copy has no more to do with the age of its component parts than has the date, when a modern reader buys a dozen books, to do with the time when these books were written. Inasmuch as the art of writing was in use in the Scandinavian countries many centuries before the fourteenth century, it is erroneous to assume that the recording of important events was deferred for three hundred years. The Latin alphabet was introduced into the North in the eleventh century, but before that time there was the runic alphabet which was adequate for making all kinds of records.

There are still in existence many runic inscriptions on stone and metal from almost every century back to the time of Christ, but their greatest frequency dates from the period immediately before and after the Norse discovery of America. From the eleventh century we have in the Scandinavian countries more than 3,000 runic inscriptions which are just so many proofs that the art of expressing thought by means of alphabetic characters was known, not to mention the thousands of runic stones that have been destroyed or put to other use since that time. Some of these inscriptions are very long as, for instance, the Røkstone which contains a stirring narrative of historical events expressed in notable poetic images. It dates from about 800.

These runic stones are nearly all memorials of departed persons and required the skill of persons familiar with the cutting of stone. For these two reasons they probably represent only a small percentage of runic writings just as our own gravestones are a very small and delegated part of the writings of people of today. The runic characters were few and easily learned. With such known means of preserving records it seems unquestionable that they were in wide use. Their utility was too obvious to be ignored. In the field of jurisprudence, where each year the voluminous laws of each district were subject to emendation or addition, the needs of explicit wording would demand that these laws were written down. There still remains a copy of the provincial statutes of Skåne written in runes, comprising a printed volume of about 200 pages.[1] As this edition dates from about 1275 when the Latin alphabet was in general use, this indicates that it was a late copy of a progressively revised much earlier runic original. (For sample page see Fig. 1.)

We have an interesting mention of the literary use of runes in the saga of Egil Skallagrimson, the most famous of the old Icelandic poets. In the year 960 his son, Bodwar, perished in a storm on Borgafjord in Iceland, and Egil

[1] See *Det Arnemagneanske Haandskrift, No. 28, Codex Runicus*, Copenhagen, 1877.

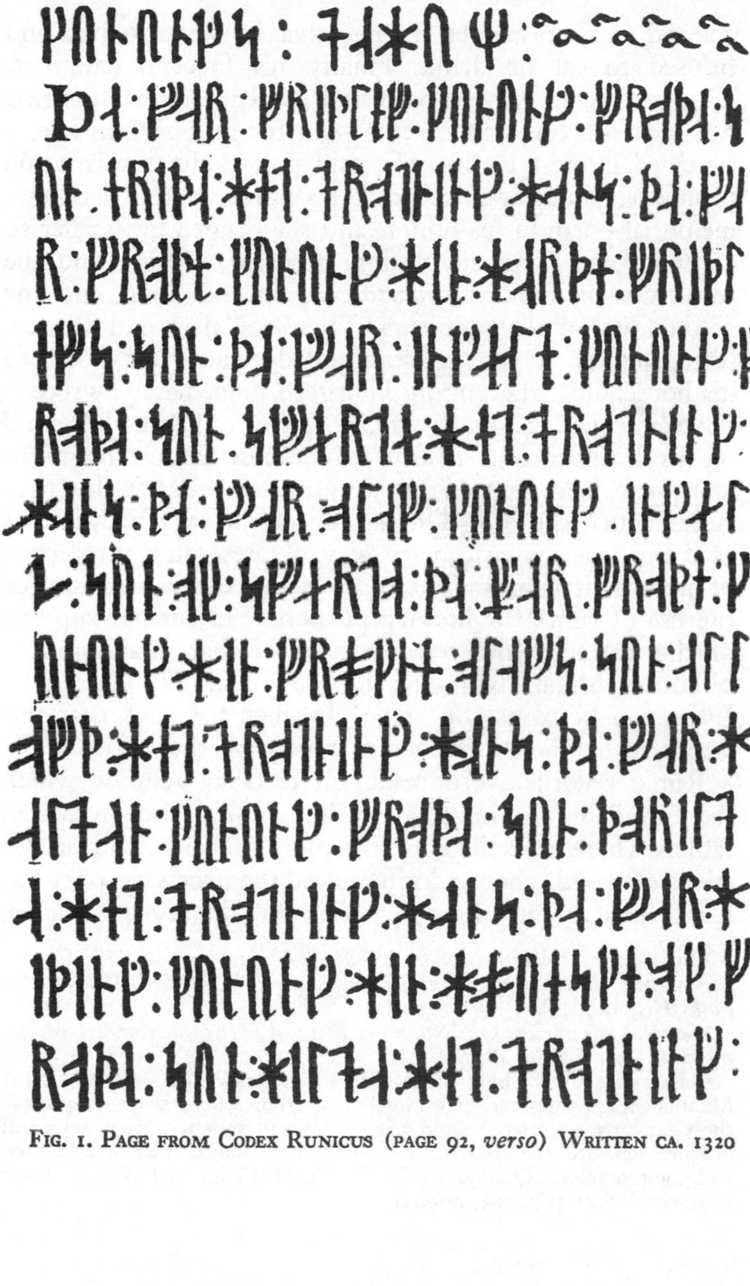

FIG. 1. PAGE FROM CODEX RUNICUS (PAGE 92, *verso*) WRITTEN CA. 1320

grieved so deeply over his loss that he went to bed and refused to eat or drink. Finally his favorite daughter, Thorgerd, who was married and lived in another district, was sent for. She conceived a plan for making him take a renewed interest in life. She said that Bodwar was a too promising young man to go to his grave without having a memorial poem in his honor, and she begged her father to compose one. This suggestion appealed to Egil, and the result was the famous *Sonartorrek*, 192 lines long, and one of the finest of elegiac poems. Then Egil arose and dressed, seated himself in his highseat, and declaimed the poem to his household, whereupon Thorgerd immediately wrote it down in runes.[2] Similarly in *Gretla* we read that Hallmund on his deathbed felt an urge to compose an autobiographical poem, and he told his daughter to write it down in runes which she did. The author of the saga mentions it as if this was the customary way of preserving the record of important events. There are many other instances of the use of runes for literary purposes.[3] In further support of this we have the testimony of Hraban Maur, Archbishop of Mainz, who died in 856. In his *De Inventione Literarum* he gives the runic alphabet and says that this was used by the Northmen in recording their poems.[4]

Runic records were made on calfskin vellums which were available in almost every household. Also on waxed tablets where a needle took the place of a pen, and on flat sticks of wood where a knife served the necessary purpose. Unfortunately, as these materials are highly perishable,

---

[2] *Egils Saga Skallagrimssonar*, Jonsson's edition, pp. 285-286, Copenhagen, 1886. A Norwegian translation is given in Munch, *Det Norske Folks Historie*, I, Part 2, pp. 159-163.

[3] See P. G. Thorsen, *Om Runernes Brug til Skrift udenfor det Monumentale*, Copenhagen, 1877.

[4] His words are: "These (runes) are the letters which are used by the Marcomenni, whom we call Northmen, from whom they who speak the German tongue have their origin. With these letters they, who still are heathen, are accustomed to record their songs, their incantations and their oracles." Quoted by P. A. Munch in his *Det Norske Folks Historie*, I, Part 1, p. 383, note 2.

they have nearly all perished. But, in view of the wide-spread knowledge of runes, it is reasonable to assume that the early explorers, desirous of preserving a correct log or record of their journey, would keep a daily written account of their courses as has been the custom of seamen from time immemorial.[5] We may likewise assume that their descendants, eager to preserve the memory of their ancestors' outstanding achievements, would also cause to be made written records of them.

The most favored method of preserving the records of great men was to embody the narratives in alliterative verse. There are still extant hundreds of poems, chiefly historical, some of them containing hundreds of lines, from the tenth and eleventh centuries in which the exploits of kings and heroes and remarkable events are told in verse made easy to remember by reason of certain alliterative and metric forms. As practically every line of these poems is filled with abstruse metaphors according to the usage of the times, it seems out of the question that they could have been preserved unless they were first written down in runes. The recitation and chanting of these folk songs, we are told, was one of the principal amusements in the long winter evenings. The adventures of the Vinland explorers were probably recited in the same alliterative versification for several centuries before a more prosaic age paraphrased them into prose. Rafn and Magnusen have shown that the existing prose sagas of the Vinland voyages retain innumerable vestiges of this earlier alliterative verse. In many cases the later transcriber has made no other change in the versified diction than to merely write the words in continuous lines.[6]

It is therefore reasonable to conclude that the extant story of the Norse discovery represents a continuous pres-

[5] There is still preserved a late instance of a logbook written partly in runes, see facsimile of first page in Admiral Mogens Gyldenstjerne's log in Thorsen, *ante*, pp. 85-87.

[6] See *Grönlands Historiske Mindesmærker*, I, 290-353.

ervation of the facts through the media of written accounts made shortly after the events transpired.[7] These written accounts suffered through fading ink and doubtful legibility. Such textual ambiguities would further suffer from bungling copyists of many generations and the well-meaning *übergearbeitung* of uninformed editors. But these emendations would not seriously injure the main facts of the narrative. A greater injury would happen if some late descendant of one of the principal leaders in the discovery would set to work to compile a family saga in order to extol the memory of his ancestor. In such case he would be apt to pick out only such parts of the story as concerned his ancestor and omit or condense the rest because it had little or no bearing on the family history. The result, as far as his narrative is concerned, would be a garbled account of the discovery because of his omission of the other actors.

It is precisely this kind of divergence that we find in one of the two main accounts concerning the Vinland voyages. *The Saga of Thorfin Karlsefni and Gudrid*[8] in Hauksbook was compiled by Hauk Erlendson, a high official who was very proud of his family. It is not at all a history of the Norse discovery of America, nor does it profess to be. It is a family saga beginning with the ancestors of Thorfin Karlsefni and his wife and ending with the family descendants brought down to Hauk himself. The chief hero of the family was Thorfin Karlsefni who was the leader of the largest expedition to Vinland. It is therefore easy to understand why Hauk is interested only in his ancestor's part in the discovery. Consequently we find in this saga the most complete account of Thorfin's expedition, but a much less satisfactory account of the other journeys. Several of these are merged into one ex-

---

[7] See John Fiske, *Discovery of America*, I, 201-202.

[8] This is the original title of the saga according to Arne Magnusson, but Gustav Storm has without any warrant changed it to *The Saga of Erik the Red*.

pedition. Bjarne Herjulfson, who was not in any way connected with Thorfin's family, is not mentioned in Hauksbook, and his accidental discovery is attributed to Leif Erikson who was slightly connected with Thorfin's family. Leif was Gudrid's guardian before she married Thorfin, and Thorstein (Leif's brother) was Gudrid's first husband. They therefore belong in the family history.

In the Flateybook the purpose of the narrative is quite different. This is not the history of a family or of any one great hero. It is the history of a great event—the discovery of a new land. Leif Erikson's family figures most prominently in the narrative because four of the six expeditions which are mentioned were led by members of his family. But there is no attempt to glorify it. On the contrary, the picture of Freydis, Leif's half-sister, is most abhorrent.

The negligible importance of Hauk Erlendson's narrative as a record of the discovery of America is well illustrated by the paucity of his account about Leif Erikson's discovery. The following lines are all that he tells about this discovery of a new world:

Leif put to sea when he was ready. He was driven about for a long time and lighted on lands whose existence he had not before suspected. There were self-sown wheatfields and vines. There were also those trees called *mösur*, and they had some samples of all these things.

There are only two possible reasons for this brevity. (1) Either this was all that Hauk knew about Leif's discovery, in which case he clearly was not qualified to write a history of it; or (2) It was all he cared to say about it, in which case he was not trying to give a history of it. When we compare these meagre lines with the thirteen-page recital about his ancestor's, Thorfin's, later visit to the same region, it is evident that Hauk's mention of Leif's voyage is just incidental to the introduction of his real story—the marriage of Hauk's ancestors, Thorfin and Gudrid, and their voyage to the new land.

A comparison of the different viewpoints of the two sagas may be had by tabulating the amount of space devoted to the characters and events in each of the two narratives. Omitting the story of Erik's colonization of Greenland, which is the same in both and borrowed from *Landnama*, II, 14, the tabulation is as follows:

Matter not concerning the discovery

Hauksbook	Pages	Flateybook	Pages
Gudrid's ancestral history....	1½		
Her father's personality......	3½		
Gudrid and the Sybil........	3½		
Leif goes to Norway........	2	Leif goes to Norway......	⅔
Thorstein's death and prophecies......................	3	Thorstein's death and prophecies	3
Thorfin Karlsefni's genealogy	½		
Thorfin's marriage with Gudrid	2		
Thorfin's descendants	1		
Total....................	17	Total....................	3⅔

Concerning the discovery

Hauksbook	Pages	Flateybook	Pages
		Bjarne's discovery.........	3
Leif discovers Vinland......	⅙	Leif discovers Vinland.....	5
		Thorwald discovers Vinland	2½
Thorstein's voyage..........	1	Thorstein's voyage........	¼
Thorfin's expedition.........	13	Thorfin's expedition.......	3½
		Freydis' expedition	5
Total....................	14⅙	Total....................	19¼

This analysis shows that less than one-half of Thorfin's Saga in Hauksbook is devoted to the discovery of America, and nearly all of this smaller one-half deals with Thorfin's expedition—the big event in the family history. The Flateybook version, on the other hand, is almost exclusively devoted to the history of the discovery, taking up one expedition after another in systematic order.

The relative merits of these two versions have been the subject of heated debate between many commentators.

Some of them, particularly Gustav Storm [9] and H. P. Steensby,[10] have gone so far as to claim that the Flateybook version is to be rejected in every particular except where it agrees with Hauksbook. Most of the commentators, however, have failed to see why, in the case of parallel versions—both of which no doubt were subject to editorial patchwork of numerous copyists—one should be considered authoritative and the other worthless. This misunderstanding would have been avoided if the critics had understood that Thorfin Karlsefni's saga is a family saga whose plan is not concerned with a survey of the Norse discovery of America as a whole. Except for the part dealing with Thorfin Karlsefni's voyage, Hauksbook is of little value in shedding light on the Norse discovery. Its sailing directions and time periods are hopeless, and what it has to say about other participants is negligible. Most of the recent commentators and all of those who have treated the Norse discovery most fully are now agreed that the Flateybook contains the most helpful and reliable version.[11]

Besides these two narratives concerning the discovery of America, there are also about a dozen references to Vinland made by different Icelandic writers of earlier dates, one going as far back as Ari the Learned, the earliest historian of Iceland (aside from the poets) whose writings in part are still preserved. He was born in 1067. All of these brief mentions of Vinland are of the casual kind, indicating that Vinland was a well known country, like Ireland, Friesland or Russia, about which it was unnecessary to go into explanatory detail.

[9] *Studier over Vinlandsreiserne*, Copenhagen, 1887.
[10] *Norsemen's Route from Greenland to Vinland*, Copenhagen, 1918.
[11] *Cf.* A. W. Brögger, *Vinlandsferdene*, Oslo, 1937; Richard Hennig, *Terrae Incognitae* (Düsseldorf, 1938); Edward F. Gray, *Leif Eriksson, Discoverer of America*, Oxford, 1930; G. M. Gathorne-Hardy, *The Norse Discoverers of America*, Oxford, 1921; William Hovgaard, *The Voyages of the Norsemen to America*, New York, 1915; John Fiske, *The Discovery of America*, Boston, 1892.

As an illustration of the great significance of these scattered notices may be cited Ari the Learned's brief reference to Vinland, contained in his account of the discovery of Greenland, written about the year 1120. He was a meticulous historian who did not base his conclusions on the current traditions or folk-songs, but cites his own relative, Torkel Gellison, who had been in Greenland. Ari writes:

The land which is called Greenland was found and settled from Iceland. Erik the Red was the name of a man from Breidafjord who sailed from Iceland and took land there in what was later called Eriksfjord. He gave the land its name and called it Greenland, saying that people would be more inclined to emigrate thither if the land had a good name. There they found, both east and west in the land, building sites, boat-remains and stone implements by which one could understand that such people had lived there as now live in Vinland and which the Greenlanders call *Skrællings*. He (Erik) began to build the land fourteen or fifteen winters before Christianity was adopted in Iceland, as was told to Torkel Gellison, in Greenland (by a man) who personally accompanied Erik thither.[12]

This shows that Vinland about the year 1120 was a reasonably well known country. It is not an account of the discovery of Vinland, but only a reference to archeological remains in Greenland which presupposes a knowledge of Vinland. As John Fiske so aptly remarks: "Unless Ari and his readers had a distinct recollection of the accounts of Vinland, such a reference would have been an attempt to explain the less obscure by the more obscure." [13] Ari makes three other mentions of Vinland which in the same way implies a general knowledge of the discovery of Vinland.

The earliest literary references to the discovery of

[12] *Islendingabok*, Ch. 6. According to Ari, Christianity was introduced in Iceland in the year 1000.
[13] *Discovery of America*, I, 206.

America are not found in Icelandic documents, but in German and Norwegian records made shortly after these discoveries were made. Reference has already been made to Adam of Bremen's ecclesiastical history, completed about 1070, in which the author mentions that Vinland had been discovered by many. The earliest mention of Vinland is found on a stone inscribed with runes in an inland parish in Norway. The date of this inscription is about 1050.

VII. THE VIKING GRAVE AT LAKE NIPIGON

IT has been the common opinion of all students of the Vinland voyages that these journeys were merely brief visits to the shores of America, and that explorations into the hinterland were not to be thought of. But recently a sensational discovery made far inland seems to call for a drastic revision of the ideas held concerning the scope of these journeys. A grave containing three weapons from the eleventh century has been found near Lake Nipigon, which is 1,040 miles from Vinland in air line distance and 3,500 miles by the most probable land and water route. This discovery was made by James E. Dodd of Port Arthur, Ontario, a freight conductor on the Canadian National Railway. He is also interested in mining and it was while he was engaged in digging on his claim that he found this grave near Beardmore, a railroad station about 130 miles northeast of Port Arthur.

In the spring of 1930 or 1931 he was engaged in digging a trench on a promising spot on his claim. It was immediately below a dike of dark rock rising about a dozen feet above the ground. This dike was marked by a vertical vein of white quartz a foot wide. He decided to follow this white vein to see what it would lead to. He removed about three feet of soil at the bottom of it and came to a layer of schist, and then found that the white vein extended out from the dike in a horizontal direction.

Being eager to follow the horizontal direction of the vein, Dodd decided to loosen up the overlying soil with dynamite. This done, he noticed a strip of rusty iron "imbedded" in the schist (cemented to it?). He tried to pry it loose, but it broke in two, and then he found it was an old-fashioned sword. He also found an axe and a strip of metal bent like a handle. This came off easily. There was also a shallow iron bowl, but this broke in many fragments when he pried on it. He first thought that some previous miner must have been there long ago, and then decided that they were Indian relics and threw them on the dump. Being at the time on the quest of the alluring gold, supposedly hiding somewhere in the vein he was following, he practically forgot the "rusty iron" fragments which were left in the dump in the mine.[1]

For some time these articles lay there unheeded. Then in some way his interest in them was awakened. He took them to his home in Port Arthur and decided that there might be persons who would be willing to pay something for them. Shortly after he had taken them to his home he was visited by Mr. John Jacob of the Fish and Game Department of the Province of Ontario who had heard of the find from one of Dodd's neighbors. Mr. Jacob was so impressed by the possible significance of the find that he made a trip to the scene of the find. He found the local conditions to be as described by Dodd and also discovered a mold of rust left by the sword as it was pried loose from the rock. He sent word concerning the find to Dr. C. T. Currelly, Director of the Royal Ontario Museum of Archaeology, but apparently the message was never delivered.

Several years went by, and Mr. Dodd met with no responsive enthusiasm among the people with whom he associated. On the contrary, he became the butt of many

[1] The above description of his discovery is as he told it to Mr. O. C. Elliott, formerly a teacher in Fort William Collegiate Institute, in the summer of 1936. Mr. Elliott was one of the first to give any information to the public about the find. In September 1936 he sent a report of it to the present writer and about the same time it came to the attention of Dr. E. M. Burwash of the Ontario Department of Mines who communicated the information to the Royal Ontario Museum in Toronto.

mild jokes because of his interest in his new hobby. This tended to make him less communicative and his relics were rarely mentioned.

But in 1936 he came in touch with a sympathetic listener. It was Dr. E. M. Burwash of the Department of Mines who came to Port Arthur to hold an annual class in mining. Mr. Dodd told Dr. Burwash about his discovery, and the latter reported it to Dr. Currelly. Mr. Dodd was then persuaded to come to Toronto and the articles were bought by the museum. At this time Dr. Currelly asked Mr. Dodd if he had found anything else at the time of the discovery. The answer was yes, he had found a bowl of iron but it had broken in many pieces and he had almost forgotten it. This was later identified as the boss of the shield of which he had found the handle, and a couple of fragments of the boss were later found in the dump.

The museum authorities were much interested in this find and planned to write an official report on it. But these weapons represented a field of research with which Dr. Currelly's staff had had very little contact, and considerable correspondence and study were a preliminary necessity. In the meantime no photographs were given out and very little information. In the fall of 1937 the present writer was permitted to inspect the articles on condition that he say nothing about them to the public, as the museum had not yet finished its investigation of the circumstances of the discovery and therefore reserved the right to make the first report about it. I saw at once that these articles represented the standard type of Scandinavian swords and axes of the eleventh century, of which the museums of northern Europe have many specimens.

In spite of the Museum's caution, some fragmentary news of the find leaked out, and, because of its sensational nature, it was mentioned in many papers. Then in January, 1938, came a sudden anti-climax. A public lecturer mentioned the find in an address in Winnipeg, and a few days after this a newspaper in that city printed an interview with a former railroad pal of Mr. Dodd by the name of Eli Ragotte in which the latter declared that Dodd's discovery was a fake—that he, Ragotte, had found the relics himself in the basement of a house into which Mr. Dodd had just moved in 1931. Quickly the reporters hunted up the owner of the house, a Mr. Hansen, and he said yes, the implements had been given to him by Johan Bloch, an educated young Norwegian who had come there a few years previously. This seemed to be conclusive. Another historic bubble had burst.

If it had not been for Mr. J. W. Curran, editor of the Sault *Daily Star*, Sault Ste. Marie, Ontario, it is probable that nothing more would have been heard of the Lake Nipigon find. He is a lover of history and for some time had been investigating the tradition concerning early white men on Hudson Bay whom Samuel Champlain in 1610 heard referred to as *mistigoche*, "the wooden-boat men." In September, 1938, he was in Port Arthur and spent some time in probing into the story of Dodd's discovery in which he, like all others, had lost all faith. In company with Dr. George E. Eakins, president of the local historical society, and Judge Alexander McComber, both old residents of the city, he began an investigation which soon assumed extensive proportions.

He first got in contact with Mr. Carl Sorenson, Royal Norwegian Vice Consul in the neighboring city of Fort William, who had known Mr. Bloch for many years. Mr. Sorenson was confident that Mr. Bloch had nothing to do with the Lake Nipigon relics and this was corroborated by a number of local Norwegian engineers who also had known Bloch very well. He then interviewed Mr. Hansen in Port Arthur and Mr. Ragotte in Winnipeg and found that they had both made false statements. Mr. Hansen admitted that he had never seen the relics, and Mr. Ragotte signed an affidavit to the effect that he had just told the story "to have a little fun with Dodd." Finally he was able to find several witnesses who could testify to the fact that Mr. Dodd had had the relics a year or two before he had moved into Mr. Hansen's house where Ragotte and Hansen had claimed that they had been found.

Mr. Curran also visited the site of the find in company with Dr. Eakins, Mr. Fletcher Gill and Mr. Dodd. They found it was about 200 yards south of a small stream known as Blackwater River which flows into Lake Nipigon on the east side of the lake. The Canadian National Railway tracks are close by and the village of Beardmore is three miles to the northeast. Mr. Dodd was asked to see if he could find any of the fragments of the boss of the shield, and after some digging he unearthed a piece about 2½ inches in length and about an inch in width. This was taken to the museum in Toronto where it was learned that Professor McIlwraith of the museum staff had already been up to the site of the find and found a similar small fragment.

Mr. Curran's report on his investigation was originally printed in the Sault Ste. Marie (Canada) *Daily Star*, October 4, 6 and 8, 1938. Recently it was republished with much additional matter in a volume entitled *Here Was Vinland*. In this volume [2] are presented eight affidavits from different persons who all saw the implements in 1930 and 1931 shortly after they had been found by Mr. Dodd and before he had moved into the house rented from Mr. Hansen. These affidavits were obtained chiefly through the agency of A. J. McComber, Senior Judge of the Thunder Bay District.

Altogether, Mr. Curran's and Judge McComber's investigations have been so thorough, with results so convincing, that there seems to be no doubt about the authenticity of the find.

The fact that this warrior was buried with all his weapons at considerable depth shows that he was not a

[2] Sault Ste. Marie, Canada, pp. 175-184.

lone wanderer or a prisoner among the Indians, for in that case his weapons would not have been buried with him. Probably he would not have been buried at all, for the digging of deep graves was among Indians too hard work to be spent on prisoners or enemies. He must have been accompanied by other Norsemen who solicitously buried him according to their custom. Moreover, they must have been as well armed as he, or they would have kept his weapons. These conclusions are self-evident.

But now comes a question which is not so easily answered: What was this band of Norsemen doing in this remote inland wilderness in the eleventh century?

Three possibilities present themselves. One is that a company of early visitors to Vinland decided to explore the great waterway to the West—the St. Lawrence River. By ascending this river and the Great Lakes above, they would come, if they followed the north shore of Lake Superior, within a hundred miles of the place where the Viking grave was found. This is the way the French in the seventeenth century penetrated to the center of the American continent.

But there are several objections to this theory. While the French followed this waterway to its ultimate ends, they did not do it upon their first attempt. Theirs was a progressive exploration dictated and governed by their trade in beaverskins and other hides, which led them farther and farther inland. The Norsemen in the eleventh century had no such commercial motive, and it seems extremely improbable that they would go to the labor of carrying their heavy boats over a large number of portages, including that of Niagara Falls, without an important motive. This improbability becomes an impossibility when we think of their turning north from Lake Superior into the barrens of northern Ontario. What would they want there?

A second possibility is that these men were Greenlanders who on their way to or from America were driven far north into Davis Strait, then 500 miles north-west through Hudson Strait, and finally 900 miles south to the head of James Bay. Here they may have suffered shipwreck whereupon they may have wandered inland.

But all this is highly improbable. It does not seem likely that a storm or a series of storms could have driven them so far on such a circuitous route when there was no lack of harbors where they could have sought safety. Along the shores of Labrador and in Hudson Bay there are thousands of headlands and islands behind any one of which they could have lain in safety until the storm had passed. According to the *Coast Pilot* this is not a dangerous coast to follow except in winter and early spring. This theory does not seem reasonable.

The third possibility is that these men were members of an exploration party who purposefully set out to circumnavigate this new land of the West. Of course, they would have had no conception of the fact that America was a vast continent. To them, as to Adam of Bremen, it was "another island" whose unseen shores would beckon to the curious. There is nothing improbable in such a purpose; we find several examples of it in early Norse history. In or about the year 865 Naddod left the Faroe Islands for Norway and was carried by storms to Iceland—a country up to that time unknown to Norsemen. Curious to see how big it was, Naddod sailed completely around it, a distance of a thousand miles. It was late in fall when he left it, and as a heavy snowstorm was covering the whole country with a blanket of snow, he called it Snowland. A year or two before or after this—the exact date is unknown—another sailor had the same experience. Gardar, a Dane, left Denmark for England but was carried to Iceland. He, too, prompted by the same curiosity, sailed completely around it, whereupon he sailed away and called it Gardarsholm after himself.

Such an impulse—to see how big a new land is—is one of the most common forms of curiosity. Erik Thorwaldson felt it when he sailed hundreds of miles northward toward the Arctic after he discovered Greenland. To him and the people of his time, Vinland was "another island," and sooner or later some of them would set out to circumnavigate it. When such time came they would sail northward following the coast, push through Hudson Strait and then turn southward along the sterile coast of .western Labrador. When they arrived there they would have reason to think that they had come to the other side of "the island," for the shore here runs due north and south for 900 miles. But when they reached the head of James Bay and saw the large rivers which poured into it—the Nottawa, the Moose and the Albany—the last with a flow far larger than any they had seen in Europe, they would have realized that this was no island but a large continent. For further progress they needed more extensive equipment.

Two possible courses would now present themselves. One would be to return as they had come, past 2,000 miles of barren shores—a route that would have no appeal to the alert men who had planned the enterprise. The other would be to send the ship home and with a smaller company to ascend the large river, the Albany, to its source. Inasmuch as they had now sailed southward for almost a thousand miles, they would have reason to believe that the overland route would not be so long. As this route suggested not only a change from the cramped conditions on board the ship but also new scenes and adventure, there is little doubt that there would be plenty of volunteers for the journey.

The Albany River is reported to be an easy river to ascend, being almost free from portages. Finding that it had a continuous westward trend, the supposed explorers would eventually turn into some tributary coming from the south. While the country west of James Bay is depressing and worthless for agriculture, it is rich in game and fish, and they would have little difficulty about food supplies. Eventually, after a journey of about 500 miles, they would reach the dividing ridge between the waters of the Albany and the St. Lawrence. From this point they could practically float back to the more familiar shores of the Atlantic, but here one of their number died. Inasmuch as his grave lies at the foot of the white vein of quartz which rises like a twelve-foot monument above his grave, it is probable that he was carried to this conspicuous spot after his death so that his grave later could be easily found. Perhaps he was the commander of this valiant company, and it was expected that his people would plan to bring his remains to Greenland to bury them in consecrated ground, just as Thorstein tried to do with the body of his brother Thorwald.

But no one came to claim the body of this first intrepid explorer of America's interior. The way back to Vinland and Greenland was exceedingly far, whether by sea or land, and it is doubtful if any of the company returned to tell the tale. Only of this man can we visualize the funeral up there on the low ridge sparsely clad with solemn spruce trees. Down to the solid rock they dug his grave, then placed him there beneath the monument that Nature had provided. His head was to the west facing the dawn whence would come the Lord of the Resurrection Morning. On his left side lay his trusty sword, on his right his axe. His arms were folded over his breast and over them lay his burnished shield. Then, perhaps, while his comrades in arms stood bareheaded around the open grave, one of them repeated as much of the liturgy for the dead as he could remember.[3]

[3] Some weeks after this chapter was written, the writer received a copy of the March, 1939, issue of the *Canadian Historical Review* which on pages 4 to 7 contains a report entitled "Viking Weapons Found Near Beardmore, Ontario," written by Dr. C. T. Currelly. As the writer's investigation was made independently of Dr. Currelly's, it is interesting to find how closely the two reports agree.

VIII. LATER EXPEDITIONS TO VINLAND AND MARKLAND

THE so-called Vinland Sagas that have been reviewed in Chapters II to V *ante* tell of six expeditions to America, and many students have therefore thought that these include all the voyages that were made. But it is not safe to assume that nothing happened because the records are silent. The fallacy of such a conclusion is revealed in the preceding chapter.

All the planned voyages to the American mainland that are mentioned in Flateybook and Hauksbook were undertaken by members and near connections of Erik Thorwaldson's family and were perhaps first recorded by some member of this family. It seems probable that other families would also have been interested in voyages to Vinland, for there is abundant evidence to show that these Norsemen were not lacking in initiative and resourcefulness. Bjørn Jonssøn, an old chronicler, relates the following of the seafaring habits of the Norse Greenlanders:

All the large landowners of Greenland had vessels built to send to the *Nordsetur* for seal hunting, with all kinds of hunting gear and hewed timber; and sometimes they themselves accompanied the expeditions—as is related in Skald-Helgi's Saga and in that of Thordis. Most of what they took was seal-oil, for seal hunting was better there than at home in the settlements. . . . *The Nordsetur* men had their booths or houses both in Greipar and in Crooked-Fjord Heath. Driftwood is found there but no growing trees. This northern end of Greenland is most liable to take up all the wood and other drift that comes from the bays of Markland.[1]

[1] From Björn Jonsson's *Grönlands Annaler*, written before 1646 and compiled from older Icelandic sources. Quotation from *Grønlands Historiske Mindesmærker*, II, 238.

Plate I. The first white man's homestead in the new world. Erik Thorwaldson's house was just on the other side of the steep knoll in the left foreground. The foundation remains.

From Poul Nörlund's BRATTAHLID in *Meddelelser om Grönland*, Vol. 88, No. 1

Plate II. Norse Axe, XI Century, found in Nova Scotia.

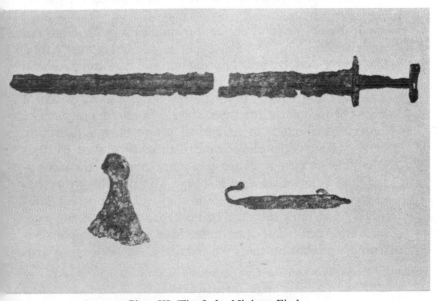

Plate III. The Lake Nipigon Find.

The *Nordsetur* stations lay very far to the north, around Disco Island and northward. In 1823 one of these seal-hunting stations was discovered a thousand miles north of the Eastern Settlement. On the island of Kingiktorsuak, north of Upernivik, in latitude 72° 57-58′, Captain W. A. Graah of the Danish Navy, the first explorer of the Arctic regions of Greenland after it was rediscovered, found three cairns; in the top of one of these he found a stone

FIG. 2. THE KINGIKTORSUAK STONE, FULL SIZE
Photograph furnished by The National Museum, Copenhagen

about three inches long, containing a neatly engraved runic inscription. The following is a translation: "Erling Sigvatsson and Bjarne Thordarson and Endridi Oddsson raised these beacons the Saturday before *gagndag* (i.e., April 25) and wrote" (here follow the last six signs which have been a puzzle for more than a hundred years). The inscription abounds in numerical proportions and cryptic signs and is a very clever contrivance.[2] Professor Magnus Olsen has written an exhaustive monograph on the inscription and believes its date is 1333. The present writer has just completed an independent study of it (not yet published) and finds the date to be 1291. As the cairns were built in April, these men must have spent the preceding winter up there on the 73rd parallel. Not until more than

[2] Norsk Tidsskrift for Sprogvidenskap (Oslo, 1932), V, 189-257.

300 years later did any other explorers penetrate so far north.

The greatest need of the colonists in Greenland was timber for they built large houses and needed wood products for roofs, floors, paneled walls and fuel. They also needed lumber for boats, furniture and many other uses. A voyage to Norway was four times as far as a trip to the inlets of southern Labrador where there were no harbor duties to pay and the timber was free. But as a journey a thousand miles north into the Arctic wastes was not thought of sufficient importance to be recorded, it is not strange if we hear little of their necessarily frequent voyages to the American mainland for timber.

In view of the fact that these Norsemen in Greenland were remarkably enterprising and capable [3] and equipped with sea-going vessels, it would be strange indeed if only one household out of a known total of 280 had the curiosity and enterprise to visit the American shores, especially as we are repeatedly told that voyages thither were profitable.

We have documentary proof of one voyage to Vinland which indicates that the contact with it was one of considerable importance. In 1112 Erik Gnupson was appointed by Pope Paschal II "bishop of Greenland and Vinland in partibus infidelium." [4] According to Ivar Bardsen, the Bishop's seat was at Sandness in the Western Settlement, and a find has been made there which supports this. [5] In

[3] There is a record of an exploration expedition which was made by them in 1266 to Lancaster Sound on the 75th parallel. See Daniel Bruun in *Meddelelser om Grönland*, 57, 107; also H. Geelmuyden, *Den Förste Polarekspedition*, in *Naturen*, VII, 178.

[4] John Fiske, *The Discovery of America*, I, 222. Professor Fiske gives the title in quotation marks but does not mention his source.

[5] Aage Roussell, *Sandness and the Neighboring Farms*, in *Meddelelser om Grönland*, Vol. 88, No. 28-30. This find consists of a rectangular piece of wood about sixteen inches long, richly ornamented on one side with expert carving of a type characteristic of the twelfth century. Dr. Roussell believes it was one of the arms of a bishop's folding chair and prints an illustration of one having the same carving upon it. This type

1121 the Bishop made a journey to Vinland as is recorded in a number of Icelandic annals of the time.

Unfortunately it is not known if the bishop ever reached Vinland, but nonetheless his journey is highly significant. It is of course excluded that he went to Vinland for purposes of exploration or adventure. His training and duties as a bishop of Greenland make that impossible. But it is quite possible that as the habitable parts of Greenland became crowded, some of the people would emigrate to the more congenial climate of Vinland as Thorfin Karlsefni had done and create temporary settlements. In such case the Bishop's journey would be eminently fitting.

Perhaps it was Bishop Erik and his missionaries who planted the Christian faith in a tribe of Micmac Indians of Gaspé, a trace of which was found by their first French missionary in the seventeenth century, as related by Dr. John Gilmary Shaw.[6]

Practically all that we know about the Norse colony in Greenland in written form comes to us through Icelandic channels. We have no literary productions whatever in Greenland manuscripts because these all perished when the colony came to an end through the double attacks of pestilence and the Eskimos. Yet it is known that these Norsemen had literary interests. At least two of the famous poems of the Elder Edda, the Atli lays, were written in Greenland, and there were several other poets, such as Skjald-Helge and Svein, whose works have been preserved in part. This is not bad for a community of only two or three thousand in that remote age. It is probably true that these writings were only a small part of the literature of the colony, in which narratives about expeditions to Vin-

of a chair was "not used by secular chiefs or the lower clergy but forms a part of an episcopal sign of dignity."

[6] LeClercq, *First Establishment of the Faith*, Shea's translation, New York, 1881, Introduction, I, 11. LeClercq's own account of this veneration of the cross is given in his *Relation de la Gaspesie*, pp. 172-199 and 266-277.

land and other distant regions may have played an important part.

A most interesting nonliterary piece of evidence of pre-Columbian contacts with America has just been noted in the cathedral of Schleswig, Germany. Professor Alfred Stange of the University of Bonn is at present engaged in restoring the wall paintings of this church which was built about 1280. In an arcade or cross passage are a series of paintings depicting scenes from the life of Christ. These are bordered on the sides by floral designs and below by a frieze showing small animals and birds. In this frieze Professor Stange found eight excellent reproductions of a strutting turkey cock. The frieze, according to Stange, dates from the time when the church was erected, and the artist is said to have been a painter from Lübeck, one of the chief centers of the Hanseatic League (see Plate IV).

There is complete agreement among scholars that the turkey was not introduced in Europe until 1530 when the Spaniards brought some birds back from Mexico. The earliest known representation of it is by Pierre Belon in 1555.[7] Its appearance in a northern European church built 275 years earlier is therefore a remarkable discovery. It not only presents independent proof of the Norse discovery of America, but also indicates later pre-Columbian visits to it. As the Hanseatic League carried on trade with Greenland, it is possible that the artist painted this strange bird from life.

The Icelandic historian, Gudmundur Kamban, who was the first to call attention to the significance of these turkeys as proof of pre-Columbian visits to America, thinks that one of the early eleventh century discoverers of America brought turkeys back with him from Vinland to Greenland. Here domestication may have been attempted but probably without success. But he assumes that before the birds perished, some local artist in woodcarving, weav-

[7] Belon, *L'Histoire de la Nature des Oyseaux*, p. 249.

ing or painting would preserve the likeness of the beautiful bird from forgetfulness. Later, according to Kamban, this pictorial image would be copied and recopied until finally after several centuries a sample would come to the attention of the Lübeck artist who decorated the walls of the Schleswig cathedral.[8]

While this theory is not impossible, it seems improbable that a series of more or less crude copies of an unknown bird would eventually result in anything as lifelike as the strutting turkey of the cathedral. His characteristic pose, his wheeled tail, the strange tubular extension dangling from the base of his beak—even the unique beard or tuft of coarse hair projecting from his breast—are all there in lifelike detail. This indicates immediate contact between the artist and the bird.

Inasmuch as there is evidence to show that the Hanseatic League carried on trade with Greenland as early as the thirteenth century,[9] it seems more probable that some captain from Lübeck on one of these trading trips obtained a turkey from a Greenlander who shortly before that time had brought it with him from the American mainland. In this way the stage would be set for the Lübeck artist to paint the bird from life as his work in the cathedral indicates that he has done. (See Note, page 86.)

The people of Greenland at this time were reasonably prosperous and had time for domestic arts and also for literature. They kept many cows besides sheep, goats and horses. They also had considerable income from the sea in the form of seals, walruses, whales and polar bears. Their shipments of walrus tusks were so large that for a time it drove ivory, which it supplanted, off the market. Their sixteen churches were large, well-built structures of stone, and the cathedral is reported to have been a fine edifice. The foundation, which still remains, shows that it was eighty-four feet long and sixty feet wide across the

[8] *Politiken* (Copenhagen), September 4, 1939.
[9] A. W. Brögger, *Vinlandsferdene*, Oslo, 1937, pp. 167-175.

transepts. The bishop's residence was even larger, and his barns, according to Dr. Nörlund, had stalls for more than a hundred cows.

The earlier impression that the Greenland colony was a forlorn settlement of semi-savages fades when we see the amazing finds unearthed by Dr. Poul Nörlund in the cemetery at Herjulfsness.[10] These finds are nearly all from the fourteenth century when the colony was beginning to decay because of the unwise restrictions imposed upon its commerce by the King of Norway. Nevertheless we find that the same fashions in clothing were in vogue in Greenland as in the best centers of Europe. The dead were buried in long gowns, tight at the waist, but with very voluminous skirts, up to fifteen feet in circumference. On their heads they have hoods with long pendant "tails" two feet long and more, hanging behind. Just such garments as these were worn by Dante, Chaucer and the best people of their time.

Up to this time (ca. 1340), the Norsemen of Greenland had lived in peace, without danger from outside enemies or contact with the Eskimos.[11] They knew from relics found on the shore that these people whom they called Skrællings (i.e., inferior people) had lived there before their time, but they had disappeared. But some time before the middle of the fourteenth century reports reached the Eastern Settlement that the Eskimos had invaded the Western Settlement, causing serious trouble. This was alarming news, and an expedition was sent from the Eastern to the Western settlement. We have the second-hand testimony of a member of this expedition as to what happened.

This eyewitness was Ivar Bardson, a priest from the vicinity of Bergen, Norway. In 1341 he was sent to Greenland by his superior, Bishop Haakon of Bergen, to

[10] *Buried Norsemen at Herjulfsness* in *Meddelelser om Grönland* (1924), Vol. 67. Note final conclusion on p. 51.
[11] H. Rink, *Tales and Traditions of the Eskimo*, 1875.

learn what had become of the Bishop's old friend, Bishop Arne of Greenland, from whom he had heard nothing for many years. Ivar reached Greenland in safety and found Bishop Arne alive and well except for the weakness of old age. He was persuaded to remain in Greenland for many years as superintendent of the properties of the bishopric.

Shortly after his arrival in Greenland, Ivar and a company of men were sent to the Western Settlement. Their mission was to repel the Eskimos. The following is a part of a sixteenth century transcript of Ivar's report of this expedition:

. . . There in the West Settlement stands a large church, which is called Stensness (Sandness) church, which church for a time was a cathedral and episcopal seat.[12] But now the *Skrællings* have occupied all the West Settlement, there are many horses, goats, cattle and sheep, all wild, and no people, neither Christian nor heathen. All this was told us by Ivar Bardson Greenlander, who was steward of the episcopal residence in Gardar for many years, that he had seen all this, and he was one of those appointed by the Lawman to go to the Western Settlement against the Skrællings, to drive the Skrællings out of the West Settlement, and when they came thither, they found no man, neither Christian nor heathen, nothing but some wild sheep and cattle.[13] [The report adds that they took some of the sheep and cattle and then returned to the Eastern Settlement.]

There has recently been much discussion as to what had become of the people of the Western Settlement. Some writers have thought that they were exterminated by the Eskimos. But as Ivar Bardson does not mention any signs of bloodshed, this theory is a mere unsupported guess. Besides, as Nansen writes: "Can anyone who knows the

[12] This church and farm was located at the inner end of Ameralik fjord, known to the old Norsemen as Lysufjord.
[13] See entire report in *Grönlands Historiske Mindesmærker*, III, 259. Ivar's commission from Bishop Haakon is printed in *Ibid.*, III, 886-889.

Eskimos imagine that they slaughtered the men but not the cattle? These represented food for them and that is what they would first have turned their attention to." [14]

Nansen's has an explanation of the disappearance of these colonists which is almost diametrically opposed to the theory of extermination. He believes that Ivar Bardson's visit took place just at a time when the Norsemen voluntarily gave up their accustomed mode of life and joined themselves to the Eskimos. He reasons that the Norsemen would eventually recognize that Greenland was better adapted for hunting than for agriculture, and that they now had taken the decisive step to adopt this supposedly easier mode of life. This theory is fully and ably supported by Vilhjalmur Stefansson. [15]

But this revolutionary change in mode of life of a large group seems very doubtful. It is quite possible that some of the Norsemen now and then voluntarily adopted the Eskimo life, just as we read of some of the early Frenchmen in America (mostly half-breeds) joining themselves to the Indians. But it does not seem plausible that a whole settlement of white people in the midst of the hostilities would bury the hatchet and join themselves to their former enemies whom they considered an inferior race. There is no apparent reason why they should, for these Norsemen had coupled hunting with agriculture for many generations. Furthermore, if such a wholesale fusion took place, the traditions of the Eskimos ought to reflect it. But they make no reference to it; on the contrary, these traditions tell only of continuing hostilities until the last Norseman was destroyed. [16]

It is beyond the province of this study to determine

---

[14] In Northern Mists, II, 109.

[15] Unsolved Mysteries of the Arctic, New York, 1939, pp. 23-25; Natural History, January, 1939.

[16] H. Rink, in Aarbøger for Nordisk Oldkyndighed (1868), p. 194; D. Bruun, in Meddelelser om Grönland, pp. 57, 144 ff.; 67, 133, 251, 257, 258, 430, 482, 518, 520.

what eventually became of the Norse population in Greenland as a whole. But concerning the disappearance of the people of the Western Settlement in 1342 we have a bit of important contemporary evidence. According to the information of the Greenlanders of that time, this disappearance was not because of extermination by the Eskimos nor because of amalgamation with them, but was due to emigration. There is preserved a seventeenth century copy or synopsis, made in Latin by Bishop Gisle Oddson, of an annalistic record of the fourteenth century which in translation for the year 1342 reads as follows:

1342. The inhabitants of Greenland fell voluntarily away from the true faith and the Christian religion, and, after having given up all good manners and true virtues, turned to the people of America (ad Americæ populos se converterunt). Some say that Greenland lies very near the western lands of the world.[17]

This copy of the old annal by Bishop Gisle Oddson supplements the report of Ivar Bardson cited above with the exception of the omission of the word *western* (Greenland). It is not strange that the Bishop was able to reproduce it from memory, for it is highly sensational from a clerical point of view. It not only corroborates Ivar Bardson's report that the people of the Western Settlement had emigrated, but also adds the startling fact that they had "given up the true faith." Finally it tells where these people had gone and what year this emigration took place.

[17] *Grønlands Historiske Mindesmærker*, II, 459-464. See also Storm, *Om Biskop Gisle Oddsons Annaler* in *Arkiv f. Nordisk Filologi*, VI (1890). Bishop Gisle Oddson was bishop of Skalholt and had spent his entire life there being the son of the former bishop, Odd Einarson. This episcopal see was in the Middle Ages the principal repository for Icelandic records. In 1630 it was destroyed by fire, and all its manuscripts perished. As Bishop Gisle had had the best opportunity of becoming acquainted with these manuscripts, he later made a synopsis in Latin of some of the more important documents that were lost. The name *America*, of course, was not in the original. But in translating the account into Latin in 1637, the Bishop also translated the name.

While Ivar Bardson's report and the Bishop's annal both refer to the same event, the references are so different in detail that it is obvious that the two reports are independent in origin.[18]

Some commentators have thought that the clause *ad Americæ populos se converterunt* means that the Norse Greenlanders gave up their former mode of life and united with the Eskimos of Greenland. But this imputes to the Bishop an anachronism of speech. As John Fiske says in his introduction to his *Discovery of America:* "In dealing with the discovery of America one must keep steadily before one's mind the quaint notions of ancient geographers." In this case the question is, What did the Bishop mean by the name of America? The answer is, of course, *continental* America. For more than a hundred years after his time, the geographers still considered Greenland as an elongation of Europe from the northeast.[19] Not even now with our better geographical knowledge would one think of alluding to the Eskimos of Greenland as the natives of America.

That the Bishop thought of the "people of America" as dwelling in a more remote region west of Greenland is indicated by him in the explanatory sentence that follows: "*Some say that Greenland lies very near to the western lands of the world.*" It is as if he had said: "They probably had not far to go, for it is said that Greenland lies very near to America." The eminent historian, Professor P. A.

[18] This charge of apostasy was perhaps an exaggeration. The priests who occasionally visited the Western Settlement would be annoyed at the superstitions and beliefs in magic formulas which flourished among the people, and would return with the report that the people there were "practically heathen." In the ruins of a single farm, Sandness, excavated by Dr. Aage Roussell, sixteen runic inscriptions were found on kitchen utensils and other objects, and a large proportion of them consist of magic formulas of a kind not approved by the church. See Erik Moltke's Appendix to Roussell, *Sandness and the Neighboring Farms* in *Meddelelser om Grönland* (1936), Vol. 88, No. 2.

[19] Fiske, *Discovery of America*, II, 549. *Cf.* Winsor, *Narrative and Critical History*, I, 117-132.

Munch, is entirely of the same view. He says: "The attacks of the Eskimos were presumably the cause of what is stated in an account of 1342, viz., that the inhabitants of Greenland fell voluntarily from Christianity and emigrated to other parts of America. . . . This account has all evidence of truth (*aldeles Troværdighedens Præg*)." [20]

This report, that these harassed people emigrated to America, not only reflects the views of their contemporaries, but also tells what would seem to have been the reasonable thing to have done. When two hostile tribes make war on each other, the usual result is that the weaker one eventually seeks refuge elsewhere. These people could not move to the Eastern Settlement, because that was already occupied. Nor could they move northward, because they would be trespassing on the haunts of their enemies, the Eskimos. The only direction that lay open to them was west or southwest. There lay a land known to them in song and story for hundreds of years, where they were accustomed to go for their timber supply (see pp. 75 and 87). There was probably no great number of these exiles, as several years of fighting must have reduced the population considerably. But these survivors, perhaps a couple of hundred in number, decided, like their ancestors before them, to seek new homes in another western land. There is nothing unique in such an emigration. It is just another link in that long series of mass migrations of which we read in Jornandes, Paulus Diaconus and other medieval historians.

The fact that Bardson found many cattle and sheep grazing in the deserted settlement indicates that the settlers must have left their homes the same summer in which he arrived, for the cattle could not possibly have survived

[20] *Det Norske Folks Historie, Unionsperioden,* I, 313, 314. The same interpretation—emigration to America—is also given by Storm in *Arkiv f. Nordisk Filologi,* VI, 356. The same view is also held by Professor Finn Magnusen, the learned compiler of *Grönlands Historiske Mindesmærker* (see Volume III, 887).

outdoors during the long winter of northern Greenland. Their few and small vessels would not permit them to take all their personal possessions in one trip. They would take their families and their best milch cows, intending to return for the other domestic animals later in the summer.

If one asks, What became of these people? there are many answers. Nicholas Tunes, who in 1656 visited Baffin Land, reported that he found two types of natives. One was of tall stature, well built and with blond complexion; the other was the common Eskimos.[21] From the same region Dr. Franz Boas has recorded a number of striking traditions of a people called *Tornit* or *Tunit* which seem to show that a people of big physique, other than the Eskimos, have lived there.[22] In the same direction go the observations made by G. M. and Robert Gathorne-Hardy [23] and Sir Wilfred T. Grenfell.[24] Then there are the "Blond Eskimos" seen by many explorers [25] and described at length by Vilhjalmur Stefansson,[26] and the blue-eyed Indians of Moose River, Ontario, and several other places.

But while any or all of these ethnologically divergent types may indicate descent from the Norse Greenlanders who emigrated to America in 1342, the evidence is not sufficiently clear to prove it. There is also the possibility that these exiles never reached continental America but perished in the crossing, or, if they did reach it, they may have been exterminated by the natives shortly after their arrival. These possibilities are too many to be answered

[21] Cesar de Rochefort in *Histoire des Isles Antilles de l'Amerique,* 1658, Book I, Ch. 18.

[22] *Bulletin American Museum of Natural History,* XV, 209-11, 315-16, 541. Some of these traditions are reprinted in Hovgaard, *Voyages of the Norsemen to America,* pp. 45-49.

[23] *A Recent Journey to Labrador,* in the *Geographical Journal,* London, 1922, Vol. 59, 153-167.

[24] *Forty Years for Labrador,* Boston, 1932, p. 102.

[25] See General Greeley's article in *National Geographic Magazine,* December, 1912.

[26] *My Life with the Eskimo,* 1913, pp. 191-202; Hovgaard, *Voyages of the Norsemen to America,* 1914, p. 50.

and really do not matter. Nor does it matter if the Norse Greenlanders did not emigrate, but joined the Eskimos. The significant thing is that the report of this alleged emigration, and, more important, the alleged apostasy, was the cause of another expedition to America, this time from Norway and Sweden, which carried its members into the very heart of the American continent 130 years before Columbus reached the West Indies. This will be told in the following chapter.

NOTE. Some time after this book was first published, a controversy arose concerning the date of the eight turkey paintings. Dr. H. Hermannsson, in a review in *American Historical Review* (January, 1942, p. 318), alleges that Dr. Erwin Stresemann has discovered that they were of recent origin, four having been painted in 1891, by an old painter in Hannover named A. Olbers, and the other four being the work of some unknown artist in 1920.

This is partly supported and partly contradicted by E. Ehrhardt, a building inspector in Bremen. He says he supervised the construction work in the cathedral for a long period and claims that Olbers painted *all* the turkey paintings in that church (*Flensborg Avis*, Feb. 26, 1941).

Most of the German and Danish experts on old church paintings refuse to accept Olbers' claim, because it presupposes that the medallions now carrying the turkey paintings were left blank for more than 600 years. This, they say, is disproved by an examination of the paintings. Olbers' work in 1890 consisted in adding fresh colors to the faded image and also, in some places, new lines. Professor Alfred Stange's restoration of the ancient paintings consisted largely in removing this line patchwork of 1891, and in so doing the old lines of the turkeys were uncovered. (W. Hennig, "Die Truthähne von Flensburg," *Marburger Jahrbuch für Kunstwissenschaft*, Band 10. J. Jörgensen in *Flensborg Avis*, December 18, 1940.)

In view of this conflicting testimony, final conclusion must wait for fuller clarification.

IX. THE PAUL KNUTSON EXPEDITION
OF 1355-1364

IT has been mentioned above that the Norsemen in Greenland in all likelihood made frequent trips to Markland (Nova Scotia, Newfoundland and southern Labrador) for timber. Such trips were, as Nansen says, "everyday voyages for the support of life, like the sealing expeditions to *Nordsetur*, and when nothing particular happened to these vessels, such as being driven to Iceland, we hear nothing about them." In 1347 an incident, out of the ordinary, happened on one of these voyages, and we find it recorded in a number of Icelandic annals:

1347. There also [besides other ships mentioned] came a ship from Greenland; it was smaller than the small Icelandic trading vessels. It came into outer Straumfjord [in Iceland]. It had no anchor. There were seventeen men on board, and they had sailed to Markland, but were later driven here by a storm at sea.[1]

According to the Gottskalk Annals these Greenlanders the next year, 1348, went to Bergen which was then the largest city in the North and the temporary seat of the Norwegian government. Their appearance here must have

[1] *Islandske annaler*, Storm's edition (Christiania, 1888), pp. 213, 353, 403. As the annalist mentions that the vessel was rather small, Professor Storm (*Vinlandsreiserne*, p. 73) thinks that the purpose of the sailors was not timber cutting but probably fishing—the trips to the northern fishing grounds having become too hazardous because of the hostility of the Eskimos. This may well be. The motive for the journey is, however, of secondary importance. As Professor Joseph Fischer says (in *Die Entdeckungen der Normannen in Nordamerika*, p. 46): "Important is and remains the fact that the people of Greenland in the middle of the fourteenth century had not forgotten Markland, and that at that time Markland was mentioned in Iceland as a well known country."

created a great stir. While no doubt there was some knowledge about America among the better-informed ·Norwegians, this knowledge was necessarily quite hazy, as it rested on traditions several hundred years old. But here, perhaps for the first time since Thorfin Karlsefni's visit more than 300 years before, were seventeen men who had personally been to America, who could describe the country from personal observation.

The principal purpose of their visit to Norway may have been to inform the King of the threatened destruction of the Norse colonies. They could tell him that the Western Settlement had already been laid waste by the Eskimos and also the more startling news that the survivors had given up Christianity and emigrated to more distant regions farther west. It is possible, as Professor Munch suggests, that these men may have been in personal contact with their exiled countrymen in Markland.[2] While in Iceland these Greenlanders had conferences with Jon Guthormson, the most prominent politician in Iceland, who was temporarily in public and royal disfavor.[3] Sensing the political value of being the bearer of important tidings, he conducted these seventeen Greenlanders to the court of the King with the hope of being reinstated in the King's favor, in which he was eminently successful.

The King of Norway (and Sweden) at that time was Magnus Erikson, noted for his missionary zeal to convert the heathen. He was the one king in Swedish and Norwegian history who spent years of his time and millions in money in attempting to convert the people of another country to the Roman Catholic faith. With such ardor for the dissemination of the faith, it must have been most disturbing news to the King to learn that his own Christian subjects in Greenland were falling away from it. The year previously, 1347, he had shown his interest in Greenland

---

[2] Det Norske Folks Historie, Unionsperioden, I, 314.
[3] Islandske Annaler, p. 354; Grönlands Historiske Mindesmærker, III, 15, 52 (note 47).

when, in making his will, he bequeathed a sum equal to about eight thousand dollars in American money to the cathedral in Greenland. Now, immediately afterward, he learned to his dismay that entire parishes of his colony were repudiating Christianity.

But just at this time the King was occupied with a much greater missionary enterprise. In 1347 he made extensive preparations for raising a large volunteer army to compel the Russians to accept the Roman Catholic faith. In 1348 he personally led this army into Russia, where he captured a fort and compelled the baptism of a large number of heretics. A premature return to Sweden, however, turned this victory to defeat.

King Magnus had no intention of dropping his project because of this defeat. But simultaneously with the news of it came the report from the western part of Norway that a pestilence had broken out, which threatened to exterminate the entire population. This was the terrible Black Death which in these years spread over all Europe and Asia, and laid many million victims in their graves. The loss of life was not so great in Norway and Sweden as in other countries owing to the more scattered condition of the population, but even there, fully twenty-five per cent of the population perished in the two years 1349 and 1350.

This terrible catastrophe did not stop but only delayed the King's attempts to Christianize Russia. He sent a delegation to Pope Clement VI, asking him to declare a "holy crusade" against Russia, and without waiting for an answer he set out with another army in 1351. This campaign was more disastrous than the former, and when he returned to Sweden the next year, it was with the loss of many men and all his financial resources.

On his return home, however, he was met with good news. The Pope had hearkened to his request and had ordered that a holy crusade against Russia be preached in

Germany and Poland as well as in the Scandinavian countries. The Pope also offered King Magnus the loan of all the tithe money for 1351 collected in Sweden and Norway, and promised to give him half of all the tithes collected during the four following years.[4]

Full of determination to plant the cross in Russia, King Magnus now hopefully awaited the collection of the papal tithes. By 1353 abundant funds were coming in, and the King began to plan another campaign. But now the report was heard that the plague had spread such death in Russia that it would be suicidal to go there. Terrified by the memory of their own experience, the people refused any inducements to take part in the proposed crusade.[5]

The King was therefore obliged to give up his great mission. But he had the funds provided through the cooperation of the Pope. This temporary affluence enabled him to carry out an enterprise which he probably had had in mind for several years. His people in Greenland were falling away from Christianity. Seeing he could not go east, he would go west, and there seek to restore his subjects to the Church. We have a copy of a letter issued by him in 1354, in which it is stated that he is fitting out an extraordinary expedition to Greenland. There is no suggestion of commerce or warfare in the stated object of the expedition—its aim is solely to see that Christianity does not perish in Greenland. At its head is placed Paul Knutson, the law-speaker of Gulathing and one of the leading men of Norway. The following is a translation of the letter:

Magnus, by the Grace of God, King of Norway, Sweden and Skaane, sends to all men who see or hear this letter good health and happiness.

We desire to make known to you that you [Paul Knutson] are to take the men who shall go in the Knorr [the royal trad-

---

[4] *Diplomatarium Norwegicum*, VI, No. 200; Vol. VII, No. 245.
[5] A. Taranger, *Norges Historie* (1915), III, Part One, 87-89.

ing vessel] whether they be named or not named, from my bodyguard and also from among the retainers of other men whom you may wish to take on the voyage, and that Paul Knutson, who shall be the commandant upon the Knorr, shall have full authority to select the men whom he thinks are best suited to accompany him, whether as officers or men. We ask that you accept this our command with a right good will for the cause, inasmuch as we do it for the honor of God and for the sake of our soul and for the sake of our predecessors, who in Greenland established Christianity and have maintained it to this time, and *we will not now let it perish in our days*. Know this for truth, that whoever defies this our command shall meet with our serious displeasure and thereupon receive full punishment.

Executed in Bergen, Monday after Simon and Judah's day [October 28th] in the six and XXX year of our rule [1354]. By Orm Østenson, our regent, sealed.[6]

According to Professor Storm and others, this expedition sailed from Norway in 1355 and did not return until 1363 or 1364.[7] If we assume that Greenland was its only objective, it becomes very difficult to explain its long absence from home. The commander, Paul Knutson, was a most important man of those times, being one of the King's *Lendermænd* and a large landowner. Part of his crew is said to be from the King's retinue, i.e., all prominent men of the best families.[8] It is inconceivable that such men of affairs and social distinction would linger year after year in the dreary little colony of Greenland.

But if in the King's words, that he "would not now let Christianity perish" in Greenland, we see a reference

[6] An ancient Danish translation of this document is printed in *Grønlands Historiske Mindesmærker*, III, 120-122. Cf. also Storm's *Studier over Vinlandsreiserne*, p. 73. The law of Norway required that all royal documents and communications be sealed by the regent, who was the principal adviser of the king and the keeper of the royal seal.

[7] Storm, *Studier over Vinlandsreiserne*, pp. 73, 74; Gjessing in *Symra* (Decorah, Ia.), 1909, p. 124; Nansen, *In Northern Mists*, II, 38; Munch, *Det Norske Folks Historie, Unionsperioden*, I, 312.

[8] P. A. Munch, *Det Norske Folks Historie, Unionsperioden*, I, 414, 415.

to the apostasy of the Greenlanders who went to settle among the people of America in 1342, then we find abundant reason for the long absence of the expedition. The only place where Christianity was threatened in Greenland was the Western Settlement. There it was not only threatened, but had completely succumbed to adverse conditions, as was witnessed by the empty churches and deserted homesteads found by Ivar Bardsen. If Paul Knutson was to restore Christian worship to these deserted temples—as was his mission according to the King's mandate—it would be necessary for him to seek these apostates among the people of America whither they had gone, and then either compel them to return or accept the Faith in their new homes.

As good Catholics, Paul Knutson and his men would be horrified at the thought of these people rejecting Christianity, and thus, according to the belief of the times, selling themselves to the devil. As devout sons of the Medieval Church, the King and his messengers would feel it their duty to follow these apostates to the ends of the earth and make every effort to save them.

We therefore see the probability, as pointed out by Professor Storm,[9] that there was actually a Norse expedition in American waters about 1360. This view is supported by Dr. Gjessing.[10] Even Professor Nansen, who is extremely skeptical about all names and dates connected with the Vinland voyages, thinks it probable that Paul Knutson's mission also required him "to explore the fertile countries further west," i.e., America.[11]

The documents and libraries of the Scandinavian countries have very little to tell, however, of what happened to Paul Knutson's expedition. But out on our own Ameri-

[9] *Studier over Vinlandsreiserne* (1888), pp. 73, 74.

[10] *Symra* (Decorah, Iowa), 1909, p. 124.

[11] *In Northern Mists* (1911), II, 38. The fullest account of Paul Knutson is presented by Dr. Anton Espeland in the Bergen (Norway) *Aftenblad*, Nov. 18, 1922.

can frontier, engraved in ancient characters upon a stone wrapped in the roots of a forest tree, has come much information about the adventures of this first missionary expedition into America. This will be presented in Part Two of this work.

Plate IV. The Schleswig Turkey, painted on a frieze in the cathedral, four times
shown from the left side and four times from the right.

PART TWO
WESTWARD FROM VINLAND

Plate V. The Finding Place of the Viking Grave, shown in the lower center of the picture. The white quartz vein is seen in the background, sloping to the right.

Canadian National Railways and J. W. Curran

X. DISCOVERY AND LATER HISTORY
OF THE KENSINGTON STONE

IN the summer of 1898 a farmer in western Minnesota named Olof Ohman made a strange discovery. He was engaged in grubbing stumps in a rough and timbered section of his farm, near the village of Kensington in Douglas County. In the course of this work he encountered one tree which gave him considerable trouble. Upon digging away the soil around the roots he found that a large flat stone lay immediately under the tree. This stone was firmly clasped in the grip of two of its largest roots. He therefore had much trouble in cutting these roots without damaging his axe against the stone.

A little later his attention was again called to the vexatious stone. His ten-year-old son, playing about and finding the stone smooth of surface, had dusted it partly clean with his cap. When this was done he found a large number of regular marks or scratches upon the surface, and he called his father's attention to them. The father could make nothing out of these marks, but assumed that they were made by some human agent. The news of this discovery was soon noised about and many persons came to inspect the stone. Someone suggested that probably these marks were made by white or Indian robbers who had buried a treasure there. Upon hearing this suggestion a number of persons proceeded to dig in the hillside with shovels and pickaxes, hoping to gain speedy riches, but nothing was found.

This discovery was much more than a nine days' wonder, and as the stone was on exhibition in one of the bank windows of Kensington it was inspected by thousands.

The discussion concerning it finally resulted in the conclusion that the stone contained a runic inscription, several persons recalling that they had seen illustrations of similar inscriptions in Scandinavian books.

Late in the fall of 1898 a careful copy of the inscription was sent to O. J. Breda, professor of Scandinavian languages in the University of Minnesota. He studied the inscription for a couple of months and made a translation of most of it, which reads as follows, the words not understood being indicated by dashes:

——Swedes and——Norwegians on a discovery-journey from Vinland west——we had camp— — —one day's journey north from this stone. We— —fished one day. When we came home found——men red with blood and dead. A. V. M. save from——have——men by the ocean to look after our ships ——day's journey from this island. Year——.

This reading was given to the newspapers, accompanied by a lengthy interview in which Professor Breda stated that he did not believe the inscription was genuine for a number of reasons.[1] The chief of these were: (1) The mixture of Swedes and Norwegians which, he said, was "contrary to all accounts of the Vinland voyages," and (2) the language of the inscription was not Old Norse but a mixture of Swedish, Norwegian and English, which was unthinkable in an inscription dealing with the Vinland voyages of the eleventh century. As is seen above, Breda was unable to read the numerals in the inscription telling when this expedition is said to have been made. He therefore assumed that the inscription purported to add some details to the Vinland voyages which took place in the eleventh century.

These objections of Professor Breda, who was the first to give some interpretation of these strange signs, had a far-reaching influence. They were repeated by others who

[1] *Minneapolis Journal*, Feb. 22, 1899; *Skandinaven*, Chicago, Feb. 22, 1899.

gained their opinions on the subject from the newspaper accounts, and thus a general belief grew up that the inscription was the product of some Scandinavian immigrant who spoke a mixed English-Norwegian dialect.

In the meantime the stone had been shipped to Northwestern University in Evanston where it came to the attention of the philologist, Professor George O. Curme. He had photographs of the inscription taken and sent to several scholars in Europe. Presumably these scholars were of the opinion that a pre-Columbian expedition into the very heart of America was not only improbable but impossible, and that an alleged runic inscription recording such a fact was a fantastic absurdity which did not merit serious consideration. At any rate no detailed account or study of the inscription was published by them. The conclusion reported by them was that the inscription was a "clumsy fraud" perpetrated by some Swedish or Norwegian immigrant who had lived so long in America that he wrote a "mixture of English and Norwegian, as shown by the presence of several alleged English words in the inscription."

This verdict was generally accepted as final, and the stone was sent back to the finder branded as a forgery. Apparently disgusted with having had so much trouble about a "lying runestone," the owner threw it down in front of his granary (fortunately with the inscribed side down), where it lay for nine years esteemed only as a fair doorstep and a tolerable place to straighten nails and rivet harness straps.

Nine years later the present writer chanced to visit the neighborhood for the purpose of gathering material for a history of the Norwegian immigration. He found that the most vivid memory of former days which the people there had to relate was the discovery of this runic stone. As I had spent much time while in college in the study of runes and Old Norse, the story of this find interested me greatly. It was therefore with eager expectancy that I hunted up the owner of the stone and asked to see it.

Out in the farm yard he showed me a large, dark-colored stone lying near the granary door, half sunken in the ground. It was thirty-one inches (78.7 cm.) long, sixteen inches (40.6 cm.) wide, and six inches (15.2 cm.) thick. The weight was two hundred and two pounds (91 kg.). There was no inscription on the upper side, but the farmer turned the stone over. This under side presented on the whole a very smooth appearance with but few fractures, and the inscription which there appeared was technically a most excellent piece of work. Most of the lines were evenly spaced and the characters were of almost uniform height—about one inch. The neat inscription continued for about three-fifths of the length of the stone. Although the characters were dark and weathered, they were quite distinct except in the lower left hand corner of the inscription. Here the characters were almost worn away. The inscription continued on the flat edge which did not have the natural smoothness of the face of the stone and showed evidence of having been trimmed smooth with a cold-chisel. Here, too, the inscription covered three-fifths of the length of the stone. Evidently the lower uninscribed part of the stone was intended to be placed in the ground.

My wonder increased when I saw the length of the inscription. It is one of the longest of all runic inscriptions. I counted 220 characters, besides 62 double dots which were used to separate the words. Evidently the writer of this strange inscription was an artist in paleography who had a long story to tell. Although I assumed that the inscription was spurious, inasmuch as it has been condemned by several scholars, I persuaded the owner to let me take it home with me, thinking it would be an interesting souvenir and exemplification of my favorite subject of study.

Some time later I began the study of the inscription. On page 102 is my copy, with an interlinear transliteration. This reading and the following translation have since received general acceptance. The words in brackets are omitted in the inscription; those in parentheses are explanatory. Nine lines appear on the face of the stone as follows:

1. [We are] 8 Goths (Swedes) and 22 Norwegians on
2. [an] exploration-journey from
3. Vinland through (or across) the West (i.e., round about the West) We
4. had camp by [a lake with] 2 skerries one
5. days-journey north from this stone
6. We were [out] and fished one day After
7. we came home [we] found 10 [of our] men red
8. with blood and dead AV[e] M[aria]
9. Save [us] from evil

The following three lines appear on the edge of the stone:

10. [We] have 10 of (our party) by the sea to look
11. after our ships (or ship) 14 days-journey
12. from this island [in the] year [of our Lord] 1362

A discussion of the language of the inscription and its runic forms will be found in Chapters XIV-XVI.

My study of the inscription soon convinced me that, regardless of whether the inscription was true or false, it had been condemned largely on erroneous premises. For instance, the most common objection, that its language was not Old Norse and therefore the inscription must be a forgery, was manifestly a misconception, for Old Norse had ceased to be the language of Sweden and the greater part of Norway long before 1362.[2] In presenting my translation of the inscription, I therefore called attention to some of these misconceptions and urged that the inscription be given a new and more thorough consideration. This article, which revived the subject after it had lain dead and almost forgotten for nine years, was printed in

2 In southern Sweden and southeastern Norway the language had phonetically become very much like the present, and only in southwestern Norway did the archaic Old Norse still linger.

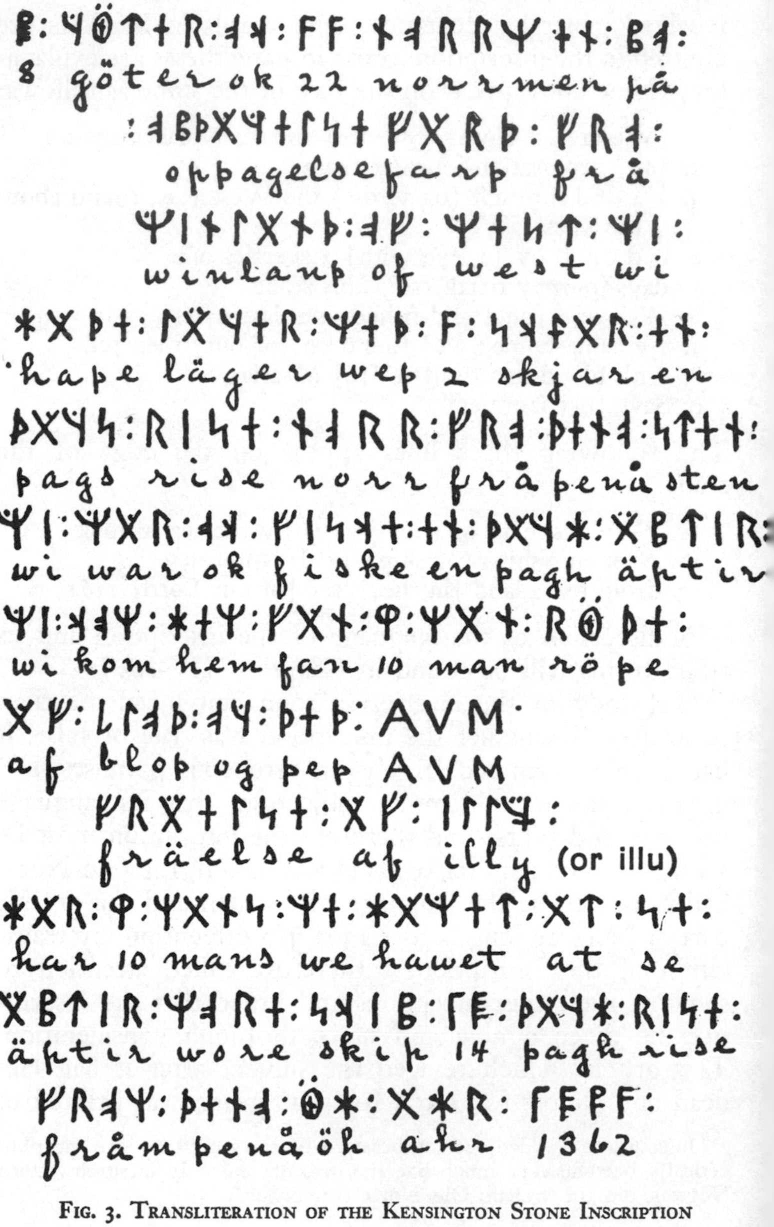

ᛔ:ᚢᛟᛏᛏᚱ:ᛀᛐ:ᚠᚠ:ᛐᛐᚱᚱᛣᛏᛏ:ᛒᛐ:
8 göter ok 22 norrmen på

:ᛐᛒᛔᚼᛐᛀᛐᛐ:ᚠᚷᚱᚦ:ᚠᚱᛐ:
oppagelsefarþ frå

ᛣᛁᛐᛀᚷᛐᚦ:ᛐᚢ:ᛣᛐᚼᛏ:ᛣᛁ
winlanþ of west wi

᛭ᚷᚦᛐ:ᛀᚷᚼᛐᚱ:ᛣᛐᚦ:ᚠ:ᚼᛐᚠᚷᚱ:ᛏᛏ:
hape läger weþ 2 skjar en

ᚦᚷᚼᚼ:ᚱᛁᚼᛏ:ᛐᛐᚱᚱ:ᚠᚱᛐ:ᚦᛏᛐᛐ:ᚼᛏᛏᛏ:
paþs rise norr frå penästen

ᛣᛁ:ᛣᚷᚱ:ᛐᛐ:ᚠᛁᚼᛏᛏ:ᛏᛏ:ᚦᚷᚼ᛭:ᚷᛒᛏᛁᚱ:
wi war ok fiske en pagh äptir

ᛣᛁ:ᛐᛐᛣ:᛭ᛏᛏᛣ:ᚠᚷᛐ:ᛩ:ᛣᚷᛐ:ᚱᛟᚦᛏ:
wi kom hem fan 10 man röpe

ᚷᚠ:ᛚᛁᛐᚦ:ᛐᛐ:ᚦᛏᚦ: AVM·
af bloþ og þeþ AVM

ᚠᚱᚷᛐᛀᛐᛐ:ᚷᚠ:ᛁᛀᛀᚼ:
fräelse af illy (or illu)

᛭ᚷᚱ:ᛩ:ᛣᚷᛐᛐᛐ:ᛣᛏ:᛭ᚷᛣᛐᛏ:ᚷᛏ:ᚼᛏ:
har 10 mans we hawet at se

ᚷᛒᛏᛁᚱ:ᛣᛐᚱᛏ:ᚼᛐᛁᛒ:ᛁᛖ:ᚦᚷᚼ᛭:ᚱᛁᚼᛏ:
äptir wore skip 14 pagh rise

ᚠᚱᛐᛣ:ᚦᛏᛏᛐ:ᛩ᛭:ᚷ᛭ᚱ: ᛁᛖᚠᚠ:
fråm penä öh ahr 1362

FIG. 3. TRANSLITERATION OF THE KENSINGTON STONE INSCRIPTION

Plate VI. The Kensington Stone, relic of the heroic and tragic wandering of Christian men, nearly six hundred years ago, in what is now the state of Minnesota,

Plate VII. The side view of The Kensington Stone.

Skandinaven, one of the leading Scandinavian newspapers of America, January 17, 1908.

My request that the inscription be given a new hearing was not in vain, for a very lively discussion of its faults and merits followed. Every word and character on the stone was subjected to a most searching scrutiny, and hundreds of articles for and against its genuineness were written and printed. It has been exhibited in France and Norway, as well as in numerous places in America. Geologists and chemists have made microscopic examinations of its surface and substance, and philologists and historians have made minute studies of its text and message. Very few inscriptions have received such keen study by people of all classes.

Among the first to give the Rune Stone serious attention was the Norwegian Society of Minneapolis—a literary club of the more prominent Norwegians of the city. In the autumn of 1908 the Society appointed a committee to inquire into the facts concerning the discovery of the stone. Doctor Knut Hoegh, one of the leading physicians of the city, was chairman of the committee and spent much time in investigating the subject. In December, 1908, and several times during the following year, he made trips to Kensington and the vicinity, interviewed all persons reputed to have any knowledge of the finding, and secured numerous affidavits.[3] In the autumn of 1909 the committee concluded its investigation and presented a report to the Society whose summary follows in translation:

1. The stone was found upon the spot where it was reported to have been found.
2. The stone which Mr. H. R. Holand now has is the same as the one that was found by Olof Ohman.
3. None of the persons who had anything to do with the finding of the stone, or who saw the place, the stone or the stump of the tree (under which it was found) soon afterward,

[3] These affidavits are printed in Chapter XI of this work.

can under any circumstances be supposed to have had anything
to do with carving the inscription.

4. The stone must have been in the ground long before the
present cultivation of the district took place. Its weathered
appearance, the worn appearance of the runes, and the circumstances of the roots (of the stump) seem to prove the last
point, when it is taken in connection with the stated facts.[4]

The investigation conducted by the Norwegian Society
under the direction of Dr. Hoegh concerning the physical facts connected with the discovery of the stone, while
made by laymen, was as thorough as possible, and the
findings of the committee have since been sustained by
more searching investigation. However, the report of the
committee did not have any extensive publicity, and a
lively discussion of the question involved in Paragraph 3
of the report continued. Since the first verdict concerning the origin of the inscription was to the effect that it
had been written by some Scandinavian immigrant who
wrote a mixture of his mother tongue and English, the
problem merely seemed to be to find the identity of this
forger. The neighborhood had been settled only about
thirty years, and as the early inhabitants were well known
locally, this identification did not seem impossible. Mr.
Ohman, as the finder of the stone, early came under suspicion. Professor N. H. Winchell, State Archeologist of
Minnesota, and others thoroughly investigated these rumors and found them wholly spurious.[5] The Museum
Committee of the Minnesota Historical Society who sifted
all these rumors says: "No one of all who have interviewed
Mr. Ohman, whether believers or non-believers in the
authenticity of the inscription, has seen any reason to
question his veracity."[6]

[4] *Symra* (Decorah, Iowa), V (1909), 187. The complete report is
printed on pages 178-189.
[5] A detailed account of this investigation is given in *Minn. Hist. So.
Collections*, XV, 237-245.
[6] *The Kensington Rune Stone*, St. Paul, 1910, p. 5.

Some time later a more important charge was made that a former Lutheran clergyman, named Sven Fogelblad, who spent his last years around Kensington, had made the inscription with the aid of two accomplices.[7] Professor Winchell also thoroughly investigated this report and found that it had no possible basis in fact.[8]

A more important contribution to a thorough understanding of this inscribed stone is the report published by the Minnesota Historical Society. In January, 1909, the Society felt called upon to take official notice of the stone and requested its museum committee to investigate the authenticity of the inscription. This committee consisted of the following members: Professor N. H. Winchell, geologist and State Archeologist; Rev. E. C. Mitchell, antiquarian; O. D. Wheeler, lawyer; F. J. Schaefer, President St. Paul Seminary; and Dr. Warren Upham, geologist and Secretary of the Society. This committee had the stone in its keeping for about two years and gave it a searching physical examination. Its members made several investigations in the locality where it was found, interviewed many local residents, and sifted several rumors and theories concerning the origin of the inscription. They also studied all published articles for and against the stone and submitted moot questions to experts. After more than a year of this careful inquiry, the committee on April 21, 1910, unanimously adopted a "preliminary report," which reads as follows:

Resolved, That this Committee renders a favorable opinion of the authenticity of the Kensington rune stone, provided, that the references to Scandinavian literature given in this Committee's written report and accompanying papers be veri-

[7] R. B. Anderson in *Amerika* (Madison, Wis.), May 27, 1910; *Minneapolis Journal*, June 2, 1910.

[8] See Winchell's correspondence dealing with Anderson's charges (see preceding note), printed in *Minneapolis Journal*, June 6, 1910, and reprinted in Holand, *The Kensington Stone* (1932), pp. 280-288. Other erratic theories are discussed in *Ibid.*, pp. 289-291.

fied by a competent specialist in the Scandinavian languages, to be selected by this Committee, and that he approve the conclusions of this report.[9]

About two weeks later, before the Committee had selected its specialist, it received a manuscript copy of an address on the Kensington Rune Stone by Professor G. T. Flom, delivered before the Illinois State Historical Society at its annual meeting, May 5-6, 1910.[10] This contained a formidable array of linguistic objections. With this new and important contribution to its philological material, the Committee resumed its study of the inscription. After giving detailed consideration to Professor Flom's dissertation, the Committee came to the same conclusion as before. A brief rebuttal of Flom's arguments was added to the report, whereupon Professor Gisle Bothne of the University of Minnesota was selected to act as a specialist in verifying the references mentioned above. By this time the summer vacation had begun and Bothne sent word that he could not accept the appointment as he was going away. He added that he did not believe the inscription was genuine because he considered the language was faulty. As an example he mentioned that the rune þ was not used properly.[11] The Committee did not select any other referee but published its report in December, 1910.[12]

After this report appeared in print, the inscription was the subject of much argument both at home and abroad. The Committee therefore waited about three years before rendering its final report. After all arguments on both sides

[9] *The Kensington Rune Stone. Preliminary Report to the Minnesota Historical Society by its Museum Committee*, St. Paul, 1910, p. 48.
[10] The address was later privately printed under the title, *The Kensington Rune Stone*. It contains 43 pages.
[11] This objection is discussed in Chapter 24, § 23. Bothne's letter is printed in Minnesota Historical Society *Collections*, pp. 15, 269.
[12] The report contains 66 printed pages and its title page bears the imprint *The Kensington Rune Stone, Preliminary Report to The Minnesota Historical Society by its Museum Committee*. Published by the Society, December, 1910.

seemed to have been presented, and finding no reason for changing its conclusions, the Committee added as its final verdict that "after carefully considering all the opposing arguments, the Museum Committee of this Society believe its [the Kensington Stone's] inscription is a true historic record." [13]

The Committee has been criticized for not having had a competent scholar in Scandinavian languages present at its sittings, but this was found impracticable. Instead it obtained opinions on all moot linguistic questions from scholars on both sides. As the Committee says in its report: "With one exception, the members of the Committee are all linguistic scholars and are capable of judging the force of linguistic arguments, *pro* and *con*, and we have attempted to compare judicially the evidence that has been adduced." [14]

It is thirty years since the Minnesota Historical Society published its committee's report, and since that time the study of this runic inscription has made important advances. Many points which then seemed obscure have now been clarified. Linguistic and runic usage of fourteenth century Scandinavian has been subjected to intensive study, and many misconceptions have been cleared up. Much new information has also been gained about fourteenth century history as far as it pertains to this subject.

This long discussion and wide publicity has served another important end. It has brought to light a number of ancient arms and implements which have been unearthed by pioneer farmers in tilling their soil. These archaic finds dating from the Middle Ages have all been discovered in the general region where the stone was found. In 1911 and again in 1928 the present writer made a study of such arms and implements in a large number

[13] Both reports with many illustrations are printed in the *Minnesota Historical Collections*, XV, 221-286. The final verdict is given on page 286.

[14] *Ibid.*, p. 256.

of museums in six European countries. It is believed that these finds will be found to have great significance in the question of the authenticity of the Kensington Rune Stone.

In addition to the runic inscription of Kensington and a number of fourteenth century war implements, there have also been found no less than five other landmarks of an unexpected kind which show that white men visited this part of Minnesota hundreds of years before the arrival of the earliest settlers. These various indications of white men's presence in Minnesota in pre-Columbian times will be discussed in the following pages.

The stone has now been returned to the county where it was found and is on exhibition in Alexandria, the county seat.

XI. THE CIRCUMSTANCES OF THE STONE *IN SITU*

THE region around Kensington, Minnesota, where the rune stone was found in 1898, was of comparatively recent settlement by white men, as for that matter was the entire state of Minnesota. The first farmers came into Minnesota about 1850. By 1870 the tide of home-seekers had rolled three hundred miles westward and the advance guard of pioneers had taken possession of the lands around the later village of Kensington. Most of the land in this part of Minnesota consists of rolling prairies of fertile soil, but the farm on which the stone was found, with its immediate surroundings, is of a different character. This land consists of hilly, stony moraines, which were covered with stunted timber and surrounded by marshes, and the pioneers therefore thought that this rough land would never be wanted for farming and used it only as a community woodlot. In 1886 a railroad was built through the district, a station was established called Kensington, and the less desirable lands began to be homesteaded and developed into farms. Thus it happened that Ohman came in 1891, preferring the labor of carving a farm out of this wilderness to going far out into Dakota where good land could be had cheap.

Seven years later while clearing some forest land on the edge of a swamp, he discovered the so-called Kensington Stone.

In determining the question of the authenticity of the Kensington inscription, the circumstances surrounding the discovery of the stone are of prime importance. If these show that the stone could have been placed in its finding spot recently, the authenticity of the inscription becomes suspicious. On the other hand, if the condition of the stone *in situ* shows that it was there before that part of the state was settled, it is important proof of the genuineness of the inscription. It is impossible to conceive of any scholar, having a knowledge of runes and Scandinavian philology, risking his life by penetrating far into a savage wilderness, inhabited only by hostile Indians, and then sitting down to chip for days upon a stone that would bring him neither honor nor riches. If the inscription is a fraud, it must have been perpetrated after western Minnesota had been made safe by the settlement of the pioneers.

Fortunately the circumstances of the discovery of the stone have been recorded in five affidavits made by persons who were present at the discovery or soon afterwards. Our information concerning this basic fact is therefore ample and reliable. These affidavits were personally obtained by Dr. Knut Hoegh (see page 103, *ante*). The following is the affidavit of Olof Ohman, the man who discovered the stone: [1]

I, Olof Ohman, of the town of Solem, Douglas County, State of Minnesota, being duly sworn, make the following statement:

I am fifty-four years of age, and was born in Helsingeland, Sweden, from where I emigrated to America in the year 1881, and settled upon my farm in Section Fourteen, Township of Solem, in 1891. In the month of August, 1898, while accompanied by my son, Edward, I was engaged in grubbing upon a timbered elevation, surrounded by marshes, in the southeast corner of my land, about 500 feet west of my neighbor's, Nils Flaten's, house, and in the full view thereof. Upon removing an asp, measuring about 10 inches in diameter at its base, I discovered a flat stone inscribed with characters, to me unintelligible. The stone lay just beneath the surface of the ground

[1] Mr. Ohman's affidavit was first printed in *The Journal of American History*, IV, 178 (1910).

in a slightly slanting position, with one corner almost protruding. The two largest roots of the tree clasped the stone in such a manner that the stone must have been there at least as long as the tree. One of the roots penetrated directly downward and was flat on the side next to the stone. The other root extended almost horizontally across the stone and made at its edge a right angled turn downward. At this turn the root was flattened on the side toward the stone. This root was about three inches in diameter. Upon washing off the surface dirt, the inscription presented a weathered appearance, which to me appeared just as old as the untouched parts of the stone. I immediately called my neighbor's, Nils Flaten's, attention to the discovery, and he came over the same afternoon and inspected the stone and the stump under which it was found.

I kept the stone in my possession for a few days; and then left it in the Bank of Kensington, where it remained for inspection for several months. During this interval, it was sent to Chicago for inspection and soon returned in the same state in which it was sent. Since then I kept it at my farm until August, 1907, when I presented the stone to H. R. Holand. The stone, as I remember, was about 30 inches long, 16 inches wide, and 7 inches thick, and I recognize the illustration on page 16 of H. R. Holand's History of the Norwegian Settlements of America, as being a photographic reproduction of the stone's inscription.

(Signed)   OLOF OHMAN.

Witness:
    R. J. RASMUSSON.
    GEORGE H. MERHES.

State of Minnesota,
County of Douglas.

On this 20th day of July, 1909, personally came before me, a Notary Public in and for Douglas County and State of Minnesota, Mr. Olof Ohman, to me known to be the person described in the foregoing document, and acknowledged that he executed the same as his free act and deed.

(Signed)   R. J. RASMUSSON,
                  Notary Public,
(Seal)
          Douglas County, Minnesota.

When Mr. Ohman discovered the stone, he called his neighbor's, Mr. Nils Flaten's, attention to his discovery. Mr. Flaten, who lived only a few hundred feet away across an open marsh, immediately went over to inspect the curious find. The following is his affidavit, setting forth some additional information:

I, Nils Flaten, of the town of Solem, Douglas County, Minn., being duly sworn, make the following statement:

I am sixty-five years of age, and was born in Tinn, Telemarken, Norway, and settled at my present home in the town of Solem in 1884. One day in August, 1898, my neighbor, Olof Ohman, who was engaged in grubbing timber about 500 feet west of my house, and in full view of same, came to me and told me he had discovered a stone inscribed with ancient characters. I accompanied him to the alleged place of discovery and saw a stone about 30 inches long, 16 inches wide and 6 inches thick, which was covered with strange characters upon two sides and for more than half their length. The inscription presented a very ancient and weathered appearance. Mr. Ohman showed me an asp tree about 8 inches to 10 inches in diameter at its base, beneath which he alleged the stone was found. The two largest roots of the asp were flattened on their inner surface and bent by nature in such a way as to exactly conform to the outlines of the stone. I inspected this hole and can testify to the fact that the stone had been there prior to the growth of the tree, as the spot was in close proximity to my house. I had visited the same spot earlier in the day before Mr. Ohman had cut down the tree and also many times previously—but I had never seen anything suspicious there. Besides the asp, the roots of which embraced the stone, the spot was also covered by a very heavy growth of underbrush.

I recognize the illustration on page 16 of H. R. Holand's History of the Norwegian Settlements as being a photographic reproduction of the inscription on the face of the stone.

(Signed) NILS FLATEN.

Witness:
    R. J. RASMUSSON.
    GEORGE H. MERHES.

State of Minnesota,
County of Douglas.

On the 20th day of July, 1909, personally came before me, a Notary Public in and for Douglas County and State of Minnesota, Mr. Nils Flaten, to me known to be the person described in the foregoing document, and acknowledged that he executed the same as his free act and deed.

(Signed) H. J. Rasmusson,

(Seal)   *Notary Public,*

Douglas County, Minnesota.

At the same time (July 20, 1909) affidavits were also obtained from Edward Ohman who as a child had been the first to notice the inscribed characters on the stone, Roald Bentson and S. Olson.[2] These witnesses were separately interviewed by Dr. Hoegh and the writer. Dr. Hoegh took down three of these statements in writing, whereupon they were read by the witnesses and signed. Mr. S. Olson, a cautious jeweler in Kensington, preferred to write his own, and his statement was also signed by Mr. Bentson.[3]

[2] These three affidavits are printed in Holand, *The Kensington Stone,* Ephraim, Wis., 1932, pp. 292-295.

[3] Mr. M. M. Quaife in an article printed in the *New England Quarterly,* December, 1934, pp. 628-632, rejects all these five affidavits as being misleading and erroneous. Instead he accepts without a doubt a statement made by Professor G. T. Flom, an early opponent of the inscription, to the effect that Mr. Olson in April, 1910, told him (Flom) that the tree in question was only four inches in diameter. (See Flom, *The Kensington Stone,* Springfield, Ill., 1910, p. 120.) Flom's assertion is made without any supporting evidence and can only be a misapprehension, for Mr. Olson had personally written his own statement and sworn to the fact that the tree was "from eight to ten inches in diameter." When Mr. Olson was shown the statement made by Professor Flom, he became very indignant and declared he had made no such statement as Flom attributed to him. Upon being shown four cross sections of poplar trees cut by Mr. Ohman to show the size of the tree (see page 116, *post*), Mr. Olson wrote another statement in which he declares that the rune stone tree was a little larger "in its oval diameter than section *b*" (Holand, *ibid.,* p. 294). This statement is also spurned by Quaife on the grounds that "a normal aspen is not 'oval' in shape" (Quaife, p. 630). However, whether normal or not, it cannot be denied that aspen trunks are sometimes "oval" in circumference as is witnessed by Mr.

These affidavits make it clear that the stone was found on a timbered elevation, almost surrounded by marshes, wrapped in the roots of a tree eight to ten inches in diameter. It is also clear that the stone must have been there at least as long as this tree had grown there, for its largest roots exactly conformed in shape to the surface of

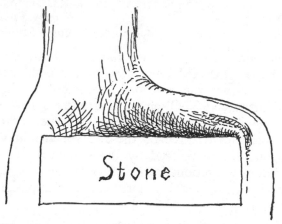

FIG. 4. SKETCH SHOWING POSITION OF KENSINGTON STONE BETWEEN ROOTS OF TREE WHEN FOUND

the stone at the place of contact and were flat on the inside where they curved around the edges of the stone.

The important question is now: How old was this tree? The stump had been destroyed during the ten years while the stone humbly served as a doorstep to Mr. Ohman's granary. The tree was an aspen (*populos tremuloides*), and this variety grows rapidly under favorable conditions. The following statement on the growth of aspens in a

Willoughby Babcock, curator of the Minnesota Historical Society Museum where the same section *b* may still be seen. See Babcock's statement in footnote 5, *post*. From these things it appears that Mr. S. Olson is a meticulous witness who would not be likely to make such a statement as Flom attributes to him. For further discussion of this and other objections by Mr. Quaife, see Holand in *New England Quarterly*, March, 1935, pp. 42-62.

bulletin on aspens published by the U. S. Forest Service
is pertinent:

The Aspens are commonly considered among the most rapidly growing trees of northeastern United States and this is
undoubtedly true of young trees in favorable situations. The
rate of growth, however, is frequently very much over-
estimated, especially in the case of full-grown trees . . .
The age may be obtained with reasonable certainty directly
from the tree itself by counting the rings of growth, since it is
established beyond doubt that, except in rare cases, one ring
is regularly added each year. Such counts show that while
aspen ordinarily exceeds in rapidity of growth the spruce, fir,
beech, sugar maple and even paper birch during the first 20 or
30 years, its growth rate decreases thereafter, while many of
the other species are still in their period of rapid development.[4]

In the summer of 1910, Dr. Knut Hoegh of Minneapolis and the writer went to the finding place to learn
something about the age of similar trees. We reasoned that
trees of the same species, grown on the same elevation and
soil, having the same conditions of shade and moisture,
would be, if equal in diameter, approximately equal in age.
Unfortunately, we found that all these conditions no
longer obtained. While Mr. Ohman still had a large
woodlot, this had been logged and cut over many years
previously.

Mr. Ohman kindly consented to cut down such trees as
were deemed necessary. As the exact size of the tree was
somewhat uncertain, we requested him to select a tree
which most nearly compared to his mental image of the
tree beneath which the stone was found.

He found two trees which were approximately of the
right size, but objected that as these trees were healthy,
they would not correctly represent the tree under which
the stone was found as that was a stunted, sickly tree. In
lieu of anything better these trees were cut down and

[4] U. S. Department of Agriculture, *Forest Service Bulletin*, No. 93
(1911), pp. 16, 17.

marked *a* and *b*. Later on he found a stunted tree which in its growth, but not in its size, resembled the "rune stone tree." Two cross sections of this were cut and marked *c* and *d*. They measured five and a half inches. One of these is shown in Plate VIII.[5] The following is a signed statement which Mr. Ohman gave us with the four cross sections.

Kensington, Minn., July 16, 1910.

The sections *a, b, c, d*, were all cut on my property in the vicinity of where the rune stone was found, under the same timber conditions. The section *a* is of the same size as the tree which grew over the stone; but both *a* and *b* are from much more luxuriant trees than that which stood over the stone. Sections *c* and *d* are from a tree which in its growth is more comparable with the rune stone tree but is about three inches less in diameter than that.

(Signed)   OLOF OHMAN.[6]

These cross sections were given to Professor N. H. Winchell, Minnesota State Archeologist, who caused them to be dried and varnished. When this was done the annual growth-rings appeared quite distinctly and, according to Winchell, showed the following number: *a*, 37 rings; *b*, 42 rings; *c*, 38 rings. (*d* showed a cross section from the same tree.) At least five years must be added to all these figures for the decayed and blurred centers where the growth-rings could not be counted.

As the stump under which the stone was found was not preserved, we do not know the exact diameter of the tree. But we have seven affidavits and statements describing this stump and made by people who inspected it immediately

[5] "Mr. Willoughby M. Babcock, curator of the Minnesota Historical Society Museum where the three cross sections, *a*, *b* and *c*, may be seen, under date of September 12, 1931, sent me the following statement of the measurements of the cross sections:

"Section A measures 8¾ inches in diameter.

"Section B measures 9 inches and 7⅞ inches in diameter.

"Section C measures 6 inches and 5½ inches in diameter."

[6] *The Kensington Rune Stone*, Report of the Museum Committee, *Minnesota Historical Collections*, XV, 223, and plates III and IV.

after the stone was found. In these statements the estimates of the diameter vary from 8½ to 10 inches in size. We cannot tell which of these estimates is the most correct, but if we take the mean average of them all, we shall probably be close to the exact size. These seven estimates are as follows:

O. Ohman's affidavit, "about 10 inches"........... 10 inches
N. Flaten's affidavit, "about 8 to 10 inches" .... 9 "
R. Bentson's affidavit, "from 8 to 10 inches"....... 9 "
S. Olson's affidavit, "from 8 to 10 inches" .... 9 "
E. Ohman's affidavit, "about 10 inches" .... 10 "
O. Ohman's sample (Sec. a) "approximately same size" .... 8¾ "
O. Ohman's second sample (Sec. b)............. 8½ "

Taking the mean average of all these estimates we find that the tree under which the stone was found had a diameter of 9.2 inches at its base. As *c* (Plate VIII) with a diameter of 5.5 inches was 43 years old (five years being added for the decayed center), then the tree under which the stone was found, having a diameter of 9.2 inches, would be 72 years old, for 5.5 : 9.2 :: 43 : 72.

The age of the tree reached by this computation seemed so high to us who were unfamiliar with the rate of growth of trees under forest conditions, that Dr. Hoegh feared we had made some error in our figures. In order to avoid such a possibility, he recommended a more conservative and general statement of the results of this investigation and suggested that a statement be used to the effect that the tree was at least forty years old. This estimate was therefore used pending the collection of further information on the growth of aspens.

Fortunately the United States Department of Agriculture has made two independent and thorough researches concerning the growth of aspens, published in two separate monographs which are of great value in this investigation. Table I, given below, is from a bulletin published by the Department, showing the rate of growth of aspens in the New England States. The data were obtained by counting the rings of growth of 409 aspens which grew in Franklin and Somerset Counties, Maine. The investigators have divided the trees into three classes—maximum, average, and minimum growths—based on the soil quality and locations of the trees:

TABLE I (FROM MAINE) [7]

Age	Quality I Diameter breast-high	Quality II Diameter breast-high	Quality III Diameter breast-high
Years	Inches	Inches	Inches
10	2.7	1.6	1.0
20	5.3	3.8	2.4
30	8.0	5.8	3.6
40	10.4	7.8	4.7
50	12.7	9.4	5.8
60	14.8	10.9	7.0
70	17.0	12.3	8.2
80	19.2	13.4	9.3
90	21.3	14.3	10.5
100	23.3	15.1	11.7

This table shows age of tree based on diameters breast-high, whereas the diameter of the tree under which the rune stone was found was measured at stump height. These two measurements must therefore first be brought into conformity. Frederick S. Baker, U. S. Forest Examiner, covers this point in the following words: "Pronounced stump swelling is shown in aspen at an early age, amounting to as much as an inch at the base of trees of 8-inch diameters breast-high. By the time the breast-high diameter is 16 inches the swell at the stump is nearly 2 inches." [8]

[7] U. S. Department of Agriculture, *Forest Service Bulletin*, No. 93, p. 17.
[8] *Aspen in Central Rocky Mountain Region*, U. S. Dept. of Agric. Bulletin 1291, Feb. 20, 1925, p. 6.

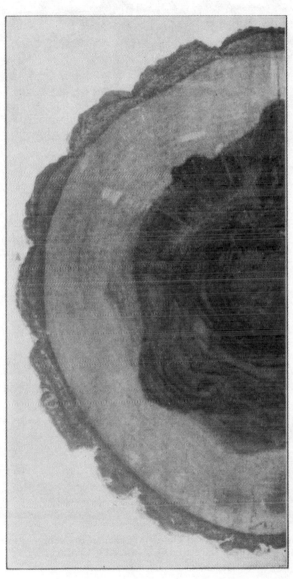

Plate VIII. Section C. Section of poplar tree of a stunted growth. Similar to the tree growing above the rune stone but three inches smaller in diameter. Original cross section in Minnesota Historical Society Museum.

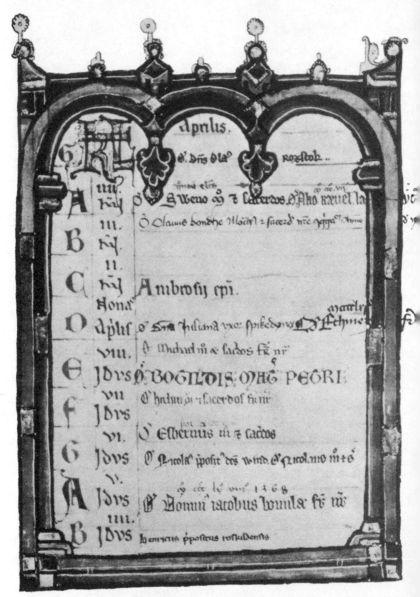

Plate IX. Page from the Nestved Obituary Calendar Showing Various ways of writing the letter Ø in the XIV Century.

In order to get the breast-high diameter of the rune stone tree, it is therefore necessary to subtract a maximum of one-eighth from its diameter at its stump. The result is 8 inches which would be its diameter breast-high.

As the tree under which the stone was found was of stunted growth, its rate of growth would be comparable with the rate shown in the *Quality III* column above. According to Table I above, a tree of this quality grown in Maine would be about 68 years of age when attaining a diameter of 8 inches. Abundant moisture is one of the requirements of the aspen. As Maine has a rainfall of 41 inches per year, while Minnesota's annual rainfall is only 26 inches, it is probable that the annual growth of aspens is greater in Maine than in Minnesota. If five per cent is allowed for this supposed slower growth of aspens in Minnesota, we arrive at the age of 71 years or a little more, which is very close to the result (72 years) reached by the inspection of the tree (section *c*) which was cut by Mr. Ohman.

That the rate of growth of aspens is largely dependent upon the amount of rainfall is shown by a comparison with the rate of growth of aspens in Utah. The Department of Agriculture has published a bulletin dealing with the growth of aspens in the West. It is entitled "Aspen in the Central Rocky Mountain Region." Below is given Table II taken from this bulletin, showing the rate of growth of aspens in that region. The trees are here divided into five classes, based on the quality of the soil and other growth factors. Four classes are given below, the fifth (the poorest) not being given in the bulletin.

This table shows that an aspen of third-rate quality, 8 inches in diameter breast-high, when grown under the lesser rainfall of Utah, would be 115 years old.

The conclusion of this inquiry is that the tree under which the stone was found was at least 70 years old. This conclusion is reached by two independent studies. A comparison of its age with the age of another sickly tree

TABLE II (ROCKY MOUNTAINS) [9]

| Age | Quality I | Quality II | Quality III | Quality IV |
| | Diameter breast-high | Diameter breast-high | Diameter breast-high | Diameter breast-high |
Years	Inches	Inches	Inches	Inches
40	4.5	4.0	. . .	. . .
50	5.3	4.8	4.1	. . .
60	6.1	5.4	4.7	4.2
70	7.0	6.1	5.3	4.8
80	7.8	6.8	5.8	5.3
90	8.7	7.5	6.5	5.8
100	9.5	8.2	7.1	6.3
110	10.4	8.9	7.7	6.9
120	11.2	9.6	8.3	7.4

(Plate VIII) growing in the same vicinity gives its age as 72 years. Practically the same age (71 years) is reached from the tables of the Forestry Bureau based upon the study of thousands of aspens graded as to quality. There can therefore be little doubt that the tree was at least seventy years old. Seventy years back from 1898, the year the stone was found, brings us back to 1828. This was about twenty years before the state of Minnesota was settled by white

[9] "For their best growth, the aspens require deep, fresh or moist, but porous and well-drained, soils. Sandy loams mixed with decayed vegetable matter are the best. In the Rocky Mountains, thrifty stands of quaking aspen are often considered good indications of agricultural soil. The aspens are not, however, absolutely restricted to fertile soil. They are often found in abundance on thin, fairly dry soil, as well as in poorly drained situations. In such places, though there are commonly more trees to the acre, they never grow so rapidly, so large, or to so perfect a form as in the better situations. Thus, in northern Maine, a 31-year-old aspen stand growing on deep, loose, sandy loam, contained 672 trees per acre, about 60 feet high and from 6 to 8 inches in diameter, while on a dry, gravelly ridge, within 10 rods of the other, a stand of the same age contained 1,224 trees per acre, but averaging only about 25 feet in height and from 2 to 5 inches in diameter." *Forest Service Bulletin* No. 93, pp. 14, 15.

The rune stone tree was growing near the top of a dry, gravelly knoll, about 44 feet from its base.

men. Douglas County, where the stone was found, had no white settlers of any kind until 1858, when a few Yankee trappers and townsite speculators settled in the vicinity of Alexandria, about fifteen miles from the finding place of the stone.[10] The first Scandinavian pioneer in the county was a Mr. Nils Mickelson, who settled in the neighboring township in 1864. He also was a trapper. In 1867 came the first group of farmers. The rune stone in all likelihood was therefore in its finding place almost forty years before the pioneer farmers settled there. After 1867 the settlement of the county advanced steadily. The first railroad reached the county in 1878 at Alexandria. Kensington was reached by a railroad in 1886.

Several European scholars, impressed by the circumstances of the stone *in situ* and by the weathered appearance of the inscription (see Chapter XII), have suggested that the inscription was probably made about a hundred years before it was found. But in so doing they have forgotten that Minnesota at that early time was practically an uninhabited wilderness as far as the presence of white men is concerned. Only a few scattered fur traders then sojourned in Minnesota, and these men are all known, for they had to get their supplies from, and bring their peltries to, the agencies of the fur companies. Among these early fur traders not a single Swede or Norwegian is known.

Another matter of importance in deciding the question of the authenticity of the inscription is the change in physiography which the region around Kensington has experienced during the last few centuries. A study of Fig. 5, which gives some idea of the topography of the vicinity where the stone was found, will help to make this clear. This sketch was made on the spot and shows in the center Mr. Ohman's farm of ninety-eight acres enclosed by a dotted line. This farm is morainic and very

[10] See Constant Larson's *History of Douglas County, Minn.*

hilly, being made up of three elevations, marked A, B and C, rising from forty to sixty feet above the nearby marshes, and separated by lower areas from twelve to fifteen feet above the marshes. On the north and south sides are extensive marshy areas which now are under partial cultivation. In periods of heavy rainfall the larger marsh drains through a rather narrow gully shown in the northwestern corner of the sketch.

In the extreme northwestern corner of the farm is shown the location of Mr. Ohman's house. The finding place of the stone is indicated by a black quadrangle in the extreme southeast corner of the farm, three-quarters of a mile in a straight line from Mr. Ohman's house. Here it was found near the top of elevation A, forty-four feet above the marsh. Almost due east of this spot, 500 feet across the open marsh, is shown the site of Mr. Flaten's house.

The inscription speaks of the finding place as an "island," but it is not now in any sense an island. Nor would any visitor to the place as far back as the region has been settled be likely to have called it an island. Elevation A on which the stone was found slopes toward the southeast into a plain, 600 feet wide at its narrowest point and from twelve to fifteen feet above the marsh. When the first pioneers came this plain was covered with trees centuries old. A similar tract of timber extended toward the west until it climbed the slope of elevation B. The drainage in the northwest corner of the big marsh was the same then as now. It therefore seems most improbable that any modern forger would call such a region of timbered rolling country an island.

In order to explain the discrepancy between the term used in the inscription and the existing conditions, we must therefore assume that the inscription was written at a time when the (formerly) timbered lands to the southeast and west of elevation A were covered with water. But such a condition was impossible while the gully in the

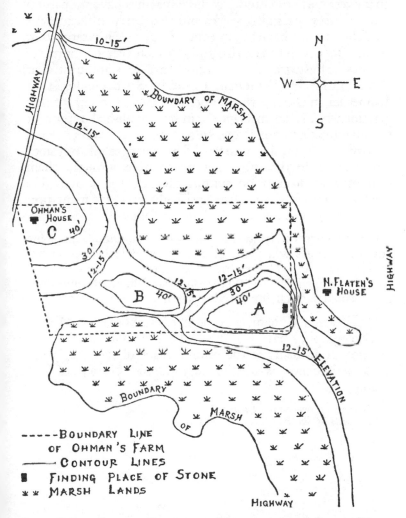

FIG. 5. SKETCH SHOWING TOPOGRAPHIC CONDITIONS OF THE FINDING PLACE
OF THE STONE AND VICINITY

northwest corner existed. As these marshes have no natural watercourses the gully serves only to carry off excessive rainfalls. It must have taken centuries for such intermittent erosion to have eroded the gully fifteen feet or more.

These physiographic conditions are so significant that Professor N. H. Winchell, formerly State Geologist of Minnesota, mentions them several times as proof of the genuineness of the inscription in the published report of the investigating committee. In a letter to the writer dated August 17, 1911, he writes: "The changes of physiography are such that no faker could have wrought them into such an inscription within the last 100 years." He expresses himself even more positively in a statement prepared for publication which reads as follows:

I am convinced from the geological conditions and the physical changes which the region has experienced, probably during the last 500 years, that the stone contains a genuine record of a Scandinavian exploration into Minnesota, and must be accepted as such for the date named.[11]

Dr. Warren Upham, a recognized authority on Minnesota geography, has also affirmed his conviction that the mention of an island as the finding place of the inscription is in accordance with the topographic history of the vicinity.[12]

[11] *Journal of American History*, IV, 180.
[12] *Records of the Past*, IX, 6 (January, 1910).

XII. THE WEATHERING OF THE INSCRIPTION

AN analysis of the rate of growth of aspens indicates, then, that the stone was probably in its finding place in 1828. The next question is, Is there any way of determining whether or not the stone with its inscription was there before that time? A study of the epigraphic condition of the inscription may answer this question.

It is a known fact that the stone when found lay a little beneath the surface of the ground. It must have been similarly covered by soil in 1828 when the tree began to grow above it, for the seed which afterward grew into the tree above it would require a layer of moist soil above the stone for germination and growth. It is also known that the stone when found lay with its inscribed face down.[1] It follows, therefore, that during these seventy years the inscription was protected from the action of the elements and suffered but little change by weathering. According to Winchell, boulders which have not been exposed to surface influences show little or no signs of corrosion. Speaking of limestone boulders he writes:

> Such boulders when freshly taken from the till in deep excavations are not rotted, but are fresh and firm and smooth as marbles, and show distinctly the fine glacial scratches which they received during the Ice age, which ended about 7,000 or 8,000 years ago.[2]

As an illustration of the absence of weathering on inscriptions which have been protected from the action of

[1] *The Kensington Rune Stone*, Report of the Minnesota Historical Society's Committee, p. 1. Also corroborated by Mr. Ohman.
[2] Museum Committee's *Report on the Kensington Rune Stone*, in *Minn. Hist. Collections*, XV, 235.

the elements may be mentioned two Egyptian inscriptions now in the Metropolitan Museum of Art in New York. These appear on the sarcophagi of Wen-Nofer and Uresh-Nofer which are from the period of 378-341 B.C. These two sarcophagi contain thousands of inscribed characters and figures which show very little weathering. The symbols on the inside of the sarcophagi look as fresh as if cut today.

As the inscribed face of the rune stone also was protected during the seventy years when the tree grew above it, the inscription, if made shortly before that time (1828), should show a fresh unweathered appearance. This, however, is not the case.

The Kensington Stone is of the kind known to geologists under the name of *greywacke*. According to Professor Winchell about five per cent of the stones around Kensington are *greywacke*. At some remote time this stone must have split off from a large boulder, leaving a fine, smooth surface, excellently adapted for receiving a carved inscription. Because of this smooth surface the characters on this face of the stone are not deeply incised. The inscription is continued on the broad edge of the stone, which evidently was not so well suited for chiseling, as it bears plain evidence of having been trimmed smooth by help of a cold-chisel. Even this smoothing left the surface much rougher than the main face, and it was necessary to chisel the characters much deeper on the side of the stone. Owing to this deeper chiseling, the characters on the edge of the stone when found were quite solidly imbedded with a hard clay. An iron tool of some kind was thoughtlessly used to scratch out this clay.

Mr. G. M. Gathorne-Hardy has pointed out [3] that the dressed surface of the edge of the stone speaks strongly against the theory that the inscription is the work of some modern forger. He observes that the region where the

[3] In a letter to the writer.

stone was found was in the heart of the territory of a particularly savage tribe of Indians, the Sioux, until 1864, and the alleged forgery must have been done long before that time. Working in such a dangerous neighborhood, the imaginary forger would naturally go to no unnecessary labor in chiseling his inscription. If he needed to add a date or a fact, there was plenty of room on the face of the stone, as there was no need for him to set it upright in the ground. Under such circumstances he would not go to the labor of chiseling the edge smooth in order to continue his story there.

Greywackes are very hard stones and therefore weather very slowly. This is particularly true of this specimen, as is shown by the pronounced glacial markings on the back of the stone made many thousand years ago. Notwithstanding this durability, the inscription on the face of the stone presents a noticeably ancient, mellow and weathered appearance, approaching the time-worn appearance of the untouched face of the stone. The very worn appearance of the characters in the calcite has already been mentioned. In marked contrast to these two aspects are some of the characters upon the edge of the stone which were scratched with an iron implement when the stone was found. After thirty years, during many of which the inscribed edge of the stone was exposed to the elements while lying in front of the finder's granary, these characters on the edge are almost as white and fresh as if cut today. A few of the characters on the edge escaped this scratching, and they appear just as weathered as the uninscribed surface around them.

The lower left hand third of the face of the stone is covered with a deposit of calcite (shown on the photograph by the lighter color). A number of runic characters are cut in this calcite. These characters are so worn down by the disintegration of this softer rock as to be practically illegible except by help of the context. They are much more legible on the photograph than on the stone itself, as all the characters were traced over with a soft pencil to make them appear more distinctly in the photograph.

Through some mistake Professor Flom has erred in representing the appearance of the runes inscribed in the calcareous incrustation on the stone. He writes: "The runes of this particular part of the stone are as clear and distinct as they are on the upper part which is of greywacke." [4] The following is a description made in 1930 by Mr. Constant Larson, an attorney of Alexandria, Minn., where the stone is now preserved in a local museum:

I have your letter of February 10th asking me to send you a careful copy of the rune inscription on the lower left hand corner of the Kensington Rune-stone which is covered by a calcareous deposit.

I have inspected the stone but find it impossible to comply with your request. There are three lines of runes on the part of the stone covered by the calcite. The first line has only one or two characters on this surface and I cannot definitely make out either one of them. The second line has more characters on it but the only one that I can make out is the following: X. The third line has several runes and the only one I can definitely make out is also X.

The characters on the stone, except that part covered by the deposit of calcite, are very clear and every one of them can be easily made out. The calcareous surface, apparently, because of the exposure to the weather and the elements, has become so worn down that it cannot be made out by anyone who is not an expert in reading runes.

This description indicates how blurred these characters have become by the chemical disintegration of the calcite. Of the eleven runic signs on this part of the stone, a layman of trained observation was able to make out only two and these two he only got approximately right.

The stone was lying with its inscribed face down and protected from the weather, not only when it was found, but also during the eight or nine years while it lay in front

[4] G. T. Flom, *The Kensington Rune Stone*, p. 7.

of Mr. Ohman's granary. Yet in spite of this protection
from the elements, its corroded appearance was mentioned
in the first published reports we have about the stone. The
stone was sent to Northwestern University in the latter
part of February, 1899, and a few days later one of Chicago's daily papers had a long news account about it in
which occurs the following passage concerning the weathered appearance of the inscription:

Wherever the characters of the inscription have not been
disturbed, they have precisely the same color as the general
surface of the stone. But, as Professor Curme pointed out, it
can be plainly seen, that most of the letters have been
scratched over with a sharp instrument after the stone was
unearthed.

The letters of the inscription were evidently carved with a
sharp instrument, for they are clearcut and distinct in outline.
But the fact that the upper edge of the incised lines is rough
and rounded as a result of the disintegration of the stone,
while the bottom of the scratched incisions is sharp and clear
shows plainly that many years must have elapsed since the
inscription was cut.

In other words, the external appearance of the Kensington
rune stone, so far from speaking against it, is such that the
inscription may well be six hundred years old.[5]

We also have proof that Mr. Ohman who discovered
the stone was impressed by the weathered appearance of
the inscription. He writes:

Upon washing off the surface dirt, the inscription presented
a weathered appearance, which to me appeared just as old as
the untouched parts of the stone.[6]

Nils Flaten, who saw the stone the same day it was dug
up, likewise says that "the inscription presented a very
ancient and weathered appearance."[7] Roald Bentson and

[5] *Skandinaven*, Chicago, May 3, 1899.
[6] See his affidavit in preceding chapter.
[7] See his affidavit in preceding chapter.

S. Olson, who saw the stone a few days later, also state in their affidavit that the inscription had a weathered appearance "similar to the uninscribed parts of the stone." [8]

In 1909 and 1910 the stone was exhibited in Chicago, Madison, St. Paul and Minneapolis and was inspected by many geologists. Although at that time it was generally discredited by philologists, not a single geologist found reason to add his weight of opinion to the condemnation. Three nationally known geologists, in fact, were so impressed by the evidence of the weathered appearance of the inscription, that they voluntarily wrote opinions favoring the authenticity of the inscription. Thus Professor W. O. Hotchkiss, then State Geologist of Wisconsin, wrote as follows:

I have carefully examined the various phases of weathering on the Kensington Stone, and with all respect for the opinions of philologists, I am persuaded that the inscription cannot have been made in recent years. It must have been made at least fifty to a hundred years ago and perhaps earlier.[9]

Dr. Warren Upham, the eminent glacial geologist, who had the stone under observation in his office for more than a year, wrote in 1910: "When we compare the excellent preservation of the glacial scratches, shown on the back of the stone, which were made several thousand years ago, with the mellow, time-worn appearance of the face of the inscription, the conclusion is inevitable that this inscription must have been carved many hundred years ago." [10]

Winchell, after having had it under close scrutiny for more than a year, wrote a lengthy report on it and summarized his observations with the following conclusions: [11]

[8] See their affidavits in Holand, *The Kensington Stone*, pp. 292, 293.
[9] Statement on file in the archives of Minn. Historical Society.
[10] First published in the *Journal of American History*, 1910, IV, 180.
[11] *The Kensington Rune Stone* in *Minn. Hist. Society Collections*, XV, 236, 237.

There are six stages of weathering of *greywacke* which are exhibited by the stone, and they may be arranged approximately in a scale as follows:

1. A fresh break or cut................................ 0
2. Break or cut shown by the runes of the face.......... 5
3. Edge-face, which was not engraved, but was apparently dressed by a rough bush-hammering................. 5
4. The inscribed face of the stone...................... 10
5. The finely glaciated and polished back side and the non-hammered portion of the edge...................... 80
6. The coarse gauging and the general beveling and deepest weathering of the back side....................250 or 500

These figures are but rough estimates and are intended to express the grand epochs of time through which the stone has passed since it started from the solid rock of which it formed a part prior to the Glacial period; and to a certain degree they are subject to the errors of the personal equation of the person who gives them. Prof. W. O. Hotchkiss, State geologist of Wisconsin, estimated that the time since the runes were inscribed is "at least 50 to 100 years." If the figures in the foregoing series be all multiplied by 100, they would stand:

$$(1) \quad (2) \quad (3) \quad (4) \quad (5) \quad\quad (6)$$
$$000 : 500 : 500 : 1,000 : 8,000 : 25,000 \text{ or } 50,000$$

Since 8,000 years is approximately the date of the end of the latest glaciation (5), the numbers may all be accepted as the approximate number of years required for the various stages of weathering. Hence stages (2) and (3) may have required each about 500 years.

The opinion of Professor O. E. Hagen, the well-known Assyriologist, may also be cited. Bringing to the study of the inscription his highly developed skill in determining the genuineness of cuneiform tablets of questionable authenticity by the patina and weathering, Hagen became so convinced of the genuineness of the Kensington inscription that he began an extensive study of the whole subject. Unfortunately, before the completion, his home and all its contents were destroyed by fire. He also suffered bodily injuries and died shortly afterward. In the interval he wrote a letter to his friend, Mr. W. Ager, editor of *Reform,* a newspaper published in Eau Claire, Wis., in which he tells of his loss. The letter was printed in *Reform,* April 29, 1926, and reads as follows:

All my notes concerning the discussion of the Kensington stone also became a prey to the flames. This loss I felt so much more deeply as I some time ago publicly announced that I would make known my views concerning it. As the circumstances are now I cannot attempt any exhaustive dissertation, and for the present I can only make the following categorical statement.

In epigraphic respects I find in the inscription no evidence that it is anything except what it purports to be. I worked over the stone for a whole day under different kinds of light and found the runes on the whole to be what I looked for from that time and the people that are mentioned in the inscription.

In linguistic respects the inscription presents certain peculiarities, perhaps also errors in writing, but real philological errors showing it to be a forgery I do not find. The negative side of this protracted discussion concerning the authenticity of the inscription has, however, often made use of assertions and argumentations which to speak as mildly as possible must be stamped as scientific irresponsibility. It is not disputed that the inscription is before us as a comprehensible document and it therefore behooves the negative side to present actual valid evidence to show that it is a forgery. Such evidence, in my opinion, has not yet been presented. On the contrary there has been found in the Kensington region a number of remarkable finds which in a surprising manner seem to corroborate what the inscription relates.

My advice is therefore that the Kensington stone be placed in a safe repository where it can be preserved as an important epigraphic document concerning American History.

O. E. HAGEN.

XIII. A COMPARISON OF THE PAUL KNUT-SON EXPEDITION AND THE KENSINGTON INSCRIPTION

WHEN Professor O. J. Breda of the University of Minnesota late in the fall of 1898, received the first photographs and copies of the Kensington inscription, just as he was preparing to resign from his position as professor of Scandinavian Languages and Literature, he no doubt received these things with the greatest interest. After several months of study he presented the first faulty translation, and with it the conclusion that the inscription was a modern forgery. His two principal reasons were the following: (1) The mixture of Swedes and Norwegians was "contrary to all accounts of the Vinland voyages," (2) the language was not Old Norse but a mixture of Swedish, Norwegian and English which was unthinkable in an inscription dealing with the Vinland voyages of the eleventh century.[1] This shows that even so well informed a man as the professor of the Scandinavian department of the University had never heard of the Paul Knutson expedition of 1355-64 and could therefore only think of the Vinland voyages of the eleventh century.

These two objections continued to be the chief arguments against the inscription for many years. If the alleged forger had had the discretion to use any one of the many common formulas that are seen in hundreds of runic epitaphs and omitted his reference to the *Goths*, there would have been little objection to the acceptance of his product. But when he used this strange date and the still more strange mixture of two nationalities, he aroused grave sus-

[1] See *ante*, p. 98.

picion. Inasmuch as this mixture of Swedes (Goths) and Norwegians in an overseas expedition is so challenging, some remarks on the subject are necessary.

The term Goths refers to the inhabitants of the old *Gøtaland* (not Gotland), and more particularly West Gothland in the southwestern part of Sweden. Although this province by 1362 had been a part of Sweden for centuries, its inhabitants were still known as Goths, and continued to be so called until about 1500.

Strange as it may seem to find representatives of two different nations engaged in an expedition purporting to have taken place in the Middle Ages, no detail of the inscription is more fitting. In order to make this clear it is necessary to take a glance at some historical developments in the Scandinavian countries in the fourteenth century.

King Magnus Erikson, by whose command the Knutson expedition was fitted out, became by inheritance the first joint King of Sweden and Norway. This union of the two kingdoms was distasteful to the Norwegians for several reasons, and in 1343 the Royal Council compelled him to abdicate the throne of Norway in favor of his son Haakon, to take effect when the latter reached his majority in 1355.[2] In the meantime King Magnus was permitted to hold the royal power in trust only. In Sweden there was no objection to the union, but the King personally became exceedingly unpopular. This was partly because he showed little disposition to respect the old-time prerogatives of the nobles, and largely because of his lack of circumspection in distributing his royal favors.

King Magnus was a descendant of the famous *Folkunga* family of West Gothland and here he spent most of his time. The close association with the prominent people of his paternal province resulted in an unfortunate favoritism.

[2] P. A. Munch, *Det Norske Folks Historie, Unionsperioden*, I, 289-295. This thousand-page volume by Professor Munch is a detailed biography of King Magnus from his cradle to his grave.

Ignoring local expectations, he placed the government of various parts of his kingdoms in the hands of his favorites, the nobles and clergy of West Gothland and vicinity. For instance, Orm Øisteinson, who had large possessions on both sides of the Gøta River and was considered both a Goth and a Norwegian, was made Vice-gerent of Norway. Vinalde Hendrikson, another Goth, was made chancellor of Norway. Johan Karlsson and Nicolas Markusson, the King's two successive Swedish chancellors, were both Goths.[3] So, too, was Israel Byrgeson whom the King appointed as his Vice-gerent to act during his war with Russia.[4] Benedikt Algotsson, another Goth but little known, was made Duke of Halland and Finland and Governor of Skaane.[5] This last act of local favoritism in particular alienated the discontented magnates of other parts of Sweden so completely that open rebellion broke out. The seventeen-year-old Prince Erik was persuaded to raise the standard of revolt, and the result was that King Magnus had to give his rebellious son the greater part of his kingdom.

Erik was king for only three years when he died in a small-pox epidemic. But the nobles, whose pawn he was, were as implacable as ever. Rather than make peace with King Magnus, they chose Duke Albrecht of Mecklenburg to be their ruler. Thus for the first time in its history was Sweden ruled by a foreigner.

Although disinclined to use force, King Magnus made some efforts to drive Albrecht from his throne. But only the people of West Gothland remained faithful to him. With a small army from this province, augmented by volunteers from Norway under the command of his son, King Haakon, he sought battle with King Albrecht and

---

[3] *Ibid.*, pp. 544, 646.
[4] *Ibid.*, p. 488. He was on his mother's side a member of the King's family, the *Folkunga*, from West Gothland.
[5] *Ibid.*, pp. 589-594, 640.

the powerful nobles.[6] The result was disastrous. King Magnus was captured and languished in prison for six years. When at last peace was restored and he was ransomed, his kingdom was restricted to the province of West Gothland.[7]

In view of the above facts, i.e., the King's ancestry and place of residence and his unfortunate favoritism to the Goths which alienated from him the nobles and prominent people of other parts of Sweden so that finally he was deserted by all except his faithful Goths, it is reasonably certain that his *hirdmenn*, or personal retinue, in the latter part of his reign consisted largely of Goths.

Going back now to the letter which King Magnus in 1354 wrote to Paul Knutson (see page 90), it will be seen that he commanded Paul Knutson to select the men for the crusade to Greenland from two sources: (1) "from my retinue" (*fra mine haandgangne menn*) [8] and (2) from the retainers of other men. If Paul Knutson did not wish to offend the King and his retinue, he would select some of his companions from among the nobles who made up the King's retinue, who were largely Goths.[9] As Greenland was a Norwegian colony, and as he personally was a Norwegian of much prominence, Paul Knutson would

[6] H. Hildebrand, *Sveriges Historia, Medeltidan*, p. 288. Munch, *op. cit.*, p. 765. Styffe's *Bidrag til Skandinaviens Historia*, No. 36, pp. 62-118.

Munch gives a list of the prominent Swedes who remained faithful to Magnus. These were almost all from West Gothland, Dal and Vermland. The two last districts were up to that time considered a part of West Gothland. Munch, *op. cit.*, pp. 750, 751.

[7] Hildebrand, *op. cit.*, p. 292.

[8] Dr. Hildebrand describes the *haandgangne menn* or *hirdmenn* as follows: "They were chosen among the best families in the land, paid by the King, and mutually joined together in a close fraternity." *Sveriges Historia, Medeltidan*, p. 114. See also *Gjerset's History of the Norwegian People*, I, 259, 260.

[9] Participation in such missionary enterprises for the propagation of Christianity was eagerly sought by the soldier of the times because it meant complete absolution from all sins. It was perhaps with a view to their eternal welfare that the King directed Paul Knutson to give members of his retinue a place in the expedition.

presumably also avail himself of the opportunity offered in the second clause, and select some Norwegians of his own acquaintance. The expedition would therefore be composed partly of Goths and partly of Norwegians. On the Kensington Stone we read of eight Goths and twenty-two Norwegians. The greater dignity of the Goths, as members of the King's bodyguard, is implied by the fact that they are mentioned first, although they were a minority in numbers.

These Goths are therefore not a historical misfit, serving as an insurmountable objection to the identification of the Kensington expedition with the Knutson expedition. Instead they are quite indispensable to the inscription when it is viewed in the light of the peculiar political conditions of the times. The little understood presence of these Goths in the inscription seems rather an excellent internal evidence of its truth. It is one of those little hall-marks of genuineness which an imitator fails to appreciate, but which so naturally marks the true producer.

As has been shown in Chapter IX, *ante*, we know that a Norse expedition was sent to Greenland about the time of this date. The object of this expedition is unique in the history of Greenland. Its purpose was not trade or taxes, but, as expressly stated in the letter of King Magnus, to reestablish Christianity in Greenland. As suggested by Storm, Gjessing, Nansen and other writers, this purpose probably included "an exploration of the lands farther west." [10] Let us now see what points of agreement or dis-

[10] Professor Storm's remarks are as follows: "We have a copy of a royal diploma from October, 1354, which indicates extraordinary preparations. Paul Knutssøn of Onarheim, a member of the King's bodyguard [*Hirdmand*] is appointed leader of the expedition and he is given extraordinary authority to fit it out and choose the members of it. The purpose of the enterprise is to maintain Christianity in Greenland, i.e., a fight with the Eskimos, and to strengthen the colony in general, perhaps also to explore the new lands. In any case we can be sure that the conditions in the Greenland colony and its fate was in these years debated

agreement there are between the Kensington inscription and the holy crusade led by Paul Knutson.

I. The date. The Paul Knutson expedition took place in the years 1355-1364. The Kensington inscription is dated 1362.

II. The personnel. It has been shown above that the Knutson expedition was made up partly of Norwegians and partly of Goths. The Kensington inscription mentions eight Goths and twenty-two Norwegians.

III. The presence of priests. The Knutson expedition, being an enterprise for the maintenance of Christianity, would count among its members one or more priests. The presence of a priest is indicated in the Kensington inscription by the pious character of the inscription, and by the knowledge of Latin words and characters as shown in the letters A V M, and also by the fact that the explorers were able to leave an inscription in writing—an accomplishment almost unknown to all but the clergy.

IV. Headquarters in Vinland. Nothing was known of the apostate Greenlanders except that they had moved away, leaving no signs of warfare behind them. It was therefore a voluntary, orderly emigration whose only object could have been to better their conditions. Their destination must have been somewhere in the West or Southwest as there was no other place to go. Paul Knutson knew by reports, both written and oral, of these lands in the West. One was Helluland, a region of desolation. Another was Markland, the land of forests. The third was Vinland, which, according to all reports, was a good land with a mild climate and abundant products. Acting on the reasonable assumption that people, when driven by hardships to

in Bergen from whence the expedition departed and whither it after a number of years returned. We have no direct information as to when it returned. We know that it had not returned in 1357. It appears most probable that it did not return until 1363 or 1364 for in the last year Ivar Bardsen reappears again in Norway and not before 1365 is a new bishop to Greenland consecrated." *Studier over Vinlandsreiserne*, 1888, pp. 73, 74.

emigrate, would go to the best land within reach, Paul Knutson would presumably first seek these exiles in Vinland. The Kensington inscription definitely states that its people came from Vinland.

V. A protracted stay in Vinland. The location of Vinland must necessarily have been somewhat hazy to Paul Knutson and his men. However, all accounts agreed that Vinland lay beyond Markland. Markland means forestland, and Nova Scotia was probably the original Markland, being the first land where travelers coming from the north could see forests. By the middle of the fourteenth century the Greenlanders would have discovered that abundant timber was to be had in the interior of the long bays of southern Labrador and Newfoundland. This would cause the appellation Markland to be moved north to apply to these nearer sources of timber supply. The first region beyond Markland would therefore be the southern shores of the Gulf of St. Lawrence. Here, perhaps in Gaspé Bay which is the first good harbor he would come to, was probably the place where Paul Knutson established his winter quarters while searching the neighboring shores for signs of the emigrants. But this search would require a long time, for nowhere on the Atlantic coast line is the land so cut up by bays and promontories as is the region around the Gulf of St. Lawrence. This long gulf and the St. Lawrence River, up which they could sail for 500 miles, must have seemed an ideal region to Paul Knutson and his men, being so much like the more favored parts of southern Norway and Sweden. They would therefore presumably search its shores carefully. This search, including that of all the other bays and islands in this region, would take several seasons which they must have spent in what they supposed was Vinland.

This long sojourn in Vinland, which incidentally explains the long absence of the Knutson expedition, is clearly implied in the Kensington inscription when it speaks of "8 Goths and 22 Norwegians on a discovery-

journey *from Vinland.*" Unless their stay in Vinland had
been of long duration the inscription would have read
"from Norway."

VI. The route. Eventually Paul Knutson would be convinced that the emigrants were not in those parts. But that
would not terminate his efforts. To him as to other people
of his times this new land was a large island, and somewhere on the shore of this island these apostates whom he
was seeking must be found unless God had struck them
down in their iniquity. The thing to do therefore was to
follow the shore until he found them. Eventually he would
reach Hudson Bay and then he would have reason to believe that he had gotten to the other side of the "island,"
for here the coast runs due south for many hundred miles.
But when he finally reached the southwestern corner of
Hudson Bay, he would learn that he was not skirting the
fringe of an island, for here the Nelson River pours a flood
of waters of continental dimensions into the sea.

Assuming that the expedition reached the Nelson River,
the commander by this time would have had ample reason
for realizing that his quest for the Greenland apostates was
hopeless. But with the conclusion of this mission he would
conceivably see the beginning of another enterprise which,
while it promised less of celestial glory, held more interest
for this world. This great continent the coasts of which
he had been skirting so long—what did it look like in the
interior? Was it a desert wilderness or was it a vast world
of strange sights and treasures like the marvelous Asia,
whose wonders had just recently been revealed? The age
of great explorations had begun, and echoes of the great
overland journeys into the heart of Asia by Marco Polo,
Friar John, and William Rubruquis had reached every
court and capital of Christendom. To intelligent, capable
men like Paul Knutson and his associates, eager for the
honor of their king, the call to explore this new country
would have been appealing and probably persuasive.

The initial exploration of new regions has almost always

been accomplished by means of great rivers. They lessen the labor of transport and provide unmistakable highways through the wilderness. Thus was America explored by the pathfinders Joliet and Marquette, Robert La Salle, and

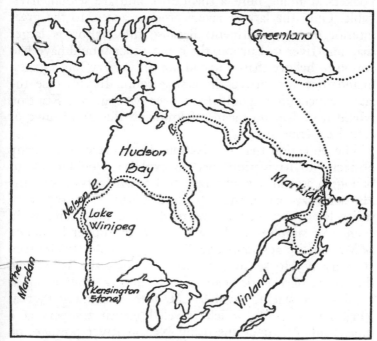

FIG. 6. SKETCH SHOWING ROUTE BY WAY OF HUDSON BAY

Lewis and Clark. These men, all of them, penetrated thousands of miles into the interior of the continent by ascending the course of one large river to its source and thence portaging across to the head-waters of another flowing in the opposite direction. Paul Knutson would have been right in reasoning that by ascending the Nelson he could find another river that would carry him back to Vinland. If the commander's only thought was to return to his headquarters in Vinland, he would probably have gone up the Nottawa or the Albany rivers. But if he contemplated an exploration of this new country, he would avoid the small rivers and seek the largest drainage basins, as explorers always do. The small rivers are usually blind pockets, draining only a small area, and are seldom navigable. Only the largest rivers promise access to the great interior of any continent. Because the Nelson is larger than any river in Europe, the commander would have had reason to believe that it would not only carry him farthest inland, but also prove the easiest route. In this case the latter expectation would have been wrong, but Knutson would have had no means of knowing this in advance of actual experience.

The objection that the Nelson River presents so many obstacles to navigation that no explorer would think of trying to ascend it is contrary to known facts. When the Hudson's Bay Company organized its fur trade some centuries later, the Nelson was used for a long time as an avenue of supplies to the stations on the upper branches, as Mr. Quaife acknowledges.[11] In 1934 could still be seen at Norway House, at the north end of Lake Winnipeg, the wreck of a York boat, "a long clumsy scow as big as a miniature yacht," which had been nailed together at York Factory, "in which traveled eleven trappers at a time, hauling it over the many Nelson River portages on log rollers."[12]

Here the reader may pause to ask: Is it not more probable that the explorers ascended the St. Lawrence River and left their boats at the west end of Lake Superior?

There are a number of obstacles to this theory. The inscription says that the vessels were left "by the sea," that is, the ocean. The St. Lawrence is navigable for shipping as far up as Montreal, about 500 miles from the ocean. As the explorers naturally would sail their ships as

[11] *New England Quarterly*, VII, 637, note 54.
[12] A. E. Sevareid, *Canoeing with the Cree*, p. 118, New York, 1935.

far as possible, they would not leave them until they reached the rapids near Montreal. But in that case they would not say that they had left their ships by the *ocean* seeing they had brought them 500 miles inland. Another obstacle is that the word *havet* in the inscription, which is translated "the sea" or ocean, always refers to a body of *salt* water, and this does not fit Lake Superior. Finally the distance mentioned in the inscription—"14 day-journeys"—cannot be made to agree with the distance from Lake Superior to Kensington, but it agrees closely with the distance from Hudson Bay. This will be elucidated in Chapter XVII.

This Hudson Bay route is implied in the peculiar wording of the inscription: "an exploration-journey from Vinland *through* (or *round about*) the West." If the explorers had come straight west, there would have been no reason for adding the words "through the West." But having arrived by a circuitous route, they indicated this route by saying that they had come from Vinland by way of the West.

VII. The time of return. The historians who have discussed the Paul Knutson expedition are agreed that it returned in 1363 or 1364, more probably the latter year. There is no explicit statement in historical documents concerning the time of the return, but we find in an Icelandic annal covering the years 1328-1372 that Bishop Alf was ordained bishop of Greenland in 1365.[13] As the needs of diocesan administration and the canonical rules of the Church demanded that a new bishop be ordained forthwith after the news of his predecessor's death, and as Bishop Alf's predecessor, Arne, had died in 1348 or 1349, this implies that no vessel had returned from Greenland in the intervening years until shortly before 1365.[14]

This time of return compares closely with the Kensing-

---

13 Storm, *Islandske Annaler*, p. 227.
14 *Grønlands Historiske Mindesmærker*, III, 30, 59, note 86.

ton inscription. The ten men who in the summer of 1362 were left in charge of the ships would in the nature of things be instructed to remain there for some time. Even if only for two months, this would probably make it too late for them to get out of Hudson Bay before it would freeze up. Consequently they would not be able to return to Vinland until 1363. Here they would likely expect to find the overland party safe and sound. Not finding them there they would wait until the spring of 1364. By that time they would understand that the major part of the expedition had come to grief. To search for them would be utterly futile. The only thing they could do would be to return and report to their King. Thus they would arrive in Norway in the summer or fall of 1364.

So far a comparison of the Kensington inscription shows perfect agreement with what is known of or can be deduced from the Knutson expedition. There remains, however, one point which indicates a disagreement: The Kensington inscription refers to "our ships," while the King's letter mentions only *one* ship.

This discrepancy, however, is not vital. When the letter was written October 28, 1354, commanding that the expedition be fitted out, all details concerning its equipment and scope were necessarily in their infancy. The King mentions the royal *knorr* because this vessel was the one that usually made the trip to Greenland. The *knorrs* were bulky vessels intended for carrying large cargoes of freight, but with freeboards so high that oars were practically useless. As preparations for the expedition went on, it probably occurred to the commander that circumstances might lead him into unknown and shallow waters where he might meet with enemies. In such a case where easy mobility might be imperative, he would be helpless in the *knorr*. He would therefore decide to take two or more light war vessels that were easily propelled by oars. We shall see, in fact, that there actually was a plural number of war vessels in Greenland at this time.

These coincidences are so many and striking that they can hardly be the results of chance. The Kensington inscription must either be the work of some person in recent years who knew of the Paul Knutson expedition, its personnel, purpose, duration and course, or else it is a true record of the date it bears.

The first supposition seems scarcely tenable. The first time any reference in print is made to this specific expedition is in *Grønlands Historiske Mindesmærker*, III, published in Copenhagen in 1845.[15] But it does not seem probable any possible forger could have based his inscription on the information which is given there. The editor merely prints a late and distorted copy of King Magnus' letter to Paul Knutson because the name of Greenland occurs in it, just as he mentions every other reference to Greenland to be found in old documents. He makes no editorial comment shedding light on the subject from other sources. He does not suggest the possibility that an exploration journey to America was involved, nor does he say anything about the time of its return or of its peculiar bi-national personnel. These things are not hinted at until Professor Storm briefly alludes to some of these items in 1888.[16] In order to account for this perfect historical corroboration, the opponents of the inscription have therefore insisted that it must have been written shortly after Storm's book was published.[17]

Against this hypothesis we have a signed statement from Mr. Nils Flaten, a neighbor of Mr. Ohman, in which he declares that he lives in a house which faces directly toward the spot where the rune stone was found; that this house is only 500 feet away from that spot; that there was no intervening timber or other obstruction preventing a clear view of it, and that he had lived in this house unin-

---

[15] Vol. III, 122.
[16] *Studier over Vinlandsreiserne*, pp. 73, 74.
[17] Gjessing in *Symra*, V, 125; J. E. Olson in *Minneapolis Tidende*, Aug. 24, 1911; and others.

terruptedly since 1884.[18] It therefore would have been impossible for anyone to have sat in full view of Mr. Flaten's house and chiselled the inscription without being detected.[19]

We have seen, moreover, that the stone was in its finding place as early, approximately, as 1828. Furthermore, the weathering of the inscription, as stated by several geologists, shows that it was made at least a hundred years before the time of their examination in 1910 (see Chapter XII).

The objection has been made to the writer in a private communication that there is no evidence to show that the Paul Knutson expedition ever took place.

Few documents bearing on the Paul Knutson expedition remain, it is true. It should be pointed out, however, that the four centuries that followed this date were preeminently Norway's "dark ages." Little interest was taken in copying the records of the past, and more and more of them went up in flames in their scattered repositories.[20]

In spite of the paucity of public documents, there are to be found a few items which corroborate the fact of the expedition. Mention has already been made of the Icelandic annals wherein it is learned that Bishop Arne's death in Greenland in 1349 did not become known until 1364, when a vessel must have brought the news from Greenland. This is considered by Storm and others as evidence

[18] Following is Mr. Flaten's statement:

"Kensington, Minn., July 20, 1909.

"This is to certify that I live only 500 feet from the spot where the rune stone was found. This house faces directly toward this spot and there is only the open swamp between. I have lived in that house since 1884 and there has not been a day or night but that the house has been occupied by some members of my family.

"(Signed) NILES FLATEN."

[19] As the stone weighs 202 pounds it must have been carved at or near the spot where it was found.

[20] Björn Jonssön, Lyschander, Olavus Magnus and Peder Clausen all refer to books and documents dealing with affairs in Greenland which are now lost.

that the Paul Knutson expedition returned that year or in 1363. Paul Knutson, who as the lawspeaker (judge) of *Gulathing* is frequently mentioned up to 1354, is last mentioned as the commandant of the expedition. Presumably he was among those who perished on the journey.

We have definite testimony to the fact that an expedition was sent to Greenland in these years. This is found in Bishop Olaus Magnus' once famous work *Historia de gentibus septentrionalibus*, and is evidently an echo of Paul Knutson's expedition. He writes:

. . . Here [in Greenland] live a kind of pirates who make use of skin boats . . . in which they attack merchant vessels, seeking to sink them by piercing their hulls from below instead of attacking them from above. In the year 1505 I personally saw two of these skin boats above the western portal within the cathedral dedicated to the Sainted Halvard where they were put up on the wall for general exhibition. It is stated that King Haakon captured them when he with his battle fleet passed the coast of Greenland just as they [the natives] prepared to sink his vessel in the sea. . . .[21]

This passage is highly significant. It was, of course, an error when the cicerone of the cathedral told the bishop that King Haakon had personally commanded this expedition. The years of his reign, 1355-1380, were filled with wars and intrigues, first with the Hanseatic League and later with Sweden in his vain attempts to secure his legitimate right to the throne of Sweden. It is therefore hardly conceivable that he would personally lead an expedition into the distant and dangerous waters of Greenland. Divested of this embellishment the information conveyed is that a royal naval expedition operated in Greenland waters in King Haakon's reign which was not of a commercial nature but sailed in war vessels and had unfriendly relations with the Eskimos. This is a brief characterization

[21] *Historia de gentibus septentrionalibus*, Rome, 1555, Book II, Ch. IX. The above passage is a translation from the Swedish edition *Historia om de Nordiska folken*, Uppsala & Stockholm, 1909-16, II, 92.

of the Paul Knutson expedition. It took place in King Haakon's time,[22] it was a royal expedition sent to Greenland, and it was not of a commercial nature. It was therefore easy for tradition to dramatize this expedition for the redemption of the Greenland apostates into a royal battle fleet with the King himself in command.

But why did the bishop of Oslo give these Eskimo kayaks a place of honor in his great cathedral? In those days there was no scientific interest in the customs of barbaric peoples, and a cathedral would be the last place for the exhibition of the crude craftsmanship of the savages. But there is a religious reason which perfectly justified the presence of these kayaks on the wall *within* the cathedral. St. Halvard was the patron saint of Oslo, and he had been canonized, among other merits, for having lost his life in attempting to save a person in distress.[23] His church was therefore the proper place to preserve these kayaks, which, because they were the only mementos of the Paul Knutson expedition, symbolized the self-sacrifice of these men who had lost their lives in their crusade to save the apostate Greenlanders from eternal damnation. Professor Munch believes that the kayaks were placed on the wall of the cathedral by the command of King Haakon [24] who had additional reason for doing so. The same year (1364) that the survivors of the Paul Knutson expedition returned, the sovereignty of Sweden was lost to Magnus and Haakon when the Swedish nobles chose Duke Albrecht of Mecklenburg as king. The following year King Magnus was captured by King Albrecht and languished in prison for six years. King Haakon had a very difficult time in raising the huge ransom demanded—almost a million dollars.[25] It was probably at this time that he caused the kayaks to be

[22] King Haakon became king of Norway in 1355. The Paul Knutson expedition occupied the years 1355-1364.
[23] Ludvig Daae, *Norges Helgener*, II, 163.
[24] *Det Norske Folks Historie, Unionsperioden*, II, 106.
[25] Gjerset, *History of the Norwegian People*, II, 18.

placed in the cathedral to remind the people of his father's pious enterprise and thus obtain not only their contributions but also their prayers for his liberation. In this and other ways of building up his father's reputation for good works, he was so successful that when King Magnus two years after his liberation perished at sea, he was worshipped as a national saint.

It also appears that King Haakon caused two similar mementos to be placed in the great cathedral in Throndheim. Claudius Clavus, the Danish cartographer, who was born in the latter part of the fourteenth century, made a map of Europe in which for the first time Greenland is shown—with a very good outline. Among the many annotations on this map (made some time after 1427) he has the following: "There is hanging in the cathedral of Nidaros [Throndheim] a little hide-boat. There is likewise a long vessel of hides which was also once taken with such Pygmies [as live in Greenland] in it." [26] This is the first time an *umiak* is mentioned in history.

There is also other cartographical information which suggests a connection with the Paul Knutson expedition. In 1605 Hans Poulson Resen made a map of Greenland which he states is a copy of one made several centuries before his time. Although he has added a couple of items of more recently gained geographical information, there is good internal evidence to show that his prototype was much older. This evidence lies in the fact that he places both the Eastern and the Western Settlements of Greenland, as well as Herjulfsness and Eriksfjord, in their true location on the *western* coast of Greenland. This is as it should be, but it was quite foreign to the understanding of his time. For a hundred years before Resen's time and well into the nineteenth century, it was believed that the Eastern Settlement with Herjulfsness and Eriksfjord lay on the *east* coast of Greenland. The map therefore reflects a conception of Greenland geography which was alien to

26 Quoted by F. Nansen, *In Northern Mists,* II, 269, 270.

Resen's time and indicates that the map he had copied was based upon information gained by persons who had been to Greenland and knew the true facts. It also shows the proper locations of Markland and Vinland and reveals a knowledge of Baffin Land. All this supports his statement that the map he was copying was made *aliquot centenos annos* before his time, and this brings us back to the time of the Paul Knutson expedition.

XIV. THE LINGUISTIC ASPECTS OF THE INSCRIPTION

THE language of the inscription, being the principal means by which the writer reveals himself, presents one of the best fields for testing its authenticity. It has therefore from the first been closely scrutinized. This scrutiny has produced many criticisms of which the following are the most important: (1) The presence of five alleged English words (*fråm, mans, of* [*west*], *þeþ* and *illy*), which from the beginning was an argument against the inscription. (2) The absence of inflection in conjugations and declensions. However, the warrant for each of the sixty-two words as they stand in the inscription can only be fully demonstrated or disproved by a minute comparison with the text in manuscripts of the fourteenth century; and as this involves hundreds of difficult quotations whose validity can only be fully gauged by a scholar familiar with this field, it has been thought best to relegate this minute analysis to the Appendix. In the present chapter will be presented a brief survey of linguistic conditions in Norway and Sweden in the fourteenth century, and a consideration of the probable language habits of the supposed members of the expedition who are said to have left the inscription.

The philological questions presented in this inscription are peculiar and beset with unusual difficulties. This is due, first of all, to the complexity of dialectic usage which must have existed among the members of the expedition if we, for a moment, assume that it is a true record. If these explorers were all Goths, it would be a simple matter to check the vocabulary, grammar and syntax of the inscription with the considerable number of diplomataria from West Gothland of the fourteenth century that still remain. But besides the eight Goths there were twenty-two Norwegians. We have no inkling of what part or parts of Norway these twenty-two men hailed from. As the dialectic differences of various parts of Norway are now and were even then very marked, this opens the way for many linguistic forms. Moreover, if it was written by a member of the Paul Knutson expedition, its members must by 1362 have been in close daily contact for seven years. This constant intercourse would have a tendency to destroy the distinctive characteristics of the various dialects represented and to fuse the differences of speech into an idiom more common to the entire company. Finally it must be emphasized that these adventurers, selected for their practical fitness to cope with unknown difficulties and dangers, were no doubt soldiers and sailors instead of clerks. As such their mode of speech would undoubtedly be the most recent *colloquial* usage rather than the stilted literary style favored by the clerks who have left us most of the literary remains of the Middle Ages.

This mixture of *colloquial* dialectic usage in the process of fusion must therefore be given due consideration in testing the inscription.

In determining the question of the linguistic fitness of the Kensington inscription, only two tentative premises present themselves: Either the inscription was written in the fourteenth century, or it was written in recent years by a person of considerable philological learning. Remarks about an "illiterate bungler" are no longer pertinent. The fact that the writer was able to produce a lengthy inscription in an ancient dialect, which for forty years has survived criticism, in runic characters accompanied by the very rare runic numerals, is proof enough that he must have been an able student of philology, unless he lived at the time of the date of the inscription. Assuming for a moment that he was a person of modern philological training, he must have gotten his learning from such textbooks as were available from fifty to a hundred years ago. In compiling his inscription he would naturally follow the rules and paradigms of such textbooks most carefully in order to meet with the approval of future critics. Having gone to the toil and study of making such an inscription, it is hardly thinkable that he would place self-made obstacles in the way of the acceptance of his fabrication.

But this assumption falls down when we study the inscription. Instead of the antique inflected forms like *wi haffthom, wi warum, wi komum*, etc., which he must have learned in the textbooks that existed in the nineteenth century, we find *wi hade, wi war, wi kom*, etc. Instead of writing his date in Roman notation, he uses the decimal system. Instead of writing *ein, stein, heim*, he writes *en, sten, hem*. Such a spelling as *þeþ* for *død* is entirely foreign to a person of present-day philological training. So also is such an apocopated preterite form as *fiske* instead of *fiskadhi*. No less than thirteen words are omitted and some are misspelled. The inscription starts out without either subject or predicate. Three times the subject of the sentence is omitted. The term, days-journey, is spelled both *þags-rise* and *þagh-rise*. We find both *og* and *ok*, *weþ* and *we, frå* and *fråm*. It seems incredible that a modern student concocting his inscription by help of textbooks would make such errors.

All these objections disappear, however, if we assume that the inscription was written in the colloquial usage of the fourteenth century. In those days carelessness in spelling was the rule instead of the exception. The omission of the subject was characteristic of the times, and numerous illustrations may be cited (see Appendix) to show that inflected endings had mostly been dropped from the vernacular of West Gothland. Sometimes we also find them quite ignored in documents written by the clerks. Henrik Henriksson, a priest from West Gothland, who in 1371 was King Haakon's household chaplain, wrote intimate letters to the King which phonetically are almost modern.[1] Ancient colloquial usage also explains the use of those ancient words, *fråm, mans, of west* which puzzled the critics for so long a time. In the fourteenth century these old words still lingered in the speech of the people, although they have since dropped out.

The date on the Kensington Stone, 1362, belongs to a period which is rather obscure in the Scandinavian North, particularly in a literary way. The eleventh, twelfth and thirteenth centuries constitute the golden age of Scandinavian history, and produced an impressive literature. The language of this earlier period is therefore well known through its runic inscriptions, manuscript literature, and the grammatical works of the present day dealing with it. Eventually this period of literary florescence came to an end, in Norway about 1300, in Iceland somewhat later. The literary remains of the fourteenth and fifteenth centuries are few and mediocre. Because of this meagre quality, no textbooks illuminating its grammar and syntax were published until after the time when the Kensington Stone was found. Owing to this paucity of information concerning the language and dialects of the fourteenth century, many persons have assumed that these dialects were marked by the same attention to declensions, conjugations and inflections which characterize the period that preceded it.

But the language of Sweden and eastern Norway by 1362 had changed very materially from the Old Swedish and Old Norse. Speaking of the language of Norway in the fourteenth century (which was the more archaic of the two), Professor Munch writes:

The languages of the two kingdoms [Sweden and Norway], which had always much resembled each other, were now [due

---

[1] See his letter of 1371 in *Diplomatarium Norwegicum*, VI, No. 278. See also his letter of 1370, written at the dictation of Queen Margaret. A facsimile of this is printed in Taranger's *Norges Historie*.

to the Union in 1319] in the process of amalgamation. The numerous [Swedish] clergy appointed to Norway, the many new connecting links, and the constant association between Norwegian and Swedish families, caused the spoken language, and in part the written language, of the upper classes of Norway to approach that of the Swedes. . . . The melodious and highly inflected Old Norse language was being displaced by a less elegant transition language, marked by lacerated word forms and the lack of strict grammatical rules and therefore probably not written the same way by any two writers. In part it resembled Old Norse, in part Swedish and in part the provincial dialects. . . . The regular grammatical inflections which distinguish all old languages were the first to be discarded. . . . The neglect of inflectional endings and the substitution of particles or the use of certain modified sentence structures became characteristic.[2]

Professor Amund Larsen has also called particular attention to the great transition and resultant irregularities which mark the Norse writings after Sweden and Norway became united under one king. He writes: "In Norwegian from the latter part of the Middle Ages it is even more difficult than in the neighboring languages to reconstruct the real sound and forms of the spoken languages, in that we find not only the traditional forms of writing preserved along with reproductions of the most decadent phonetics of the times, but old and later Swedish and Danish is mixed with the native speech. . . . We can see from this that people attempted to write as they had learnt, not as they spoke. What the spoken language was can therefore not be found by statistics, but by comparison with the dialects of the present from the same or nearby places." [3]

Falk and Torp also dwell on the disintegration of the sonorous Old Norse language through foreign influences

[2] P. A. Munch, *Unionsperioden*, I, 596-597, 363-364. See also Prof. Brøndum-Nielsen in *Arkiv f. Nor. Filologi*, 1918, pp. 105-137, for similar conclusions.

[3] Amund B. Larsen, in *Arkiv f. Nor. Filologi*, 1897, p. 244.

as represented in writings of the fourteenth century. They say: "From 1360 and onward the Norwegian shows a strong *Swedish* influence. The Royal Council of Norway in its documents of that time regularly makes use of a kind of Swedish; the language of the clergy is not seldom strongly colored with Swedish; private documents from or to the Norwegian nobles are often half or wholly Swedish. . . . German influence on the Norwegian language is of an old date. . . . Just as in Sweden and Denmark, the Hanseatic League occupied a dominant place in Norway in the fourteenth and fifteenth centuries. . . . In the documents scores of German words crowded in through Swedish and Danish channels. . . . There are numerous examples showing that many dialects in the fourteenth century had given up plural verb forms." [4]

These four eminent authorities are therefore in agreement to the effect that the language of Norway in the fourteenth century is characterized by a marked decadence of ancient grammatical usage and a growth by accretion from Swedish and German. In Sweden and Denmark foreign influence had caused even greater disturbance to the vocabulary and syntax of the native languages than in Norway. It is therefore apparent that this is a most difficult period in which to place a literary imitation. The recognized literary stability of the Old Norse period, easy of imitation, had passed away and was succeeded by a period of decay, resulting in a reconstruction of the languages. The great linguistic difficulties of the period, together with the dearth of information about it, render its literary style one which even an expert philologist a generation ago would scarcely be tempted to imitate.

These characteristics of fourteenth century language development are all manifest in the Kensington inscription. While much of its vocabulary is archaic, it exhibits the "decadent phonetics," mentioned by Larsen, and the "la-

[4] *Dansk-Norskens Syntax*, 1900, pp. XII and XIII.

cerated word forms and the lack of strict grammatical rules," mentioned by Munch. It also shows the presence of German words and illustrates the lapse of plural verb forms mentioned by Falk and Torp. This mixture of old words and new forms is just what should be expected, for while "grammatical inflections were the first to be discarded," as mentioned by Munch, archaic words and ideograms continued to linger in the speech and writings of the people, being much more a part of the thought of the people than the rules of grammatical syntax. Even now in the days of general education and standard usage, grammatical rules are observed very indifferently in colloquial usage.

All things considered, the Kensington inscription seems linguistically to be a logical fourteenth century product of such a personnel as the inscription mentions. Dialectically the inscription seems to be predominantly Gothic, which probably means that the artisan who inscribed the stone was a Goth. This assumption is supported by the fact that the eight Goths are mentioned first in order instead of the more numerous Norwegians. Mixed with this Gothic dialect there are a number of words of probable Norwegian usage which may be echoes of the dictation of the commander of the expedition or some other Norwegian member.

In view of positive evidences favoring the authenticity of the inscription, linguistic peculiarities should not be unduly stressed. The circumstances of the stone *in situ*, the physiographic changes, and the weathered appearance of the inscription all point to the conclusion that the inscription must have been written hundreds of years ago. In this connection, the statement of Dr. Gustav Indrebø, professor of Old Norse at the University of Bergen, which he gave the writer for publication, is of especial interest:

If it can be proven that the inscription on the Kensington Stone is as much as a hundred years old, then one must, in my opinion, because of historical reasons, assume that it is in fact much older, and genuine,—in spite of the fact that it contains various uncommon and unexpected linguistic things.[5]

Oslo, September 14, 1928.

Gustav Indrebø.

[5] Professor Indrebø's statement as written by him in Norwegian reads: "Dersom det kann provast at innskrifti paa Kensington-steinen er so mykje som 100 aar, maa ein etter mitt skyn av historiske grunnar gaa ut ifraa at ho i røyndi er mykje eldre, og ekte,—til traass for at ho inneheld ymse uvanlege og uventa spraaklige ting."

XV. THE RUNIC SYMBOLS

A RUNIC inscription is a phenomenon in America, but in northern Europe there are thousands. Runic symbols are a cultural product of the early Scandinavians, and for a thousand years were practically their only means of expressing themselves in writing. The earliest runic alphabet contained twenty-four characters, but later was shortened to sixteen. Usually a new technology is more simple in its primitive beginning, and increases in detail of classification with its advancement. But here we see the reverse, in that the more complex alphabet precedes the more simple. The explanation is probably that the early alphabet of twenty-four characters was borrowed, ready made, from a people of greater culture than the Goths. In their new habitat these symbols were used infrequently, and the result was that one-third of them were found unnecessary and eventually forgotten.

More than eighty per cent of the runic inscriptions in the Scandinavian North are written in the alphabet of sixteen signs. In the eleventh century, when the vogue of making runic inscriptions was at its height, these sixteen characters were practically standardized because of their frequent use. Augmented with the so-called dotted runes to express the letters e, d, g, p, and ø, it continued in general use for more than two hundred years. It would therefore be an easy matter to make a short inscription purporting to date from this period which would be faultless both in the matter of runic types and linguistic forms, inasmuch as there are thousands of prototypes to borrow from. Later, especially in the thirteenth and fourteenth centuries, when the knowledge of the Latin [1] alphabet was

---

[1] In this chapter the term *Latin* is used to refer to the letters of the Latin alphabet as opposed to the Runic or Greek alphabets and does not refer to any of the specific forms in which it may be written such as Roman, Gothic, etc.

spread through the agencies of the Church, the use of runes became more infrequent, the old types were modified through errors in memory and because of the change in vocalic sounds, and new types were borrowed from the Latin alphabet. While the practise of runic writing continued sporadically for several centuries, the old alphabet became more and more distorted, until finally in the eighteenth century, we find in Dalarne, Sweden, a hybrid runic style of characters which are chiefly distorted Roman characters.

The Kensington inscription is technically an excellent piece of work. The lines are straight, the characters are of uniform height and boldly chiselled, which indicates considerable skill in the art of cutting runes or similar handicraft. This is also indicated by the fact that while the inscription linguistically shows many errors, it has epigraphically none.

It is to be expected that an inscription from as late a date as 1362 would show many of the late characteristics mentioned above (i.e., changes in form and additions from the Latin alphabet). These we find in the Kensington inscription. Comparing the Kensington runes with the old standard runes in use in the thirteenth century we have the following alignment:

	The old *futhork* of sixteen runes	Dotted runes added in the XII century
Runes in use about 1200	ᚡᚠᚦᚠᚱᚢ:᛭᛬ᛁᛅᚼ:ᛏᛒᚤᚱᛚ	ᛏᚠᚡᛒᛏᚠ
Latin equivalents	*f u th o r k h n i a s t b m l R(y)*	*e d g p æ ø*
Kensington runes	ᚡᚤᚦᛐᚱᛉᚼᛁᚼᛇᛏᛒᚤᚱᚤ	ᛏᚼᛒᚷᚯᚠ
Latin equivalents	*f w d o n k h n i a s t b m l y*	*e g p æ ø j*

This comparison shows that fourteen of the Kensington runes are the same in form as the equivalent runes in use in the twelfth and thirteenth centuries. (The reversed position of some of these runes is found in so many other inscriptions that it needs no discussion.) The fifteenth differs from its prototype only in the absence of the two dots. This absence may be due to oversight or, more probably, to the fact that the space within the two loops of the sign was too small to permit the successful introduction of the two dots. These fifteen characters may therefore be disposed of as acceptable.

There remain six characters which are dissimilar to the equivalent characters in the old alphabet, and one which is new to it. These are ᚷ (a), ᛘ (w), ᛪ (k), ᛩ (y or u), ⊕ (ø), ᚷ (æ) and ᚴ (j).

Two alternative explanations are possible to account for these divergent types. (a) They were written by some modern runic scribe who did not know the correct runic symbols. (b) They were written by someone in the fourteenth century who did not know or had forgotten the correct forms. There is also the additional possibility that these forms represent a restricted local divergence in form, but this probably applies to only three of them—the runes for *a*, *æ* and *y* (*u*).[2]

The first alternative does not seem reasonable. Assuming that the inscription is a modern product, it seems almost inevitable that its author would first carefully compile it in the quiet of his study from such books on runes as were available. Even if these were few and meagre, he could not have failed to learn the approved forms for at least the three letters *k*, *u* and *y*, as they may be seen in almost any runic inscription. After having carefully copied his unfamiliar runic symbols on paper, he would later proceed

[2] Such local divergent forms are frequently found in runic writings. Magnus Olsen discusses a number of such new forms found in Greenland inscriptions, see *Norsk Tidsskrift for Sprogvidenskap* (1932), V, 237 ff. The latter part of *Codex Runicus* (pp. 92-100 which according to its editors was written about 1320) contains a number. See edition of 1877, p. XX, which contains a note concerning line 8 of page 98. See also P. G. Thorsen, *Om Runernes Brug til Skrift*, p. 43 (Copenhagen, 1877).

to copy them onto the stone. A forgery involving so much study and labor (expert stone cutters have estimated that it would take at least two days to carve the inscription), would not be undertaken except with great preparation. It is therefore very difficult to imagine how a modern student of runes would be ignorant of the most common signs in the runic alphabet which may be found in the most elementary textbooks.

Assuming that the inscription was written in 1362 by some member of the Paul Knutson expedition, the situation becomes quite different. These men did not have the opportunity of refreshing their knowledge by consulting a textbook, for no book on runes was then in existence. The use of runes was very infrequent in the fourteenth century as the Latin alphabet had by that time become the means of writing. For seven years these men had toiled amid strange scenes with probably no thought of runic symbols, and under these circumstances it is not strange if the rune-master could not recall all the ancient forms. Only the fact that runic characters are much easier to carve upon stone than Latin letters could have recommended the use of these almost obsolete signs, and there were perhaps only one or two men among them who could claim any knowledge of the almost lost alphabet.

The very forms that are used for the forgotten runes are good evidence that they were written in the fourteenth century. They are not modern forms or inventions of the scribe. They are, with two exceptions, adaptations of the equivalent Latin letters, *the way these letters were written in the fourteenth century*. This will be shown below.

ᚠ . This sign, representing *j*, occurs once in the inscription in the word *skjar*. Up to the date in this inscription we know of no runic sign for *j*, the sign for *i* being used for both *i* and *j*. Nor was the *j* used in writing with the Latin alphabet until in the beginning of the fourteenth century, when, particularly through Queen Euphemia's encouragement of the translation of French romances, the use of *j* as a consonant became known in Sweden and Norway.

This *j* (⸚) in the inscription is not an invention of its writer, as some critics have thought, but may be seen in several MSS. of the fourteenth century. At that time the letter *j* was written as ⸚ , ⸚ and ⸚ .

Its form occurs on the *primstaver* or perpetual calendars of the fourteenth century which would aid the memory of the runic scribe.[3] In *Flateyjarbok*, MS. of the second half of the fourteenth century, the *j* of the inscription occurs innumerable times. It consists of an upright line with a short transverse line across its middle and has a short (sometimes curving) line extending downward to the right in an oblique direction from the top of the letter. As expressed in the artistic writing of this beautiful MS. it usually appears as ⸚ .[4]

⸚ . This rune is a fourteenth century Latin *k* in reversed position. In the Roman minuscules of that period the lower arm of the *k* never extends to the foot of the vertical stave but, like in the rune under discussion, extends in a horizontal direction, or nearly so, from a point about one-third of the way from the bottom. The upper arm forms an acute angle with the stave. A dozen illustrations of this *k* may be seen in the portion of *Magnus Eriksons Statslag* (MS. of 1387) reproduced in Fig. 7, *post*. The reversed position of this *k* was probably intentional to mark it as a rune in conformity with the writer's *g* (⸚).

⸚ . This character appears to be a runic adaptation of

---

[3] See column one, Fig. 10, *post*.

[4] See *The Flatey Book* (published by the Norrøna Society, London, 1906), photostatic reproductions, p. 21, line 31; p. 39, lines 41, 50 and 54; p. 45, line 9; p. 51, line 36, 38; p. 63, lines 34, 39 and 50; p. 87, line 43; p. 93, line 18. The line numbers in this reference are taken from the line numbers given on the first printed page after each facsimile.

the Latin *w* which at first was written as two *u*'s. As there was no symbol for *v* or *w* in the runic alphabet, the rune-master may have borrowed the sign from the Latin alphabet. The common form of the *w* at that time was ω. As all runes have staves he has added one to this character. The result would be ᛘ. But as this character was already in use with the value of *m,* he has added a dot to the sign to differentiate it from runic *m.*

It is possible and probable that the rune-master did not add this stave to his *w.* (ᛘ). In some manuscripts previous to this time the *v* is already provided with a stave. One of the master penmen of the thirteenth century was a secretary of Bishop Nikulas of Oslo who wrote a most artistic hand with every letter of printlike uniformity. In *Diplomatarium Norwegicum,* Vol. I, is a letter from him (No. 7) in facsimile, wherein the *v* a dozen times is written ᛉ. Such an accomplished artist must have had many imitators. The *w* made after this model would therefore be ᛘ, which is practically the same sign as is used in the inscription.

Another explanation is that this sign is meant to represent the new runic sign ᚥ which in the first half of the fourteenth century was widely used for *v* or *w.* It frequently occurs in the latter part of the Scanian Law (*Codex Runicus*) which part is supposed to have been written shortly after 1319.[5] The learned Ole Worm (1643) also gives many illustrations of its use in discussing the Gotland rune-calendar of 1328.[6]

ᛦ. This character represents *y.* In fourteenth century writings this letter is usually written ᛦ, and this is the character the rune-master has borrowed. However, as the runic symbol ᛦ represents *g,* he has added another dot and

[5] See edition of 1877, pp. 92, 93. The date is discussed by P. G. Thorson, *Runernes Brug til Skrift,* pp. 36-52, Copenhagen, 1877.

[6] *Fasti Danici,* pp. 125, 127, 131, Copenhagen, 1643.

also a transverse line near the bottom, probably influenced by his ᚨ (*j*), to differentiate it from the runic *g*.

The letter *y* is found written ᛦ in manuscripts of the fourteenth century from all over the North, from Iceland to the Baltic Sea. See, for instance, its occurrence several times in the fragment of *Magnus Eriksons Statslag* (MS. of 1387), reproduced in Fig. 7, *post*. The dotted *y* occurs as early as 1224 in a document from Oslo.[7] Kock mentions that *y* with one dot above occurs as early as 1220.[8] It is probable that the *y* was also written with *two* dots above in manuscripts of that time, for we find it thus twice printed in *Via Catherinæ*, the first book printed in Sweden (1475).[9]

As the word in which this character appears is in the dative case and therefore calls for the spelling *illu*, it may be that this sign is meant for a *u*. According to Professor Wright, the *u* in German was written with two dots above it,[10] like the sign under discussion. There were also several other ways of writing the *u*. In *Codex Runicus* we find, besides the common sign for *v* or *u*, two others which are entirely different in form. One, which is used very often, is precisely like a runic *f*, with the addition of a dot between the stave and the first twig. The other has no dot, but the stave is crossed by a short line near the bottom.[11] (See *ante*, p. 55, line 8, which shows both signs. This sign is not unlike the character in the inscription.

ᛰ . Objection has been made to the two dots above the *o*, and doubt has been expressed that the umlaut of *o* was ever thus expressed until after the art of printing

---

[7] See facsimile of No. 7, in *Diplomatarium Norwegicum*, I. A West Gothland manuscript of 1280, showing the same dotted *y*, is given in Hildebrand's *Svenska Skriftprof*, I, No. 30.

[8] *Ljudhistoria*, II, 354.

[9] Hildebrand, *Sveriges Medeltid*, p. 401.

[10] Frederick Wright, *Historical German Grammar*, p. 42.

[11] *Codex Runicus*, edition of 1877, p. 92, line 1; p. 92, *verso*, line 8.

was introduced. Mr. J. A. Holvik states this objection as follows: "The letters *æ* and *ø* are the results of jointly-written [*sammenskrevne*] *ae* and *oe*. In manuscript and print we often find the letter *e* placed above the *a* and *o* to express the umlauts *æ* and *ø*. Thus in the first print-types both in Sweden and Germany. As the printed types from the beginning were formed with the common manuscript forms as models, there is reason to believe that no other signs were used in manuscript than the letter *e,* to indicate the umlaut." [12]

In answer it may be stated that it is doubtful if a single old Scandinavian MS. can be found where the *e* is written above the *o*. Instead, we find a very small inverted *v* (^) above the *o*. This little hook may be traced back as far as 1230,[13] and may represent an abortive remnant of the superimposed *e* which is rarely if ever found in Scandinavian manuscripts, but is common in German. In *Flatey-jarbok*, MS. of the latter half of the fourteenth century, the *ø* occurs very frequently. The superimposed inverted *v* is generally written with a very light stroke of the pen and its arms are almost parallel.[14] Sometimes the arms fail to meet at the top and the *ö* is written thus ȯ. Whether or not the writer of the Kensington Stone meant to write two dots or two short parallel lines like the writer of the *Flateyjarbok* is impossible to say, but his marks are fully justified by the transitional forms in the latter manuscript which illustrates the evolution of the two dots as the mark of the o-umlaut.

But there were also many other ways of writing *ø*. Kock has given a number of illustrations of this unstable

[12] *Decorah-Posten* (Decorah, Iowa), Jan. 23, 1925.

[13] See page from *Liber Daticus Lund Vetustior* (MS. of 1230) reproduced in Kaalund's *Palæografisk Atlas*, Copenhagen, 1903, Plate III.

[14] See p. 9, line 7, and the last two words in the third line of page 15 in *The Flatey Book* (photostatic reproductions of the MS.), London, 1906.

form, and calls particular attention to *Sødermannalagen* (*Cod. Havniensis*, number 2237, MS. of the first half of the fourteenth century), whose writer uses three different signs for ø "without any indication of different phonetic values." [15] These three signs are Ø, ∅ and ȯ .

The last sign is perhaps the most common form, and is much the same as is illustrated in the page from the Nestved obituary calendar (Plate IX), except that in the latter the little mark above the *o* has been joined to the oblique line through rapid writing. Sometimes the oblique line is omitted and the little mark above is merely a dot or rather two short fine lines which have been run together so as to appear like one dot. Following are some of these forms:

In the accompanying photographic reproduction of a portion of *Magnus Eriksons Statslag* (MS. of 1387), the ø occurs eleven times. In the hand of its accomplished penman, the earlier curve or inverted *v* (⌃) has changed into a mere dot in every instance. A close inspection of the photograph by means of a magnifying glass seems to show that there has been a double movement of the pen in writing the dot above the *o*, as if the clerk's intention was to make two fine lines, which have run together. It would be physically impossible for the rune-master chiselling upon a stone with rough tools to duplicate such short fine lines close together. The nearest he could come to it would be two dots or short lines spaced some distance apart.

Judging from the eleven specimens in *Magnus Eriksons Statslag* (see Fig. 7), it may be inferred that the inverted *v* above the *o* (ȯ) early changed to one or two dots, as the fancy of the clerk preferred. The single dot occurs frequently, but as the double dot became the sur-

---

[15] *Svensk Ljudhistoria*, II, 1, 2.

viving mark for the umlaut of *o*, it must also have been frequently used. It appears on a wax tablet from Sogn, thus ö. The double dots on the tablet are recognized by Kristian Kaalund, the editor, who dates the writing from about 1300.[16]

In *Onarheims Gildeskraa* (MS. of 1394) the *ø* has a single dot, but the *u* has a double dot (ü).[17]

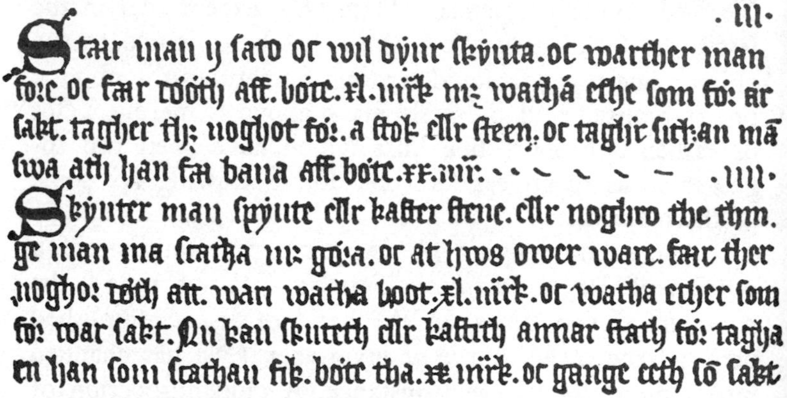
. iii.
Skar man y sato or wil dyur skyuta. oc warther man
fo:r. oc far dödh aff. bote. xl. mrk m: watha ethe som fo: ar
sakt. tagher th: noghot fo:. a stok ellr steen. oc taghir sithan ma
swa ath han far bana aff. bote. xx. mr. - - - - - . iiii.
Skyuter man spyute ellr kaster stene. ellr noghro the thin.
ge man ma scatha m: go:a. oc at hwos ower ware. far ther
noghor dödh att. wan watha boot. xl. mrk. oc watha ether som
fo: war sakt. Nu kan skutetth ellr kastith annar stath fo: tagha
en han som scathan fik. bote tha. xx. mrk. oc gange eeth so sakt

FIG. 7. PORTION OF MS. OF Magnus Eriksons Statslag (1387)
SHOWING NUMEROUS DOTTED *ö*'s, *ä*'s AND *y*'s
From Hildebrand's *Svenska Skriftprof*, Stockholm, 1894,
Plate XXII, No. 34.

In *Den Norske Landslov* (MS. of 1325) the *ø* usually is written with one dot (ȯ), but once it is written with two dots (ö).[17]

The last three illustrations are from manuscripts from Bergen, which, in the fourteenth century, was the headquarters in the North for the German Hanseatic League. It is probable that the use of the double dots above o was introduced into the North through these merchants, whose mercantile connections in their home country would early make them familiar with new usage in other parts. Professor Joseph Wright says: "In early MHG the umlaut of

[16] *Palæografisk Atlas*, No. 49, third line, last page.
[17] *Ibid.*, Nos. 22 and 11.

a, o, u, was represented in Upper German by å, ȯ, u̇ and from the fourteenth century onwards by ä, ö, ü." [18] The o with two dots occurs, for example, in *Der Schwabenspiegel*, MS. of 1410 (*der Bischof von Kölne*), and in a letter from Markgraf Johan von Brandenburg, MS. of 1428.[19]

Inasmuch as we find there was no standard form in the fourteenth century for the ø, but find it written both with and without interior lines, and also with and without dots above, and finally with both one and two dots, there can be no legitimate objection to any one of these forms. As has already been pointed out, it is probable that the writer of the inscription was a priest (see page 138). He may have known of no runic model to follow in writing the *ö*, because it was little used in runic writing before his time. In this dilemma he may have recalled the obituary calendars kept in all monasteries for use in saying mass for the dead. These obituary calendars were sheets of parchment, one or more for each month, whereon was recorded, next to the proper date, the death of the members of the brotherhood. These mortuary entries were uniform in record and began thus:

Ø[*bit*] *Dom*[*inus*] *Jacobus*, etc. (see Plate IX above for illustration). This imposing array of continually recurring capital Ø's, page after page, may have impressed itself so much on the scribe's mind that he adopted this form of the letter in his alphabet.

Of the thirteen obituary notices shown in the *Obituarium Nestvediensis*, six or seven begin with an ø which in type is practically the same as the one in our text.[20]

---

[18] *Historical German Grammar*, p. 42.

[19] Wilhelm Arndt's *Schrifttafeln*, III, Plate 100.

[20] The characters referred to are (1) in line G; (2) in line A (the second obituary, Ako's); (3) in line D (the second obituary, Ethmerus'); (4) in line F; (5) in the second G, second line; (6) in the second obituary in the same line; (7) in the second line A. See Plate IX above which is reproduced from *Palæografisk Atlas*, edited by Kr. Kaalund, Copenhagen, 1903.

These six or seven obituaries, according to Professor Kaa-lund, the commentator, all date from the fourteenth century. They are made up (like the Kensington ∅) of a large elliptic O, inside of which is a perpendicular line which is crossed by an oblique line. Above the O is a dot or short line. In the obituary calendar, the oblique transverse line is irregular in length and direction and usually is connected to the mark above as a fine flowing tail. Such fine cursive lines would, of course, be difficult to duplicate when chiselling with rough tools upon a stone. Instead of this he put in the runic e (+) to show that he was writing the umlaut of o. The same character appears in a Norwegian letter of 1321 in the name *Ollingi* of which a facsimile is shown in *Dip. Norweg.* I (fourth line, first word). The form in the inscription is much like the next to the last obituary shown in Plate IX which dates from 1368.

The presence of these paleographic forms in the inscription is highly significant. Very few facsimiles of fourteenth century Scandinavian paleography were published until about 1900.[21] As the inscription (assuming it to be a forgery) must have been written long before that time (see Chapters XI and XII), this supposed forger had no means of knowing how these Latin letters were written in the fourteenth century unless he was a specialist in Scandinavian paleography. But in such case he would also have known the correct runic forms, and there would have been no necessity for him to have substituted Latin letters. These fourteenth century Latin letters in the inscription therefore appear to be good evidence in support of the authenticity of the inscription.

There remain now the two signs X and X̷ which represent the letters *a* and *æ*. These signs apparently represent

[21] Hildebrand's *Svenska Skriftprof* was published in 1894; Kaalund's *Palæografisk Atlas* in 1903; *The Flatey Book* in 1906. In *Diplomatarium Norwegicum*, I (1847), two pages of facsimiles are given, but these have apparently been selected to illustrate the *dissimilarity* in writing and would be of little use in selecting standard types.

a local divergence in form of which there are several. The Kensington *a* is unique, however, in that its upper right hand branch has a well-marked hook.

In making a dotted *a* for *æ* (X) the rune-master follows the custom of expressing the umlaut with a small sign or dot above the root vowel, which became general in the fourteenth century. This manner of writing *æ* is used twenty-five times in a manuscript of the old *Vestgøtalag* from 1280.[22]

The runic *a* in the inscription (X) is found, minus the distinctive hook, as stated above, in several different regions. It is also found in late inscriptions from Dalarne in Sweden (thus X). This similarity has led Professor G. T. Flom of the University of Illinois to make the positive assertion, presented with much elaboration, that the Kensington inscription is the product of some modern immigrant from Dalarne.[23]

For proof he refers to the Dalecarlian alphabets as given by Liljegren and Ihre-Gøtlin. In the accompanying table, I give not only the two alphabets mentioned by Flom, but also all other runic forms which appear in Dalecarlian inscriptions. This table was compiled by Professor Noreen, and the illustration is a photographic copy of Noreen's table as it appears in *Fornvännen* for 1906.[24]

An inspection of these alphabets will convince the reader that the writer of the Kensington inscription would hardly get his runic lore from them. Instead of identity we find here such disparity in form that no runic characters of the Middle Ages are more dissimilar to the Kensington alphabet than are the Dalecarlian. Only b, f, h, i, m, and r are the same in form.

In order to show how great is the disparity between

[22] Hildebrand, *Svenska Skriftprof*, I, No. 30.
[23] G. T. Flom, *The Kensington Rune-Stone, An Address*, pp. 24-30.
[24] See Johannes Boethius, Lars Levander and Adolph Noreen, *Dalska Runinskrifter från nyare tid*, pp. 63-91.

these runic alphabets, the writer gives below in parallel columns the alphabets of the Kensington Stone and the Ihre-Gøtlin alphabets, in which Flom claims to have found such remarkable agreement. For further comparison the writer has added a column containing the alphabet of the Scanian Law (*Codex Runicus*) of the thirteenth century. A comparison of these various alphabets (see Fig. 8) shows the following differences:

The Kensington and the Ihre Gøtlin alphabets differ in a, e, g, k, l, n, o, p, s, t, v (w), y, æ, ö—total 14.

The Kensington and Liljegren alphabets differ in a, e, g, k, l, n, o, p, s, t, v (w), y, æ, ö—total 14.

The Scanian Law and Ihre-Götlin alphabets differ in a, e, g, k, l, o, p, s, t, v (w), y, æ, ö—total 13.

The Scanian Law and Kensington alphabets differ in a, k, n, t, y, æ, ö—total 7.

This comparison yields the following: (1) There is a minimum of similarity between the Kensington and the Dalarne alphabets. (2) The Scanian Law shows almost the same differences from the Dalarne alphabets as does the Kensington alphabet. (3) The Scanian Law differs from the Kensington alphabet in only 7 characters. If Flom was seeking an alphabet similar to that of the Kensington Stone, why did he pass by the Scanian Law where there are only seven divergences, and select the Dalarne alphabet where there are twice as many differences?

When we compare the *linguistic* forms of Dalarne with those of the Kensington inscription, Flom's theory proves equally untenable. To be brief, there are two convincing proofs that the Kensington scribe has not employed the dialect of Dalarne. The first reason is that for the last three hundred years, the aspirate *h* has dropped out of the Dalecarlian speech.[25] In contrast to this, we find the Kensington inscription abounding in aspirates, such as *hem*, *har*, *hade*, *havet*, *dagh*, *öh*, *ahr*, etc. The other reason is that

[25] See *Dalska Runinskrifter från nyare tid*, in *Fornvännen*, Stockholm, 1906, pp. 68, 71, 76, 86, 89.

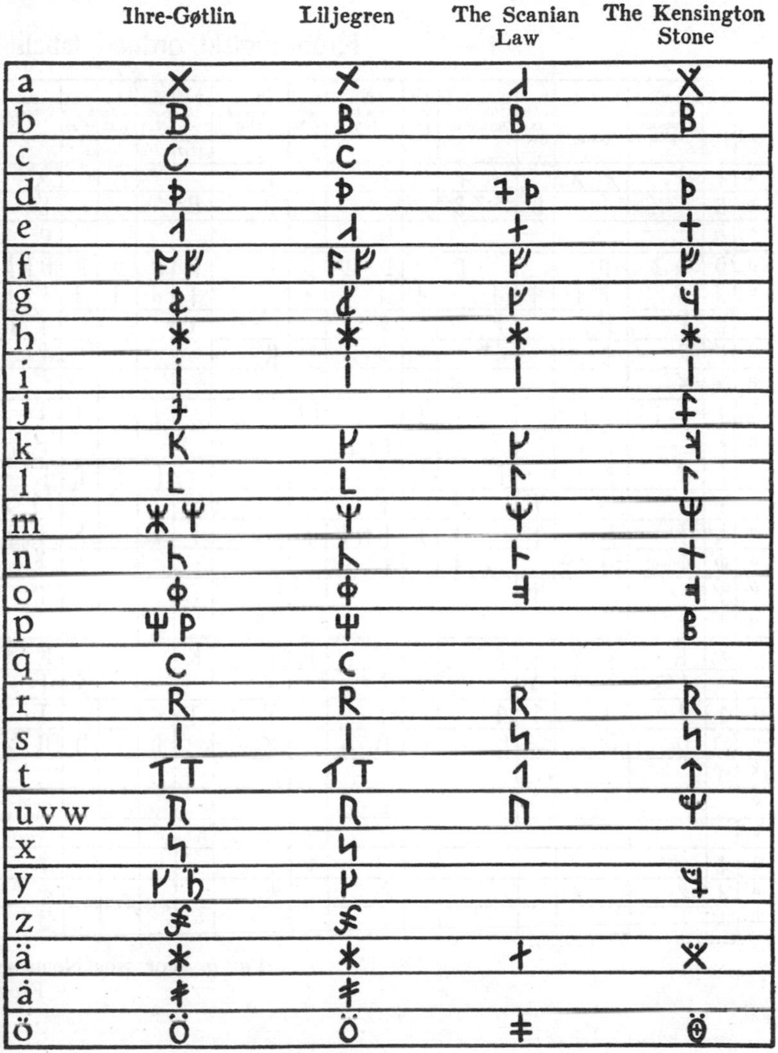

	Ihre-Gøtlin	Liljegren	The Scanian Law	The Kensington Stone
a	✕	✕	⅄	✕
b	ᛒ	ᛒ	ᛒ	ᛒ
c	ᚲ	C		
d	ᚦ	ᚦ	⊦ ᚦ	ᚦ
e	⅄	⅄	✝	✝
f	ᚡ ᛈ	ᚡ ᛈ	ᛈ	ᛈ
g	ᚵ	ᚵ	ᛈ	ᚨ
h	✳	✳	✳	✳
i	ᛁ	ᛁ	ᛁ	ᛁ
j	ᛁ	ᛁ		ᚠ
k	ᛣ	ᛈ	ᛈ	ᚨ
l	ᛚ	ᛚ	ᚱ	ᚱ
m	✳ ᛘ	ᛘ	ᛘ	ᛘ
n	ᚻ	ᚻ	⊦	✝
o	ᚦ	ᚦ	ᚴ	ᚴ
p	ᛘ ᛈ	ᛘ		ᛒ
q	ᚲ	ᚲ		
r	ᚱ	ᚱ	ᚱ	ᚱ
s	ᛁ	ᛁ	ᚼ	ᚼ
t	ᛏ ᛏ	ᛏ ᛏ	ᛏ	ᛏ
u v w	ᚲ	ᚲ	ᚲ	ᛘ
x	ᚼ	ᚼ		
y	ᛈ ᚽ	ᛈ		ᚨ
z	ᚴ	ᚴ		
ä	✳	✳	✝	✕
å	✳	✳		
ö	Ö	Ö	✢	Ö

FIG. 8. FOUR RUNIC ALPHABETS OF THE MIDDLE AGES

Kronologiskt ordnad tabell

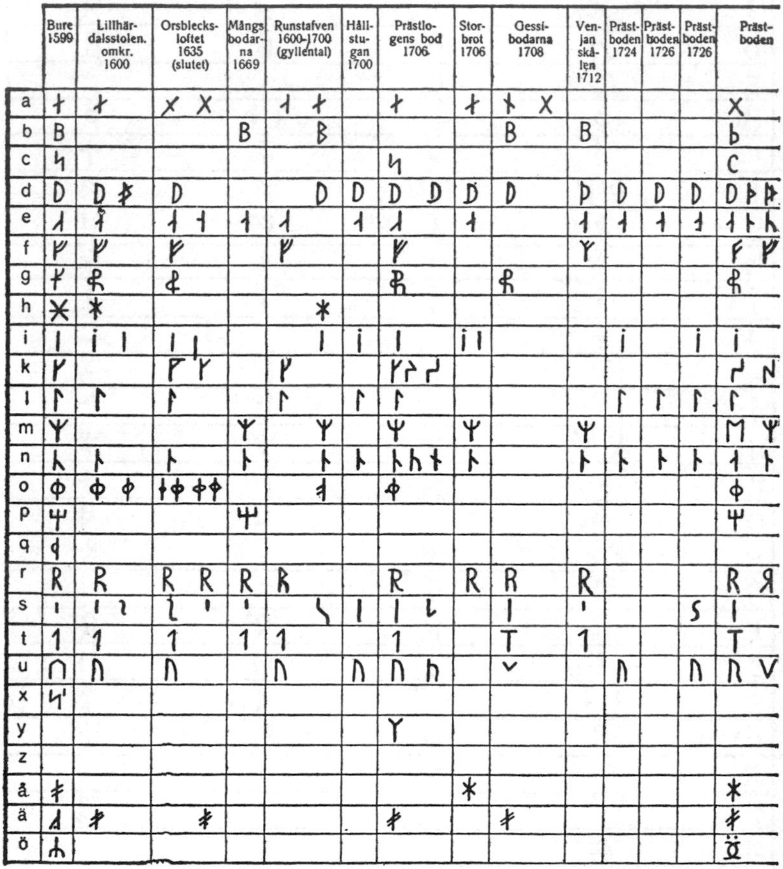

	Bure 1599	Lillhärdalsstolen. omkr. 1600	Orsblecksloftet 1635 (slutet)	Mångsbodarna 1669	Runstafven 1600-1700 (gyllental)	Hållstugan 1700	Prästlogens bod 1706.	Storbrot 1706	Gessibodarna 1708	Venjan skälen 1712	Prästboden 1724	Prästboden 1726	Prästboden 1726	Prästboden
a														
b														
c														
d														
e														
f														
g														
h														
i														
k														
l														
m														
n														
o														
p														
q														
r														
s														
t														
u														
x														
y														
z														
å														
ä														
ö														

FIG. 9. PROFESSOR NOREEN'S
From

öfver dalrunornas olika former.

Prästboden	Åsenboden 1726	Mångsbodarna 1738	Åsenskålen 1749	Baltzar 1750	Lillhärdalsdyfveln 1759	Baltzar 1768	Baltzar	IhreGötlin 1773	Kassticka 1790	Refstickorna 1795	Liljegren. (1832)
X ⌁	X	X ⌁	⌁	X		X	X	X	X	X	X
	ß		ß	ß				ß	ß	ß	ß
	C		Ϸ Ϛ					C	C		C
Þ	D	Þ	D P	D P				Þ	D D D	D Þ P	Þ
⟨	⟨ ⊦	⟨	⟨		⟨ ⟨	⟨	⟨	⟨	⟨	⟨	⟨
	ⶃ		ⶃ ⶃ	ⶃ ⶃ	ⶃ	ⶃ	F ⶃ	F	ⶃ	F ⶃ
⯪⯪⯪	⯪		⯪	⯪⯪⯪		⯪	⯪	⯪	⯪	⯪
		⁂					⁂	⁂ ÅÅ	⁂
ı ı	ı	ı ı	ı	ı	ı	ı	ı ⌁	ıı	ı	ı
⯚	⯚	⯚					K	K	⯚	⯚
⌐	⌐	L ⌐	⌐	⌐		⌐	L L	⌐	L
Ψ	Ψ		Ψ Ψ		Ψ	⁂ Ψ	Ψ	Ψ	Ψ
⌐	⌐ ⌐	⌐	⌐ ⌐			⌐	⌐	⌐⌐	⌐	⌐
φ	φ		φ 0 0			φ	φ	0 ⊕	φ	φ
Ψ		Ψ					Ψ P	P	P P Ψ
							C			C
R	R	R R	R	R	R R R	R	R	R	R
ı	ı		ı	ı			ı	ı ı	ı	ı
T	1	1	1		T 1	1 T	1 T	⌁⌁	1 T
⌐ ⌐	⌐		⌐	⌐	⌐ ⌐	⌐	V W	⌐	⌐
						⌐			⌐
	⊤		⊤		⌐	⌐⌐⌐ ⌐	⌐
						⯲		⯲
	⁂		⁂	⁂		⁂	ÅÅÅ⁂ ⁂	⁂
⯲	⯲		⯲ ⯲	⯲ ⯲	⯲	⯲	⯲⌇	⯲	⯲
	Ö					Ö	Ä Å	Ö

TABLE OF DALECARLIAN RUNES
Fornvännen, 1906

the word-forms in Dalarne are in many cases very different. If the inscription were in the dialect of Dalarne, we would find *ema* for *hem*, *ela* for *illy*, *menn* for *man*, *ar* for *ahr*, *sjå* for *se*, *vesto* for *vest*, *nordo* for *nord*, *resa* for *rise*, *duo* for *dedh*, *voro* for *var*, *bluæ* for *blodh*, *kumo* for *kom*, *ver* for *vi*, *sker* for *skjar*, *esu* for *deno*, *sen* for *havet*, etc.[26] No Swedish dialect is further from the Kensington inscription than the Dalecarlian.

[26] See Noreen's *Ordlista öfver Dalmålet*.

XVI. RUNIC NOTATION AND GOTHIC LETTERS

THE most interesting runic feature of the Kensington Stone is the presence of a series of strange numerals. These were so little known when the stone was discovered that the scholars who attempted to read the inscription were obliged to skip these mystic signs as undecipherable. When at last they were interpreted they were pointed to as strong proof of the modern authorship of the inscription, since the rune-master "was unable to write dates and numbers except in a system of his own invention." It was not until 1909—eleven years after the stone was found—that Helge Gjessing, a philologist of Oslo, was able to show that these numerals were not an invention of the runic scribe, but were in perfect accord with runic numerals used in the Middle Ages.[1]

The numerals in the Kensington inscription are the following in the order in which they occur: ᛆ, ᚠᚠ, ᚠ, ᛈ, ᛈ, ᚠᛈ, ᚠᛈᚠᚠ. The last group occurs at the very end of the inscription and is preceded by the word *ahr* (English *year*). This group must therefore represent the date when the inscription is supposed to have been written. The stave, or upright line, is common to all these numbers; their values must therefore be sought in the transverse lines. A little study of these transverse lines will soon make plain the system.

To each stave is added one transverse line for each unit; thus ᚱ = 1, ᚠ = 2, etc. But as there would scarcely be room to add transverse lines to the number of ten, the first five units are collectively represented by a semi-

[1] See his article in *Symra*, Decorah, Iowa, for 1909, No. 3, pp. 116-119.

circle which is joined to the stave instead of a transverse line. 6, 7, 8, etc., are made by adding more cross lines below the semi-circle. By the same system, 10 is represented by two semi-circles, one on each side of the stave. ᚱᚠᚹᚠ therefore represents 1362.

We are indebted to a Danish writer by the name of Ole Worm for information concerning the use of these numerals. In 1643 he published a work in Latin, entitled *Fasti Danici*, in which he illustrates their usage. This work has never been translated or reprinted and is very rare. As to these numerals, Ole Worm in one part of his work discusses the ancient *primstaver* (also called *runstaver*), or household almanacs, which were in use in the Scandinavian countries in the Middle Ages. This *calendarium perpetuum* most often consisted of a flat stick of wood about thirty inches in length and two inches in width. On it, lengthwise, were three lines of symbols. The middle line contained the runes ᚠᚢᚦᚨᚱᚴᚼ. (the first seven letters of the runic alphabet), repeated 52 times, with the addition of an ᚢ at the end. In this way an ordinary year of 52 weeks and 365 days was represented.[2]

Worm has given us an illustrative table showing the various kinds of numerals shown on different *primstaver*.[3] This table is herewith reproduced photographically (see Fig. 10).

In this illustration, columns one and two show runic letters having the numerical values given in column six. Columns three and four are runic numerals, and column five shows a staveless improvisation of the signs in the two preceding columns.

[2] A brief but lucid explanation of the runic calendar is given in von Friesen's excellent work *Runorna i Sverige*, Uppsala, 1928, pp. 82-84. According to Professor Bugge, *Norges Indskrifter med de ældre Runer*, II, 499, and Gjessing, *Runestenen fra Kensington, Symra*, No. 3, p. 117, the use of these *primstaver* with runic numerals goes back as far as the beginning of the fourteenth century. Numerous illustrations of its use in the fourteenth century is given in *Fasti Danici*.

[3] *Fasti Danici*, Copenhagen, 1643, p. 69.

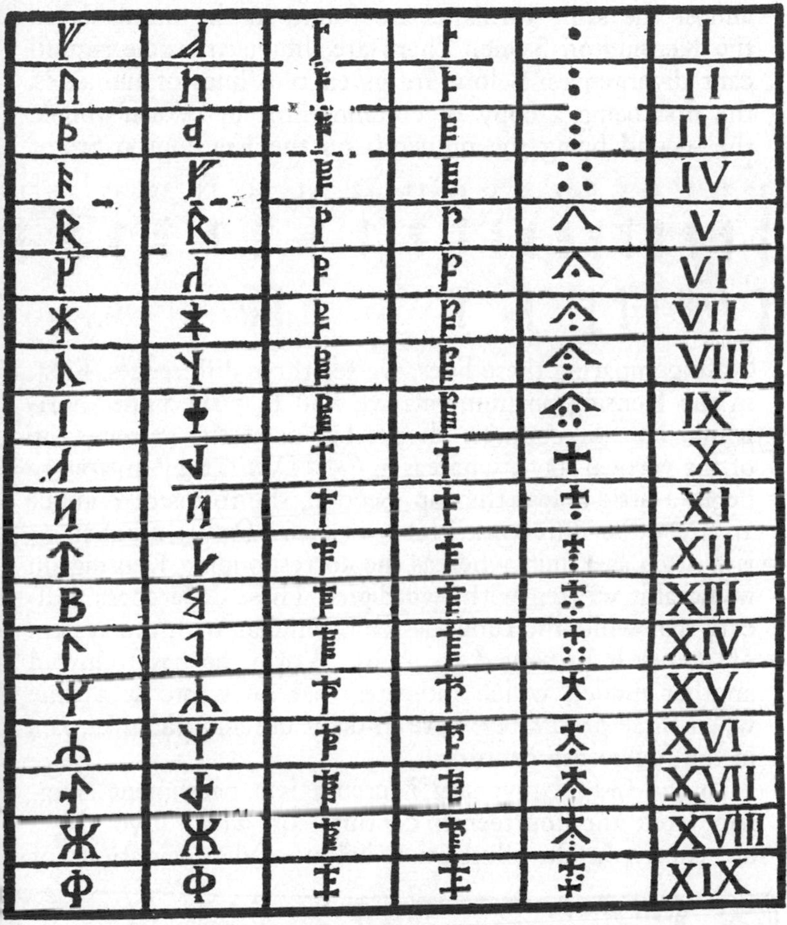

Fig. 10. A Page from Ole Worm's *Fasti Danici* Showing Runic Numerals in Use on the Perpetual Calendars of the Middle Ages

As the reader will notice, columns three and four show almost the same forms as are found in the numerals on the Kensington Stone. There are, however, some significant divergences. Below are given two lines of numerals, the first being a copy of column three in Worm's book, the second being the numerals on the Kensington Stone.

By comparing these lines, we see three differences. First, in the Kensington numerals we find that the upper horizontal line, or counter, always begins at the extreme top of the vertical stave, whereas in *Fasti Danici* they invariably begin a little below the top. Second, the forms of number 10 are quite different. Third, in *Fasti Danici* number 14 is written as a unit, whereas the corresponding Kensington numeral is written with two digits. These differences indicate that while the rune-master is familiar with the system of numerals preserved to us by Worm, he has followed another model; which indicates that he wrote at a time when these *primstaver* were in daily use and plentiful, *i.e.*, in the fourteenth century.

In the Oslo University Museum is a parchment almanac from the fourteenth century, of which two pages are shown in the illustration below. Other variations of

FIG. 11. PAGE FROM PARCHMENT ALMANAC OF XIV CENTURY

the runic numerals are here shown. The representations of the almanac are the same as on corresponding sections of the *primstaver*, except that Latin minuscules are here used instead of runic signs. The Arabic numerals have probably been added later. The illustration represents the month of November.

Some critics have condemned the inscription because it shows the use of the decimal system (14 and 1362). They claim that this system was unknown in northern Europe as early as 1362.

The decimal system was of comparatively recent introduction into the North in the fourteenth century. The most common style then was to state the number of the year of the king's reign (for instance, "in the twentieth year of King Magnus"). If the Anno Domini enumeration was used it was usually given in Roman numerals (for instance, MCCCLXII).

Another not infrequent method of giving the date was by writing it out in the historical style such as is sometimes done now. We have examples of this both in runic inscriptions and in other historical documents, showing that the usage was current in many parts of the Scandinavian North.

Upplands-lagen, MS. of 1300, concludes its introductory authorization by King Birger thus:

Giwit war breff þættæ j Stockholmi æptir wars hærræbyrþ þusænd arum, twem hundræþ arum, niutighi arum, ok sæx arum.[4] (This our letter is given after the birth of our Lord one thousand, two hundred, ninety and six years.)

The Arabic numerals were introduced into western Europe at least as early as 982 when it is known that Pope Sylvester II introduced them.[5] His numerals are

[4] *Upplands-lagen* (Cod. Upps. L. 12), Schlyter's edition, Stockholm, 1834, Corpus III. Numerous examples of this manner of dating occur in *Flateyjarbok*, MS. of 1387. See also letters of 1326 and 1330 in *Diplo. Norveg.* VI, Nos. 128, 134, 135.

[5] *International Encyclopedia*, article *Notation*.

in part like their equivalents in use at present. They were presumably introduced into the Scandinavian countries in the beginning of the fourteenth century. According to Thatcher and Schwill the decimal system was invented in the twelfth century by an Arab mathematician, Muhammed Ibn Musa, who also invented the zero.[6] We have an excellent record of the early use of the decimal system with Arabic numerals in the North in a manuscript entitled *Algorismus*—a treatise on numbers—preserved to us in *Hauksbok*, a Norse manuscript of about 1320.[7] This monograph explains the significance of the decimal system, and treats in detail of addition, subtraction, division, multiplication, and rules for finding the square and cube root of numbers. In working out illustrations of the above, the treatise uses Hindu or Arabic numerals throughout. P. A. Munch, who has given us a complete translation of the treatise, adds: "After Hauk Erlendsson's time, in the beginning of the fourteenth century, the Arabic numerals are frequently found in Norwegian and Icelandic codexes, partly as chapter numbers in the margin, partly also as dates and sums. There are several indications that Arabic numerals were regularly [*stadigen*] used in working out accounts, but in the finished documents there have been inserted the different figures in Roman numerals."[8]

Similar dates in decimal notations are also to be found in the Swedish *diplomataria* of the same period. A letter written by a German residing in Sweden begins "Int jair ons Heren 1352."[9] Another is similarly dated 1355.[10] Plate IX *ante* is a facsimile page from the *Calendarium Nestvediense Obituarium* wherein the obituary notices are

---

[6] Wells, *Outline of History*, II, 37.

[7] A translation of a paragraph of *Hauksbok* showing the use of numerals in decimal notation is given in Reeves, *The Finding of Wineland the Good*, opp. p. 104, London, 1895.

[8] The translation is given in *Annaler for Nordisk Oldkyndighed*, 1848, pp. 353-375. See also Gjessing in *Symra* (Decorah, Iowa), V, 117, 118.

[9] *Diplo. Sveca.* VI, No. 4788.

[10] *Ibid.*, No. 5128.

recorded synchronously with the events they mention. Here (second line from bottom) the year of the death of Dominus Jacobus is given in Arabic numerals—1368.

Abundant evidence of the knowledge and use of the decimal system in the fourteenth century is found in several Icelandic *annals* of the Middle Ages. *Annales Vetustissimi*, which come to a close with the year 1314, contains numerous dates and numbers written in decimal notation.[11] Professor Munch believes that this manuscript was written by a secretary of Hauk Erlendsson (died 1330).[12] Professor Storm is of the opinion that it was written by another clerk "of the same time and style of penmanship."[13] *Skalholts Annaler*, which according to Storm was written "about 1362 or a little later,"[14] contains scores of dates written in decimal notation.[15] *Rymbegla*, a manuscript of about 1300, has many numbers in decimal notation.[16]

The inscription contains three symbols written in Latin characters of the Gothic type. Evidently the runic scribe meant to show particular respect or veneration for the word or name that they represent. Inasmuch as the prayer, "save us from evil," follows immediately after these Latin characters, it is assumed that they represent Ave Maria or Ave Virgo Maria. In the manuscripts of the Middle Ages it is everywhere to be noticed that the scribes used great reverence whenever they had occasion to write a divine name. Usually it was done with the aid of various colored inks and many ornamentations. The Kensington scribe, chiselling upon stone in the wilderness, could not emulate the examples of the clerks. But he bethought him-

---

[11] G. Storm, *Islandske Annaler*, 1888, pp. 33-54.
[12] *Samlede Afhandlinger*, I, 319 f.
[13] Storm, *Islandske Annaler*, pp. VIII, IX.
[14] *Ibid.*, p. XV.
[15] *Ibid.*, pp. 159-215.
[16] Ed. of 1780, Havniæ, see f. i. Part 4, §§ 75, 76.

self of Latin, the language of the Church, and thus dignified his appeal to the holy mother.

The *Angelica Salutatio*, of which Ave Maria (Hail,
Mary!) is the familiar beginning, is not, strictly speaking,
a prayer for deliverance from bodily peril, but a greeting
of adoration, a divine salutation. All educated persons of
the present day know this, and a modern philologist en-
deavoring to frame an inscription and prayer of the fourteenth century would therefore most likely select a more
logical mode of appeal for divine assistance than to say,
"Hail, Mary!" But a study of religious practices of the
fourteenth century shows us that the Angelic Salutation
was then held in especial veneration. In those comparatively illiterate times the frequent intonation of the Angelic Salutation had given the expression, *Ave Maria*, an
almost talismanic significance and was largely used coupled
with prayers of all kinds. Archbishop John Ireland, who
was an intimate student of religious practices in the Middle
Ages, was much impressed by the peculiar wording of this
prayer, and publicly stated before a meeting of the Minnesota Historical Society that it was proof to him that the
inscription could not have been written by a modern
forger.[17] The fact that the three letters AVM are written
without any separating marks, whereas all other words in
the inscription are separated by double points, indicates
strongly that the rune-master did not look upon them
as separate words of a salutation, but as the initial letters
of the first three syllables of one holy name: thus
A—V(e)—M(aria), although A(ve)V(irgo)M(aria) is not
impossible.

The form of these letters, however, have been severely
criticized by the eminent archaeologist, Professor Oscar
Montelius, on the grounds that such unornamented Gothic
forms were not in use in the fourteenth century; the cus-

[17] St. Paul *Dispatch*, Dec. 14, 1909.

tom at that time, when writing Latin capitals, demanding the majuscule type of letters.[18]

If the inscription had been written upon parchment in a quiet monastery, this criticism would be very much to the point, for it is quite true that the majuscules were very much in vogue among the clerks of the fourteenth century. We also find them generally used by the artistic engravers of seals. But if the Kensington Stone is genuine, it was written under quite other circumstances. For several days its writer had labored with crude tools to chisel his account into the surface of a very hard rock. He was working in a strange and sinister region, surrounded by unseen enemies. Only a few days earlier he had found ten of his companions—one-third of the entire company—"red with blood and dead," brutally slain by these mysterious enemies. To expect that a man writing under such tragic and laborious circumstances should stop to ornament his letters with unnecessary flourishes, merely to follow the fashions of literary artists, is expecting too much. As a pious Catholic, he felt it incumbent upon him to show his reverence for the holy name of the Virgin by writing it in the capital letters of the Church, but even then he takes time only for the first letter of each syllable. Circumstances were not propitious for further elaboration.

If the majuscules used by the clerks were different in *type* from the Gothic, the criticism would be valid. But this is not the case. Up to the close of the twelfth century, almost all the inscriptions in churches and upon seals were in plain classical forms of the Roman alphabet. After this begin the more ornamented forms of the same type known as the majuscule, but, as Hildebrand says, "many of these majuscule inscriptions were mixed with Gothic forms." [19] The basic Gothic form is and was easily recognized in all majuscules, and such unornamented forms occur quite fre-

[18] *Chicago Daily News*, June 10, 1911.
[19] Hildebrand, *Svenska Sigiller från Medeltiden*, Stockholm, 1867, Introduction, p. VI.

quently among them. Three or four instances may be cited:

The seal of Ingeger Philipsdatter, widow of the knight Magnus Gregerson, from 1326, reads:

(S' IN) GI (GER) DIS FILIE PHILLIPI

in practically plain Gothic forms.[20]

The gravestone of Ragnild, the daughter of the priest Jon, from ca. 1350, contains the words AVE MARIA in almost pure Gothic forms.[21]

A seal of 1330 shows all three letters (A V M) in un-ornamented forms.[22]

In the Bergen, Norway, museum is a seal of Rostock from the fourteenth or fifteenth century which contains only plain Gothic letters.[23]

A study of the runic symbols seems to present quite strong evidence that the inscription was written in the Middle Ages. Its alphabet agrees most closely with that of *Codex Runicus* (ca. 1275), its nearest neighbor in date. The differences are such as may be expected from the fact that the Kensington inscription is dated about a hundred years later. Furthermore, the use of the very rare runic numerals in somewhat divergent forms from the published types does not suggest a modern authorship, but rather that the rune-master has followed models of his own observation.

[20] Hildebrand, *Svenska Sigiller från Medeltiden*, third series, No. 702. See also No. 69 from 1288; No. 96 from 1295; No. 711 from 1335, and No. 766 from 1316. In the last, both the majuscule A and the plain Gothic A are shown.

[21] Reproduced in Øverland's *Norges Historie*, III, 890.

[22] Peterson, *Danske Adelige Sigiller*, Copenhagen, 1897.

[23] Taranger, *Norges Historie*, III, Part One, 21.

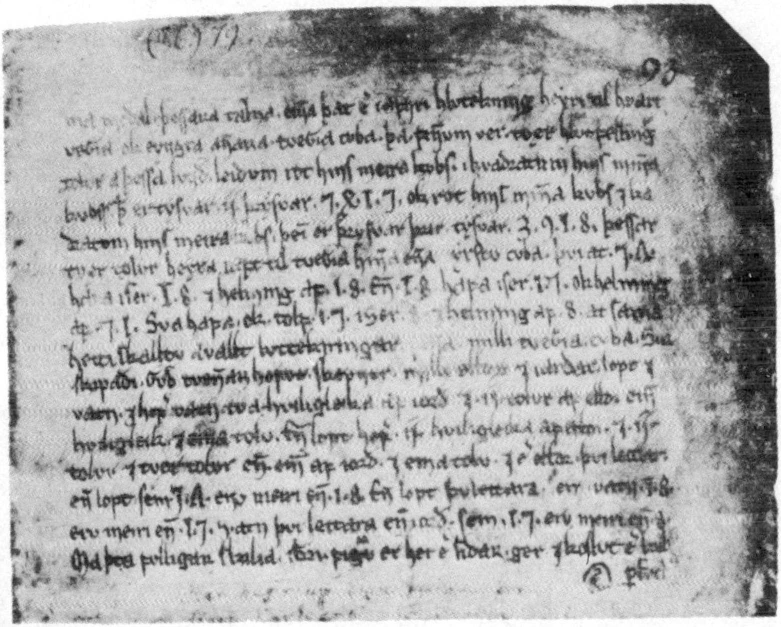

Plate X. Page of Hauk Erlendson's *Algorismus* showing Arabic numerals.
MS. ca. 1320.

Plate XI. The mooring stone at Cormorant Lake showing hole seven inches deep
Photo by Esther Henderson

Plate XII. The three boulders on the shore of Cormorant Lake. The positions of the holes are shown by the three white sticks.
Photo by Esther Henderson

XVII. THE PLACE OF MASSACRE

SO far this study of the Kensington inscription has chiefly been devoted to a consideration of the arguments advanced against its authenticity—the date, the bi-national character of its personnel, the linguistic aspects, the runic characters and the notation. The reader will by this time have a comprehensive idea of whether or not these arguments prove that the inscription is a modern forgery. But in addition to this largely internal evidence there are a number of other finds which bear upon the authenticity of the inscription. These new factors will be briefly discussed in this and the following chapters.

An attentive reading of the inscription will show that its writer did not so much think of it as a record of a great exploration expedition as of an obituary record of his ten dead companions. The inscription divides itself into three parts. The first sentence is introductory. Here, in twelve words, he briefly tells who he and his companions are and what they are doing:

[We are] *8 Goths and 22 Norwegians on* [an] *exploration journey from Vinland through the western regions.*

In the last eighteen words he states that another group of the same party are down by the sea taking care of their vessels; and, as an afterthought, comes the date of this adventure at the end of the inscription:

[We] *have 10 men by the sea to look after our ships 14 days' journey from this island; year 1362.*

All the intermediate portion, numbering thirty-six words, which is more than half the length of the inscription, is used to describe the known circumstances surrounding the death of the ten men. He mentions with some detail the location of the fateful camp, explains his inability and that of his companions to help his unfortunate comrades, and gives a photographic impression of the mutilated appearance of the ten victims. Presumably these men had been suddenly overwhelmed, killed and scalped by a party of Indians, and the blood from their riven heads had flowed down and covered their features. The returning fishermen had been horrified by such a gory manner of mutilating the dead. The rune-master therefore reverses the logical order of narration and describes the scene as he saw it—first he saw the blood-stained features of his friends; then he found that they were dead. Even several days after this disaster the gruesome sight of his murdered companions is so vivid in his mind that he feels urged, in the middle of his inscription, to invoke the aid of the Holy Virgin in prayer:

We had [our] *camp by two skerries one day's journey north from this stone. We were* [out] *and fished one day. When we returned home* [we] *found ten* [of our] *men red with blood and dead. Ave Maria! Save* [us] *from evil!*

The sudden extinction of these ten men was therefore the big thing the writer of the inscription wanted to record. He is apparently not conscious of the fact that he is a member of a great expedition. The immediate loss of his friends has dimmed any such thoughts if he ever had them.

When a serious calamity overtakes us, it is relatively of little importance to describe the precise geographical spot where it happened. But it is an old-time habit of man to give the location of such an accident a prominent place in the narrative of the trouble. So it is with the writer of the inscription. He feels impelled to describe the location of the camp. It was "by two skerries one day's journey north from this stone." In other words, the camp was on the shore of a lake wherein two skerries were visible. If this lake with the two skerries could be found, we would have promising corroboration of the truth of the inscription.

At first sight this does not seem so difficult. The skerries are said to be one day's journey north of the place where the rune stone was found. Assuming that a day's journey would be the distance a group of travelers would travel in a day, these skerries ought to be found from fifteen to thirty miles north of Kensington.

With this thought in mind an extensive search was made of all the lakes lying between fifteen and thirty miles north of the finding place of the stone, but without success. The question then arose, What did the writer of the inscription mean by the term *daghrise* (day's journey)?

This term occurs twice in the inscription. In the last sentence it is stated that ten men had been left in charge of their vessels down by the ocean, and that this was fourteen *daghrise* from the "island" where the stone was found. In a preceding chapter it has been shown that the vessels must have been left on the shore of Hudson Bay, most likely at the mouth of the Nelson (or possibly the Hayes) River. From here to the spot where the stone was found—up the Nelson, Lake Winnipeg and Red River of the North—is about a thousand miles or a little more by the meandering river route. This distance the rune-master calls "14 *daghrise*." Therefore one *daghrise* would be about 75 miles. Was any such unit of distance in use in the late Middle Ages?

This question remained unanswered for several years. Then in 1914 Professor Wm. Hovgaard published his *Voyages of the Northmen to America* in which he presents abundant evidence to show that the Norsemen had a unit of distance known as *dægr sigling* (day's sailing) which was roughly equal to about 75 English miles.[1] This unit was based on the average distance covered in a day's sail of twelve hours with a fair breeze, irrespective of how

[1] See Hovgaard's Chapter 4 entitled *Navigation of the Norsemen*. The use of the term is still more fully elucidated by Gathorne-Hardy in *The Norse Discoverers of America*, pp. 198-211 (Oxford, 1921). See also A. Fossum, *The Norse Discovery of America*, pp. 80, 91 (Minneapolis, 1918).

many days it took to make this distance. This suggested the possibility that the *daghrise* in the inscription was used in the same meaning.

A study of the units of distance in use in the Norse Middle Ages shows that there were five such units. They were as follows:

1. *Mila* (mile). This was almost unknown as it occurs only once or twice in the old writings according to Vigfusson.[2]

2. *Röst* (rest). This term was used to denote "the distance between two resting places" in reckoning travel on land, or about six English miles. The distance was variable, however, depending on whether one traveled in a flat or mountainous country.[3]

3. *Vika*. This term was widely used in reckoning short distances on sea or water and roughly corresponds in length to the *röst* used on land. Twelve *vika* made one *dægr sigling* or journey.[4]

4. *Dægr sigling*. This term, as mentioned above, denotes a distance at sea equal to approximately 75 English miles. It was based on the coastwise sailing of Norway where it was customary to put into harbors at night, thus making a sailing day of twelve hours. This *dægr* was also called a *tylft*, or dozen, because it was equal to twelve *vika*.

5. *Dægr haf* (day's sail on the open sea). After Iceland, Greenland and other northern islands became settled, the sailing period of twenty-four hours became more common, and this brought with it a unit of 150 miles. This was also sometimes called a *dægr sigling*, but the historian, Ari Frodi, more accurately distinguishes between the two units and calls the longer one *dægr haf*.[5]

It has been objected that the term *daghrise* could not

[2] *Icelandic Dictionary*, art. *mila*.

[3] *Ibid.*, art. *röst*. Falk and Torp, *Etymologischer Wörterbuch*, art. *rast, röst*. Heidelberg, 1910.

[4] Gathorne-Hardy, *op. cit.*, pp. 196-199.

[5] *Landnamabok*, I:1.

be used in the meaning of 75 miles of travel on land because the *dægr sigling* was a nautical term. A writer of the fourteenth century, it is claimed, would have used the term *rastir* (the plural of *röst*) to tell the distance traveled.[6]

To this it may be answered that if the writer of the inscription had used the terms *röst* or *rastir*, it would have been strong evidence that the inscription could not have been written in the Middle Ages, for this unit was never used in measuring distances on lakes or rivers. It was only used in describing travel on *land*, on foot or on horse. Distances on inland waters were always reckoned by *vika* just as it was also used in mentioning short trips at sea. There are numerous passages to illustrate this. Thus Ivar Bardsen, about 1350, describes a small lake as being two *vika* wide.[7] Another writer says: "The lake was half a *vika* wide." [8] The term was used whether the journey was made by sailing, rowing or swimming. Thus we read that a kinsman of Erik Thorwaldson swam to an island a long half *vika* from shore in order to get fresh mutton with which to feed his visitor.[9] A writer of the fourteenth century gives an implication of the meandering course of a voyage around Iceland direct from headland to headland as amounting to fourteen dozen *vika*.[10]

Just as this man who circumnavigated Iceland day by day added up the number of *vika* he had sailed or rowed, so the explorers of Paul Knutson's party in ascending the rivers added up their *vika* and translated the number into the larger measure. For seven years they had been counting their *vika* and adding them up into *dægr sigling*, and they would have no reason for changing their system. The only thing they did change was to adopt the more accurate synonymous term *day's journey* as they were not

[6] L. M. Larson in *Minnesota History*, XVII:28 (1936).
[7] *Grönlands Historiske Mindesmærker*, III, 254.
[8] *Fornmanna Sögur*, pp. 8, 32.
[9] *Landnama*, p. 107; *Flateyjarbok*, I, 554.
[10] *Biskupa Sögur*, II, 5.

sailing up the rivers. But they continued on the water in boats as before. When the explorers reached Lake Winnipeg, they came to a vast expanse of water 300 miles long, and so wide that for much of the time they could not see the other side. As the journey continued by boat practically up to the place where they left their inscription, this would leave only the portages that could be reckoned in *rastir*.

If "day's-journey" means seventy-five miles in one part of the inscription, it must have the same meaning when used in another part. When the rune-master says that the skerries are "one day's-journey" north from the finding place of the stone, they should be looked for about seventy-five miles north of Kensington.

When this problem was finally solved, it was with much anticipation that the writer set forth one day in the summer of 1919 to look for the two skerries.

He left the train at Detroit Lakes in Becker County which lies at approximately the right distance north of the finding place of the stone, and found he had arrived in the heart of the beautiful Lake Park Region of Minnesota. The surroundings were therefore quite as charming as his quest was exciting.

Southern Becker County has a hundred or more lakes, but most of them are too small to require any attention on this mission. Evidently the camp of the explorers must have been on the shore of a large lake inasmuch as the men who were out fishing knew nothing of the massacre of their ten companions until they returned and found the victims "red with blood and dead."

Several days passed in inspecting the larger lakes with many inquiries for rocky islands, but in vain. Finally the writer came to Cormorant Lake in the southwestern corner of Becker County which seemed to be bigger than any of the lakes he had previously visited. It was surrounded by steep, timbered hills alternating with somnolent swamps dotted with clumps of shrubbery and dron-

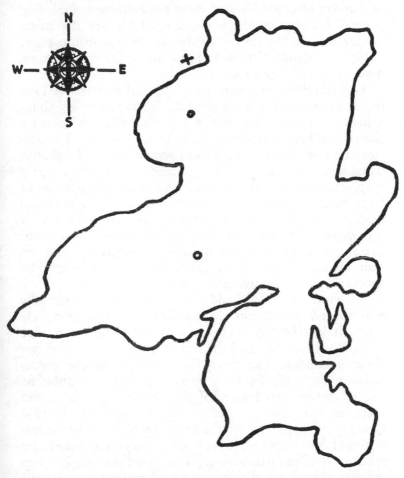

Fig. 12. Outline Map of Cormorant Lake, Becker County, Minnesota
The cross marks the probable site of the camp. The skerries
are indicated by two small circles.

ing with the monotonous chirping of crickets. The peace
of Sunday afternoon rested over the landscape, including
a small country store by the wayside where the store-
keeper was dozing on the shady side of his little cottage.

"Rocky island? Yes, there's one not so far up the shore.
You can see it from the road."

The traveler continued his walk, and it was not long
before he came in sight of the little island which lay about
a mile from the shore. It had a perfect likeness to many
skerries he had seen along the coast of Norway. He borrowed a boat from a farmer and rowed out to the skerry.
Then he found that while it appeared like the outcropping
of place rock, it really consisted of a conglomeration of
large boulders which was smoothed over by gravel and
sand, upon which was growing a few scattered reeds. It
was about a hundred feet long, gently sloping and about
five feet in elevation at its apex. Upon returning with the
boat he learned from the farmer that "there might be
another" skerry in the north end of the lake.

The road which had paid a momentary visit to the lake
now turned inland, but the traveler continued along the
shore. It was heavily timbered without a house for three
miles. Finally he reached the top of a very steep hill rising
about a hundred feet from the lake level at the northwestern angle of the lake. From this high elevation he
had an unobstructed view of almost the entire lake, and
there, in a straight line before him, he saw two skerries!
One lay near the base of the hill on which he was standing, and the other (the one previously inspected) lay
about two miles farther away. These two skerries are such
unusual phenomena that one can well understand why the
writer of the inscription recalled them in seeking to make
a pithy description of the spot where his friends had perished. They lie so low and one lies so close to the shore
that only from this one spot on the shore can both
skerries be seen. As the inscription mentions two skerries,
the probability is that the fatal camp was on the spot

Plate XIII. Mooring stones shown in Olaus Magnus' *Historia* of 1555.

Plate XIV. The Björndahl mooring stone seven miles south of Hawley, Minnesota.

whence the two skerries can be seen. Here, presumably, is the grave where these ten men were buried, as prudence would dictate a quick burial and departure from this sinister vicinity. No excavation has been done due to the fact that the grave, if there, may be anywhere within an area of two acres. The excavation has therefore been postponed until funds are available for a thorough job.

This hill lies eighty-one miles from the spot where the rune stone was found as measured by the speedometer of an automobile.

The location of this camp at the northwest angle of Cormorant Lake indicates that the explorers left Red River at its junction with Buffalo River and followed the latter stream southeastward as this leads directly toward Cormorant Lake. In making this journey of less than forty miles, the travelers made an ascent of almost 500 feet, and they may have thought that they had gained the dividing ridge on the other side of which they would find streams that would carry them eastward toward Vinland. This probable assumption was correct for Becker County lies on a continental watershed. The small streams in the western part are tributaries of Red River which through the Nelson empty into Hudson Bay; while the streams in the eastern part of the county flow east and are the headwaters of the Mississippi. A short overland journey would therefore have brought them to a great waterway, down which they could have glided for hundreds of miles in the right direction.

But the massacre of their comrades and the physiography of their new surroundings prevented this. A glance at the accompanying physiographic map of Minnesota (see Fig. 13) will make this clear. Practically up to the time when the explorers reached Cormorant Lake they had traveled through a prairie country where reasonable watchfulness would protect them from surprise attacks by enemies. But now, at Cormorant Lake, they had left the prairie region behind, and entered a forest region which

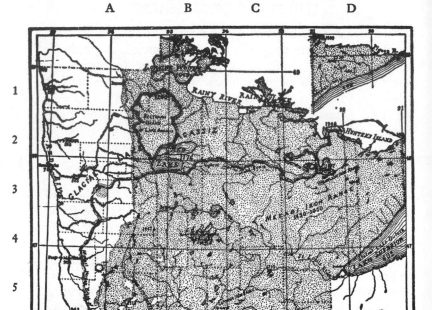

FIG. 13. Physiographic map of Minnesota, from Folwell's *History of Minnesota* by courtesy of the Minnesota Historical Society. A circle at A-5 shows the location of the camp at Cormorant Lake. A square at A-7 shows the finding place of the Stone near Kensington. These two features have been added to the map.

stretched eastward for hundreds of miles. While they would know nothing about the size of this forest, its ominous presence was there as a forbidding physical fact. Their comrades had been struck down immediately after entering the shade of this forest, and prudence would dictate the advisability of going around these woods where enemies could steal in upon them from every side. How did they travel? If on foot, they could not avoid leaving a trail, whether on the prairie or through the forest. But if they traveled by boat and followed the streams, they would avoid this difficulty. This question will be answered in the next chapter.

XVIII. THE MOORING STONES

THE discovery of the skerries—the landmarks of a tragedy 600 years ago—marked a significant advance in the investigation relating to the Kensington Stone. But Cormorant Lake had other evidence in store for the investigator.

In the fall of 1919 the writer made another trip to Cormorant Lake in company with several other men. Mr. John Johnson, the owner of the hill from which the two skerries can be seen, then came to us in great excitement and said he had found a stone which had a strange-looking hole chiselled in its upper surface. He guided us to the beach and here, directly below the hill where the camp presumably must have been, he showed us a large boulder. It was about six feet long and on thrusting aside the thick underbrush that grew around it, we saw a neat little hole drilled in the surface of the rock. It was triangular in outline with the angles rounded off, about an inch and a quarter wide at the widest point. The depth was about an inch and a quarter, and, as the interior was distinctly visible in the bright sunlight, it could be seen that the inner surface of the hole was just as worn and mellowed by the slow weathering of time as was the general surface of the stone.

As we were discussing the significance of this discovery, our attention was called to another large stone half concealed in the brush only six feet away. This stone also had a small triangular hole in its upper surface pointing toward the lake. It had the same diameter and shape as the former, but was seven inches deep. Like the first, its inner surface showed an ancient weathered appearance (see Plate XI).

Still another large stone with a similar hole in it was later discovered. This was found by Mr. Johnson on a subsequent visit, only eight feet distant from the first stone, but hidden by the dense underbrush, which we at the time did not attempt to penetrate. Like the other stones this also was a very large boulder, having a hole in its upper surface pointing upward and outward toward the lake. The hole in this stone is only about a half inch deep. The three stones lie practically side by side on the old beachline, and the little holes were all about five or six feet above the level of the lake as it was in 1919 when these measurements were taken.

What could have been the purpose in drilling these holes? Depressions in rocks are sometimes caused by dripping water or other natural agents, but it is hardly conceivable that any natural agent could have made a narrow triangular hole seven inches deep. Moreover the precise similarity of the holes and their presence in angular positions in detached free-lying granite boulders lying side by side excludes such a possibility. Nor can the presence of these holes be explained by fossiliferous agency inasmuch as the boulders are igneous rock masses in which fossils are never found.

The first theory of the reader is probably that someone planned to obtain building material by blasting. But no one in that vicinity, or visitors to the place, will admit the possibility of this idea. These stones lie at the foot of a precipitous hill almost a hundred feet high, so inaccessible that they could not be approached with horse and wagon except in winter on the ice. Inasmuch as there is an abundance of stone of all sizes scattered about in the fields, it seems unreasonable to suppose that anyone would go to the most inaccessible part of the lake shore to get them.

Another hypothesis is that some boys made these holes in the boulders for the purpose of filling them with gunpowder to be exploded on the occasion of a Fourth of July or other celebration. But this surmise is no more satisfactory than the former. In the first place it does not seem probable that boys would go to the considerable labor of drilling a hole seven inches deep merely for the purpose of detonating some gunpowder when a tin can or other receptacle would serve equally well. Moreover, if the seven-inch hole had actually been used in that way, fragments of the rock would most certainly have been blown off by the explosion. But the stone shows no indications of such fractures or chippings.

Finally, both of these hypotheses are further nullified by the weathered appearance of the interior of the holes, which clearly shows that they were drilled a long time ago. We have the testimony of Mr. Ole Larson, an old settler, who distinctly recalls seeing these holes in the spring of 1879. The following is a letter received from him:

Barnesville, Minn., Dec. 5, 1927.

Your mention in your address last night of the boulder with the deep hole in it on the shore of Cormorant Lake reminded me of the first time I saw that stone almost fifty years ago. It was in April, 1879, when we went to Cormorant Lake on a fishing trip. We had come from southern Minnesota a month earlier and were living with Peder Staum who had settled here before us. He had a flat-bottomed skiff which he loaded on his wagon and, with provisions for several days, we set out drawn by a pair of oxen prepared to stay a week if necessary. The party consisted of my father, Anders Larsen, Peder Staum and his two boys, Anders and Gulbrand, Stephen Furua and myself. I was then just twelve years of age. After we had spent some time in fishing in West Cormorant Lake,[1] we three young boys, the Staum boys and myself, went on a walk along the west shore of Big Cormorant up to the north end, and on this walk we discovered the large boulder with the triangular hole in it at the foot of the big hill. It made such an impression on us that we at once returned to the fishing camp and persuaded our elders to go and see it. I remember when they had done so that there was much talk among them to the effect that white people must have been there a long time before us, see-

[1] West Cormorant Lake was formerly a large extension of Cormorant Lake to the west. It is now separated from the main body of the lake by an isthmus a few feet wide. The main part of the lake is now usually called Big Cormorant to distinguish it from West Cormorant Lake.

ing the hole showed that it had been cut a long time before we saw it. The lake was then much higher than it is now, the hole in the stone not being more than four or five feet above the lake level. Since then I have seen this stone almost every spring as it was our custom to go to Cormorant Lake every year and fish for a few days. We brought salt with us and salted down several barrels of fish which we pioneers thought was good food for summer. At that time no one lived around the lake, but there were many Indian tents and campfires to be seen.[2]

[Signed]   OLE LARSEN.

The evidence in this inquiry therefore indicates that these holes were made by persons having steel tools, that is, white people, before the neighborhood was settled, and, judging by the weathered appearance of the chiselled surface, a long time before the coming of the earliest pioneers. The next question is, Who were these early men carrying chisels?

It is most improbable that the occasional hunters and trappers who may have visited this region carried cold chisels. They may therefore be excluded.

The drivers of the Red River carts, which were built wholly of wood, probably also had little use for cold-chisels. However, they had room for them in their carts. But as their main route reached the Red River at Ft. Abercrombie, forty miles to the southwest, and as their "Pembina" route passed fifteen miles east of Cormorant

---

[2] The township in which Cormorant Lake lies is largely taken up by Big Cormorant Lake and its big appendage West Cormorant Lake. The land around these lakes is hilly and was all covered with timber. When the first wave of pioneers reached this part of the state in 1870 and 1871 the few choice claims in the township were taken up. In 1872 there were ten settlers in the township. From 1871 to 1877 this and many townships near by suffered from an annual scourge of grasshoppers, and the settlers were constantly on the verge of starvation. This caused many to move away and deterred others from settling in. Moreover the pioneers that followed did not care to struggle with the heavy timber and work for years grubbing stumps, when they could get land ready for the plow a little farther on. The rough lands around the lake were therefore not settled upon until some time in the eighties.

Lake, the connection of these teamsters with these holes appears highly unlikely.[8]

Assuming, however, that the Kensington inscription is genuine, we can see a feasible origin and significance of these holes. On top of the hill from which the two skerries are visible was the camp of the Norse explorers; at the bottom of this hill lie the stones with their mystic holes. We know that these men carried cold-chisels, because they required such tools to cut the inscription on the stone. Besides having these points of agreement there is ample reason to believe that they made this seven-inch hole at just this particular spot.

We get some inkling of the significance of this hole in the statement that they were out fishing. That means that they had a boat (possibly more than one). It was not only laborious but also unsafe and injurious to the boat to pull it up on shore. Instead, they would secure it in the manner more approved by seamen—a line from the stern to the shore to keep the boat from drifting off, and the bow anchored in deeper water to keep the boat from pounding on the shore.

On the coast of Norway fishermen safeguard their boats, when not in use, in two ways. Those who can afford it have boat houses. Those who have none content themselves with drilling a hole in the rocky beach, into which is driven a bolt holding a large ring. The stern-line of the boat is tied to this ring, while a rope from the bow is fastened to an anchored buoy.

Mr. Gustav Wiig of Minne, near Bergen, Norway, who for forty-six years was a fishermen's merchant on one of the outermost shores of Söndmöre, told the writer that in olden times it was common for people who had no boat houses to tie their boat to an iron ring which was fixed to the shore by means of a bolt driven into a hole chiselled

[8] W. W. Folwell, *A History of Minnesota*, St. Paul, 1921, Vol. I, 226; A. H. Wilcox, *History of Becker County, Minn.*, St. Paul, 1907, pp. 217-219.

Plate XV. Mooring stone near Kensington, Minnesota. The upper part of the stone containing the greater part of the chiseled hole has been knocked off.

Photo by Esther Henderson

Plate XVI. Close-up view of same stone showing bottom of hole.

Photo by Esther Henderson

Plate XVII. The Kensington Stone was found on top of the hill above the stone pi
shown near the left side of the photograph.

from seven to nine inches deep in the rock and cemented
with sulphur. K. M. Johansen, captain of the small steamer
on which the writer traveled through Nordfjord, Norway,
stated that all along the coast to North Cape it was common to use such rings fastened in the rocky shore for tieing
up boats. He said it was customary to paint a large white
circle around the ring to make it conspicuous to strangers.
He pointed out a number of such rings while passing along
the shore.

This method of mooring boats was in use as far back as
the fourteenth century and much earlier. C. G. Styffe, in
discussing economic conditions in the Middle Ages,[4] points
out that wagon roads were few in number and transportation was mostly by means of boats along waterways and
portages. Since then the land (in Uppland, Sweden) has
risen many feet, but Styffe says that these old water
courses can still be traced by means of the iron rings
which were used for mooring boats and which still sometimes remain. He says: "Iron rings, fastened in the rocks
and used for securing boats are found, with other evidence
of former boat routes, in places now so high (above the
sea) that it is improbable that these water courses have
existed since the beginning of our historic time." [5]

Olaus Magnus, the last Catholic archbishop of the North,
also describes such mooring places. In 1555 his great work,
Historia de Gentibus Septentrionalibus, was published,[6] and
the following is related in Book II, Chapter 13:

. . . It now remains to tell how the seafarers who sail the
deep bays (of Norway) with their many sudden turns and
skerries can remain in safety at their chosen spots without
using anchors. For this purpose one finds in many places along
the passages rings of iron, larger than a warrior's shield, fas-

---

[4] *Skandinavien under Unionsperioden*, Stockholm, 1911.

[5] *Ibid.*, p. 115, 329 n. 8, 330.

[6] It was translated into Swedish in four bulky volumes in 1909 with
the title *Historia om de Nordiska Folken*. The illustrations are the same
as in the Latin original.

tened to the rocks with molten lead . . . especially near the prosperous city of Bergen. Good kings generously paid for them. When the tide or a storm is imminent, they (the sailors) put out their cables, and even large ships lie as safe as if they were in hidden caverns. But those who want to undertake the passage of this dangerous labyrinth ought to know their way.

He also prints a picture showing no less than ten of these mooring places (see Plate XIII). As will be noticed, the mooring rings in this illustration are fixed in relatively the same position on the rocks as are the holes in the Minnesota stones.

It can only have been this purpose that prompted the chiseling of the seven-inch hole. Long before the discovery of this pierced rock, the trail of the explorers led to this particular spot on the shore of Cormorant Lake. As the explorers had a camp at this place, and as it was customary in their day to moor boats in this manner, it should not greatly tax the reasoning to put the two together. It may seem a laborious manner in which to make fast a boat, but help was abundant. In a party of thirty men, it is likely that each man had his appointed duty, not the least important of which was the care and protection of the boat. These men had to find their food day by day, and this demanded that the boat be ready for use at all times. It was much more efficient to make a boulder serve as a pier. This was accomplished by drilling the hole into which could be slipped an iron pin with an attached ring and a rope fastened to the boat. Upon embarking the pin was simply pulled out and tossed into the boat.

As mentioned above, there are two other boulders at this spot which also have such holes in similar positions but of much smaller depth. These two holes presumably represent abortive attempts to make the desired mooring as described below.

Plate XII shows the positions of the three boulders, and the holes are marked by white sticks inserted into them. The photograph was taken on a line almost parallel to the shore line which is to the right. When the man whose duty it was to provide a safe mooring for the boat selected the rock which was to serve as a pier, he apparently chose the uppermost (boulder C) as being of the best height above the surface of the lake. But immediately in front of and below this boulder lies a large flat rock with sharp edges which is not visible in the photograph. As it was then covered by probably two feet of water, he may not have noticed it at once, but when he did so (after chiseling a hole a half inch deep), he would decide that this rock might injure the bottom of the boat. He therefore rejected this boulder and began to drill his hole in boulder B (the one to the right) in front of which the bottom sloped steeply. But this rock is of very hard texture which he discovered after getting down 1¼ inches. Finding the drilling too laborious, he decided to use boulder A (the one in the foreground) which lies on about the same level as B, and here he made a hole of the required depth—seven inches. Boulder A is shown on Plate XI.

These conclusions are corroborated by the following circumstances which all three boulders and holes have in common:

1. The longitudinal directions of these holes have a declination from the vertical of about twenty-five degrees.

2. This declination is toward the lake which suggests that it had some connection with the lake.

3. The boulders are all very large (about 6′ x 4′ x 5′) which was desirable to prevent the stone from being dragged into the water by the tugging of the boat.

4. Boulders A and B both lie on practically the same horizontal plane (the hole in C is on a plane 21 inches higher) which, if the lake was up to its maximum height (see surveyor's report on page 207), would bring the openings of the holes well above the surface of the water.

5. Immediately below A and B the shore drops steeply which, if the lake level was at the assumed height, would

give five feet of water depth which would be ideal for mooring.

6. They all lie immediately below the hill upon which the camp was presumably located, and near which would be the most desirable place to moor the boat.

However, the validity of this exposition all depends on the height of the lake level 600 years ago. If this was higher than the seven-inch hole, the explanation is all in vain.

Cormorant Lake has an altitude of 1,354 feet and is the largest lake in the county. It has no tributaries, and its drainage basin is limited to the hills that enclose it. Two miles south of Cormorant Lake lies Pelican Lake with an altitude of 1,318 feet, or thirty-six feet lower than Cormorant Lake. The intervening area consists of a marshy plain with some morainic deposits. The waters of Cormorant Lake are prevented from rushing down through this lowland by a low ridge on its south margin a few hundred feet long and about ten feet high above the present (1930) level of the lake.[7] There are no signs that the lake has ever had a natural outlet through this ridge of beach gravel.[8] A short distance south of it a spring gives rise to a small stream which runs through the swamp and finally becomes a creek (Spring Creek) which empties into Pelican Lake. When this region in 1870 was surveyed by government surveyors the lake was also without an outlet, for the original surveyor's plat places the source of Spring Creek a short distance south of Cormorant Lake, just as is the case at present.[9]

[7] Ths paragraph was written in 1930 when an engineer's survey of the lake was made.

[8] In 1875 a mill was built some distance below the lake and as water-power was insufficient, a five-foot ditch was dug through this ridge. See A. H. Wilcox, *History of Becker County*, 1907, pp. 547, 548. H. R. Holand, *The Kensington Stone*, 1932, pp. 153, 154.

[9] See original surveyor's plat in the Capitol in St. Paul and certified copy of same in the office of the Register of Deeds for Becker County in Detroit Lakes, Minn.

It is evident by this that the level of the lake could never have been higher than this ridge on the south, or about ten feet higher than the present (1930) lake level. The indications are that the highest ancient lake level was about a foot below the top of the ridge, or about nine feet above the present lake level. The skerries are also about nine feet above the present level. The openings of the holes in the boulders described above are a little more than nine feet above the present lake level. The skerries must therefore have appeared as true skerries in the fourteenth century, and the boulders, where the boat is supposed to have been moored, lay at the water's edge with the opening of the seven-inch hole a few inches above the surface of the water when it was at its highest possible stage.

In order to check these personal observations, another trip was made to the lake in May, 1930, and the services of a professional surveyor were secured. The following is his report:

Alexandria, Minn., June 18, 1930.

Acting upon the request of Atty. Constant Larson of this city I did on the 19th day of May, 1930, in the presence of Mr. Larson, his daughter Lorayne, Mr. J. L. Fitzgerald, and Mr. and Mrs. Holand make certain investigations along the shore of one Cormorant Lake in Becker County, Minnesota with the following results:

1. At the outlet, near the southerly end of the lake I found that the lake could not have been at any time more than 10.6 feet above its present level of the above date and the level apparently longest retained was approximately 9.00 feet above its present level.

2. At the northwesterly side of the lake are three large boulders with holes drilled into them which I shall list as "A," "B" and "C." The hole in "A" is 7 inches deep and is 9.65 feet above present water level, the hole in "B" is 1½ inches deep and is 9.68 feet above present water level, the hole in "C" is ½ inch deep and 11.43 feet above present water level.

From the above findings it is evident that the water level of the said Lake Cormorant was at one time at or near the same elevation as the above-mentioned chiseled holes in the boulders "A," "B" and "C."

(Signed)   PAUL R. JOHNSON, County Surveyor,
Douglas Co., Minn.

These three finds—the inscription near Kensington, the site of the camp at Cormorant Lake and the mooring stone below the campsite—mark two stations on the journey of these explorers. But recently there have been discovered several other landmarks—four more mooring stones have been found, so that it is now possible to point out a series of successive campsites.

One of these was found on the farm of O. N. Björndahl, in section 12, Skree township, Clay County, Minnesota, seven miles south of Hawley. It is a granite boulder about 3½′ x 4′ which has a triangular hole about nine inches deep. A wooden plug, whittled to fit the hole in the stone at Cormorant Lake, fitted this second stone precisely. Just as at Cormorant Lake, the interior of the hole is so weathered that the chisel marks have entirely disappeared (see Plate XIV).

Upon inquiry it was learned that the stone was found on the south side of a lake which has now been drained. The lake was about a mile long and wide and abounded in fish when the first settlers came in the late seventies.[10] It was receding year by year, and shortly afterwards the fish froze out. In 1906 a drainage ditch was dug, and the lake bottom became a meadow.

This lake was formerly joined to several other smaller lakes and sloughs which practically extended to the big bend in the Buffalo River, about four miles northwest. With these facts before us, it is possible to reconstruct the route of the explorers.

The channel of Buffalo River runs approximately straight southeast for about twenty-five miles from the Red River.

[10] It is on record that Tosten Torkelson, a neighbor of Ole N. Björndahl, in 1877 caught a wagonload of fish in this lake. See *Fargo Forum*, June 7, 1939, p. 23.

Then it makes a 90° turn to the northeast. At this point the explorers must have been confronted with the question of the choice of two routes. One was to follow the river northeastward, which would seem the easier as the labor of portaging was not immediately necessary. But this direction would not be acceptable except for a short distance as their later trail shows that they were pushing on in a general southeasterly direction. The other route was to portage over to the chain of lakes which stretched southeastward as far as they were able to see. Apparently the latter course was followed because the mooring stone is found on the south side of the last of these lakes toward the southeast. From here they continued eastward to Cormorant Lake, twelve miles away. There are several small lakes between these two which would lessen the labor of portaging, but nevertheless it must have been one of the most laborious sections of their entire journey as Cormorant Lake lies several hundred feet higher than the Björndahl lake.

Southward from Cormorant Lake lies a series of lakes and rivers with almost negligible portages, and here the explorers could make easy and rapid progress. The writer has followed this waterway with the hope of finding another campsite, but nearly all these lakes have receded so much that their old margins cannot now be definitely determined.

Eventually they reached the little "island" with its steep slopes near the present village of Kensington, and this may have been the first place where they found the conditions safe enough to permit them to inscribe a memorial in honor of their dead comrades.

I have visited that spot many times, but each time I have been so occupied in contemplating the events that took place on top of the hill, that I have given little or no thought to what might be seen at its base. But in 1937, after seeing the mooring stone in Clay County, it occurred to me that "the island" where the rune stone was found was preeminently the place to look for a mooring stone. The explorers camped there for several days while the stone was inscribed and while they were renewing and replenishing their outfit and supplies, and they must have had a mooring place for their boat unless this in the mean-time had been left behind. This expected mooring stone should be found about fifteen feet above the present level of the marsh, if Winchell and Upham were right when they said that the lake level in 1362 was about fifteen feet higher than the present marsh. However, two successive inspections failed to reveal any mooring stone either at the fifteen-foot level or at the bottom of the hill.

The thought then occurred that if the boat was moored near the spot where the rune stone was found, this moor-ing place would be on a very steep hillside (see topo-graphical sketch, p. 123, *ante*). Such a hillside would be subject to considerable erosion, and eventually the stone, overbalanced by the action of frost, might have rolled down like many other stones now at the bottom of the hill. If this mooring stone in hurtling down the hillside struck another stone, it might well have broken and parts of it bounced farther out over the lower land.

With this thought in mind another search was made in 1938 and this time it was successful. A short distance from the base of the hill, on top of which the runic stone was excavated, lies a large pile of stones made up of boulders of all sizes which have tumbled down from the hillside. In this pile is a large boulder which at some time must have met with a severe collision because several large "chips" have been knocked off its rounded surface (see Plate XV). This accident appears to have happened several hundred years ago for the fractured surfaces show just as much weathering as the uninjured part of the boulder. In the very obtuse angle left by one of these detached parts is a chiseled hole about one inch deep and three-quarters of an inch in diameter. The inside of this hole has also been made perfectly smooth by weathering (see Plate XVI).

Plate XVIII. The mooring stone near Alexandria, Minnesota.

Photo by Esther Henderson

Plate XIX. Mooring stone two miles east of Hawley, Minnesota.

If this angular cavity was filled up by a piece which approximately conformed to the rounded contour of the boulder, and if a hole was drilled through this supposed section in line with the inch-long hole that now is there, the hole would be seven or eight inches deep and would in every way correspond to the chiseled holes already described. There can therefore be little doubt that here we have another mooring stone left by the explorers of 1362. The possibility that the boulder may have been moved to its present resting place by horse power is excluded. The boulder weighs several thousand pounds and it would be hardly possible to move it over the mucky surface of the marsh.

The explorers, upon leaving this former island with its little monument fixed near the apex, must have gone eastward. This is indicated, not only by the fact that this is the general direction which they wished to follow, but also because in this direction they found a string of lakes through which they could pass with almost no portaging.[11] For about twenty-five miles they could continue by water until they reached Lake Carlos, three miles north of the present city of Alexandria. Lake Carlos connects with Lake L'Homme Dieu which in turn connects with Lake Geneva. This lake extends southward for two miles, where it receives the waters of Lake Victoria, which lake has the shape of a crescent. Following the eastern branch one

[11] At the north end of Grant's Lake, which is a part of this waterway, in the village of Holmes City, is a high and very steep bank. About thirty years ago the owner of a lot in the village made an excavation in this steep hillside, twelve feet above the lake level which was then quite high, to make room for a stable. In so doing he found the decayed remains of one end of a boat which he believed must have been of large size judging by its stout ribs and heavy stern post. It had a round bottom which was thought very strange as the boats of the old settlers were all very crude punts with flat bottoms and straight sides. It is therefore believed by many that this boat must have been left there by the explorers of 1362. The writer collected a number of statements concerning this find, but as these documents were all destroyed by fire, it is impossible at this time to present any conclusive evidence about this find.

reaches Lake Jessie, a small lake about a mile long. On the eastern shore of this lake, near its southern end, at the bottom of a steep hillside, is still another mooring stone.[12] This stone may be seen five miles southeast of Alexandria, Minn. It is 4 feet wide, 2½ feet thick and of unknown length or depth as it is deeply imbedded in the soil (see Plate XVIII). The chiseled hole is 22 inches above the lake level which apparently could never have been more than a few inches higher than at present because of the free drainage. The waters of this lake, after making several successive drops through the other lakes mentioned above, flows to the Mississippi through Long Prairie River. The hole in this last mooring stone is 7½ inches deep, of the same size and form, and like the others shows ancient weathering. Like the hole in the mooring stone at Cormorant Lake and the two in Clay County, it has a declination from the vertical toward the lake of about 25°.

To the thoughtful observer these mooring stones are just as significant as so many additional runic inscriptions. They plainly tell that here these early explorers had their successive camps on their journey through the wilderness. Of their further progress nothing is known. It is said that a narrow slough runs from the south end of Lake Jessie to or toward Lake Osakis. Another possible course would be to make a three-mile portage to a branch of the Long Prairie River which joins the Mississippi.

Just as this chapter was going to the printer, word was received from the above-mentioned Mr. Björndahl of Hawley, Clay County, Minnesota (see p. 208), that another mooring stone had been found near there. It was reported that the stone and its hole in all essential points corresponded with the Björndahl stone and the Cormorant Lake stone. In order to get more and independent information about this discovery, the writer wrote to Rev. S. G. Hauge, who for forty years has served as pastor to

---

[12] The existence of this mooring stone was called to the writer's attention by Professor R. B. Harvey of the University of Minnesota.

a group of congregations in and around Hawley, to investigate the report. Mr. Hauge gave immediate attention to the request, and the following is his report:

Hawley, Minn., Nov. 13, 1939.

I have never heard of this stone until I got your letter today. Guided by Mr. Björndahl, I drove out to its finding place which is two miles east of Hawley and about twenty rods south of Buffalo River. The stone lies on a steep slope on the east side of a narrow coulee which has a smooth, even bottom that slopes gently toward Buffalo River. This coulee may have been the bay of a former lake because it comes to an abrupt end at its head toward the south. This region is a wilderness of high, stony hills inhabited only by wolves, and no settler would think of clearing land there. Although I have been a pastor here for forty years, living only two miles away, I have never been in this waste before, and William Olson who found the stone only chanced to discover it by following a wolf.

The stone is very large, the part above ground weighing perhaps two tons [see Plate XIX]. The hole which is eight inches deep and triangular is weathered so smooth as to seem like glass on the inside. Björndahl, who had measurements with him, found that in its diameter and position it was just the same as the hole in his own stone and in the stone at Cormorant Lake. It is about twenty feet above the water level. It is not difficult to understand that the water may have been that high as it has been almost that high since I came here. It is a most remarkable discovery for it is plain to everyone that the hole was not bored or drilled since white men settled in this region.

S. G. Hauge.

The discovery of this stone further up the river gives us more information on which to base our reconstruction of the route which the explorers followed. Upon reaching the bend in the river, they apparently continued southeastward through the chain of lakes, because these led in the right direction. At the end of this waterway they camped and left the mooring stone found on the Björndahl farm. Finding themselves confronted by many miles of uplands, over which they would have to carry their boat, they returned to the river and continued upstream for about seven miles and then camped at the stone described by Rev. Mr. Stange. A few miles above this spot, the river is joined by a tributary from the southeast which leads into the immediate vicinity of Cormorant Lake.

There is one long stretch along the route of these explorers where they must have left a number of mooring stones, some of which could probably be found. This is the rock-bound east shore of Lake Winnipeg. It must have taken them many days to make the voyage as the lake is more than 300 miles long, and their progress may have been interrupted by storms as well as delays caused by the need of procuring food. It is the opinion of geologists that the level of Lake Winnipeg cannot have changed materially during the last 600 years, and if this be so their campsites could be found in some of the inlets. These should be sought on the east shore of the lake as the explorers manifestly were seeking a waterway leading eastward to their headquarters somewhere on the Atlantic coast.

XIX. CORROBORATIVE FINDS UNEARTHED IN MINNESOTA

FROM time to time the writer has received a number of ancient articles that have been unearthed in various parts of America. They have been sent by people who have heard of the Kensington Stone and have thought that perhaps their finds may have some relation to the narrative that is engraved upon it. Most of them have proved to be Indian artifacts, in some cases stone implements, but more often copper weapons. A number of articles from the French and English occupation of the Northwest have also been received.

⌊ Among these many finds there are a few iron weapons of strange and antique shape which have proved very interesting. A study of Norwegian and Swedish history and archeology shows that they are of Scandinavian origin of the late Middle Ages, that is, ca. 1200-1500. Another remarkable fact about these finds is that nearly all have been unearthed in northwestern Minnesota, in the region from Kensington, Douglas County, northward. Affidavits have been secured concerning the circumstances of their finding. The following is the list of these Scandinavian finds presented in the order of their discovery.

1. Plate XX, a fire-steel made from a narrow file. The photograph shows full size but for a small part broken off. The fire-steel was found by the leader of the first group of white pioneers who settled in Polk County, Minnesota, about five miles north of Climax and on the shore of a bayou about a half mile off the Red River. The following letter from the finder states the circumstances of the discovery.

Climax, Minn., June 8, 1914.

I have your letter concerning the fire-steel which I found. I settled here in June, 1871, and we were the first to take land around here. A short time after I settled here I was boring holes with a six-inch post-hole auger. When I got about two feet down I heard something scrape against the auger and I pulled it up thinking I had struck a stone. The dirt clung to the auger and I examined it looking for the stone and found the little fire-steel. It was much rusted and there was also some charcoal and ashes. It must have been there a long time, because the place where this hole was bored was on a dry elevation. The fire-steel is just the same size and form as the fire-steels which my grandmother used 65 or 66 years ago. And now I will tell you how it is used [here follows an account of its usage and how to prepare tinder].

[Signed]   OLE JEVNING.

Some years later Mr. Elias Steenerson of Crookston obtained the following affidavit:

Climax, Minn., Dec. 29, 1920.

My father-in-law, Mr. Ole Jevning, came to this part of the Red River Valley in June, 1871. There were no settlers for many miles near this region before him. The same year, before the land was plowed, he was one day engaged in digging fence post holes with a post-hole auger. About two feet beneath the surface of the ground he unearthed a small fire-steel, similar to the ancient fire-steels which he had seen in Norway where he was born and brought up. The spot where the steel was found is on a high dry knoll, which lies about a half mile east of the Red River and about four and a half miles north of the present village of Climax. The steel was quite rusty when he found it and there was also some charcoal and ashes in the hole where it was found. It was four inches long and a quarter inch thick.

I hereby testify that the above is a true summary of what Mr. Jevning told me about this steel upon several occasions. He later loaned it to Mr. H. R. Holand for inspection.

[Signed]   A. O. STORTROEN.

Subscribed and sworn to before me this 5th day of January, 1921.

[Signed]   C. M. DAVIDSON, *Notary Public.*

Fire-steels were early introduced among the Indians by fur traders, and specimens may be seen in many museums. However, upon investigation it was found that the fire-steels of the fur trade were different. They were very crudely made and very small, usually permitting only two fingers of the hand to be inserted within the fire-steel.[1] Extensive inquiries failed to reveal any fire-steels of this (Climax) type anywhere in America.

In 1928 the writer made an extensive trip visiting a large number of museums in Europe for a comparative study of this fire-steel and other finds. Only in the Scandinavian countries were any such fire-steels found, and in the University Museum in Oslo the Minnesota fire-steel was at once recognized as a Norse implement of the Viking Age. The Museum kindly gave the writer the following statement identifying the fire-steel:

Upon request I will state that the fire-steel which carries the same mark in its entire form with the spiral ends is of exactly the same type as the fire-steels which in great numbers have been found in Norwegian graves from the Viking Age. . . .

Oslo, September 18, 1928.
[Signed]   Eivind S. Engelstad.[2]

Inasmuch as the Climax fire-steel is of the Norwegian type which goes back to the Viking Age, there remain only two reasonable explanations of its presence here. It was either brought over by one of the first settlers in the Climax area, or it was left by some Norwegian explorer who penetrated to the Red River before this region was settled. In any case it is not an Indian or a French fire-steel.

The first alternative is impossible because it was found by the first settler in the Climax vicinity, deep in the soil,

---

[1] C. E. Brown in *The Wisconsin Archeologist*, p. 10, No. 2 (1930).
[2] Holand, *Kensington Stone*, p. 176. The Norwegian text of Dr. Engelstad's statement is as follows: "Paa Opfordring skal jeg faa meddele at det ildstaal some berer samme merke ved hele sin form med de spiraloprullete ender er av ganske samme type som de ildstaal der i mengdevis er funnet i norske graver fra vikingetiden."

and before the land was plowed. There remains the second alternative—that it was brought in by an early explorer. This explorer must have left it there a very long time ago, because it was found two feet down in the ground in a layer of charcoal and ashes. This implies that it was lost while a fire was being made, and it would presumably take many hundred years for two feet of soil to accumulate above the fire-steel. We know of only one party of Norwegian explorers who are reported to have visited this part of America hundreds of years ago. They were the explorers mentioned on the Kensington Stone as having visited this region in 1362. They must have carried just such fire-steels as this, and their route lay right past the spot where the fire-steel was found. The most reasonable conclusion, therefore, is that this fire-steel is a memento of the explorers who penetrated into the present state of Minnesota in 1362.

2. Plate XXI, a Norwegian axe of the Middle Ages found in northern Michigan in 1880. The owner, Mr. Morgan H. Stafford, Boston, Mass., made the following report under date of August 15, 1936, concerning the discovery:

This axe was found about the year 1880, possibly in 1878, by a man, probably a prospector, as he stooped to drink from a small stream near Republic, in the Upper Peninsula of Michigan (about 35 miles west of Marquette, Mich.). As the story came to me, he reached down to pick the axe up from the bottom of the stream on which it rested, but upon grasping the handle or piece of haft which protruded, the wood seemed to dissolve. Realizing that it was something unusual, he took it with him on his return to Marquette and sold it to one T. Meads, a curio dealer and collector, who in turn sold it some years later to my brother, Walter K. Stafford, from whom I eventually obtained it with his collection of ancient copper tools, silver crosses of Jesuit origin, and other relics of the Lake region.

It originally bore a label to the effect that it was a Spanish axe, probably attached by Mr. Meads who jumped at that attribution as a possibility, although why he did not ascribe it to the French who were so numerous in that part of the country is strange. In the early nineties I showed it to Professor Rasmus B. Anderson, the well known writer on Scandinavian mythology, when I met him at my home in Marquette, and he said quite positively it was of Norse origin.

[Signed]   MORGAN H. STAFFORD.

Upon request Mr. Stafford kindly sent the axe to the writer for inspection. It proved to be neither Spanish nor French, but an exact duplicate of an axe seen by the writer in the great museum, *De Sandvigske Samlinger*, in Lillehammer in Norway (see Plate XXII). A visit was made in 1928 to about twenty Scandinavian museums, but only one such axe was found. Apparently the Michigan axe and the Lillehammer axe were made by the same armorer because they are alike in every detail. The length of the axehead is $5\frac{7}{8}$ inches, but the length of the "eye" in the axe is $7\frac{1}{16}$ inches. This is because the "eye" is prolonged in the form of an iron sleeve for the protection of the axe-handle. Its weight is $3\frac{1}{2}$ pounds.

This axe was evidently not intended for cutting timber for it has a blunt edge, and the "blade" is a full inch thick immediately back of the edge—about like the point of a crowbar. It was more effective as a club than as an axe for chopping. The probability is therefore that it was a battle-axe. A lusty swing with such a heavy axe could easily break the bones beneath chain armor and prove very effective.

This conclusion is supported by the long iron "sleeve" enclosing part of the handle. Icelandic sagas mention many combats between warriors, in which one is armed with a sword and the other with an axe. Frequently it is told that the swordsman cut off the handle of his opponent's axe, thus rendering him helpless. To guard against this it became desirable to reinforce the handle of the axe with a protective covering of iron. In this case we find the haft enclosed in an iron casing seven inches long.

The most important fact about the axe in determining the time when it was brought to America is the seemingly paradoxical evidence presented by the condition of the wood in the handle. As stated above, the handle was so decomposed that it "seemed to dissolve" in the hand when it was grasped. But the wood inside the iron tube, on the contrary, had become mineralized. The axe was sent to Professor W. C. Darrah of Harvard, a world authority on vegetable microstructure. His report is as follows:

May 15, 1937.
The wood in the handle of the axe found near Republic, Mich., is of subarctic spruce and might well have come from Norway or northern Canada, but not from as far south as the Great Lakes. It is significant that spruce is not strong or durable, and one can justifiably infer that spruce was used because other woods were scarce. The wood as now preserved in the axehead is dense, mineralized and obviously decomposed. As to the reported fact that the protruding handle was decomposed to a paste-like substance, it is my opinion that this indicates a submergence in water for several hundred years.

This set of conditions makes recent age out of the question.
[Signed] W. C. DARRAH,
Research Curator of Paleobotany,
Botanical Museum of Harvard University.

The question now arises: Is this axe a relic of another unknown pre-Columbian expedition of the late Middle Ages, or is it a memento of the Paul Knutson expedition of 1362?

The first alternative is highly improbable. While the Knutson expedition had a definite objective based upon historical facts which accounts for its presence in Minnesota, it is impossible to account for a second expedition in the same general period of time, and none such is referred to in the documents that remain. It therefore remains to examine the possibility that this axe belonged to a member of the Knutson expedition.

The finding place of an implement like this, which could have been useful to Indians, is not of much help in determining the approximate locality where it was lost by its white owner. It may have traveled far as part of the equipment of an Indian. In this case a consideration of the movements of the Indians that occupied the Upper Peninsula of Michigan where the axe was found may prove helpful.

As far back as Indian history goes, or about 300 years, it is known that the Chippewa were in indisputed possession of the Upper Peninsula. They engaged in many wars, but unlike nearly all other tribes, they were never dislodged from their ancestral possessions. Their principal warfare was with the Sioux, a confederation of tribes infinitely more numerous than the Chippewa, but not such good fighters. The result was that the Chippewa eventually drove the Sioux out of Wisconsin and eastern Minnesota. As the dominant ambition of the Chippewa youth was to equal their fathers in winning Sioux scalps, which involved repeated forays into the West, we can well see how this ancient Norwegian axe may have reached the Upper Peninsula. The Knutson expedition lost its men and weapons in Sioux territory, and the Sioux warrior who had captured this axe may in turn have been slain by a Chippewa who carried it to the Upper Peninsula.

3. Plate XXIII, a battle-axe found three miles southeast of Erdahl, Minnesota, or about fifteen miles northwest of Kensington. It weighs 5⅓ pounds. The edge is 8¼ inches long and the width of the axe from poll to edge is 6¾ inches. The eye of the axe is almost doubled in length by a prolongation below which may be called the neck, and is 4½ inches long. This opening tapers considerably from the opening in the neck where it is 1⅞" by 1⅝" to the upper edge of the axe where it is 1⅛" by 1". On the poll of the axe is superimposed a hammerlike addition 2¼ by 1⅜ inches in size and about ¼ inch thick. The blade of

the axe has a long downward extension. The axe referred to is the lower specimen on Plate XXIII.

The reason this implement is called a battle-axe is that it is clearly not meant for chopping. The edge is like that of a crowbar, the blade being ⅞ inch in thickness 1½ inches from the edge. It is a little thicker at the lower point of the blade than at the upper. Most of the great weight of the axe is in the blade near the edge. It is therefore more a heavy maul than a tool for cutting. Apparently the only use it could have been put to is to smash helmets. Against a steel helmet an arrow, a spear, or a sword would be harmless, being too light in the impact of the blow, but a blow from such a clublike axe with the bulk of the weight near the edge directing the blow would smash any helmet if properly delivered. There is sufficient edge on this battle-axe not only to stun the opponent, but also to fracture the skull. The following is an affidavit setting forth the circumstances of its finding:

Minneapolis, Minn., Dec. 11, 1928.

About thirty-five years ago my late husband, Julius Davidson, and I purchased a farm about five miles southwest of Evansville, Minnesota, and about three miles southeast of Erdahl. Being in need of more tillable land, Mr. Davidson in 1894 decided to clear and break up part of a piece of native woodland which was on the farm.

The trees had been cut some years before, and the stumps were pulled up by Mr. Davidson by means of a stump-puller. Beneath one of these stumps he found a heavy axe of strange shape, the like of which he had never seen before. The top of the stump under which the axe was found was more than two feet in diameter, and my husband said that it must have been several hundred years old. The axe lay quite deep in the hole, about a foot and a half below the surface of the ground. None of our neighbors had ever seen or heard of this axe before.

The axe was in my possession until last summer when I loaned it to Mr. H. R. Holand.

[Signed]   MARTHA DAVIDSON.

State of Minnesota,
  County of Hennepin.

Subscribed and sworn to before me a notary public this 15th day of December, 1928. [Signed] CHAS. A. PALMER.

In May, 1930, I visited the spot where this axe was found in company with Mr. Emil Skog, the postmaster of Evansville, Minn. We found that the axe was found on or near the south margin of a large tract of native timber, a few rods from a small pool. We learned that this grove in pioneer times comprised about a thousand acres. Nels Christenson, an old settler who came there in 1869, told us that the farmers for many miles around came to this grove to get logs. No buildings have ever been erected on the quarter section where the axe was found, the land being gravelly and almost unfit for cultivation. The exact finding place is in the northeast corner of the northeast quarter of the southeast quarter of section 24, township of Erdahl, Grant County.

The many excellent museums of the Scandinavian countries are rich in weapons of the Viking Age, but they have very few arms from the subsequent period of the Middle Ages. In pagan times it was customary to bury the dead with their weapons and other implements which were thought necessary for their journey through the underworld on their way to Valhalla. But when Christianity became established, these burial customs ceased, and the graves from the following centuries yield very few implements of warfare. Many battles were fought during the later Middle Ages, and thousands of arms were left on the battlefield. But instead of being buried with the slain, these arms were thriftily saved until at last they were sold to the blacksmiths for junk long before any museum was established. For this reason there are very few weapons remaining from the five centuries beginning with about 1050, and the writer found it a much slower process to identify the Minnesota finds than he had anticipated.

None of the largest museums in the Scandinavian countries had any axes on display of the type shown on Plate

XXIII. But in the Historical Museum in Stockholm a wooden duplicate was found. This museum, like the others, had very few arms from the period after the Viking Age, but it had a large number of carved reredoses from old churches. On one of these screens Dr. B. Thordeman, curator of the Museum, pointed out a figure of King Olaf (later known as St. Olaf, who died in 1030) who held in his hand an exact wooden image of the axe shown above in Plate XXIII. The size of the reredos and the lack of good light made it impossible to obtain a good photograph, but Dr. Thordeman gave me the following statement:

The axe marked B. Thm. [see Plate XXIII] is in type practically identical with St. Olaf's axe on the reredos from Østeråker (originally from Storkyrkan in Stockholm), now in the National Historical Museum, dated 1468.

Stockholm, Sept. 6, 1928.
[Signed]   BENGT THORDEMAN.[3]

With reference to the date of the reredos (1468), it may be remarked that the wood-carvers of that period did not have the same opportunity of presenting their images historically correct that artists of our day have. They had but scant means of knowing what clothing and arms were worn and carried at the time of Christ, for example, and we therefore find the soldiers of Pontius Pilate pictured as if they had lived in the Middle Ages. The best they could do in the absence of source material was to give their figures as old-fashioned clothing and arms as they were familiar with. This knowledge of old patterns seldom went back more than a hundred years. When therefore the reredos shows an axe in the hand of St. Olaf who died in 1030, it does not mean that it is a true copy of axes

[3] The following is the Swedish text of Dr. Thordeman's statement:

"Yxan märket B. Thm. är praktiskt taget till typen identisk med S. Olafs yxa på altarskåpet från Østeråker (ursprungligen från Stockholms Storkyrkan), nu i Statens Historiska Museum, dateret 1468.

Stockholm den 6te Sept. 1928.
[Signed]   BENGT THORDEMAN."

from that period. We know from hundreds of battle-axes found in the graves from the Viking Age that it is not. It rather means that it is modeled after an axe perhaps a hundred years older than the date of the reredos, 1468.

It is likely that the explorers camped on the spot where this axe was found as the finding place lies on the most direct and probable route that they would follow in traveling from Cormorant Lake to the "island" near Kensington.

4. Plate XXIV, a battle-axe found near Brandon, Minnesota, about ten miles north of Kensington. It has the same weight as the former (Plate XXIII) and practically the same striking shape and measurements. This axe shows more superior blacksmithing, however, than the other. The bulk of its weight is in the blade near the edge like the other, but instead of being embodied in a thick blade, the weight is concentrated in a ridgelike projection on both sides. The thickness of the axe at the ridge is one inch at the lower end of the blade and three-quarters inch at the upper. Its use was clearly the same as that of the other.

The following affidavit tells what is known of its history:

State of Minnesota,
County of Douglas. ss.

T. A. Jensen, being first duly sworn, on his oath states as follows:

I live at the Village of Nelson in Douglas County, State of Minnesota, where I have lived for forty years.

About in the year 1915 I attended an auction at the home of John Nelson near the Village of Brandon in said Douglas County, Nelson having then recently died. Among his effects was an old axe of a very peculiar shape, something that was like the picture of battle-axes that I had seen in books and in the museum at Copenhagen where I lived when a boy. The axe was entirely useless for any practical purpose.

Wondering where Mr. Nelson could have obtained such an axe, I inquired of his daughter about it. She told me that her father had had this axe in his possession for a long time and her father had told her that he had received it from an Indian far back in the pioneer days of Minnesota, when her father used to go hunting with the Indians.

I personally knew Mr. Nelson, who was one of the earliest settlers of Douglas County. He wore very long hair and lived much like an Indian.

I kept the axe in my possession for some time and then placed it in the Museum Room of the Alexandria Public Library. I had a talk with Mr. H. R. Holand about the Kensington Rune Stone and then turned the axe over to him. Mr. Holand kept it in his possession until it was placed in the case containing the Rune Stone in the Chamber of Commerce at Alexandria, Minnesota, where it now is.

[Signed]   T. A. JENSEN.

Subscribed and sworn to before me this 18th day of July, 1930.

[Signed]   CONSTANT LARSON, *Notary Public*,
Douglas County, Minn.

Hon. O. J. Berg, Judge of Probate, Douglas County, Minn., knew Mr. Nelson very well and the following letter from him is of interest:

Alexandria, Minn., July 19th, 1930.

Replying to your inquiry about Mr. John W. Nelson who is reported to have been the owner of the old battle-axe which is now here in Alexandria, I have the following to say:

I personally knew Mr. Nelson very well, as he was our near neighbor. My father, together with another party, came through Douglas County in 1866 looking for homestead lands and in 1871 came back and settled on a quarter section near Nelson Lake, two miles east of Brandon and about a mile from John W. Nelson. Mr. Nelson lived there when father made his first trip through Douglas County and had been here for some time. According to information I have, Mr. Nelson must have settled here in 1863. Mr. Nelson was therefore one of the first, if not the very first settler in that part of Douglas County.

Mr. Nelson was an Irishman, a professional auctioneer, good

natured and an excellent neighbor. He preferred to hunt and trap rather than till the soil and he was very friendly with the Indians. He always permitted them to camp on his land and he probably was a greater favorite with them than any other man in the country. I can easily understand how they would present him with the old battle-axe.

In appearance Mr. Nelson was of the Wild West type, with long whiskers and long dark hair that reached down over his shoulders. He was respected for his honesty and loved for his good humor and breezy reminiscences of Indian ways and pioneer days. He died in 1915.

[Signed] OLE J. BERG, *Judge of Probate Court.*

This axe, as the illustration shows, is in excellent state of preservation, and the first impression one has on seeing it is that it cannot possibly be 600 years old. But the state of preservation of an antiquarian object is not always a safe criterion of its age. The famous Gokstad vessel which was unearthed in a burial mound in Norway a few years ago was filled with hundreds of household objects of wood and metal many of which were in excellent state of preservation as was also the vessel. Yet that vessel and its contents were placed in the mound more than a thousand years ago. Still more remarkable is the state of preservation of a sword recently found in a burial from the Bronze Age, more than 2,000 years old. Speaking of this sword, Dr. Sigurd Grieg of the Oslo Museum says it is so well preserved that "it might well have come from the armorer's shop a couple of days ago." If this axe had been used as a ceremonial weapon by the Indians for a long period, this would well account for its well-preserved appearance.

This type of heavy axes, having a thickness of about an inch at the ridges immediately behind the edge, is very rare. After making the rounds of nearly all the museums in Sweden and Norway, only three were found. Two of these were in *De Sandvigske Samlinger* in Lillehammer (see Plate XXII) and one was found in the museum in Skara, Sweden (see Plate XXV). Herr S. Welin, curator of the museum, kindly gave me the following statement in writing:

Skara, Sweden, October 3, 1928.

We have in Westgothland's museum in Skara a battle axe which in all important features is identical with the axe shown in the photograph marked S. V.[4] [see Plate XXIV]. The axe has the long opening for the helve which is characteristic of axes from the late Middle Ages, with a large opening in the lower end and a smaller opening in the upper. The hammer consists of a heel-like appendage fixed to the back of the axe and, what is of greatest importance, the axe has the same projecting ridge on both sides near the edge, just as is shown on the photograph shown by Mr. Holand. See further the photograph of the Skara axe [Plate XXV]. The axe has undoubtedly been used as a battle axe, especially for smashing helmets.

[Signed]   S. WELIN.

A battle-axe with the same prominent ridge is shown in an illustration from an Icelandic MS. of the late Middle Ages.[5]

It has been suggested that this axe was perhaps a broadaxe for smoothing logs and making boards. A broadaxe would no doubt be a useful implement on an exploring expedition for it might be necessary to build a boat. But

---

[4] The identification mark did not reproduce because of the nature of the ink used. The same is true of marks which should appear on Plates XX, XXIV (the upper axe), and XXX. The photographs with the original identification marks may be seen in the office of the Minnesota Historical Society.

The following is the Swedish text of Herr Welin's statement:

"Skara den 3 Oktober 1928.

"Vi har i Västergötlands fornmuseum i Skara en stridsyxa, som i allt väsentligt är identisk med yxan, som forekommer å et fotografi, märket S. V. Yxan har den långa holk, som är karakteristisk för yxar från medeltiden, med en stor öppning i den nädra enden och en helt obetydelig öppning i den övre. Hammaren har en utanpålligende klack, och, hvilket är av störste vikt, yxan har den framträdande kam eller rygg på bägga sidorna nära eggen, liksom på det av Herr Hjalmar Rued Holand visade fotografiet. Se förövrigt fotografi av Skara-yxan. Yxan har utan tvifvel väret brukad som stridsyxa, särskilt till at krossa hjälmar med.
                                        "S. WELIN, Museumsintendant."

[5] See Nansen, In Northern Mists, II, 15.

a heavy axe with a blade an inch thick would be a sorry substitute for a broadaxe. This takes the place of an adze or plane and, like these tools, calls for a light, thin blade. It is impossible to make thin shavings with an axe edge like the point of a crowbar.

5. Plate XXVI, a beautifully wrought spear-head of steel, considerably pock-marked or honeycombed with rust. The point is seven inches long and one and one-half inches wide at the widest part. The midrib is present, but not prominent. At the base of the blade is a conical socket three and one-half inches long (outside measurement), into which the head of the shaft was introduced. The socket has two tongs $\%6$ inch in width for securing the shaft. These tongs are 4¾ inches long, but were originally longer, as the ends of both have been broken off. This weapon was found about forty miles east of the Mississippi River in Trempealeau County, Wisconsin, in a small coulee among the steep ridges of Pigeon Creek. The land had been covered with timber and was recently cleared by the owner. It was while breaking up his first field that he found the spear among the roots of the clearing. The following affidavit gives an account of its discovery.

I, Nils Windjue of Whitehall, Trempealeau County, Wisconsin, being under oath, make the following statement, to-wit:

In the fall of 1899, while breaking up some new land on my farm in Sjuggerud coulee, town of Pigeon, Trempealeau County, Wis., I found an ancient steel spearhead. The spearhead was actually found by my adopted son, George Windjue, then about five years old, who was playing about and saw the spearhead turned up by the breaking plow.

The spearhead was covered with a thick layer of rust when found, but by polishing and filing I removed this rust except what is honeycombed into the metal. The spearhead is 15 inches long, having a blade about 7 inches long and 1½ inches wide at its base. The blade is of one piece with a hollow shank which is 3½ inches long.

This shank or socket is cylindrical in form, hollow and about three inches long. The opening is hexagonal in form at the mouth; at this point it is one inch in diameter, while it is about one-half inch in diameter at the point where it connects with the blade. The shank is prolonged in the form of two strips of steel, one-half inch in width, and about 4½ inches long, extending from opposite sides of the shank for the purpose of reinforcing the handle. These strips have two holes for purposes of riveting.

When the spearhead was found one of these strips was about two inches longer than it is now, but I inadvertently broke this part off.

This spearhead was found near the southwest corner of the northeast quarter of the southeast quarter of section twenty-one (21) township twenty-two (22) and north of range seven (7) west, about five miles northeast of Whitehall, Wisconsin.

No part of this farm of one hundred twenty acres had been farmed or cleared until I bought it in 1893.

In 1925 I gave the spearhead to Mr. H. R. Holand.

Dated at Whitehall, Wisconsin, this 12th day of May, A. D. 1928.

[Signed] NILS WINDJUE.

Subscribed and sworn to before me, a notary public, in and for Trempealeau County, Wisconsin, on the 12th day of May, 1928.

[Signed] CHAS. B. MELBY.

This spear was recognized in many museums as a true specimen of Scandinavian spears. In the Folk Museum of Lund, Sweden, were about a dozen of the same type. The accompanying photograph from the National Museum in Copenhagen (Plate XXVII) shows three spears with the same type of blade, shank, socket and attachment as the Whitehall spear.

There remained the possibility that the spear is of English or other origin. A visit was made to the Tower of London where there is a large collection of spears. However, all the spears there are distinctly of another type, quite wide, with heavy midribs. They all have long shanks because the shaft is held in place by the shank only. The

Plate XX. Norwegian fire-steel of medieval type, found near Climax, Minnesota.

Photo by Milwaukee Public Museum

Plate XXI. Medieval Norwegian axe found near Marquette, Michigan.

Photo by Morgan H. Stafford

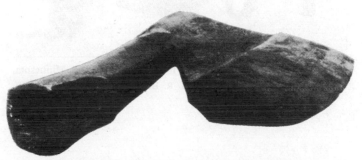

Plate XXII. A precisely similar axe in the Lillehammer Museum, Norway.

Photo by De Sandvigske Samlinger

Plate XXIII. Fourteenth Century implements found in Minnesota.

Photo by H. R. Holand

same is true of the German spears shown in the Zeughaus in Berlin. Norwegian and Swedish spearheads are characterized by very short shanks, only three or four inches long. The shank is provided with two opposite strap-like extensions of steel, about seven inches long, which hold the shaft firmly by means of clinched bolts. These straps are never seen on English and French spears, and rarely on German. It is an error to suppose that "individual smiths had their own patterns." The shape of the spear, which in the Middle Ages was almost as much a part of a man's attire as a necktie is now, was prescribed by well-established national customs.

6. Plate XXIII (the upper), an axe, known in the Scandinavian Middle Ages as a *skjæg-øks*, because of the extremely long projection of its lower part. It is generally classed as a battle-axe, but may have had other uses. Like the other two axes, the neck for the helve is about the same length as the eye of the axe, and, like them, it calls for a tapering helve. The measurements of the hammer-head are exactly the same as those of the axe shown in Plate XXIV.

The strikingly divergent feature of this axe is the "beard" or long prolongation of the lower part of the blade. It continues downward and inward for about ten inches until it meets the helve. Here it forks so as to form a clamp for the two sides of the helve to which it has been fastened by a bolt. Unlike the other two axes, it has a very thin blade, this being nowhere more than three-sixteenths of an inch in thickness and in most places only one-eighth inch thick. It weighs just five pounds. The length of the cutting edge is sixteen inches.

This axe was found near the extremity of a long and narrow point of land projecting from the south about a mile into Norway Lake in Kandiyohi County, Minnesota (about fifty miles southeast of Kensington). This peninsula consists of a broad base beyond which is a low neck of land, terminating in a higher and broader elevation. When the early settlers came this terminal elevation was an island. The history of this island is well known since

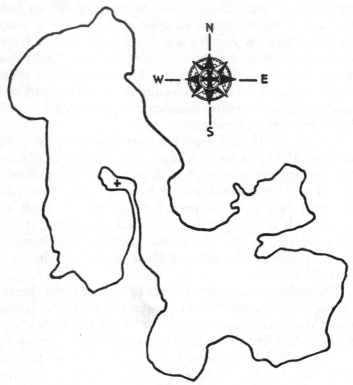

FIG. 14. OUTLINE MAP OF NORWAY LAKE, MINNESOTA
The cross marks the place where the axe was found.

the coming of the first white settlers. It was preempted in 1857 by Even Railson, who was the first white man to select land in the northern part of Kandiyohi County. The base of the peninsula is made up of very choice farming land and here Mr. Railson had his buildings and fields. The island north of it (now the terminal end of the peninsula) seemed to be a favorite camping-ground for the Indians, so Mr. Railson reserved it for their use, and the land has never been cleared. It was near the middle of this "island" that the axe was found and it was presumably left there by some Indian. The Indians camped here year after year and adopted Mr. Railson into their tribe under the name of "Big Chief." Mr. Railson lived here for half a century until his death. It then passed into the possession of his daughter whose son now has the farm. The "island" or northern part of the peninsula is in the same state of nature as when Mr. Railson purchased the land. The following statement, obtained through the kindness of the Rev. D. C. Jordahl, Ridgeway, Iowa, who was then pastor of the local Lutheran congregation, tells the story of its discovery.

Norway Lake, Minn., July 30, 1912.

I hereby certify to the following facts:

In the summer of 1908, on one of my fishing trips to the peninsula projecting into Norway Lake, in section 6, township 121 north, range 35 west of the principal meridian, being in the town of Lake Andrew, in Kandiyohi County, Minnesota, I came, near the middle of said peninsula, across an iron implement of a peculiar form and shape. I picked it up and looked at it, and concluded it must have been a part of a drill [seeding-machine] or some other machinery; so I left it and went out on the lake fishing, thinking nothing more about the find I had made nor bothering myself with carrying it home about a mile distant.

During the following two years my attention was drawn to articles appearing off and on in the newspapers in regard to a remarkable stone discovered near Kensington, Minn., said to contain an inscription to the effect that some old vikings had roamed about in this country in the fourteenth century. The idea then occurred to me that possibly this axe over in the peninsula had been one of the weapons employed by some roving vikings of old. So, in the summer of 1910, I looked for it again and readily found it, took it home and placed it in my machine shed. I mentioned the fact to my neighbors and others. At the request of Senator L. O. Thorpe, of Willmar, Minn., I have now loaned it to Hjalmar R. Holand, of Ephraim, Wis.

[Signed] OLE SKAALRUD.

In presence of
D. C. JORDAHL.
P. A. GANDRUD.

Rev. Horatio Gates, a clergyman of Willmar, Minn., interviewed several of the first settlers to learn what was known about the axe. The following affidavits set forth the results of his inquiry.

State of Minnesota,
County of Kandiyohi. ss.

I, the undersigned Ole Skaalrud, do further declare under oath, in addition to the affidavit already made, that I have never heard of anyone in this neighborhood or elsewhere in this state or country having had in their possession such an axe as the one found by me on the peninsula extending into Norway Lake; neither have I knowledge of anyone who could have brought it or whose relatives brought in such an axe from the old country.

I have been a resident of Andrew and Arctander townships in Kandiyohi County for 36 years. I was born in Land, Norway, in 1866.

[Signed] OLE SKAALRUD.

Subscribed and sworn to before me this 26th day of August, 1912.

[Signed] R. W. STANFORD, *Notary Public.*

This large axe found at Norway Lake was a familiar object to most of the museum people with whom I talked, and was to be seen in several museums with minor differences in detail of blacksmithing. This led me to hope that I would find an exact duplicate, of which I could get a photograph, but in vain. In the National Museum in Copenhagen, which was the last Scandinavian Museum I visited, were also some of these excessively broad battle-axes with their unique socket and double attachment to the helve,

Plate XXIV. Swedish battle axe of the Middle
Ages found near Brandon, Minnesota.

Photo by Milwaukee Museum

Plate XXV. Swedish battle axe of the late Middle Ages in
the Museum of Skara, Sweden.

Photo by F. Thesslund, Skara

Plate XXVI. Scandinavian Spearhead found near Whitehall, Wisconsin.

Photo by Milwaukee Public Museum

Plate XXVII. Spearheads in National Museum, Copenhagen, Denmark.

Photo by the National Museum, Copenhagen

but with a small divergent detail. Dr. Matthiessen, one of the curators, gave me the following statement which mentions this difference:

Copenhagen, Oct. 10, 1928.

Upon given opportunity the museum will not neglect to state that the photograph marked XX [Plate XXIII] shows an axe which in type shows a certain similarity with some specimens which are to be found in the collection here which date from the Middle Ages. While the axe in the photograph has two holes for the helve, the specimens in our museum, which likewise have a double attachment to the helve, have the lower attachment to the helve by means of an iron band.

[Signed]   Hugo Matthiessen.[6]

Dr. Matthiessen's reference to the two holes is in error. He did not see the axe itself, but only the photograph. In this it appears as if the axe has two sockets, but this is misleading. It has only one true socket, the lower apparent socket being a broad iron band which circles the helve two-thirds of the way around and is bolted to it. The attachment is therefore practically the same as in the Copenhagen axes, the difference being that in the Minnesota axe the band is fastened by means of a bolt through the transverse diameter of the helve while in the Copenhagen axes the bolt goes through the longitudinal diameter of the helve. Two axes of the same type are also illustrated in a painting from about 1450 in Kumla Church, Västmannland, Sweden [7] (see Plate XXVIII).

7. Plate XXIX. A sword found three miles west of

[6] The following is the Danish text of Dr. Matthiessen's statement:

Kjøbenhavn 10 Oktober, 1928.

"Paa given Foranledning skal Museet ikke undlade at udtale, at det med XX mærkede Fotografi viser en Økse, some i Type frembyder en vis Lighed med enkelte Eksemplarer, som findes i Samlingen her og skriver sig fra Middelalderen. Medens den paa Fotografiet viste Økse har to Skafthuller, har Nationalmuseets Eksemplarer, der ligeledes har haft dobbelt Fæste til Skaftet, forneden Tilslutning til denne ved en Jernskinne.   P. D. V.

[Signed]   Hugo Matthiessen."

[7] Hildebrand's *Sveriges Historia, Medeltiden,* Fig. 387.

Ulen, Clay County, Minn., in the spring of 1911 on the farm of Hans O. Hanson Strand.[8] He was a recent settler, but his farm had not been under cultivation before he settled there. In an interview which the writer had with Mr. Strand at the spot where the sword was found, Strand said he had plowed that field several times, but very shallow, as was the practice in that vicinity. Then, at a Farmer's Institute meeting, he had heard a speaker dwell on the benefits gained by deep plowing and, much impressed, he had returned to his farm and set his plow point several inches deeper. Shortly afterward the sword was turned up, deeply incrusted with a heavy layer of rust. He stated in his affidavit that he had spent much time in removing this rust.

Rev. Horatio Gates who accompanied the writer secured affidavits from Mr. Strand, his neighbors and others concerning the discovery of the sword and the settlement of the neighborhood. These affidavits brought out the fact that none of them had ever seen the sword before, nor had any knowledge of how it had come there. Unfortunately, these affidavits perished in 1934 when the writer's home was destroyed by fire.

The length of the blade at present is 16¼ inches, but originally it was longer, as it shows signs of having been cut off in a crude manner. The bronze handle, including the cross-bar which serves as hilt, is 6½ inches long and has spiral ornamentation. It has some resemblance to the Roman style of swords which were used for a time in the U. S. Army about a hundred years ago and were known as Foot Artillery swords.[9] The blade of this (Army) sword is short and heavy with an oval contour. It has a long shallow central groove near the point and two narrow

[8] The sword is now in the possession or keeping of State Teachers College, Moorhead, Minn.

[9] T. T. Belote in *U. S. National Museum Bulletin* 163, "American and European Swords in the Historical Collections of the U. S. National Museum." See Plate 15 and p. 42.

parallel grooves near the hilt. The quillons are straight with rounded ends. The surface of the grip is corrugated in imitation of eagle feathers. While there is a superficial resemblance, the sword found near Ulen, Minn., according to the opinion of the Smithsonian Institution, given below, is of a different type from the Foot Artillery sword:

Washington, D. C., March 4, 1939.

Referring to previous correspondence and particularly to your letter of February 13, I regret to say that we have been unable to find any information whatever concerning the sword of which you submit a photograph.

Captain Charles Carcy, Assistant Curator of History, states that he will keep the specimen in mind and we shall be glad to supply you with any information that we may discover concerning it. [Signed] J. E. GRAF, *Associate Director*.

Aside from the temporary revival a hundred years ago of the Roman type, there are two principal differences between the sword of the Middle Ages and the later sword. One is the double edge which was prevalent down to the sixteenth century and later. This older sword was primarily a cutting weapon. In the course of the sixteenth century the blade became narrower and more pointed until the rapier form was reached. The other difference is the protection for the hand which became increasingly necessary as the sword was less used for cutting and more for thrusting. The sword of the Middle Ages had no other protection for the hand than a short crossbar, usually rectangular, known as quillons. In the sixteenth century a cup-shaped guard was added to the quillons which proved more serviceable. The Ulen sword is of a type which antedates these changes and is characteristic of the fourteenth century or earlier.

While no other specimen of this type of sword has hitherto been found in America and only few in northern Europe, there are numerous illustrations of it in old books, manuscripts, wood carvings, and on sarcophagi which are abundant evidence that this type was in use in the Scandinavian countries in the thirteenth, fourteenth and fifteenth centuries. Archbishop Olaus Magnus in his *Historia de gentibus septentrionalibus* (published in 1555) shows many illustrations of them.[10] A sarcophagus in the Uppsala cathedral shows an identical specimen.[11] A manuscript ornamentation of the fourteenth century gives an illustration.[12] The carved doors of the Hyllestad church (ca. 1200) in Norway show four swords like the sword from Ulen. According to Professor Worsaae, these portals date from beginning of the thirteenth century.[13]

The cross-bar of the Ulen sword has an ornamentation in the middle on each side. On one side appears a cuirass, behind which can be seen two battle-axes and a dagger in crossed formation. On the other side is the bearded head of a man surmounted by a helmet. The form of this helmet appears numerous times in the illustrations of Olaus Magnus in his work cited above.

There is one interesting point about this sword which indicates that it was not brought into Minnesota by immigrants of the nineteenth century. This is the manner in which a part of the sword has been cut off. Originally the blade must have been about two feet or more in length, which was the usual length of swords of the Middle Ages. But when it was found it was only about sixteen inches long.

Evidently the person who cut off the missing part did not have any cold-chisel or other white man's tool to help him. Instead he set to work with a round-headed hammer to pound the blade in two. Not succeeding in this, he snapped off the end. In so doing he also fractured a corner of the remaining blade, which may have become thin by the pounding.

[10] See pp. 95, 161, 171, 173, 178, 182, 190, 227, 348, 450, 660.
[11] H. Hildebrand, *Sveriges Historia*, II, 193.
[12] Reproduced in Nansen, *In Northern Mists*, II, 246.
[13] *Aarböger for Nordisk Oldkyndighed*, 1870, Plate 14.

This indicates that an Indian was the blacksmith. If an Indian acquired it, let us say at the massacre at Cormorant Lake about twenty miles away, he would feel that his booty was insignificant, because a sword is not an Indian weapon. But soon he would see that a part of the blade would make a good hunting knife, and he appears to have taken his stone-headed tomahawk to break the blade in two. The concave marks from the round head of the supposed tomahawk are still visible for a distance of about 1½ inches on the remaining stub of the blade, and this has been flattened and widened by the impact of the blows (see the enlarged tip of the sword shown in Plate XXIX).

If the sword was in its finding place before the advent of white settlers, it probably belonged to one of the ten men who were killed at Cormorant Lake. It was found only twenty miles from that campsite, and this type of sword was in use in their time. It could not have belonged to any later French or English trappers or travelers because, if they carried swords at all, theirs would have been of the rapier type in use in their time.

8. Plate XXX. A hatchet found near Thief River Falls, Minnesota. The hole for the helve is precisely the same in length as that in Plate XXIII, and the lower, larger opening is also the same. It tapers more so that the upper opening is only one inch by five-sixteenths inch. Like axes in Plates XXIII and XXIV, the neck is the same length as the eye. The hammer-head is two and one-half inches by one inch. The following affidavit has been received from the finder.

State of Minnesota,
  County of Pennington. ss.

Sam S. Brandvold, being first duly sworn, on oath says that he is a resident of the city of Thief River Falls, Minnesota, and has lived there for many years last past;

And affiant further states that some time ago, in the month of June in the year 1919, he was walking across the garden patch on the Ole Sandness farm in section 22 in the township of Rocksbury, in Pennington County, Minnesota, located about three and a half miles south of the city of Thief River Falls, Minn.;

And affiant further states that while so walking in said garden, he found an old, badly rusted iron axe, the like of which I have [he had] never seen before. The axe apparently had been plowed out of the ground. The axe was found on a little knoll in an otherwise flat country, while the renter of the farm, named Halvor Olson, was plowing in the garden. The owner of the land and the renter had never seen the axe before, and were ignorant of its presence there until I picked it up. I later presented the axe to H. R. Holand as I thought this axe might have been left in the place where found by the same people who are mentioned on the so-called Kensington Stone.

Further affiant says not save that he makes this affidavit for the express purpose of showing the place and circumstances under which he found the said iron axe.

[Signed]   SAM S. BRANDVOLD.

Subscribed and sworn to before me this 13th day of December, 1928.

[Signed]   H. O. BERVE, *Notary Public*.

Several hatchets like the Thief River Falls axe (Plate XXX) were seen in different museums. The following statement by Dr. Engelstad, assistant curator of the University Museum in Oslo, shows the age and home of these finds:

Upon request I shall state that there are in the University Museum in Oslo a number of iron axes from the Middle Ages which typologically are closely related to the axe marked E-S-E [Plate XXX].

In characterization of the axes in the Museum it can be stated that they have a prolonged socket, the back line of which is continuous with the neck, which, in some, is very broad and heavy. The upper line of our axes is quite straight, while the lower very often has an extension downward at the edge and the part of the axe immediately back of this.

At the same time I will state that the fire-steel which carries the same mark [Plate XX] in its entire form with the spiral ends is of exactly the same type as the fire-steels which in great numbers have been found in Norwegian graves from the Viking Age.

Oslo, September 18, 1928.

[Signed] EIVIND S. ENGELSTAD.[14]

This axe, as mentioned by Dr, Engelstad, is typologically of the late Middle Ages, and there are illustrations of its identical form in old drawings. Its fourteenth century age is also indicated by the fact that its socket has the same singular form as have those of the other four axes described. This socket calls for a pointed helve which is at sharp variance from the later manner of helving axes. But these points of identity are not entirely sufficient to prove that it was brought into Minnesota by the Paul Knutson expedition as such a hatchet may have remained in use until the present time and then brought to America by an early immigrant who later lost it. While it seems inconceivable that an axe should have survived continued usage for 600 years, the possibility should be given consideration.

But this doubt, scant though it be, does not apply to the other seven relics as the circumstances of their discovery show that they were here long before the pioneers came. The condition of the wood in the Republic axe (Plate XXI), found about 1880 in an unsettled wilderness, shows

[14] The following is the Norwegian text of Dr. Engelstad's statement:

"På opfordring skal jeg få meddele at man ved Universitetets Oldsaksamling i Oslo har en rekke jernøkser fra Middelalderen som rent typologisk står øksen merket E-S-E nær.

"Til karakteristikk av øksene i Oldsaksamlingen kan meddeles at de har et forlenget Skafthullparti hvis bakre linje går i ett med nakken som tildels er meget bred og kraftig. Bladets øvre linje er helt rett, mens den nedre ofte har et nedhengende skjegg ved eggen og partiet umiddelbart bak denne.

"Samtidig skal jeg få meddele at det ildstål som bærer samme merke ved hele sin form med de spiraloprullcte ender er av ganske samme type som de ildstål der i mengdevis er funnet i norske graver fra vikingetiden.

Oslo 18 September, 1928.

[Signed] EIVIND S. ENGELSTAD."

Concerning the marks mentioned by Dr. Engelstad, the reader is referred to note 4 of this chapter.

that it must have been lying in damp soil or water for centuries. The battle-axe found near Erdahl was found underneath the stump of a tree estimated to be several hundred years old. The battle-axe from Brandon was presented to one of the earliest settlers by an Indian. The third battle-axe was found far out on an out-of-the-way peninsula which formerly was an island. No road led out there nor was any pioneer's cabin there. We know the history of this tract of land since the first pioneer preempted it. The sword was found by the first person who plowed the soil of the farm where it was found, and its blade shows definite signs of having been hammered and broken off by an Indian without white man's tools. The spear was found in the first plowing in a rough and narrow timbered coulee whither no road led, and where the finder himself was the first to clear the land. The fire-steel was found by the first Norwegian settler in the northern part of the Red River Valley in unplowed soil, two feet beneath the surface. The presence of the charcoal with the fire-steel shows that the soil above it must have accumulated since the fire was made. It must have taken a very long time for the wind and vegetation of the prairie to accumulate such a deposit above the remains of the fire. All these things taken together seem to show conclusively that these articles were not brought in by the pioneers of the present age.

The only explanation that will satisfy all the conditions is that these articles were brought in by the explorers who left the Kensington inscription dated 1362. These finds belong to the same period. Their place of origin is southern Sweden and Norway just as the members of this expedition are stated to have come from southern Sweden and Norway. They are found in just that region where these explorers traveled and they are just such things as were needed on their journey.

Some readers may think it strange that so many of these implements should be found after a lapse of 600 years. But the conditions for preserving ancient relics of the kind

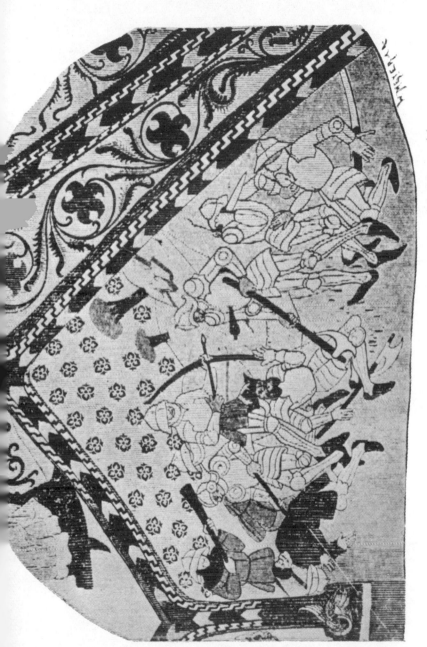

Plate XXVIII. Painting in Kumla Church, Sweden, showing two axes of the Norway lake type.

From Hildebrand's Sveriges Historia

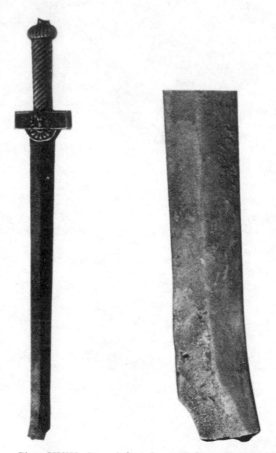

Plate XXIX. Sword found near Ulen, Minnesota,
and broken end of the same showing round-headed
hammer marks.

Photo by Wm. Westman, Alexandria, Minn.

mentioned above were really more favorable in America than in Europe. Here were no junk dealers and black-smiths to gather and transform these antiquated relics, and they could not easily be destroyed. When the Indians who acquired them eventually lost them, they would be quickly hidden in the new vegetation and thus lie undisturbed until the pioneer turned them up with his plow. As a large part of that section of Minnesota over which these explorers traveled is tillable, it is likely that other relics from the same expedition will turn up. These thirty men probably all carried spears and fire-steels, but so far only one of each has been uncovered. Most of them, if not all, also carried swords, but only one of these has been found. Five axes have come to light (one of which may possibly be a recent importation), but as these axes were really different kinds of fighting weapons, there were probably more axes than men in the expedition.

XX. THE VERENDRYE STONE

IT may be that the Kensington Stone is not the only runic inscription left by the Paul Knutson expedition. Two hundred years ago Pierre Gaultier de Varennes, Sieur de la Verendrye, the first white man known to have visited western Minnesota and the Dakota plains since 1362, found in that region a stone inscribed with unknown characters of a description which indicates that this also was a runic inscription.

La Verendrye, one of the greatest of the distinguished French explorers of America, was born at Three Rivers on the St. Lawrence in 1685. In his youth he served for several years as an ensign on the battle fields of France. Later he was commandant of a fur-trading post on Lake Nipigon, the most distant of all French frontier posts. Here the lure of the great mysterious West seized him and he determined to explore its unknown wilds, partly to add new provinces to the French dominion and partly to search for a short and feasible route to the Pacific Ocean. He applied to the king for support in this great enterprise, but was only granted permission to undertake the expedition at his own expense. In 1731 he set out from Quebec with fifty men after turning all his resources and credit into cash. The following year he reached the western shore of Lake of the Woods on the boundary between Minnesota and Manitoba. Here he built his headquarters, Fort St. Charles, and pushing out to the west and north built several other frontier forts. Years of distress and disaster followed, caused by the failure of supplies to arrive, the mutiny of his men and the attacks of the Sioux Indians. But with dauntless perseverance and resourcefulness La Verendrye maintained his hold on the region and extended the do-

minion of France in every direction. He heard strange
stories from the Indians of a nation of white people who
were not hunters but agriculturists living far to the southwest. In 1738 he made a journey to this strange people
and found them to be the Mandan Indians occupying the
region between the present cities of Minot and Bismarck,
North Dakota. Somewhere on the plain between Lake of
the Woods and the Mandan Indians near central North
Dakota he discovered a pillar of stone in which was fixed
a small stone inscribed on both sides with unknown characters. As he was unable to decipher the inscription and
had seen nothing like it before, he brought it with him
when he in 1743 made a trip to Quebec. He submitted
the inscribed stone to the scrutiny of the Jesuit scholars
there. They were likewise unable to read the inscription;
but on comparing it with illustrations of Tatarian inscriptions which they found in books in their college library,
they found the characters "perfectly alike." Esteeming this
discovery a matter of state importance, the stone with
its mystic inscription was sent to Paris to Count de Maurepas who then was one of the king's ministers.

The record of this remarkable discovery is preserved
to us by Professor Peter Kalm, a member of the Swedish
Royal Academy of Sciences, who about that time was so-
journing in America. While here he kept a diary of his
keen and interesting observations which later was published in three volumes.[1] In 1749 he visited Quebec where
he not only heard the story of the discovery of this inscribed stone from the Jesuit scholars in the city, but also
received an account of it from La Verendrye himself who
happened to be there. The account that he gives of it is
therefore practically firsthand. The following is what Professor Kalm tells about the matter:

The history of the country can be traced no further than
from the arrival of the Europeans; for everything that hap-

[1] *Travels into North America*, etc., translated into English by J. R.
Forster, London, 1771.

pened before that period, is more like a fiction or a dream, than anything that really happened. In later time there have, however, been found a few marks of antiquity, from which it may be conjectured that America was formerly inhabited by a nation more versed in science, than that which the Europeans found on their arrival here; or that a great military expedition was undertaken to this continent, from these known parts of the world.

This is confirmed by an account, which I received from Mr. de Verandrier, who has commanded the expedition to the South Sea [the Pacific] in person, of which I shall presently give an account. I have heard it repeated by others, who have been eye-witnesses of everything that happened on that occasion. Some years before I came into Canada, the then governor-general, Chevalier de Beauharnois, gave Mr. de Verandrier an order to go from Canada, with a number of people, on an expedition across North America to the South Sea, in order to examine how far those places are distant from each other, and to find out what advantages might accrue to Canada or Louisiana, from a communication with that ocean. . . . As they came far into the country, beyond many nations, they sometimes met with large tracts of land, free from wood, but covered with a kind of very tall grass, for the space of some days' journey. . . . When they came far to the west, where, to the best of their knowledge, no Frenchman, or European, had ever been, they found in one place in the woods, and again on a large plain, great pillars of stone, leaning upon each other. These pillars consisted of but one stone each, and the Frenchmen could not but suppose that they had been erected by human hands. Sometimes they have found such stones laid upon one another, and, as it were, formed into a wall. . . . At last they met with a large stone, like a pillar, and in it a smaller stone was fixed, which was covered on both sides with unknown characters. This stone, which was about a foot of French measure in length, and between four or five inches broad, they broke loose, and carried to Canada with them, from whence it was sent to France, to the secretary of state, the Count of Maurepas. What became of it afterwards is unknown to them, but they think it is yet [1749] preserved in his collection. Several of the Jesuits, who have seen and handled this stone in Canada, unanimously affirm, that the letters on it are the same with those which in the books, containing accounts of Tataria, are called Tatarian characters, and that, on comparing both together, they found them perfectly alike. Notwithstanding the questions which the French on the South Sea expedition asked the people there, concerning the time when, and by whom these pillars were erected? what their traditions and sentiments concerning them were? who had wrote the characters? what was meant by them? what kind of letters they were? in what language they were written? and other circumstances; yet they could never get the least explication, the Indians being as ignorant of all those things, as the French themselves. All they could say was, that these stones had been in those places, since times immemorial. The places where the pillars stood were near nine hundred French miles westward of Montreal.[2]

It is evident from this account that this inscribed stone was not an Indian pictograph. Pierre la Verendrye had spent more than fifty years in Canada,[3] mostly among the Indians, and probably had seen hundreds of such pictographs. The Jesuits, likewise, many of whom had spent years among the Indians as missionaries, were also familiar with their pictographs. Indeed, the picture writing of the Indians has so little in common with the appearance of the writing of more civilized peoples, that even one who sees it for the first time would not confuse it with the alphabetic characters of any other people. Professor Kalm states that the Jesuits, upon comparing the writing on the stone with illustrations of Tatarian inscriptions found the characters "perfectly alike." This comparison is helpful, but of course, it could not have been a Tatarian inscription, for the Tatars, living east of the Caspian Sea with no known interest in seafaring and exploration, would be among the last peoples on earth to have found their way into the interior of North America.

[2] *Travels into North America*, etc., III, 122-128.
[3] His father, René Gaultier, Sieur de la Varennes, a captain in the French army, settled at Three Rivers, Canada, in 1665.

It happens, however, that Tatarian inscriptions and runic inscriptions have a remarkable superficial resemblance. This has already been noted by Sir Charles Eliot who in his article in the Encyclopaedia Britannica on Turks calls attention to this resemblance.[4] The letters in both modes of writing are most often formed on a vertical staff and they are mostly rectangular in form. Several runic signs have their duplicates in Tatarian characters which occur in inscriptions on the upper Yenesei and Orkhon rivers. The similarity of runic and Tatarian inscriptions is shown in the illustration of a Tatarian inscription (see Plate XXXI).[5]

As the Jesuit scholars found these characters in an illustrated book on the Tatars, it may be possible to get a definite image of Verendrye's inscription by consulting the illustrated books on Tatars that were published before 1743. While several books on the Tatars were published before this date, there was only one, according to the Librarian of Congress, which shows specimens of Tatar writing. This is Philipp Johann von Strahlenberg's *Das Nord- und Östliche Theil von Europa und Asia*, published in German in Stockholm, 1730, 4to. Strahlenberg was a Swedish officer who for thirteen years had been a captive among the Tatars, and his book was by far the most popular of its kind, being translated and published in many editions, among them being an English translation in 1736, another in 1738, and a French in 1757. This must therefore have been the book on the Tatars in which the Jesuit scholars in 1743 found illustrations of writing "perfectly like" the writing on the Verendrye stone. On *Tab. V*, section D (see Fig. 15), may be seen a Tatarian inscription containing ten different characters.[6] Six of

[4] See article *Turks*, language, p. 3.

[5] *Inscriptions de l'Orkhon*, published by the Société Finno-Ougrienne, Helsingfors, 1892, Plate 8.

[6] I am indebted to Mr. Philip Ainsworth Means for sending me photographs of cuts in Strahlenberg's book.

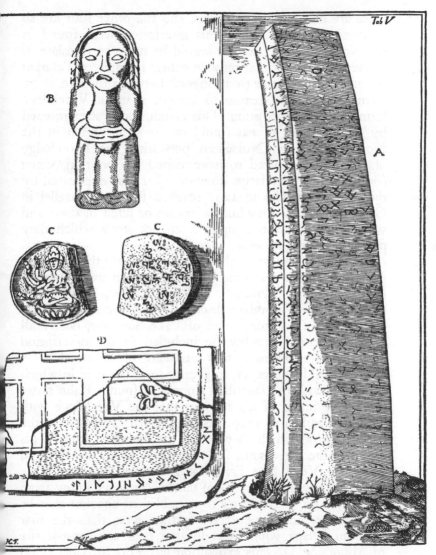

FIG. 15. TATARIAN INSCRIPTION FROM STRAHLENBERG'S BOOK

these are common runic forms, and the other four are so suggestively runic that if this inscription were found in the North, valiant attempts would be made to translate it. In view of the fact that only an expert in runic or Tatarian writing would be able to distinguish between the two, there seems to be good reason to believe that La Verendrye found a runic inscription. This conclusion is strengthened by the fact that it was found in the same region in the Northwest which Norsemen possessing the knowledge of runes are reported to have visited. Its position, when found, on top of a large stone or pillar was duplicated by the Norsemen who in 1291 reached the 73rd parallel in Greenland where they built a beacon or pillar of stone and wrote their inscription upon a smaller stone which they placed upon it (see *ante*, page 74).

Professor Kalm states that the place where these discoveries were made was nine hundred French miles west of Montreal. This statement is not of much help in localizing the site, as the Verendrye discoveries covered several thousand miles of territory west of Lake Superior, nearly all of which could roughly be included in the description "nine hundred French miles westward of Montreal."

It is possible, however, to greatly limit the field in which the pillar with the inscribed stone was found. Kalm states in the beginning of his account that the Verendrye with whom he talked in 1749 was in personal command of the expedition on which they found the inscribed stone. This excludes the three sons, for they were all in the West in 1749. La Verendrye Sr. must therefore have been the Verendrye with whom Kalm talked. Now we know from the senior La Verendrye's own published account that he did not personally penetrate farther west than the first Mandan village which was located near the present site of Minot, N. D. This expedition left Fort St. Charles on the Lake of the Woods September 11, 1738, and proceeded to the site of the present city of Winnipeg where La Verendrye had built a station called Fort Maurepas. They then went up the Assiniboine River to the site of the present city of Portage La Prairie, where La Verendrye built another station called Fort La Reine. From here La Verendrye and his men accompanied by a large number of Indians traveled southwestward to the Turtle Mountains and after following a circuitous route reached the village of the Mandans on December 3, 1738. Somewhere between Fort St. Charles and the Mandan village they must have seen the large pillars which they believed had been erected by human hands. "At last," says Kalm (that is, near the end of their journey), "they met with a large stone, like a pillar, and in it a smaller stone was fixed, which was covered on both sides with unknown characters." This significant pillar and inscribed stone must therefore have been found in the vicinity, and probably to the north or east, of the village of the Mandans.

This mystic inscription was sent to Count de Maurepas and probably baffled the count and his advisers as much as it had bewildered the learned Jesuits in Quebec. While something was known of Tatarian inscriptions, the day of runic interpretation had not yet arrived. But if a thorough search of Paris archives could be made, it is possible that the stone could be found. And if found it is more than probable that its message would not only throw further light on the Paul Knutson expedition, but would also give an important clew to the origin of that strangest of all Indian tribes, the Mandans.

XXI. SUMMARY

IN the preceding pages an effort has been made to discuss frankly all arguments for and against the authenticity of the Kensington Rune Stone. This study has led to the following conclusions:

1. No valid evidence to show that the inscription is a forgery has been presented.

2. The theory of a forgery is highly improbable.

3. External evidence shows that the theory of a forgery is impossible.

4. Numerous Scandinavian arms and implements of the Middle Ages unearthed in western Minnesota indicate that this region was visited by Norse explorers several hundred years ago.

5. The discovery of ancient Scandinavian mooring stones along the probable route in Minnesota, and other corroborative evidence separately testify to the presence of Scandinavian travelers in Minnesota long before the arrival of the earliest settlers.

A brief review or summary of the arguments which have led to these conclusions will be presented in this chapter.

1. THERE IS NO VALID EVIDENCE TO SHOW THAT THE INSCRIPTION IS NOT AUTHENTIC.

Most of the arguments that have been presented against the inscription are of a linguistic nature. These arguments—which chiefly deal with the absence of inflected word forms—are based on the assumption that the stilted literary style of the clerks of the Middle Ages represents the true vernacular of the people. The proponents of these objections forget that then, as always, there was, besides the literary language, a colloquial and dialectic speech, which presumably was the medium of expression of the great

majority of the people. Just what were the differences between the literary language of the fourteenth century and
the colloquial speech of the times, we do not know; but
from the intermittent lapses into colloquial usage—of which
even the best of the clerks were occasionally guilty—we
can infer that the sonorous inflections of earlier days had
largely passed out of use. This is corroborated by the
statements from Professors Munch, Larsen, Falk and Torp
cited in Chapter XIV.

Other linguistic objections have been examples of pal-
pable error on the part of the critics, such as when one
writer claims that *æptir* was never used as a conjunctive
adverb, or when another declares that the letter *d* was
never expressed by the thorn (þ).

One very interesting objection which has often been
advanced is that the words *fråm, mans, þeþ, of (west)* and
illy are English words. These words have proved to be
archaic Old Swedish words of unquestionable autochthony
which in the fourteenth century still lingered sporadically
in the speech of the people.

On the whole, the inscription with its many omissions
of subject, its numerous faulty spellings, its colloquialisms,
and its archaic vocabulary seems to be in close harmony
with fourteenth century colloquial usage. Indeed, many of
its criticized word forms could be cited as positive indication of the authenticity of the inscription by reason of
the fact that their rare occurrence in literary remains of
the fourteenth century makes their use by a forger highly
improbable.

When we examine the runic objections, we find the
same lack of evidence to sustain them. The runic numerals,
which in the early years of the discussion were severely
criticized as an invention of the runic scribe, were later
proved to have been in widespread use in the fourteenth
century. The inscription shows practically no agreement
with the Dalecarlian inscriptions of the seventeenth and
eighteenth centuries such as one writer has attempted to

prove. It agrees in all but a few characters with the runic alphabet of the Scanian Law of about 1275. The presence of these divergent forms does not agree with the theory that the inscription was written in modern times, for in such case a forger would borrow his symbols from books, and his runes would all be correct. Such divergent forms are easily accounted for, however, if we assume that the inscription is genuine, because a lapse of memory as to particular forms would be natural in travelers who had not seen runic forms for at least seven years of travel (1355-1362). This supposition is strongly supported by the peculiar types of the Latin alphabet that have been used in place of the true runes. These types are all such forms of the Latin alphabet as were in use in the fourteenth century and are quite different from their modern equivalents. As very little paleographic facsimile material illustrating these forms was published before the end of the nineteenth century, this shows that the theory of a forgery is improbable.

The historical objections have likewise been proved to be untenable. The date—1362—at first considered an erratic plunge into a misty past, has been eminently justified, inasmuch as many recent historians are agreed that a Norse expedition appears to have spent the nine years from 1355 to 1364 in western waters. The mixed personnel—"8 Goths and 22 Norwegians"—whose bi-national character for a long time was considered an absurdity, has also been proved to be in exact harmony with what would be expected in the expedition of 1355-1364, due to the peculiar political position of King Magnus, who commissioned it.

At first sight it seems strange that such an expedition should have been fitted out so soon after the Black Plague. But for King Magnus this was an exceptionally opportune time. As shown in Chapter IX, the King was at this time in possession of a large fund, provided by the Pope for carrying on the holy crusade against the Russian heretics. This (last) campaign against Russia failed to be carried out. The possession of this fund for the work of the Church therefore enabled King Magnus to carry out his plans to safeguard Christianity in Greenland and to restore its apostates to the faith.

2. THE THEORY OF A FORGERY IS HIGHLY IMPROBABLE.

Even if we admit the remote possibility that among the earliest pioneers in Minnesota, or before their time, there was a scholar with the abstruse knowledge necessary to fabricate a runic inscription of this length, there are several considerations which make it extremely improbable that this inscription is his product. Let us review a few of these improbabilities. One is the *place* in which the stone was found. Any conceivable forger would naturally plan to have his creation come to the attention of the public; otherwise there would be no motive in making it. He would therefore place the stone in a spot where it would be most likely to be discovered. But the stone was not found in any such place. It was found in a wilderness of marshes and precipitous timbered knolls which gave no promise of ever being settled. The early settlers were all of this opinion, and for twenty years this tract of land was used as a community woodlot. Even now after all the land has been taken up, there are still patches of timber on those steep hillsides which presumably will never be cleared. Thus it was only by an accident that the stone was found near the top of a steep hill on the edge of a swamp.

Secondly, it is highly improbable that a forger would use such an obscure unit of distance as "day's-journey" in the meaning of 75 English miles. One might say impossible, for the ancient meaning of this term was not elucidated by expert research until fifteen or twenty years after the stone was found (see Chapter XVII). But even if this suppositious learned forger had been able to dig this meaning out of old records, there would be nothing to gain and much to lose by using a term which would in all eventuality convey an entirely misleading meaning to the people whom he planned to deceive.

The improbability of a modern fabrication is greatly increased by the fact that it is almost impossible to think of anyone who could have perpetrated it. Considered as a modern product, this lengthy inscription written in the difficult and little understood language and runic symbols of the fourteenth century is a literary marvel, a philological work of art, which it would be very difficult for any philologist of today to equal. Where could such erudition be found among the early pioneer Scandinavians of America? The only person against whom suspicion has been directed was Sven Fogelblad. But aside from other disqualifications, he will not answer as a forger, inasmuch as he did not come to the vicinity of Kensington until 1885-1890. The stone was found by Mr. Ohman directly in front of Nils Flaten's house and in plain view of it. As we have an affidavit from Mr. Flaten that he has continuously occupied this house since the spring of 1884, without having ever observed any suspicious activities about, Mr. Fogelblad and his imaginary lore appears too late upon the scene to play the part ascribed to him.

As the stone could not have been carved while Mr. Flaten's house was occupied, the alleged forgery must have been made before 1884. This brings us back to the early pioneers of the region, the very first of whom came in 1864. All these pioneers are well known and wholly above suspicion. Going back beyond them we reach the not distant period when this region was the hunting ground of the Sioux Indians, and the field of possibilities shrinks to the vanishing point.

Finally there is an improbability which grows bigger, the more one looks at it. This improbability is concerned with the entire lack of motive for any such forgery. Crimes and deceptions are motivated by greed, lust, revenge and kindred impulses, but what could have been a sufficient motive to prompt a learned scholar to go far out into the wilderness and there sit for days, chiseling on a stone that would bring him neither honor nor riches, all the time exposed to hardships and probable death at the hands of savage Indians? It is true that archeological frauds are not infrequent, but they are usually copies of ancient artifacts that have a recognized commercial value. Occasionally a more novel and ambitious fraud appears, like the Cardiff Giant, but such forgeries are always the work of clumsy amateurs whose hope of gain is the most noticeable feature of their performance. But whoever was the author of this long and circumstantial inscription, he was certainly not a *clumsy* forger, for his work has withstood the criticism of keen scholars for more than forty years. Nor is it conceivable how its assumed author could have profited by it. Such a hope would demand the energetic assistance of a fellow conspirator, presumably the finder, on whom the burden of publicity would rest. But Mr. Ohman, the finder, proved to be an exceptionally stolid individual, and neither he nor anyone else around Kensington has endeavored to exploit the stone.

3. External evidence shows that the theory of a forgery is impossible.

These improbabilities are fully vindicated when we consider the circumstances of the finding of the stone. The stone was found gripped between the largest roots of a tree in such manner that it must have lain in its finding place at least as long as the tree had stood there. In Chapter XI it is shown that this tree was about seventy years old. Seventy years anterior to 1898, when the stone was found, brings us back to 1828, which is more than twenty years before Minnesota was settled by white people and thirty-six years before the first Scandinavian reached Douglas County, where the stone was found. The earliest Scandinavians did not penetrate as far west as Chicago until 1834. If there were no Swedes or Norwegians in the Northwest at that early date (1828), the theory of a forgery is manifestly impossible.

This conclusion is fully substantiated by the testimony of geologists cited in Chapter XII. As the stone lay with its inscribed face down at least as long as the tree grew above it, it could not have been subject to any appreciable weathering influences after 1828. Yet geologists estimate that the inscription has been subject to at least a hundred years of weathering. This weathering must have taken place before the stone was covered by soil. The hundred years of previous weathering therefore brings us back to 1728 as the latest possible date when the stone could have been inscribed.

In addition to his testimony on the age of the weathering, Professor Winchell, who for thirty years was State Geologist of Minnesota, declares that the physiographic changes, which the region around Kensington has experienced, preclude the possibility that the inscription was written by a forger.

4. A NUMBER OF SCANDINAVIAN ARMS AND IMPLEMENTS OF THE MIDDLE AGES UNEARTHED IN WESTERN MINNESOTA INDICATE THAT THIS REGION WAS VISITED BY NORSE EXPLORERS SEVERAL HUNDRED YEARS AGO.

Turning from the stone and the circumstances of its discovery, there are a number of other antiquarian finds which indicate that western Minnesota was visited by Norse explorers about the time of the date in the inscription (see Chapter XIX). There is the battle-axe found on a point of land projecting into Norway Lake, twelve miles south of Brooten. This battle-axe is of such strange design that the finder, a practical farmer, did not recognize it as an axe. There are the two heavy, club-like battle-axes found near Kensington, one of which was found underneath the stump of a huge tree which must have been several hundred years old. There is the fire-steel found near Climax by the first settler in the vicinity, in unplowed soil, in a layer of charcoal, two feet down in the ground. There is the ancient hatchet of marked fourteenth century characteristics found near Thief River Falls, Minn., and the steel spearhead found near Whitehall, Wis., during the first plowing of a field just cleared from its ancient growth of timber. According to the statements of curators of European museums in which similar types are found, all these four axes are typical of the Scandinavian Middle Ages and similar expert testimony is also at hand about the other two finds.

These and other arms and implements must either have been brought in by the white settlers after that part of the Northwest was opened for settlement, or they must have been brought in by the people to whose time they belong—that is, by the men that left the Kensington inscription. In Chapter XIX a number of reasons have been presented showing-that they could not have been brought in by the pioneers of the nineteenth century. The chief of these reasons is that most of these ancient weapons have been found deep in the soil, beneath growing trees, by the first settlers in their respective localities. These finds therefore each bear independent witness of the presence of white men in these parts, long before Minnesota was settled.

These implements are all, in minute detail, the same as are known to have been in use in the Scandinavian countries in the fourteenth century. They are all specimens of such equipment as these explorers of 1362 would have reason to believe they would need on their journey. They have been found in just that part of America said to have been visited by these explorers. Finally no such articles have been reported found elsewhere on the continent. These four facts seem to present indisputable evidence that Minnesota was visited by Scandinavian explorers in the Middle Ages.

5. THE MOORING STONES AND OTHER CORROBORATIVE EVIDENCE.

Besides these eight remarkable finds there are certain other collateral evidences which point in the same direction. There are first of all the skerries mentioned in the inscription as a topographical identification mark to show the location of the place of massacre. When after many years of bewilderment, it was found that the obscure term "day's-journey" was used as a unit of distance equal to approximately 75 English miles, these skerries were quickly found in the place indicated, and the precise site of the fateful camp is probably circumscribed within a few acres.

Immediately below this campsite, where would be the most natural place for the explorers to moor their boat or raft, is found a large boulder with a hole drilled into it seven inches deep (see Chapter XVIII). This hole was drilled into the boulder before the first settlers came, because it showed even then a weathered appearance. The Indians who preceded them could not have bored such a hole, for they had no tools which would enable them to drill a deep hole in a granite boulder. This hole provides a facility for mooring purposes exactly similar to the method used along the rocky shore of Norway and Sweden from time immemorial. Its presence in this particular spot therefore seems to be corroborative evidence of the presence of the Kensington explorers who, according to the inscription, here went out on the lake to fish. Four similar mooring stones have been found along the probable route marking the campsites of the explorers.

Perhaps the most significant confirmation of the inscription is the perfect agreement which it shows with all that is known of the royal expedition sent to American waters in 1355. In Chapter XIII a parallel has been traced, showing that the two expeditions agree in all particulars such as the time of their departure and time of return to Norway, and also in their personnel, purpose and probable route of their journey while in America. The writer of the inscription must therefore have known all about the Paul Knutson expedition either by reading about it or through personal contact with it. However, in 1828 when this inscribed stone was lying in its finding place covered by soil and the little seedling was beginning to wrap its

roots about it, not a word had been published about Paul
Knutson and his expedition. It was not until 1887 that
Professor Storm saw in it an allusion to a possible explora-
tion of America.

Finally we have the record of the inscribed stone found
by the La Verendrye expedition (see Chapter XX), on
its journey to the Mandans in central North Dakota in
1738. This stone is now lost, but there is strong reason to
believe that it was another runic inscription. It could not
have been an Indian pictograph, for the French explorers
must have seen scores of such tracings in their extensive
travels. It is stated that the scholars in Quebec thought it
was a Tatarian inscription. This means that it looked like
a runic inscription, for Tatarian and runic inscriptions
have a remarkable superficial likeness, and these scholars
presumably were unable to read either. This probability is
supported by what is said about its finding place. It was
found in the top of a stone "like a pillar." It is known that
runic inscriptions were sometimes placed in exactly such
positions. For instance, the Kingiktorsuak inscription found
in 1823 on the west coast of Greenland near the 73rd
parallel, was also found in the top of a pile of stones like
a pillar.

In the absence of tenable arguments against the authenticity of the inscription, and in view of the preponderance
of evidence in its favor, only one conclusion seems possible: That the Kensington rune stone is a genuine record
left by Norse explorers in Minnesota about 1362.

This runic inscription is perhaps the most important that
has ever come to the attention of man. It is the only legible
runic inscription found in America. It belongs to a period
almost devoid of runic monuments, and is a valuable addition to runic literature. Of particular importance is the
fact, demonstrated by this inscription, that Leif Erikson's
discovery of America in the beginning of the eleventh
century was not an isolated incident without historical
sequence, but was known and followed by other expedi-

tions to America for almost 400 years afterward. Furthermore, it possesses great individual interest in that it tells of one of the greatest exploring trips in the world's history, a great enterprise undertaken with daring and carried out with a tragic dénouement.

Finally it has a priceless significance in that it is the oldest native document of American history written by white men.

It is to be hoped that funds will soon be provided to make possible a thorough search for the remains of the ten men who were killed at Cormorant Lake, and that a fitting monument may be erected over the grave of these first white martyrs of the West.

XXII. THE END OF THE TRAIL

AMONG the readers who have followed this discussion so far there may be some who feel that the authenticity of the Kensington inscription has been vindicated by the preponderance of arguments in its favor. If this be so it may be of interest and perhaps of importance to try to answer a question which is very often asked: What became of the survivors?

Before attempting to answer this question it should be emphasized that what follows is not presented as evidence in support of the authenticity of the inscription. The writer believes that this authenticity has been sufficiently demonstrated in the preceding chapters. But the material discussed in this chapter is of such peculiar significance, that if it is correctly interpreted, it not only answers the question of what became of the survivors, but also explains a most interesting and puzzling question in Indian ethnology.

The inscription states that there were thirty members of this expedition into the western interior of the continent. It is almost certain that these men never reached their headquarters in Vinland; for not only is it highly improbable that they would be able to traverse in safety the fifteen hundred miles of wilderness which separated them from the Atlantic coast, but no reference to their adventures is found in existing records, although these indicate that a part of the original expedition returned to Norway in 1364. The probability is therefore that these thirty men were either killed by the Indians or captured and adopted by them. If the latter was the case, it is not unlikely that they, because of their superior intelligence and ability, would rise to positions of importance in the tribe and leave some evidence of their presence and influence behind them. Now it happens that in this very part of America there was until recent times a tribe of mixed white and Indian origin of such superior civilization and peaceful disposition that it seemed like an oasis of comfort and gentleness in a desert of savage and warring Indians. These strange and pleasing people were the Mandan Indians, who occupied stationary villages on the upper Missouri in central North Dakota.

The Mandans are probably the greatest ethnological enigma in the study of the North American Indians. Unlike other Indian tribes in their region who were nomadic hunters, the Mandans lived in large and well fortified towns in roomy dwellings of relatively permanent construction and subsisted largely by agriculture. They were a peaceable people with much skill in domestic arts. Most remarkable of all is the fact that they were of mixed origin, many individuals among them being almost white in color. They are reported as showing many physiognomies unlike the typical Indian features, and individuals with blue eyes and fair hair were not uncommon among them. Finally their traditions, customs and religious beliefs showed influences of a different sort from those found among other northern Indians. All travelers who have visited the Mandans are unanimous in describing them as the most intelligent, well mannered and hospitable of all the tribes of the North.

The widespread reports of the advanced culture of the Mandans and their strange physical characteristics early caused many travelers of both high and low degree to visit them.[1] Captain Pierre la Verendrye, the first Frenchman

[1] Many of these travelers have left records of their observations which all in the main agree concerning the points mentioned in the preceding paragraph. The most important are Pierre la Verendrye's *Journal* (1738) printed in *South Dakota His. Colls.*, VII, 340 ff. This *Journal* is also printed in Margry, *Découvertes et Etablissements des Francais*, VI, 585-595. McIntosh *Report* (1773) to the U. S. Indian Bureau summarized in Schoolcraft's *History, Condition and Prospects*, III, 253-254. *The*

known to have penetrated into the region west of the upper Mississippi in Minnesota, was the first of these. In 1732, after pushing hundreds of miles beyond the farthest earlier advance, he built a fort on the west side of Lake of the Woods. During the following years, in which he was preparing to seek a way to the Pacific, he heard from the Indians many strange tales of a people farther west who were said not to be Indian but white people and French like himself. In 1738 he therefore set out on a journey several hundred miles to the southwest to visit these people. He found the Mandans, comfortably settled in six large villages on the Missouri some distance southwest of the present city of Minot, N. D. His hope of meeting countrymen was quickly dispelled when he arrived in the first village, but he was nevertheless deeply impressed with the fact that he had here reached a tribe very different from those he had previously seen in his lifetime among the Indians. The following is a part of his description of this Mandan village.

M. de la Marque and I walked about to observe the size of their fort and their fortifications. I decided to have the huts counted. It was found that there were 130 of them. All the streets, squares and huts resembled each other. Several of our Frenchmen wandered about; they found the streets and squares very clean, the ramparts very level and broad; the palisades supported on cross-pieces morticed into posts of fifteen feet to twice fifteen feet. There are green skins which are put for sheathing where required, fastened only above in the places needed, as in the bastion there are four at each curtain well flanked. The fort is built on a height in the open prairie with a ditch upwards of fifteen feet deep by fifteen or eighteen feet

Manuscript Journal of Alexander Henry (1806), Elliott Coué's edition, I, 322-343, 363-366. George Catlin's *North American Indians* (1841), I, 79-184; II, appendix A. Maximilian, Prince of Wied-Neuwied, *Voyage en l'Amérique du Nord* (1834), translated and reprinted in *Early Western Travels*, XXIII, 252-367; XXIV, 11-84. Will and Spinden, *The Mandans*, in *Papers of the Peabody Museum*, III, 85-219.

wide.[2] Their fort can only be gained by steps or posts which can be removed when threatened by an enemy. If all their forts are alike, they may be called impregnable to Indians. Their fortifications are not Indian. This nation is mixed white and black. The women are fairly good-looking, especially the white, many with blond and fair hair. Both men and women of this nation are very laborious; their huts are large and spacious, separated into several apartments by thick planks; nothing is left lying about; all their baggage is in large bags hung on posts; their beds made like tombs surrounded by skins. . . . Their fort is full of caves [caches] in which are stored such articles as grain, food, fat, dressed robes, bear skins. They are well supplied with these; it is the money of the country. . . . The men are stout and tall, generally very active, fairly good-looking, with a good physiognomy. The women have not the Indian physiognomy. The men indulge in a sort of ball play on the squares and ramparts.[3]

Unlike the ordinary Indians who take but little thought for tomorrow, the Mandans were good providers who had large stores of "wheat," corn and other foodstuffs stored away. When La Verendrye came there he was accompanied by a large number of Assiniboines, but this horde of greedy visitors did not seriously threaten the commissariat of the Mandans. They kept on serving feasts without end. La Verendrye says "they brought me every day more than twenty dishes of wheat, beans and pumpkins, all cooked." This, together with the fact that their villages were of a permanent nature, shows that they were an agricultural people in a far broader sense than other northern Indians.

[2] La Verendrye's remarks about the ramparts, bastions and wide ditches are verified by Will and Spinden's excavations, see *op. cit.*, p. 151. See also Bougainville, *Northern and Western Boundaries of Ontario*, p. 83.
[3] From La Verendrye's *Journal*, Brymner's translation in *Report on Canadian Archives*, Ottawa, 1889, 1890, p. 3 ff. See also *South Dakota His. Colls.* VII, 340, 341. O. G. Libby is of the opinion that La Verendrye visited the Minnitarie (Hidatsa), but his evidence seems purely hypothetical. See *North Dakota His. Colls.* II, 502-505.

Unfortunately Verendrye lost his interpreter the day after he arrived among the Mandans. He was therefore unable to converse with these strange people and missed a unique opportunity of learning something about their history, traditions and beliefs.

Verendrye's description of the Mandans, brief as it is, is of the greatest importance because he was undoubtedly the first white man to visit the Dakota region in post-Columbian times. The pronounced blond characteristics and advanced civilization of the Mandans could not therefore have been the result of intercourse with white fur-traders. Nor does he appear to have exaggerated these peculiarities for they are amply confirmed by later visitors and by archeological research.

During the half century after Verendrye's visit, the Mandans were presumably visited by occasional *coureurs des bois*, just as these adventurers found their way to all other tribes. But it was not until some time after 1784 that any trading post was established among them. In that year the Northwest Fur Company was organized and a few years later it established a trading post near the Mandans. Yet even before this time reports of the unusual physical characteristics, culture and Christian traditions of the Mandans reached the Atlantic coast. In the *Pennsylvania Packet and Daily Advertiser* of August 24, 1784, appears the following item:

Letters from Boston mention that a new nation of white people has been discovered about 2,000 miles beyond the Appalachian Mountains. They are said to be acquainted with the principles of the Christian religion and to be exceedingly courteous and civilized. This account was brought by the Indians to Boston, and concurs with others which were reported by two French missionaries at Montreal last year.

With proper allowance for the exaggerations that accrue to such verbal reports, there can be no doubt that this refers to the Mandans. They were the only tribe in the West remarkable for their light complexion, and they lived about 2,000 miles beyond the Appalachian Mountains as measured by the usual river route down the Ohio and up the Missouri. Here the interesting item is added that they were acquainted with the Christian religion. Verendrye learned nothing about the traditions or beliefs of the Mandans because he had lost his interpreter.

In 1806 Alexander Henry, a well known fur-trader, was persuaded to make a journey of several hundred miles to satisfy his curiosity about these strange Indians. In the meantime all the other tribes of that region had made a coalition against the Mandans and had captured and destroyed all their well built towns. The surviving Mandans had retreated a few miles below Knife River when Henry visited them. He also mentions their blond characteristics and gives many details concerning their well built houses.[4]

In 1832-1834 the Mandans were visited by two eminent observers who did much to retrieve for us the information about the Mandans which was lost to La Verendrye one hundred years earlier by the disappearance of his interpreter. These explorers were George Catlin who in 1832 spent several months in the Mandan village, and A. P. Maximilian, Prince of Wied-Neuwied, who spent the winter of 1833-1834 in Fort Clark a few hundred feet away. Mr. Catlin in particular has rendered unsurpassed service with his pen and brush in preserving the memory of the early Indians in the days when their life and character were still largely uncontaminated by the white man's whiskey and guile. In 1832 the Mandans were still living their primitive life hundreds of miles beyond the western frontier. But he found there in the central North Dakota wilderness a people of such excellent virtues and advanced

[4] *The Manuscript Journal of Alexander Henry.* Coué's edition, pp. 340-341. In 1804 Lewis and Clark on their expedition to the Pacific wintered near the Mandans but they do not say much of importance about them. But some years later when George Catlin was on his way to visit the Mandans, Captain (then Governor) Clark told him he would find a nation "half white." See Catlin, *op. cit.,* I, 93.

civilization that he always refers to them in such compli-
mentary terms as "the hospitable and gentlemanly Mandans." La Verendrye's brief description of them (which
Catlin evidently knew nothing about) is confirmed except
in certain details. They were not so extensively engaged
in agriculture as in earlier days and their fortifications were
merely a picket fence of poles set near but not close together without any "broad and level ramparts" as mentioned by La Verendrye. When the latter visited them he
found the villages surrounded by a deep and wide ditch
(15' x 18') *outside* the palisades after the civilized mode of
fortifications. Catlin found this ditch *inside* the palisades
and only three or four feet wide and deep. Here we see
the European moat of the Middle Ages, conceived as an
obstacle to the storming of the fortress by the enemy outside, give place to the Indian preference for a small ditch
inside from which he could shoot his arrows between the
pickets. This inferior mode of fortification and the de-
crease in agriculture show two significant steps backward
toward barbarism.

Mr. Catlin has given a voluminous and picturesque account of nearly all phases of community life among the
Mandans verified by statements from resident agents of the
large fur companies. This, together with his invaluable
pictures drawn or painted on the spot, make up a splendid
memorial of this interesting tribe, now gone forever. Of
their physical and mental characteristics he tells the following:

The Mandans are certainly a very interesting and pleasing
people in their personal appearance and manners, differing in
many respects, both in looks and customs, from all other tribes
which I have seen. . . . I have been struck with the peculiar
ease and elegance of these people, together with the diversity
of complexions, the various colours of their hair and eyes; the
singularity of their language, and their peculiar and unaccount-
able customs, that I am fully convinced that they have sprung
from some other origin than that of other North American

tribes, or that they are an amalgam of natives with some civilized race. . . .

A stranger in the Mandan village is at first struck with the different shades of complexions, and various colours of hair which he sees in a crowd about him; and is at once almost disposed to exclaim that "these are not Indians."

FIG. 16. MANDAN WOMEN SHOWING NORDIC PHYSIOGNOMIES
Drawn from life by Catlin (*North American Indian*, I, Figs. 52, 53).

There are a great many of these people whose complexions appear as light as half breeds; and amongst the women particularly, there are many whose skins are almost white, with the most pleasing symmetry and proportion of features; with hazel, with grey, and with blue eyes—with mildness and sweetness of expression, and excessive modesty of demeanor, which render them exceedingly pleasing and beautiful. . . .

The diversity in the colour of the hair is also equally as great as that in the complexion; for in a numerous group of these people there may be seen every shade and colour of hair that can be seen in our own country, with the exception of red or auburn, which is not to be found. . . .

The reader will at once see, by the above facts, that there

is enough upon the faces and heads of these people to stamp them peculiar—when he meets them in the heart of this almost boundless wilderness, presenting such diversities of colour in the complexion and hair; when he knows from what he has seen, and what he has read, that all other primitive tribes known in America, are dark and copper-coloured, with jet black hair.[5]

Maximilian in commenting on the complexions of the Mandans says: "After a thorough ablution the skin of some of them appears almost white, and even some color in their cheeks." He also says that the noses of the Mandans were "less aquiline" than those of other Indians and "they have less prominent cheek bones." [6]

It is not only in personal characteristics that the Mandans show indications of an ancient mixture with white people, but also in their traditions. In the main the religious traditions and superstitions of the Mandans were the same as those of other Indian tribes, but blended with these are many legends which reflect a contact with white people and Christian beliefs. Like other tribes they had traditions of an early culture hero, but unlike other tribes they represented this early ancestor as being a *white man* who had come from the west in a big canoe. This tradition loomed so big in their myths that a symbolical representation of this *big canoe* had a permanent place in the middle of the public square of the village where it stood as a sacred memorial of the greatest event in their past. Other Indian tribes in the vicinity, like the Minnitaries, copied the mode of life of the Mandans in nearly all particulars, but they had no sacred canoe nor any tradition of a *white* ancestor. To this early white ancestor of the Mandans was also attributed the introduction of several important religious

[5] *North American Indians*, I, 93, 94. In his later work *O-Kee-Pa, A Religious Ceremony* (Phila., 1867), Catlin emphasizes the blond characteristics of the Mandans, and says that "one-fifth or one-sixth of the Mandans were nearly white and had light blue eyes," p. 5.
[6] *Early Western Travels*, XXIII, 255, 258.

practices which distinguished the Mandans from other tribes. This tradition was in Catlin's time still so vivid that each year was enacted the arrival of this mysterious and powerful white man who likewise in the annual festival is represented as instructing their medicine men in their religious practices. Many other traditions embodying a more or less confused memory of Christian beliefs also indicate that the Mandans at some remote time in the past have been in touch with white people of Christian practices. Among these are strange stories of the virgin giving birth to a child who later became a savior of the people; his miracles and particularly his feeding the multitude with a small amount of food, leaving fragments of food in as great a quantity as when the feeding began; his persecutions and untimely death at the hands of his enemies; a personal devil, the transgression of Mother Eve, and biblical details of the story of the Deluge. While most Indian tribes in their creation myths have a distorted account of a vast flood which covered all things *before* the earth was created, only the Mandans have any tradition of a later flood which is similar to the account in the Book of Genesis. According to the Mandan tradition, a dove was sent out from the ark to search for dry land when the water began to subside; after a time it returned with a green twig of willow in its beak. This is just like the account in the Book of Genesis except that there the dove returns with an olive leaf. As the olive was unknown in the Mandan country, popular rendering of the story has substituted a twig of willow.

The following is Mr. Catlin's account of some of these traditions.

It would seem from their tradition of the willow branch, and the dove, that these people must have had some proximity to some part of the civilized world; or that missionaries or others have formerly been among them, inculcating the Christian religion and the Mosaic account of the Flood; which is, in this and some other respects, decidedly different from the theory which most natural people have distinctly established of that event.

There are other strong, and almost decisive proofs in my opinion, in support of the assertion, which are to be drawn from the diversity of colour in their hair and complexions, as I have before described, as well as from their tradition just related, of the "*first or only man,*" whose body was white, and who came from the west, telling them of the destruction of the earth by water, and instructing them in the forms of these mysteries; and in addition to the above, I will add the two following very curious stories, which I have from several of their old and dignified chiefs, and which are, no doubt, standing and credited traditions of the tribe.

(The first tradition tells that the Mandans originally lived inside of the earth and that a few of them managed to come to the surface by climbing up a vine. As this tradition is too obscure, it is here omitted.)

The next tradition runs thus:

At a very ancient period, O-Kee-hee-de (the Evil Spirit mentioned in the religious ceremonies) came to the Mandan village with Nu-mohk-muck-a-nah (the first white man) from the West, and sat down by a woman who had but one eye and was hoeing corn. Her daughter, who was very pretty, came up to her, and the Evil Spirit desired her to go and bring some water; but wished that before she started, she would come to him and eat some buffalo meat. He told her to take a piece out of his side, which she did and ate it, which proved to be buffalo-fat. She then went for the water, which she brought, and met them in the village where they walked, and they both drank of it—nothing more was done.

The friends of the girl soon after endeavored to disgrace her, by telling her she was *enciente,* which she did not deny. She declared her innocence at the same time, and boldly defied any man in the village to come forward and accuse her. This raised a great excitement in the village, and as no one could stand forth to accuse her, she was looked upon as *great medicine.* She soon after went off secretly to the upper Mandan village, where the child was born.

Great search was made for her before she was found; as it was expected the child would also be *great medicine* or mystery and of great importance to the existence and welfare of the tribe. They were induced to this belief from the very strange manner of its conception and birth, and were soon confirmed in it from the wonderful things which it did at an early age. They say, that amongst other miracles which he performed, when the Mandans were like to starve, he gave them four buffalo bulls, which filled the whole village—leaving as much meat as there was before they had eaten.[7] Nu-mohk-muck-a-nah (the first or only man) was bent on the destruction of the Child, and after making many fruitless searches for it, found it hidden in a dark place, and put it to death by throwing it in the river.

Such are a few of the principal traditions of these people, which I have thought proper to give in this place, and I have given them in their own way, with all the imperfections and absurd inconsistencies which should be expected to characterize the history of all ignorant and superstitious people who live in a state of simple and untaught nature, with no other means of perpetuating historical events, than by oral traditions.[8]

Maximilian's record of Mandan traditions are much the same as Catlin's with now and then some variations. In his account the reminiscences of Christian teachings also seem quite marked. Although Maximilian is a more cautious and matter-of-fact commentator than Catlin, he says: "Some of

[7] In the Mandan tradition this feeding of the multitude is done by buffalo meat instead of bread and fish. Buffalo meat, according to Catlin and Maximilian, was to the Mandans the principal staple of food. It is quite what would be expected, that if they had heard of the miracles of Jesus, this miracle of the feeding of the multitude would be the one which would make the greatest impression upon them, for such was also the case in Judea where it first was told. This miracle is thus the only one which is related by all four of the gospel writers.

[8] Catlin, I, 177-182. Catlin's veracity of observation and narration has been attested to by many persons who had spent much time among the Mandans, such as Prince Maximilian, Lewis Cass the explorer and later Secretary of State, several Indian agents and others. See *Report of Smithsonian Institution* (1873), pp. 436-438, and Catlin's *O-Kee-Pa*, pp. 47-51.

their [the Mandans'] traditions have a resemblance to revelations in the Bible, for instance, Noah's Ark and the Deluge, the history of Samson, etc. It seems highly probable that these particulars have been introduced among them from their intercourse with Christians." [9]

Catlin concludes his survey of characteristics and customs of the Mandans with the following words: "From these very numerous and striking peculiarities in their personal appearance—their customs—traditions and language, I have been led conclusively to believe that they are a people of decidedly different origin from that of any other tribe in these regions." With this opinion the reader will no doubt fully agree.

In the appendix to his second volume Mr. Catlin reverted to this subject again. After reaffirming his convictions that the Mandans were of a mixed white and Indian stock, he presents a theory concerning their origin. He suggests that the Mandans are half-breed descendants of the colonists of Madoc, a Welsh prince, who, as John Fiske says, "was dimly imagined to have sailed to America about 1170." Unfortunately for this theory, the Madoc story is pure legend without a shred of historical proof. Moreover, even if Madoc and his Welshmen had sailed to America and penetrated to the interior, they could not very well have left a blue-eyed progeny, seeing the Welsh are principally brown-eyed. This theory need not therefore detain us.[10]

Inasmuch as all the early explorers and travelers who visited the Mandans—that is, La Verendrye, McIntosh, Clark. Henry, Mitchell, Catlin and Prince Maximilian and certain unnamed missionaries (see *ante*, p. 267)—are agreed that the Mandans showed evidence of being of mixed white and Indian origin, this fact seems to be proven. These early white ancestors must have been Christians as

[9] *Early Western Travels*, XXIII, 300.
[10] For a bibliography on the Welsh emigration see Justin Winsor, *Narrative and Critical History of America*, I, 109-111.

shown by the survival of such Christian doctrines as the miracle-working child of the virgin, the biblical details of the tradition concerning the Deluge, the Mandans' belief in a personal devil "who once appeared among them but has not since been seen." Their near neighbors and imitators, the Minnitaries, knew nothing of any such Old Testament devil but had only the vague fear of evil spirits common to all Indian tribes.[11] The same medieval Christian attitude is also reflected in the Mandans' annual practice of self-mutilation for the purpose of pleasing the Great Spirit, which seems decidedly reminiscent of the flagellant practices which came into vogue in Europe in 1350 right after the Black Plague. Finally, these white ancestors must have been of the Nordic race as is shown by their fair-haired descendants, many of whom had "hazel, gray and blue eyes."

These white progenitors of the Mandans could not have been adventurers from among the early colonists of the New England states for several reasons. Although our colonial history is well known, there is no hint of any group of these early colonists thus wandering off into the wilderness away from their old associates. Moreover, the fifteen hundred miles of wilderness, teeming with warlike Indians, that they would have to cross to reach the country of the Mandans, make such a suggestion extremely improbable. Finally, this amalgamation between whites and Indians which produced the Mandans must have occurred in a much more remote period than the beginning of the seventeenth century, seeing the Mandans had lost all definite traditions of its occurrence as to time and placed the event at the end of the Deluge.

We must therefore seek this advance guard of missionaries to America among the Nordic groups in Europe. This limits our field to the Germans, the Dutch, the English and the Scandinavians. As we know of no expedition

11 Maximilian in *Early Western Travels*, XXIII, 269, 302, 328, 329.

undertaken by the first three people, which could by any stretch of imagination have left survivors in the very center of the American continent, it is reasonably safe to say that these Mandan fathers were not English, Dutch or German. When we come to the Scandinavians, the situation is different. Not only did the Norsemen make many journeys to America at a sufficiently early time, but we know from the Kensington Stone that a large party of them reached this general vicinity in 1362. The *Handbook of American Indians* has the following to say concerning the earliest known habitat of the Mandans:

Their linguistic relations to the Winnebago and the fact that their movements in their historical era have been westward up the Missouri correspond with the traditions of a more easterly origin, and would seem to locate them in the vicinity of the Upper Lakes. It is possible that the traditions which have long prevailed in the region of N. W. Wisconsin regarding the so-called "ground-house Indians" who once lived in that section and dwelt in circular lodges, partly underground, applies to the people of this tribe. Assuming that the Mandan formerly resided in the vicinity of the upper Mississippi, it is probable that they moved down this stream for some distance before passing to the Missouri.[12]

Their meeting with the Norse explorers in this location would also explain the statement in their traditions that their culture hero, "the first white man," came from *the West*. The last we know of these explorers is that they were traveling eastward.

It therefore seems highly probable that the Mandans owe their culture and their blond characteristics to the survivors of the expedition mentioned on the Kensington Stone. This has already been suggested by Professor N. H. Winchell in his great work *The Aborigines of Minnesota*.[13]

Assuming for a moment that this theory is correct, we see how perfectly all connected circumstances fit into

[12] Published by the Smithsonian Institution, 1912; II, 797.
[13] N. H. Winchell, *The Aborigines of Minnesota*, p. 574, St. Paul, 1911.

place. The Swedes and Norwegians are of the purest Nordic stock and a relatively smaller number would therefore have been sufficient to transmit the physical peculiarities for which the Mandans were noted than if any other nationality had been represented by these early culture bearers. The Mandans' great veneration for their *big canoe* is also easily understood. In being asked where they came from, the Norsemen would naturally emphasize the fact that they had come in a ship, or big canoe, over the boundless ocean. The Mandans, being an inland people, would have difficulty in comprehending the vastness of the ocean and therefore eventually associated this narrative with their myth about the flood which was a legend current among all Indian tribes. Thus they came to believe that by means of this canoe their ancestor, the first white man, had survived the flood and therefore it became a holy thing to them.

There are also several other points of connection between these explorers and the Mandans. The fact that these early white strangers, whoever they might have been, were suffered to live and attained great influence in the tribe, as shown by the fact that they greatly changed the customs and mode of life of their Indian hosts, shows clearly that they must have been men of great tact, intelligence and force of character. These virtues no doubt characterized the members of Paul Knutson's expedition, for it was the King's command that the very best men were to be selected for it.

These early visitors must also have been very religious, seeing they managed to change the beliefs of the Mandans to such an extent that evidences of this change were abundant even when Catlin and Prince Maximilian visited them. This ardent religious attitude was no doubt uppermost in the minds of Paul Knutson and his men who were engaged in a great missionary enterprise when fate changed the course of their endeavor.

Then there is the singular style of house construction

which distinguished the Mandans from other tribes east
or west. The Mandan house is so different in its design and
construction from the bark houses of the East or the tent-
like tepees of the West, that it cannot be an outgrowth
of these types. It is of course possible that a tribe of Indians could develop a radically different type of habitation from that of other representatives of their race, but
it is not probable. Seeing this unique style of housebuild-
ing is found in a tribe which is known to have been
under the influence of early white visitors, it is more
probable that this new style of dwellings was introduced
by them.[14] It is reasonable to assume that these white men
would seek to improve the comforts of their new living
quarters as soon as possible. In this attempt they would
presumably seek to reproduce a modest copy of the general type of dwelling house they had previously been used
to occupy as far as the material and circumstances of their
new surroundings would permit. Was the Mandan house
in its construction and interior arrangement analogous to
the most common type of houses in the Scandinavian
countries in the Middle Ages?

The following is a condensed description of the Mandan
house as given by Catlin, Henry and Maximilian. It was
circular in form containing one room forty feet or more
in diameter. For the outside wall short posts or studdings
were set on end about ten feet apart. These posts were
joined by horizontal timbers placed on top and the spaces
between the posts were filled with lighter material. The
wall was thoroughly braced on the outside with oblique
timbers and a solid bank of earth. Within this enclosure
and about fifteen feet from it were erected four posts ten
feet apart and about fifteen feet high. These were joined

[14] When Catlin visited the Mandans he found that other tribes in the
neighborhood such as the Hidatsa (Gros Ventres), the Omaha and the
Arickarees had similar houses. These tribes evidently borrowed this style
of habitations from the Mandans; see Catlin, *North American Indians*,
II, 260, Maximilian, *op. cit.*, p. 435.

at the top by heavy joists. A close array of poles was laid from the top of the wall to the joists to serve as rafters. These rafters were covered with a thick mat of willow boughs. This was for the purpose of protecting the rafters from the dampness of the covering of earth which was placed on top of them about a foot or more thick and finished off on the outside with a layer of impervious clay. A hole was left at the apex of the roof about four feet wide for the emission of smoke and to admit light. Immediately below this opening was the fireplace, a shallow pit curbed with flat stones set on edge. Next to the wall were the beds about two feet high. "These beds," Catlin remarks, "are uniformly screened with a covering of buffalo or elk skins, oftentimes beautifully dressed and placed over the upright frame like a suit of curtains. Some of these curtains are exceedingly beautiful, being cut tastefully into fringe, and handsomely ornamented with porcupine quills and picture writing. . . . At the head of each bed stands a large post, about six or seven feet high, with large wooden pegs or bolts in it, on which are hung with a wild and startling taste the arms and armour of the respective proprietor; consisting of his whitened shield, embossed with the figure of his protecting *medicine*, his bow and quiver, his war club or battle-axe," etc.[15] On one side of the room was a fixed high seat or broad divan cushioned with willow twigs reserved for the master of the house where he received his visitors in state.[16]

In Sweden and Norway in the Middle Ages the dwellings of the farmers and rural gentry were generally rectangular structures of logs, but round houses covered with turf like those of the Mandans were not uncommon. The well-to-do usually had several buildings used for different purposes. Of these the *stofa* was the most important, and

[15] *North American Indians*, I, 81-83; L. H. Morgan in *Contributions to North American Ethnology*, VI, 126.

[16] Alexander Henry, *op. cit.*, pp. 339-340. Maximilian in *Early Western Travels*, XXIII, 269-271.

among common people was the only dwelling they possessed. It had two V-shaped gable ends joined by a straight
ridge pole. The sod roof was supported by two rows of
upright posts which were joined at the top by heavy joists.
From the low side walls a close array of rafters was laid

FIG. 17. INTERIOR OF A MANDAN HOUSE
From Catlin's *North American Indians*, I, Fig. 46. The buffalo heads in the
background are masks used in the Buffalo Dance.

across the above joists up to the ridge. On top of these
rafters was a covering of several layers of birch bark to
protect them from the dampness of the earth or turf which
was placed uppermost. There were no windows except
sometimes in the gable ends, but there was an opening in
the middle of the roof for the emission of smoke and to
admit light.[17] Immediately below this was the fireplace in
a shallow pit in the center of the floor. This pit had a
curbing of flat stones set on edge. Along the sides of the
room were the bedsteads, not moveable, some of them

[17] Gudmundsson, *Privatboligen paa Island*, etc., p. 165.

closed in with panels or curtains, some open.[18] These panels were often richly ornamented. Above each occupant's bed hung his arms and armor.[19] On one side of the room was a special high seat reserved for the head of the house.

This, very briefly, describes the most common Scandinavian house of the Middle Ages where timber was abundant and was probably the type which the survivors of the Paul Knutson expedition would try to construct in their new homes. As is shown above, the only important difference between the two types is that the Norse *stofa* had a V-shaped gable and a ridge pole while the Mandan roof terminated in an apex. Otherwise the frame work of the two is in all essentials so much alike that a sketch of a cross section of a Mandan house shown in Winchell's *Aborigines of Minnesota* [20] is practically the same as the cross section of a Norse house shown in Gudmundsson's *Privatboligen paa Island.*[21]

The construction of a house with a V-shaped gable on the prairies of North Dakota would, however, present a serious difficulty, due partly to the absence of straight and suitable timber, and partly to the absence of building tools. Under such circumstances it is probable that they would be satisfied with a humbler type of dwelling which was also much used in Norway. This was the round house covered with turf. On the islands along the seacoast in northern Norway where timber is scarce, this was in the Middle Ages the most common type of house. Pietro Quirini, an Italian sea-captain, was shipwrecked on the coast of northern Norway in 1432, and he has given us

[18] Williams, *Social Scandinavia in the Viking Age*, pp. 127-132; Dasent, *The Story of Burnt Njal*, pp. XXVI-XXX; Linne, *Skånska Resa*, pp. 36, 37; *Folkevennen*, X, 240; Gudmundsson, *Privatboligen paa Island*, pp. 222 ff.

[19] *Ibid.*, p. 224; Linne, *Skånska Resa*, p. 37.

[20] Page 387. The illustration is from L. H. Morgan's description of the Mandan house in *Contributions to North American Ethnology*, VI, 126.

[21] *Privatboligen paa Island*, p. 119.

a long and interesting account of life among these people.[22] In this account he says that all the dwellings on the island of Røst where he spent the winter were round wooden structures with an opening in the apex through which light was admitted. Such round houses covered with turf are also described by Dr. Gudmundsson[23] and Ivar Aasen[23] and were in all details practically identical with the Mandan house. About the only difference is that in one birchbark is used to protect the timber from dampness while in the other willow boughs are used. This difference is of course dependent on the material that was locally available. As to the interior arrangement, there is only the difference that the Mandans had almost no movable furniture, which no doubt was due to their lack of carpenter tools.

While it is impossible to say positively how and with whom the Mandan house originated, it can at least be said that there is nothing in its type of construction which militates against the theory of a Norse origin.

Summarizing the results of the above study, we have the following facts:

(1) The Mandans were partly descended from white people.

(2) These white people must have had blue eyes, fair hair, and were Christians.

(3) They had come from across the sea in a *big canoe*.

(4) The Mandan house in its structural type, detail of roof covering and material is radically different from the type of dwellings used by other American tribes but is very similar to Norse houses in the late Middle Ages.

(5) Near the Mandan village La Verendrye found a

[22] J. R. Forster, *Geschichte der Entdeckungen im Norden*, pp. 251 ff.; G. Storm, *Venetianerne paa Røst i 1432*, Det norske Geografiske Selskabs Aarbog, VIII, 37 ff.; Knut Gjerset, *History of the Norwegian People*, II, 55-60.

[23] Gudmundsson, *Privatboligen paa Island*, pp. 90 ff., 105-106; Ivar Aasen's *Ordbok*, article *Kyvetak;* see also Montelius, *Sveriges Historia*, I, 259-262.

stone containing an inscription which resembled a runic inscription.

(6) The Mandans at an early time had their habitat in Minnesota not far from the place where the Kensington Stone was found.

All these characteristics and peculiarities meet in the explorers who left the Kensington Stone. They were of the Nordic race with blue eyes and fair hair. They were Christians animated by a missionary spirit. They came across the sea in a "big canoe." In their home country such round houses with the same structural details and similar interior arrangement as the Mandans lived in were not uncommon. They were the only people who could have left an inscription "like a Tatarian inscription," i.e., a runic inscription. They were last heard from in Minnesota not far from the ancient habitat of the Mandans.

With this perfect alignment of cause and effect, it seems highly probable that these Norse explorers became the white ancestors of the Mandans. It may be objected that these explorers were too few in number to have effected so great a change in the Mandan tribe as is shown in the latter's physical characteristics, traditions and mode of life. But the Mandans at the time of this union may have been greatly decimated by war or pestilence. We know from French colonial history in America that the Indian tribes waged incessant war against each other until the more unfortunate tribes were exterminated.

Just how the white men came to amalgamate with these Indians we cannot say. Many dramatic situations may have been the cause of this union. Perhaps a remnant of the Mandan tribe was at the time fleeing from the attacks of their enemies, the Sioux, and met the Norsemen. Allied by misfortune they found it expedient to seek safety in a more sparsely settled region of the upper Missouri. Here they built up a most interesting community of semi-civilized half-breed Indians. Though small in numbers this community by reason of the intelligence and experience of their white leaders [24] were able to defend themselves so well against recurring attacks of their ancient enemies, that they eventually became a numerous people well entrenched in many fortified towns as was the case when they were visited by La Verendrye.

Catlin dwells at length on the veneration which the Mandans bestowed on their ceremonial "canoe" which had a place in the center of each village. This is the more remarkable because they had very little use for canoes—in fact, they had none at all, but used round crates of wicker work covered with hides in crossing the Missouri. But this "canoe" was their memorial to that beneficent white man (or men) who had come to them from across the sea in a "canoe," and by his teachings and leadership had lifted the tribe to a higher plane of life than was enjoyed by any other in their region. It represented the aspirations he had planted in the national consciousness through his wise counsels and creative ideas, and this aspiration had grown so big that it became a tribal renaissance which enabled them to grow in ethical stature long after he had passed away. This grateful memory supplies an adequate reason for that festival of many days which was annually held in his honor. Very few monuments to departed heroes have continued so long to stir the imagination of new generations.

By a strange coincidence, the memory of these same white men was also held in veneration in their home land by similar mementos (i.e., kayaks, see page 148). These kayaks were the only tokens that were brought back to tell of these men who had sacrificed their lives for the salvation of their fellow men. Being men of social distinction sent out by the King on a holy crusade, their loss was

[24] When Alexander Henry visited the Mandans in 1806 he likewise found that one of their principal chiefs was a man of an alien people—a Cheyenne Indian who had been taken prisoner by the Mandans and later honored with a chieftainship. See Coué's ed. of Alexander Henry's *Journal*, I, 332, note 52.

perhaps felt as a national calamity. Their unwavering devotion to their holy mission was justly considered eminently suited for emulation. For this reason these tokens were hung on the richly paneled walls of the two principal cathedrals, and each year, we may assume, masses were intoned for the souls of these men, for the kayaks continued to hold their place of honor for at least 150 years.

Thus it may have been that although Paul Knutson and his men failed to find the Greenland apostates whom they were seeking, they found here in the Middle West another people just as deserving of their good works. By the introduction of agriculture and the arts of peace, Christianity and its nobler ethics, they here laid the foundation for a prosperous community which for centuries seems to have lived happily. Perhaps, after all, their expedition was more successful than they had hoped.[25]

[25] Only five or six years after Catlin visited them practically the entire nation of the "kind and gentlemanly Mandans" was exterminated by a plague of smallpox. See Catlin's pathetic account of the tragedy and heroism of their last days in his *North American Indians*, II, 257-258.

PART THREE

APPENDIX

Plate XXX. Norwegian hatchet of the late Middle Ages found **near**
Thief River Falls, Minnesota.

Photo by Milwaukee Public Museum

Plate XXXI. A Tatarian Inscription.

Photo by the British Museum, London

XXIII. LINGUISTIC ANALYSIS OF THE INSCRIPTION

THE spelling of the inscription, like other writings from the fourteenth century, is fairly phonetic. As the runic alphabet contained fewer letters than the usual script, the runic writer has borrowed some signs from the Latin alphabet, and in some cases has represented two sounds with one symbol. Thus he uses the same sign for o and å, and for d, dh and th, as the difference in sound was probably slight. The w became so popular in West Gothland about 1300 that many manuscripts use it instead of v. This is also the case in this inscription. The following is a line by line transcription with words omitted given in brackets.

1. [wi er] 8 göter ok 22 norrmen på
2. [en] opþagelsefarþ frå
3. winlanþ of west wi
4. haþe læger weþ 2 skjar en
5. þags rise norr frå þenå sten
6. wi war [ute] ok fiske en þagh æptir
7. wi kom hem fan [wi] 10 man röþe
8. af bloþ og þeþ A V M
9. fræelse [oss] af illy
10. [wi] har 10 mans we[þ] hawet at se
11. æptir wore skip 14 þagh rise[r]
12. fråm þenå öh ahr [æptir guz byrþ] 1362.

§ 1. *wi* = we, personal pronoun, first person plural; omitted in the inscription. Professors Falk and Torp state that the omission of personal pronouns in the subject of the sentence is characteristic of writings of the fourteenth century, and Professor Nygaard has written an exhaustive dissertation on this custom.[1]

---

[1] *Dansk-Norskens Syntax* § 164, 2. See also M. Nygaard, *Subjektløse Sætninger i det Norrøne Sprog in Arkiv for Nor. Filologi*, 1894, pp. 1-26.

§ 2. *er* = are. Also omitted in the inscription.

§ 3. ᛒ = 8. This and other runic numerals are discussed in Chapter XVI.

§ 4. *göter* = Goths, the people inhabiting the southern part of Sweden, known as East and West Gothland. Swedish plurals have so long been characterized by the ending -*ar* that the spelling gö*ter* seems strange. But evidence is not lacking to show that endings in -*er* were common in West Gothland in the fourteenth century. *Vestgötalagen*, MS. of 1285, does not observe any regularity of endings in *ar*. We find *saker* and *sakar*, *kaller* and *kallar*, *taker*, *takær* and *takar*; *uten*, *utæn* and *utan*; *hæreth* and *hærath*; *standæ* and *standa*; *mather* and *mathar*, etc.[2] Lydikinus, a priest of West Gothland, about the year 1300 wrote some annotations to the *Vestgötalag*. Commenting on his style, Schlyter says: "Instead of the endings *a* and *ar*, we find almost everywhere *æ* and *ær*." [3] Another priest of West Gothland has also written some notes on the same law. His MS. is from about 1325. In this we find *götær* [*vestgötær*], *ok e glæddus vestgötær af honum*.[4] This is practically the same as *göter*, as *æ*, according to Rydquist, nearly always in the old writings represents the sound of *e*.[5]

The criticized spelling of this word is really an argument favoring the authenticity. The *ar* in *götar* is now so characteristically Swedish that it would at once suggest itself to a writer of today.

§ 5. *ok* = and, conjunction. Later in the inscription it is spelled *og*. It has been considered a suspicious circumstance that the word is twice spelled *ok* and once *og*. Kock in his discussion of the laws of Swedish sound development points out that the transition of *k* to *g* had already

---

[2] *Vestgötalagen*, Collin and Schlyter's Ed., Stockholm, 1827; introduction, Corpus I, pp. IV, V.
[3] *Ibid.*, XI.
[4] Noreen, *Altschwedisches Lesebuch*, Halle, 1904, p. 14, line 3.
[5] Rydquist, *Svenska Språkets Lagar*, IV, 16-19, 93-96.

begun in the fourteenth century.[6] He gives a number of illustrations of similar alternate use of *k* and *g* by the same writers; for instance, *jak, jag; taka, tagha; sik, sigh;* etc.[7]

This uncertainty in spelling is characteristic of the Middle Ages, but is difficult to harmonize with the cultivated standards of a modern scholar.

§ 6. FF = 22. See § 3.

§ 7. *norrmen* = Norwegians. Common Old Swedish form.

§ 8. *på* = on. *På*, the later form for *pa*, is derived from the copulation of two distinct words, *up* (Eng. *up*) and *a* or *å* (Eng. on) = *upa* or *upå* (Eng. *upon*). Later the *u* was elided because of its lack of accent and the word became *på*. The only criterion of the fitness of this word lies in the question of whether the open sound of the long *a* in *pa* had changed to the open *o* sound in *på* by 1362. Kock in *Svensk Ljudhistoria*, Vol. I, published in 1906, has placed the transition in the fourteenth century. He says: "Dialectically the change of long *a* to *å* took place by the middle of the fourteenth century, at least, when accompanied by a labial consonant."[8] Noreen comes to the same conclusion.[9]

Hægstad makes the objection that the inscription cannot be older than 1470 because he is unable to find *pa* or *på* before that date. Previous to this time he has been able to find only *a* or *up a*.

Pa or *po* (på) occur a number of times in the fourteenth century. For instance, a letter of 1345 has *pa begge arwinge sidhe*,[10] a letter of 1323 has *pa nogars siida*.[11] It is of comparatively frequent occurrence.

§ 9. *en* = an. Omitted in the inscription.

[6] *Fornsvensk Ljudlära* (Studier öfver), Lund, 1882, I, 35-50.
[7] *Ibid.*, pp. 85-96.
[8] *Svensk Ljudhistoria*, I, § 430; see also pp. 352-354 and 299.
[9] *Altschwedische Grammatik*, p. 103, § 110; see also § 18, anm. 2.
[10] *Diplomatarium Svecanum*, Hildebrand's edition, Letter No. 3948, A.
[11] *Ibid.*, 2419.

§ 10. *oppagelse* = discovery. I personally called on Professor Söderwall, the great lexicographer of Sweden, for an opinion on this word, and his answer was as follows: "As far as I know this word is not to be found in the meagre literary fragments of the fourteenth century in Sweden. But that proves nothing. As you probably know, these literary fragments consist chiefly of legal documents and homilies, and it is therefore not strange if a word of such comparatively rare import as *oppagelse* is not found in such writings. The Old Norse word for this idea was *landaleita*, but this word had become obsolete when the great change from old Swedish to the Swedish of the late Middle Ages took place about 1300. As *landaleita* was dropped, some other term must have been adopted to express the same thought. The only word we know which fills this function is *opdage*."

This word is probably a loan from the Low German. But it is an error to assume that such German loans first took place in the sixteenth century. Rydquist shows that as early as ca. 1250 the Germans were officially permitted to take up residence in Sweden and to have the same rights and privileges as the native citizens of the country. This resulted in such a large immigration of Germans, that in certain parts of Sweden the law, a century later, provided that of the six burgomasters and thirty councilmen one-half were to be Swedish and one-half German.[12]

Professor Munch says that in 1352 "all the shoemakers and tailors in Oslo, Bergen and Nidaros were Germans." [13] In Sweden the Germans were even more numerous. Munch says that "the young Albrecht was greeted by the citizens of Stockholm in 1363 who were mostly Germans." [14] This large immigration of Germans into Sweden explains the

[12] *Svenska Språkets Lagar*, III, pp. I, II. See also P. A. Munch, *Det Norske Folks Historie, Unionsperioden*, I, 597, 598.

[13] *Det Norske Folks Historie, Unionsperioden*, I, 576, 577, 881, 882.

[14] *Ibid.*, p. 754. See also Styffe, *Skandinavien under Unionsperioden*, p. 341.

significance of King Magnus' proclamation in 1365, that "he would fight for the honor of God, for the welfare of the kingdom, and for the *preservation of one language in the country*." [15]

Due to this early German influence, we find that both the prefix and the suffix of this word occur innumerable times in Swedish manuscripts of the fourteenth century and even earlier. Vestgøtalagen, MS. of 1285, has *opfarelse, opstandelse, optagelse, openbare,* etc. *Lydikinus,* MS. of 1325, has *framförelse, fulkomelse,* etc. *Den Helige Birgittas Uppenbarelse,* MS. of 1360, has *understandilse, kynnilse, styrkilse, opinbarlika,* etc. Scores of other illustrations of *op-* and *-else* could be cited from the other fourteenth century manuscripts.

§ 11. *fardh* or *færdh* = journey or expedition. A recognized old Swedish word. *Gamle Eriks Krönikon* has: "Konungen börgade sina færdh." [16] In the inscription the word is spelled with an *a* instead of *æ* which may be due to an oversight in omitting the dot.

§ 12. *fro* (*frå*) = from, Old Norse *fra*. In the fourteenth century there was in southern Swedish dialects, according to Kock and Noreen, a tendency to change long *a* into *å*. See *ante* § 8.

§ 13. *winlanþ* = wineland. Old Norse name for eastern seaboard of America.

§ 14. *of* = See § 15a.

§ 15. *west* = the West, the western regions. Old Norse *vestr*. The final *r* had dropped from the dialects of southern Sweden before the fourteenth century. Fritzner classifies *vestr* both as a noun and as an adverb. As a noun he defines it as *den vestlige Himmelegn*, i.e., the western regions. [17]

§ 15a. The phrase *fro Vinland of vest* has been translated by some critics *from Vinland of the West*, and they

---

[15] H. Hildebrand, *Sveriges Historia, Medeltiden*, p. 253.
[16] Klemming's edition, line 3992.
[17] *Ordbog over det Gamle Norske Sprog*, article *vestr*.

see in this an anglicism. Inasmuch as there never was a Vinland of the East, this translation is absurd. Moreover, it reveals ignorance of a very common Old Norse preposition. *Of* is a preposition meaning over, across, through, round about. The following passages from writings of the thirteenth and fourteenth centuries illustrate this:

Of allan Noreg [18] (over all Norway).
Vestr for ek of ver [18] (westward I fared across the sea).
Han for of biskops syslu sina [19] (he traveled round about his diocese).
Fra Bjarmalands ganga land of nordrätt til Grønland tekr vidh.[20] (From B. goes land through the northern regions until Greenland begins.)

The meaning of the phrase is, therefore, *from Vinland round about the West,* which indicates that the journey thither had been by a circuitous route.

§ 16. *wi* = we. From Old Norse *ver* which in Swedish became *vir.* By 1300 we find both *vir* and *wi* in the same manuscripts. By 1347 *wi* (*vi*) is exclusively used, as illustrated in King Magnus' letter to the Kopparberg citizens (MS. of 1347).[21]

§ 17. *hafe* = had. This is the first of the five verbs in the inscription which are all in singular form while the subject is in plural. In Old Norse the verb was inflected according to person and number, and the first person plural of the present or past indicative regularly had the ending *-um* or *-dum.* This rule was so generally observed by the writers of the fourteenth century that no student of Old Norse, Middle Swedish or Middle Norwegian can fail to notice it. If this inscription were written by a modern student of philology—even of the most elementary training—it seems certain that he would have adorned his product

[18] Vigfusson's *Icelandic Dictionary*, articles *of* and *um* which are considered as variants of the same word.
[19] Cf. J. Fritzner, *Ordbog over det Gamle Norske Sprog*, art. *of.*
[20] See *Grønlands Historiske Mindesmærker*, III, 216, 220.
[21] See Hildebrand's *Diplomatarium Svecanum*, V, 636-639.

with these antique but well known plural verb endings, for these are what he would find in the textbooks and in printed manuscripts of that period. Seeing we do not find them the question arises: Had plural verb forms dropped out of colloquial usage in the fourteenth century?

The answer to this by many eminent scholars of recent date is yes. While the small coterie of clerks and clerics of the fourteenth century who were able to write, attempted painstakingly to follow the literary standards of the masters that had preceded them, they were not able at all times to do so; from time to time they forget the sonorous inflected forms and, lapsing into the vernacular, use verbs in singular with subjects in plural. If inflected verb forms had been the colloquial as well as the literary usage, there would of course have been no place or reason for a second form.

The Norwegian, Swedish and Danish languages are all children of the same parent—the Old Norse—and have passed through a similar although not quite simultaneous development. According to Bertelsen [22] the dialects of Sjælland and Jutland had lost all differences of both person and number in the past tense of weak verbs more than a hundred years before 1362. We find: iak, thu, han, vi, i, the *hade, dömdæ, spurthæ*. Thus everywhere in the *Sjællandske Lov* and the *Jydske Lov* (MSS. from ca. 1300). He cites a ten-line passage from Lucidarius (MS. of 1350) [23] where eleven instances occur in which, according to the old rule, the verbs should have been in plural as the subjects are plural. But in eight instances the verbs are in the singular, and in the plural only in three. Professor Dahlerup also speaks of the lapse of plural verb forms in the fourteenth century. He says: "Numerous verb forms . . . show that the speech undoubtedly in many parts had given up the logical use of plural forms." [24] The northern part of Jutland lies in close proximity to West Gothland and

---

[22] *Sproghistorisk Læsebog*, I, 95.
[23] *Ibid.*, p. 119, lines 20-30.
[24] *Det Danske Sprogs Historie*, 1900, pp. 37, 38.

the southeastern corner of Norway and was in close contact with them. This was no doubt the cause of the great similarity of these various dialects.

By the middle of the fourteenth century the decay of inflections and neglect of plural verb forms had become so apparent in Norwegian manuscripts that Falk and Torp say: "There are numerous examples showing that many dialects [in the fourteenth century] had given up plural verb forms." [25] Even in the West Norwegian dialects, which were the most archaic Scandinavian dialects of that period, this is apparent. Professor Gustav Indrebø has written an article entitled "Some Remarks on the Disappearance of the Plural in the Conjugation of Verbs in Norwegian" [26] supported by scores of fourteenth century citations. Professor Brøndum-Nielsen has shown that even *den Skaanske Lov*, a manuscript from Skaane from ca. 1275, frequently has singular verbs with plural subjects.[27]

In view of the definite conclusions of these experts, particular illustrations are hardly necessary, but I will add a few from Swedish and West Gothland manuscripts.

A letter from West Gothland of 1349 reads in part: [28]

Han og hans arvinge *skal* that goz ænær lika aghæ mæth swa skiæl at theer *guier* mik ater swa mangæ pæningæ som twer gother mæns af hans wæghnæ og twer af minæ sighia.

In a long letter from 1409 written in Baahus, on the border of West Gothland, plural verb forms ending in -*um* and -*dum* are entirely absent. The beginning and ending read as follows:

Wij Jacop meth Gudz nadhe biscop j Aslo Hans Kröppeliin Anwnd Lang oc Jes Jecopsson göre witerlicht meth thettæ wort opne breff at wy æfter war herres föthelsses aar thusende firæ-hundredthe vpa thet niænde aar then tiisdagh næst fore

[25] *Dansk-Norskens Syntax*, 1900, pp. XIII, XIV.
[26] *Litt um Burtfallet av Fleirtal i Verbalbøygjingi i Norsk* in *Festskrift til Amund B. Larsen*, 1924, pp. 106-114.
[27] In *Arkiv for Nor. Fil.*, XXXIV (1918), 127 ff.
[28] *Svensk Diplomatarium*, første samling, No. 4503.

pingzdaghe vpa Baholm wten fore Bahws hörthe oc saghe oc ther nær oc ower ware, etc. . . . . thet witnæ wy fore alle oc göre witerlicht meth thettæ wort opnæ breff oc til mere wissen her vm have wy ladet woræ jncigle hænges fore thettæ breff.[29]

The above letter well illustrates what Professor Munch said about the decadence of the Old Norse language in the fourteenth century—"the melodious and highly inflected language was being displaced by a less elegant transition language, marked by lacerated word forms and the lack of strict grammatical rules and therefore probably not written the same way by any two writers." All that distinguishes the verb forms of the above letter, issued by a conservative and circumspect bishop, from the most modern forms in singular is an unaccented terminal vowel which would quickly disappear in colloquial speech. And it must not be forgotten that in such transitions colloquial usage precedes the literary by many decenniums. In *Karls-Krönikon*, written about forty years later, we find *hade*, the word under discussion, in regular use with the occasional divergent spelling of *haffde*. Sometimes both spellings are found in the same sentence as in

> *Haffde the then färske mat ey fangit*
> *iac mener the hade alle forgangit.*[30]

§ 18. *läger* = camp. From Old Norse *legr*. *Karls-Krönikon* has:

Ther lot han bade planska och grafwa, som han wille ther *læger haffua*.[31]

Erikskrönikon has:

[29] *Diplomatarium Norwegicum*, I, No. 620. For similar uninflected usage see *Ibid*. VI, No. 278 from 1371; No. 357 from 1402; No. 364 from 1405; and No. 389 from 1414.

[30] *Karls-Krönikon*, line 3186-7. For similar uses of the singular verb *hadhe* with subjects in plural, see lines 3189, 3206, 3390-1, 6202-3, 7270-1, 7399, 7563, 7587, 7659, 7668, 7709, 7738, 7750, 7764, 7815-18, 7826, 7895-6, 7917, 7920, etc.

[31] Klemming's edition, Part 2, lines 8903, 8904.

Tha haffdo the thera *laghor* lagt.[32]

Söderwall, Kalkar, Torp and Falk all give this word in the meaning of *camp* in illustrations from the Middle Ages.[33] We also find it in *Magnus Eriksons Landslag*, MS. of ca. 1350, spelled *læghre* (plural), meaning *camp*, *castra*.[34]

§ 19. *weþ*, preposition, meaning *at*, *by*, or *against*. Old Norse *viþ*. Speaking of the change of *i* to *e*, Professor Kock says: "From the fourteenth century are found but very few examples of the transition *i* to *e* in accented syllables, *except* before ð [þ]." [35] In § 47 of the same work he gives a number of illustrations from the fourteenth century showing the development of *i* to *e* before ð or þ.[36]

§ 20. F = 2. See § 3.

§ 21. *skjar* or *skjær* (the fourth rune in this word is indistinct) = skerries. Old Norse *sker;* modern Norwegian, skjær; modern Swedish, skär.

Professor G. Indrebø has kindly volunteered the following comment on this word in a private letter: "k in *skjar* (*skjær*) has been palatal and because of this an i (j) has been introduced just as we in Old Swedish find *giæster*, *kiænna* alternating with *gæster*, *kænna*. See Noreen, *Altschwedische Grammatik*, § 278."

§ 22. *en* = one. Old Norse *æin* and *ein*.

The funno thær *en* troldkarl.[37]

Kock writes: "The change of the diphthong *æi* to the monophthong *e* has presumably first gone through the form *ei*, which later became *e*." He shows that the transition from *ai* to *e* began in Jutland about 950 and "by 1200

[32] Klemming's edition, Part 1, line 1722.
[33] See Söderwall's *Ordbok öfver Svenska Medeltids Språket*, article *læger;* Kalkar's *Ordbog*, Vol. III, 772, second column, line 1; and Falk and Torp's *Lydhistorie*, p. 11, No. 2.
[34] Cited by Rydquist in *Svenska Språkets Lagar*, VI, 278.
[35] *Svensk Ljudhistoria*, I, § 30.
[36] *Ibid.*, p. 41 ff.
[37] *Klosterläsning* (Cod. Oxenstierna), MS. of 1385, Klemming's edition, p. 156.

the evolution was completed in most of the districts of southern Sweden." [38]

§ 23. *þags* = day's. Old Norse *dags*. In use since the earliest times.

This word has been objected to because of its spelling: "The word for 'day' was [in the fourteenth century] pronounced *dagh* and that for 'dead,' *dödh* (*th*). To have said *thagh*, or *thödh*, would have been as impossible in the language of that time as it would be for us to say *thay* for 'day' or *then* for 'den' in English and expect to be understood." [39]

This is attributing undue circumspection to the writers of the Middle Ages. They frequently use the surd and sonant fricatives *th* (*þ*) and *dh* (*đ*) where we would expect the stop sounds of *t* or *d*. Sometimes the same word is spelled both ways by the same writer. For instance, the Saga of Didrik of Bern has, "*Thu* west ække, hwat *tw* siger"; "*Tw* later ængen wara *thin* likæ æller *tinæ* mænna." [40]

Professor Brøndum-Nielsen in discussing an inscription reading *aue ma gracia plena þominum* from ca. 1300, writes: "This spelling (þ for d in *dominum*) is presumably due to the fact that two alphabets, the runic and the Latin, which were used side by side, have influenced each other in such a manner that the rune þ and the Latin D, because of their likeness [*indbyrdes lighed*, i.e., in sound and form] became interchangeable [*sammenblandedes*]." He gives a number of illustrations of this interchange of use. He also suggests the probability that this transition (þ-d) is due to a phonological transition of these consonants, "a transition of which there are other possible evidences from ca. 1300." [41]

As to the words objected to, we find both *þagh* and *þöþæ* in *Vestgötalagen*, I (MS. of 1284). [42] *Vestgötalagen*,

[38] *Fornsvensk Ljudlära*, II, 233-238; *Svensk Ljudhistoria*, II, § 843-856.
[39] G. T. Flom in *The Kensington Rune Stone*, pp. 18 and 25.
[40] Noreen's *Altschwedisches Lesebuch*, p. 102.
[41] *Aarbøger for Nord. Oldkyndighed*, 1917, pp. 206, 207.
[42] See Rydquist's *Svenska Språkets Lagar*, IV, 285.

II, MS. of about 1350, has *đagh.*[43] *Vestgötalagen*, III (Annotations by Lydikinus), MS. of ca. 1325, also writes *þagh* (he also writes *þotter, þör, bonþæ*, and *þrenger* for *dotter, dör, bonde*, and *drenger*).[44] *Biarkoa-Rätten*, MS. of 1345, has *đagh.*[45] The *þ* and *đ* in this MS. and in *Vestgötalagen* II, as Rydquist remarks, "almost as frequently represents *d* as *dh*." [46] As Schlyter says, *þ* and *d* are frequently used interchangeably in the *Vestgötalag* MSS.[47]

But there is another probable reason why the writer of the Kensington Stone has used *þ* for *d*. This is that while there was a runic sign for *d*, this seems to have been little used except on the island of Gotland. Noreen in his *Altschwedische Grammatik* gives forty runic inscriptions from different parts of Sweden from the period before 1300. Only two of these, one an inscription from the island of Bornholm, use the runic sign for *d*. All the others have only *t* and *þ*, which occur about 700 times.[48] As the writer of the Kensington Stone presumably learned his runic lore from the runic inscriptions of the district whence he came, we can well understand why he uses *þ* for *d* inasmuch as the latter was practically nonexistent.

§ 24. *rise* = journey. This word, ordinarily spelled *rese*, is probably a loan from the Middle Low German, but this loan must have been made very early, for we find it in general use in Norway and Sweden (West Gothland) in the fourteenth century with various spellings. In *Magnus Eriksons Landslag*, MS. of the middle of the fourteenth century, we read:

j *resom* sum æmbizman hans vtsændir.[49]

[43] See Kock's *Svensk Ljudhistoria*, II, 356.
[44] *Vestgötalagen*, Collin and Schlyter's edition, p. IX.
[45] *Svenska Språkets Lagar*, IV, 293.
[46] *Ibid.*, p. 290.
[47] *Vestgötalagen*, Collin and Schlyter's edition, p. V. See also Celander, *Om judövergangen đ-d in Arkiv for Nor. Fil.*, XXII (1906), 24-78.
[48] Noreen, *Altschwedische Grammatik*, pp. 481-502.
[49] *Svenska Språkets Lagar*, III, 288.

In *Magnus Eriksons Testament,* MS. of 1346, we read:

ena *reysa* vtsændæ mot guþz owinum.[50]

In a Norwegian letter of 1344 we find it similarly used:

ef Gud krefr minnar andar nu i thessi *reiso.*[51]

In *Gamla Eriks krönikon,* written in West Gothland in 1320 (present MS. copy from 1470) we read:

tha willo the Crisno ena *reso* fara.[52]
then *reysa* war ey diger.[53]

Karls-Krönikon, MS. of 1452, has:

skulle then *resan* felig wara.[54]
Konungin . . . gjorde sidan *reisor* mange.[55]

As shown above, the spelling of the word is quite variable. We find *reysa, resom, reisu,* and *reso.* As further illustrations may be mentioned that in *Karls-Krönikon* the spelling of this word is three times *reeso* or *rese* and six times *reise* or *reyso,* all with the same meaning (journey) only a few lines apart.[56] In our inscription it is spelled *rise.*

The explanation of this spelling is probably that the writer of the inscription, like the authors of *Karls-Krönikon* and other MSS., was uncertain how the word should be spelled. This was the opinion of Professor Söderwall to whom I applied for an opinion on the word. "It is not a question of the correctness of the word," he answered, "but merely of the spelling." In the fourteenth century before dictionaries and grammars were available for guidance, there were very few writers, if any, who had developed so fine an ear for the sound of words and their

[50] *Ibid.*
[51] *Diplomatarium Norveg.,* IV, 282.
[52] Klemming's edition, Part I, line 1482.
[53] *Ibid.,* line 3371.
[54] *Ibid.,* Part II, line 6271.
[55] *Ibid.,* lines 307-309.
[56] *Ibid.,* lines 277, 309, 2024, 2997, 3285, 3315, 4533, 6271, 9448.

equivalents in written characters that they were able to spell uniformly. As an illustration it may be mentioned that the author of *Karls-Krönikon* spells the name of his hero, Engelbrekt, thirteen different ways! [57] Collin and Schlyter state that Lydikinus, the learned jurist in West Gothland (ca. 1300) frequently writes *i* for *e* and vice versa.[58] "We find *stein, stin* and *sten; ein, ien* and *en, heim, him* and *hem. Risen* for *reisen* occurs in Low German of this period." [59] Rydquist has also called attention to the frequent interchange of *i* and *e* in old writers.[60] When we therefore find *rise* instead of *rese* or *reise*, it means that the writer was uncertain as to how this vocal sound should be expressed. This uncertainty is quite characteristic of those times, but would be incomprehensible in a suppositious philological imitator of our times.

For a consideration of the special significance of the term *paghsrise*, see Chapter XVII.

§ 25. *norr* = north. Old Norse *nordr*. Noreen states that "besonders oft schwindet đ in der verbindung rđr" and cites *nor* from *nordr* as an illustration.[61] Rydquist gives numerous examples of the apocopation of this word, such as *nor, noor, norr, norro,* etc., in MSS. of the fourteenth and fifteenth centuries.[62]

§ 26. *fro* (frå) = from. See § 12.

§ 27. *penå*, demonstrative pronoun *this*.

In the phrase *frå penå sten*, the noun *sten* (stone) is masculine and *frå*, according to Noreen, governs the accu-

---

[57] See *Svenska Medeltidens Rim-Krönikor*, Klemming's edition, II, 11, 730, 736, 878, 1309, 1314, 1404, 1422, 2496, 2497, 2860, 3078, 3108, 3228.

[58] *Vestgötalagen*, Collin and Schlyter's edition, p. IX.

[59] A. Fossum in the *Norwegian-American* (Northfield, Minn.), Feb. 24, 1911.

[60] *Svenska Språkets Lagar*, Vol. IV, 46-50. On pages 94 and 95 he discusses the similar interchange of *æ* and *i*, such as *næpar* and *nipar*, *sæghia* and *sighia*, etc.

[61] *Altschwedische Grammatik*, § 244, p. 3.

[62] *Svenska Språkets Lagar*, II, 445.

sative (before 1300 it usually governed the dative).[63] The regular form would therefore be *fro pænna sten*. As to the *e* in the root syllables, Noreen, speaking of *pænna* says: "In der wurzelsilbe steht oft *e* statt *æ*." [64] *pænna* is the most common form for the singular masculine accusative, and the ending *å* is in conformity with the tendency in dialects of southern Sweden (and Norway) to substitute *å* and *o* for *a* as in "*i thesso helgho script*," [65] and "Fastbiurn *rita stin peno*." [66]

§ 28. *sten* = stone. Old Norse *stain* or *stæin*. See *ante* § 22.

§ 29. *wi*. See § 16.

§ 30. *war* = were. In Old Norse the first person plural preterite was *varum* and the third person *varu*. But as has been shown in § 17, these plural forms by the second half of the fourteenth century had dialectically been largely superseded by singular forms. *Svenska Medeltidens Bibelarbeten*, MS. of ca. 1400, has: The wrangasta dødhana som menløsom barnom *war* giordher.[67]

§ 31. *ute* = out. This word is omitted in the inscription.

§ 32. *ok* = and. In use from the earliest times.

§ 33. *fiske*, apocopated preterite form of *fiskadhi*. The plural preterites of the first conjugation of weak verbs had endings -*dum*, -*udut* and -*udu* which in the later literary language was superseded by the 3rd p. sg. ending -*ede* (older form *adi*), thus *fiskede, kastede*, etc. But in colloquial usage which still survives, these bisyllabic endings gave place to a monosyllabic *a* or *æ* (*fiskæ, kastæ*, etc.). Thus in Uppsala Krønikon, MS. of fourteenth century, we

---

[63] *Altschwedische Grammatik*, § 445. This substitution of the accusative *pænna* for the dative *pæssa* was probably less a change of case than a disregard for inflections altogether. This disregard is illustrated by many passages in this (Noreen's) paragraph and also in § 66, *post*.

[64] *Ibid.*, § 509, p. 1.

[65] *Svenska Medeltidspostillar* (MS. of ca. 1400), Klemming's edition, I.

[66] Liljegren's *Runurkunder*, No. 90.

[67] Cited in Rydquist's *Svenska Språkets Lagar*, II, 143, note.

read: "Taa *castæ* een man en brødisk." [68] Here the regular preterite form *castadhi* has been shortened to *castæ*. *Maribo Klosterklage* (MS. of 1416) has: "The meth rættæ matæ *fiskæ*." [69] Here *fiskadhi* has been contracted to *fiskæ* just as in the inscription it is *fiske*. At the present time such apocopated preterites usually end in -*a* in colloquial usage, but Professor Kock remarks that in the older *Vestgötalag* (MS. of 1285) "oftener than two times out of three the terminal vowel is *æ* instead of *a*." [70]

The clause *wi war* [*ute*] *ok fiske* therefore agrees with the colloquial usage of the fourteenth century and is perfectly justifiable if the inscription is genuine, but hardly to be expected if its author were a modern student of philology.

§ 34. *en* = one, see § 22.

§ 35. *pagh* = day. In § 23 *the* word is spelled *pag*. This vacillation in spelling is characteristic of an unlettered age and person.

§ 36. *æptir*, common Swedish and Norwegian fourteenth century form. Preposition and conjunction. Here used as conjunction (conjunctive adverb).

I have not found *æptir* used as a conjunction in writings of the fourteenth century from West Gothland, but it occurs both in Danish and Old Norse more than a century earlier. In *Konunga-Sögur*, MS. of ca. 1220: "That var tha *eptir* er Islendingar höfdo fært lög sin." [71] In *Egils Saga Skallagrimssonar*, MS. of 1260: "Han tok til forrada skipit, *eptir* er kveldulfr var daudhr." [72] In *Flateyjarbok*, MS. of 1387: "Tha var tekin til rikisstiornar Margreta . . . *eptir* er hon let fanga Albrikt." [73]

Falk and Torp mention the use of *æptir* as a conjunction

---

[68] Brandt's *Gammeldansk Læsebog*, p. 71, line 15.
[69] *Ibid.*, p. 92, line 19.
[70] *Svenska Akcent*, pp. 140, 148.
[71] *Konunga-Sögur*, Holmiæ, 1817, II, 225.
[72] See Nygaard, *Udvalg af den Norrøne Lit.*, p. 102.
[73] Edition of 1860, I, 29.

in the Middle Ages and give a number of illustrations such as: "Paa siwenda aar *æffther* han Koning wort (Eriks Krön. MS. ca. 1400)"; "*efter* du gikst af din grav"; "*effther* at mange waare faldne (Ved. MS. 1350)." [74]

Æptir as a conjunction occurs very early in Danish writings, thus twice in Riberetten, MS. of 1250: "*æffter* han havær fyrst hiemmæ waræt"; "*æfter* han havær fyrst wæræth i syt hærbærgh." In *Jens Buddes Bok*, a Swedish MS. of 1487, we read: "Nagher aar *eptir* hun jordet var . . . nödgades the röra henne helghe graff." [75]

In view of this early and widespread use it is probable that it was also used in West Gothland.

§ 37. *wi* = we, see § 16.

§ 38. *kom* = come, first person singular preterite. The plural form was *komun*. See § 17. *Gamle Eriks Krönikon* has: "The svenske *kom* först." [76]

§ 39. *hem* = home, Old Norse *heim*. *Vestgötalagen*, MS. of 1285, has *hem*. [77] For change of the diphthong *ei* to the monophthong *e*, see § 22.

§ 40. *fan* = found, first person singular preterite. See § 17.

§ 41. [*wi*] = we, omitted in the inscription.

§ 42. ꝓ = 10, see § 3.

§ 43. *man* = men, accusative plural. The runic writer evidently meant to write *mæn*, the correct form, but forgot to dot his *a* which is the only distinction between the runic letters for *a* and *æ*.

§ 44. *röþe* = red, Old Norse *raudr*. According to Kock, this diphthong by 1200 had changed to *ö* in all southern and central Sweden. A priest of Vidhem, in his annotations to *Vestgötalagen*, writing in 1325, writes: "Fyardþi war Hakun röde." *Svenska Medeltidspostillar*, MS. of ca. 1400, has: "Gudh nidhersænkte han j rödha hafuit."

[74] *Dansk-Norskens Syntax*, § 142, lb.
[75] Hultman's edition, 1895, p. 226.
[76] Klemming's edition, I, line 603 (page 191).
[77] Noreen's *Altschwedisches Lesebuch*, p. 5, line 16.

§ 45. *af*, preposition meaning *with*, *from*, *out of*, etc., which has remained unchanged from Old Norse times to the present.

§ 46. *bloþ* = blood. This word has also remained practically unchanged for a thousand years.

§ 47. *og* = and, see § 5.

§ 48. *þeþ* = dead. The plural ending (*-e*) has here been omitted. This may be due to emotional disturbance as the runemaster vividly recalled the tragic events in chiselling the climax on the stone.

Many critics have pointed to this word as proof of the theory that the inscription was the work of some modern immigrant who had been in this country so long that he had adopted a number of English words into his speech. But if so, what then shall we think of Queen Margaret or her secretary who in 1390 spelled this word the same way? Was the Queen also given to "mixing" English? In a letter from her written in Lödesö in West Gothland we read: "Effther the henne hosbonde her Jens Herne *ded* er" (as her husband, Sir Jens Herne, is dead).[78]

A better explanation of this strange spelling may be found in the apparent difficulty the untrained writers of the Middle Ages had in differentiating between the sounds of the letters *e* and *ø*. Professor Kock has given many illustrations showing the use of *e* for *ø* and vice versa. He shows that *messa*, English *mass*, is written both *messa* and *møssa*; *søvn* (sleep) is spelled both *svefn* and *svøfn*; *peper* (pepper) is frequently spelled *pøper*, etc.[79] In the second volume of his history of Swedish phonetics, he goes into the subject of the substitution of *e* for *ø* more fully. He sites *grea* for *grøa*, *bredr* for *brødr*, *hera* for *høra*, *lena* for *løna*, *bredirne* for *brøderne*, *berdha* for *børdha*, *snepa* for *snøpa*, *grepa* for *grøpa*, *fetr* for *føter*, *bret* for *brøt*, and many more.[80] Noreen in his *Altschwedische Grammatik*

---

[78] *Diplomatarium Norwegicum*, IV, No. 586. The original is preserved.
[79] *Svensk Ljudhistoria*, I, 127.
[80] *Ibid.*, II, 38-42. See particularly § 623.

also comments on the frequent interchange of *e* and *ø*.[81]

Professor Munch almost a hundred years ago pointed out the tendency in the Middle Ages toward substituting *e* and *æ* for other short vowels. He says: "[There was] in those old times an uncertainty in their manner of expressing phonetic values coupled with a tendency in those dialects to let all shorter and uncertain vowel sounds approach *e*."[82]

The only explanation for these dual spellings is, as Professor Munch says, that the uncritical writers of the Middle Ages were not certain whether the words in question should be spelled with an *e* or an *ø*. Just so also with the runic scribe of Kensington. His training in spelling was deficient, and so he substituted an *e* for an *ø*, as did many a more practised writer of his day. Such a spelling as *þeþ* for *døð* would, however, be incomprehensible in a writer of the present day having the philological learning necessary to construct a runic inscription like the Kensington inscription.

§ 49. A V M = A V (E) M(ARIA). See p. 183.

§ 50. *fræelse* = save (imperative mood).

Objection has been made to the final *e* in this word on the alleged ground that the imperative mood takes the form *fræls*. This is an error. Dr. Stefan Einarsson has pointed out (in *Speculum*, 1933, p. 405) that *frælsa* belong to the second class of weak verbs which have an *-a* or *-æ* in the second pers. sg. imperative. See also Vigfusson's *Icelandic Dictionary*, art. *frelsa*.

The whole clause, *fræelse* [oss] *af illy* (or *illu*), is a part of the Lord's Prayer in the Swedish of the fourteenth century, from which the writer no doubt borrowed it.[83]

oc laat os æi ledhæs i frestelse
utan *frælsæ* os af *illu*,

[81] Sections 136 and 146, 3.
[82] *Annaler for Nordisk Oldkyndighed*, 1846, p. 268.
[83] See Ahlquist, *The History of the Swedish Bible*, in *Scandinavian Studies*, IX, 93.

§ 51. [*oss*] = us, omitted in the inscription.

§ 52. *af* = from. *Af* is most often used in the meaning *from* in the Middle Ages. It is interchangeable with *fraa* (*fro, fran*) (see § 12) just as are the relative pronouns *som* and *der* in present Danish. Ivar Bardsen's account of Greenland has:

"Item langt öster *af* Skagefjord"; "Item öster lenger *fraa* Berrefjord." [84]

§ 53. *illu* or *illy*, the last rune is of doubtful significance, see page 165. In either case the word is here used as a dative sing. neuter substantive meaning *evil*. As *illu* is the correct dative form as illustrated in the Lord's Prayer of ca. 1300: *frælsæ os af illu* (save us from evil),[85] it would seem that this is what the runic scribe intended to write. On the other hand it appears that the dative form changed from *illu* to *illi* very early. This is illustrated in the refrain of an ancient poem harking back to the Black Plague of 1349 which reads:

> "Hjælpe os Gud aa Maria Möy,
> Aa frælsæ oss alle av illi." [86]
> (Help us God and Virgin Mary
> And save us all from evil.)

The use of *y* for *i* is very common both in accented and unaccented syllables. As illustration may be mentioned a state document of 1388, presumably written by one of the ablest clerks in the chancellor's office, in which the leading

---

[84] *Grönlands Historiske Mindesmærker*, III, 252, 253.

[85] See note 83.

[86] The ballad is printed by Prof. O. E. Hagen in *Samband*, Minneapolis, Oct., 1911, No. 42, pp. 363-369, with copious notes. Hagen said he had heard it recited in 1873 by an old Telemarking. This folksong was also communicated by Mr. Tortvei, Moorhead, Minnesota, to Mr. Torkel Oftelie, a folklorist of Fergus Falls, Minnesota, by whom it was printed in Telesoga, No. I, 1909. Mr. Tortvei was an octogenarian pioneer, now dead, who, though illiterate, remembered hundreds of old ballads which he had heard in his childhood. Mr. Oftelie sent this ballad— *Førnesbronen*—to the eminent folklorist Rikard Berge of Telemarken, Norway, who said that the ballad was *førstehands*, that is, that it was written at about the time of the events described.

men of Norway—bishops and knights—pledge their allegiance to the newly crowned Queen of Norway, Margaret. In this letter we find *y* used both for *i* and *e*, such as *Swyia* for *Swea*, *lyfsdagha* for *lifsdagha*, *ydra* for *edra*, *hafthyngia* for *hafthingia*, *thy* for *thi*, etc.[87]

This *illu* or *illi* is another word which some critics have labeled "English," but why this has been done is incomprehensible. It is just as common in the Scandinavian literature of the Middle Ages (and even at present in colloquial speech) as is its counterpart *evil* in English. *"Ulf in illi"* (Ulf the evil),[88] *"Thorgrim ille"*[89] (Thorgrim the evil), *Halfdan hinn matar illi*[90] (H. the poor feeder), all illustrate some of its uses. Professor O. E. Hagen has pointed out that it is still in common use as a substantive in Lom, a mountain parish in Norway: *me ille aa me goe* (with evil and with good),[91] *ilt ska ille fordrive* (evil shall evil banish). See further scores of illustrations in Vigfusson, *Icelandic Dictionary*, articles *illr*.

§ 54. [*wi*] = we, omitted in the inscription. This is the third time the subject of the sentence is omitted. See §§ 1 and 40.

§ 55. *har* = have (singular). For use of singular verbs with plural subjects, see § 17.

§ 56. ⁹ = numeral 10, see § 3.

§ 57. *Mans* is the gen. sg. of *madr*, the Old Norse word for man (Latin *homo*) and also people, *folk*. Its use in the latter sense is very common in Old Norse. The following are illustrations:

Til Olafs Konungs kom her *mans*, haltir oc blinder, edr a annan veg siukir (To King Olaf came an army of people, lame and blind, or otherwise sick).[92]

---

[87] The original with many seals is preserved. See *Grönlands Historiske Mindesmærker*, III, 130-34.

[88] *Flateyjarbok*, III, 457.

[89] *Ibid.*, I, 554, 557.

[90] Snorre Sturlasson, Konunga Sögur, I, 60 (1816).

[91] *Samband*, No. 42, 367 (Minneapolis, 1911).

[92] Snorre Sturlasson, *op. cit.*, II, 433, line 7.

Epter thesso aurbodi liop upp mugi *manns*, oc sotti til Medalhusa (After these tidings, ran up a crowd of people, and hurried to Medalhus).[93]

Olaf Konungr war tha j nidarosi ok hafdi med ser fjølda *mannz* (King Olaf was then in Nidaros and had with him a multitude of people).[94]

This collective genitive is still in use in Modern Icelandic. The following illustrations are taken from an article describing the emigration from Iceland to America, printed in an Icelandic almanac:

Past voru nalaegt 250 *manns* og foru med gufuskibet St. Patrick (Almost 250 persons came with the steamship St. Patrick).[95]

Aredh 1873, voru samankomnir a Akureyri hatt a annaad hundradh *manns* (In 1873, were gathered together at Akureyri almost two hundred people).[96]

It is also common in modern Norwegian and Swedish:

Alle mann pa dekk! (all men on deck!)

Skibet gik ned med mann og mus. (The vessel went down with men and mice, i.e., all were lost.)

Björnen har ti manns styrke og tolv manns vett. (A bear has ten men's strength and twelve men's wit.)

It was also in use in southern Sweden as the following excerpt from a letter written in West Gothland in 1349 shows:

Han ok hans æruinge skal that goz ænnær like aghæ mæth swa skiæl at theer guier mik ater swa mangæ pæningæ som twer gother *mæns* af hans wæghnæ og twer af minæ sighiæ, etc. (He and his heirs shall have the property with the under-

---

[93] Snorre Sturlasson, Konunga Sögur, I, 257, line 21. See also II, 301, line 10; p. 5, line 22; p. 6, line 18; p. 334, line 11, and p. 390, line 24.

[94] *Flateyjarbok*, I, 310, line 21. See also p. 454, line 3, and p. 61, line 25.

[95] *Almanak*, 1899, edited and published by Olafur Thorgeirsson, Winnipeg, p. 25. See also p. 27.

[96] *Ibid.*, 1900, p. 40.

standing that they give me back so much money as two good men on his part and two on mine shall determine, etc.).[97]

The above parallels from documents dating from the thirteenth century down to the present time from various parts of the Scandinavian countries may suffice to show that *mans* in the inscription is not an erratic English plural form but the precise word in the genitive singular denoting *people*. It is apparent that the writer of the inscription had a different conception in mind when he wrote: "We found ten men red with blood and dead," than when he said: "We have ten men by the sea." In the first instance he thinks of the ten dead men as ten individual companions now gone forever, and therefore uses the plural form *man*. In the second case he thinks of the ten men by the sea as a subdivision of the party as a whole, and therefore uses the collective singular form *mans*. This is a nice point in the linguistic usage of the time, not discussed in any textbook, and speaks strongly for the authenticity of the inscription.

§ 58. *we* = by. This is the same word which is earlier spelled *weþ* (see § 19). The *þ* is here lost because of the colloquial tendency to drop the terminal *d* or *dh* sound before an initial aspirate in the next word. This is mentioned by Noreen.[98]

§ 59. *hawet* = the ocean, the sea.

Professor R. B. Anderson in a printed article has pointed to this word as certain proof that the inscription is a forgery. According to him, the word was not in use as early as 1362.[99] This objection is typical of many superficial arguments brought against the inscription. There are few words which occur more frequently in the Scandinavian writings of the thirteenth and fourteenth centuries than *hawet*. In Snorre Sturlasson's *Heimskringla* (MS. of about 1230) it occurs on almost every page.

[97] *Svensk Dipl., 1ste Samling*, No. 4503.
[98] *Altschwedische Grammatik*, § 308, note 6.
[99] *Wisconsin State Journal*, Madison, Wis., Feb. 7, 1910.

§ 60. [*for*] = for, omitted in the inscription.

§ 61. *at* = to, the sign of the infinitive. In pan-Scandinavian usage since remote times.

§ 62. *se* = see, a dialectic variation of *sia* (*sja, sea, seia,* etc.). The usual ending of the infinitive is *a*, but Noreen states that in the old MSS. of the Middle Ages, as, for instance, in *Vestgötalagen*, the *a* when following another vowel is sometimes omitted. He cites *se* (from *sea*, English *see*) as an illustration.[100] It also occurs in *Erikskrönikon:* "At hun skulde noger tid Swerige *see*." [101]

§ 63. *æptir* = after, preposition. In general use since earliest times.

§ 64. *wore* = our. In the writings of the fourteenth century which abound in inflections this word would have been written *worum* (*skipum*). But, as pointed out in Chapter XIV, inflections had largely dropped out of dialectic usage. This neglect of inflection also occurs sporadically in the writings of that period. A Swedish letter of Queen Margaret, written in 1401, reads in part as follows:

Thenne forscrefne gardh . . . kjennes wi oss at have gifuet oc andwardet fran os oc *wore* arwinge oc efterkommere, etc.[102]

As the preposition *fran* also takes the dative, we should expect, according to ancient standards, to find *vorom arwingom*, but the clerk of 1401 was not so particular. Note also the lack of inflection in *wi kjennes*. Another Swedish letter of 1382 reads: "I *ware* byrdh oc utan *wara* byrdh." [103] *I* and *utan* take the dative (sometimes also the genitive) but the pronouns are here uninflected. Note also the dual spellings *ware* and *wara*.

§ 65. *skip* = ship. This word has been in general use in Scandinavian dialects since the earliest times.

§ 66. ℾ = 14, see § 3.

100 *Altschwedische Grammatik*, § 559; see also § 153, Anm. 2.
101 Klemming's edition, I, line 629.
102 *Svensk Dipl.*, No. 11.
103 *Dipl. Dalecarlium*, No. 41.

§ 67 and 68. *paghrise* = days journey(s). Earlier in the inscription we find *pags rise*. Here the *s*, marking the possessive case, and the final *r*, marking the plural, are both missing. Both blunders are characteristic of the inaptitude of fourteenth century writers and are in this case probably due to the rune-master's apparently nervous state of mind during the writing of the latter part of the inscription. Dr. Einarsson has pointed out (in *Speculum*, July, 1933, page 407) that Noreen in his *Altschwedische Grammatik* (321, 2 b and c) has called attention to similar omissions of plural endings.

§ 69. *from (fråm)* = from. This preposition occurs three times in the inscription. Twice it has the normal spelling *fro*, but the third time it has the criticized form *from* or *fråm*. Many critics have pointed to this word as reflecting the mixed vernacular of recent immigrants.

This *fråm* is not a loan from the English, but is an archaic form of *fro*, and occurs sporadically from the earliest days of Swedish literature down to the sixteenth century. Falk and Torp state that the form *fråm* in the meaning of *fro* occurs sporadically in old East Scandinavian.[104] Following are some illustrations of its use:

In Linköping's *Biskopskrönika*, written in 1523, we read:

Rijket kom ater til Swenske men, *fram* the uthlænske som thet ær en [105] (The kingdom came again to Swedish men from the foreigners as it is now).

In the second book of the *Maccabees*, translated in 1484, we read:

Han lot genstan upbyggia gymnasium hart undir tornit ey langt *fram* templet [106] (He immediately rebuilt the public school close by the tower and not far from the temple).

---

[104] *Etymologisk Ordbog*, article *fra*.
[105] *Svenska Medeltidsdikter*, Klemming's edition, Stockholm, 1882, p. 502, line 514; *cf.* p. 509.
[106] *Svenska Med. Bibelarbeten*, Klemming's edition, Stockholm, 1853, p. 290, line 27; *cf.* p. 424.

The *Revelations of St. Birgitta* of 1430 has:

Iak dröuis af manga handa onytellelikom thankom huilka iak forma ey bort *fram* mik skilja [107] (I am grieved by many kinds of vain thoughts which I am unable to put away from me).

Thy tha the gaa in J skola tha gar iak *fram* them [108] (For when they go into the school then I will go from them).

The preposition *fram* also occurs in Lydikinus' *Anteckningar till Vestgötalagen*, MS. of ca. 1300.[109] Other illustrations of its use are also cited and quite fully discussed by Axel Kock, who shows that this *fram* is a survival of the Gothic *fram*, which is the ancestral form of the English *from* and the Swedish *från* as well.[110]

It may be objected that in the above illustrations the word is spelled *fram*, whereas on the stone we have *from* (*fråm*).

The difference is a purely dialectic one and speaks for the authenticity of the inscription. Professor Axel Kock has shown that long *a* when joined with a labial consonant during the fourteenth century had a tendency toward *å* and *o*.[111] In another place he writes: "During the fourteenth century the long *a*-sound in Old Swedish changed to a sound more like long *å;* this transition was completed toward the year 1400." [112] The simultaneous transition in East Norwegian is illustrated by the spellings of the name of Oslo. In the earlier letters, such as from 1309, 1312 and 1321, it is spelled *Aslo*,[113] while in later letters, such as

107 Klemming's edition, Stockholm, 1857, p. 363, line 13; *cf.* p. 407.
108 *Ibid.,* p. 101, line 5; *cf.* p. 404.
109 *Vestgötalagen,* Schlyter's edition, Stockholm, 1827, p. 397, article *fram.*
110 *Några Bidrag* in *Arkiv for Nordisk Filologi,* Lund, 1890, pp. 31-34. See also Noreen's *Altschwedische Grammatik,* p. 248. *Anm.* p. 2. I am indebted to the lexicographer, K. F. Söderwall, for several of the above references.
111 *Svensk Ljudhistoria,* I, 352-354.
112 *Ibid.,* p. 299.
113 See *Dip. Norwegicum,* I, 112; III, 97, and V, 61.

from 1360, 1376 and later, it is spelled *Oslo*.[114] According to Kock, we see the tendency consummated in most writers by 1400, while in others *a* and *å* are used interchangeably (as, for instance, *fran* and *från* on the same page). The same is affirmed and illustrated by Noreen.[115]

As there was no rune for *å*, the runemaster has used the rune for *o*. This use of *o* for *å* was also common in MSS. written in the Latin alphabet. Kock cites numerous examples from the fourteenth and fifteenth centuries of words with an *å* sound which were written with *o*, as *motte* for *måtte*, *forstondit* for *forståndit*, *gorden* for *gården*, *monga* for *många*, etc.[116]

The only pertinent criticism to make of this *from* in the Kensington inscription lies in the question: Inasmuch as the writer knew the normal form *fro*, why did he also use *from*? Is this not illogical? The answer to this must be: Yes, it is illogical. But it is a sample of that erratic logic which abounds in the writings of the Middle Ages. In a letter of 1341 we find *fra* and *fron* used only two lines apart.[117] In a *Guide to Pilgrims* written about 1425 we find *fra*, *fraan* and *fran* used interchangeably.[118]

§ 70. *þenå*, demonstrative pronoun, this.

Hægstad insists that as *öh* is feminine, the phrase should read *fra thessari öy*.[119] He is apparently laboring under the impression that this inscription is Icelandic instead of Swedish. *Thessari öy* is Icelandic, and if these words were found in an inscription purporting to be in the Swedish of 1362, its presence would be sufficient to cast serious doubt on the authenticity of the inscription. *Thessari* is an impossible form in Swedish after 1300 and one will look in vain for it in the paradigms and numerous illus-

---

[114] *Ibid.*, IV, 317; III, 307, etc.
[115] *Altschwedische Grammatik*, § 1, p. 10.
[116] *Svensk Ljudhistoria*, I, 400, 401.
[117] Hildebrand's *Svensk. Dipl.*, V, part I, 10.
[118] *Gammeldansk Læsebog*, p. 307, lines 7 and 25; p. 308, lines 9 and 19; and p. 310, lines 13 and 23.
[119] *Skandinaven*, July 27, 1911.

trations which Noreen and Söderwall give of the demontrative pronouns. Its solitary occurrence in *Upplands-lagen* (MS. of 1300 or before) may best be explained as an archaism.[120]

Numerous illustrations can be cited showing that *thenna* or *thennå* was coupled with feminine nouns in writings from about 1400. In a Swedish letter of about 1400 we find, "af *thennæ* fornempdo jordh." [121] Here *jordh*, which is feminine dative, is coupled with *thennæ* which is the masculine form. Likewise also in Erikskrönikon, written in 1320 but MS. of 1470: "I *thenne* bok." [122] *Thenne*, the old masculine nominative form, is joined with *bok*, which is feminine accusative. In *Flores och Blanzeflor*, MS. of 1430, we find, "ij *thenna* graff." [123] *Graff* is feminine. Noreen cites numerous illustrations of the use of the masculine accusative *pænna* with feminine nouns from *Codex Bureanus* (MS. of 1340), *Seelentröst* (MS. of 1430), *Codex Holmiæ D. 4* (MS. of ca. 1400), *Codex Oxenstiern* (MS. of 1385), *Codex A. M. 787* (MS. of ca. 1400), *Codex Verelianus* (MS. of 1457), and others.[124] As Professor Fossum says: "The use of the same form for the masculine and feminine is just what we would look for at the period when the language made the transition to the common gender." [125] See further § 27.

§ 71. *öh* = island, Old Norse *ey*. Kock shows that the diphthong *ey* had changed to the monophthong *o* as early as the twelfth century.[126] He cites several examples of *ö* (island) to illustrate the change.

§ 72. *ahr* = year, Old Norse *ar*. Kock points out that an *h* was sometimes used in the thirteenth and fourteenth

120 Noreen's *Altschwedische Grammatik*, § 509.
121 *Svensk Dipl.*, No. 193, dated 1401.
122 Klemming's edition, I, line 1903.
123 Noreen's *Altschwedisches Lesebuch*, p. 61, line 15.
124 *Altschwedische Grammatik*, p. 400, No. 4 and § 398, Anm. 3.
125 *Norwegian American*, Feb. 24, 1911, paragraph *peno öh*.
126 *Fornsvensk Ljudlära*, II, 492, 493; *Svensk Ljudhistoria*, II, § 894.

centuries to prolong the vowel.[127] Expressions like "Da schref man *ahr* epter gudz födelse tidh "[128] are not uncommon in the Swedish literature of the Middle Ages.

§ 73. [*æptir*] = after, omitted in the inscription.

§ 74. [*Guz*] = God's, omitted in the inscription.

§ 75. [*byrþ*] = birth, omitted in the inscription.

§ 76. ᚱᚠᛈᚠ· = 1362, see § 3.

[127] *Svensk Ljudhistoria*, II, 355.
[128] *Svenska Medeltidens Rim-Krönikor*, Klemming's Edition, III, 233, line 6220.

XXIV. BIBLIOGRAPHICAL NOTES

THE bibliography on the Kensington Stone has become quite extensive, and recently many prominent scholars have expressed their views on the subject. Readers interested in the early stages of the investigation will find a bibliography of six pages compiled by the investigating committee of the Minnesota Historical Society and appended to its report printed in the Society's *Collections*, XV, 221-286. A supplementary bibliography of thirteen pages was added in 1932 when the writer published *The Kensington Stone*, a volume of 316 pages. This was the first comprehensive study of the subject and represented twenty-four years' of diligent study. In spite of its challenging contents it had a generally favorable reception. Since then eight years have elapsed, giving much time for further consideration of the thesis, and many readers have inquired as to what is now the attitude of the historians, the Scandinavian philologists and the experts on pre-Columbian discoveries of America.

In answer to this question I am giving below a list, alphabetically arranged, of the writers in the three classes mentioned above who have made public statements for or against the authenticity of the Kensington inscription since my book was published. There is also appended a brief quotation from the writings of these scholars showing their attitude toward the problem under discussion. The list is probably not complete as some public statements may have escaped my attention.

1. James Truslow Adams, historian. In *The March of Democracy* (1932), pp. 2 and 3, he writes:

One of the most interesting relics, and one which seems to have some real claim to authenticity, is the *Kensington Stone* found in the roots of a tree at Kensington, Douglas County, Minnesota, in 1898. The runic inscription on it indicates that the point where it was found marks the southern limit of an expedition of the Norsemen who came overland from Hudson Bay in 1362, and the summing up of the evidence in 1932 would seem to give this record the best claim, which, however, is only a claim, to being the earliest monument by white men within our limits.

2. Francis J. Betten, Professor of History, Marquette University. In his book, *From Many Centuries* (1938), Chapter VII is devoted to the Kensington Stone and concludes with the following statement:

Whatever linguistic difficulties remain unsolved cannot interfere with the genuineness of the Kensington Stone and the reliability of its message.

3. Charles Knowles Bolton, historian, discusses the message of the Kensington Stone in his *Terra Nova* (1935), pp. 54-63. On pp. 62-63 he writes:

Improbable as the Norse expedition would seem to be, it has several points in its favor. It answers the natural query, Why did not the Norse settlers on the west coast of Greenland, when hard pressed by Eskimos and weakened by the severe climate, seek a home elsewhere? It fits in chronologically with Knutson's proposed mission, which had royal backing, and was to be led by a man with a reputation for action . . . but . . . after reading Dr. Flom's paper, and after corresponding with Dr. Lawrence M. Larson of the University of Illinois, one is forced, reluctantly, to believe that the runc stone is not convincing evidence that Norsemen were in the Red River Valley in the fourteenth century.

4. F. S. Cawley, Scandinavian philology, Harvard University. In a review of *The Kensington Stone*, published in *New England Quarterly*, VI, 210-217 (1933), he writes:

Skeptical as the reader may be (and properly so) when he begins the book, he will find it difficult as he proceeds to resist the force of Mr. Holand's affirmative arguments, and still more difficult to answer the pertinent questions which he puts to the advocates of the hoax theory. The very irregularities are an argument against the assumption of a learned forger, and it is hard to conceive an ignoramus who would have had the necessary knowledge of history to fabricate such a record. No impartial person will deny, at least, that this book reopens to debate a question which had been generally regarded as a *res judicata*.

5. T. P. Christensen, in *The Discovery and Rediscovery of America* (1934), pp. 70-80, discusses the Kensington Stone and says:

The Kensington Stone bears a clear, unmistakable and authentic message from the Norwegians and Swedes who in the year of our Lord 1362 penetrated North America as far as the sources of the Red River of the north.

6. J. W. Curran, author of *Here Was Vinland*, Sault Ste. Marie, Canada, 1939, 360 pp. This latest work on the Norse discovery of America deals chiefly with the investigation and authentication of the Viking arms found in a grave near Lake Nipigon, north of Lake Superior. It is of much significance in the study of the Kensington Stone because it shows that as early as the first part of the eleventh century the Norse explorers had penetrated more than a thousand miles from the Atlantic coast of America. The author also discusses the Kensington Stone and the numerous fourteenth century arms unearthed in Minnesota which he accepts as proof of the presence of Norse explorers in that region in the fourteenth century.

7. Stefan Einarsson, Scandinavian philology, Johns Hopkins University. Dr. Einarsson reviewed *The Kensington Stone* in *Speculum*, July, 1933, pp. 400-408, and dwelt chiefly on the linguistic features of the inscription in the treatment of which he points out sundry errors. His findings are summarized in the concluding paragraph:

He [Holand] has actually succeeded in producing some linguistic material not easily refuted in support of the inscription, as for instance parallels to show that the singular of verbs could be used for the plural, or that the old dative plural was supplanted by the accusative.

In view of this circumstance and of the many other facts speaking for the genuineness of the stone, the well documented story of its origin, its weathered appearance, the plausible connection with fourteenth-century Scandinavian history, etc.—it is my conviction that linguists and runologists would do well to take the matter under renewed consideration before rendering their final verdict. Let us hope that the Swedish and Norwegian scholars working on this period will give us their opinion before long.

8. Anton Espeland, historian. In "Northmen in America in the Middle Ages" in *Norsk Folkekultur*, 18: 69-72, he writes:

Holand's book on the Kensington Stone is so convincing that it ought to be translated into Norwegian and thus become available to our general public. It is a scientific presentation, and nothing is affirmed without the scrupulous weighing of all evidence. There was much misconception about this inscription, and learned men thought it was a forgery, but now most scholars who have read the book will agree with Holand that the inscription is an authentic record of 1362.

9. Joseph Fischer, author of *Die Entdeckungen der Normannen in Amerika* (1902), declared himself in a letter to Professor Richard Hennig "von der Beweisführung Holand's überzeugt. *Contra facta non valent argumenta!*" Quoted by Hennig in his article "Der Runenstein von Kensington" in *Vergangenheit und Gegenwart* (1937), pp. 27-43.

10. A. D. Fraser, archaeologist, University of Virginia, discusses the subject, "The Norsemen in Canada," in *The Dalhousie Review* for July, 1937, pp. 175-186. On page 180 he writes:

There appears to be one genuine record on stone left by the Norsemen. This is at Kensington, in western Minnesota, a place hardly worthy of the name of town. Here an inscribed stone, bearing undoubted runic characters, was discovered nearly forty years ago. Inasmuch as Kensington is far off the supposed track of the Norsemen and the runes are demonstrably not of the eleventh-century type, the document was almost immediately dismissed as an impudent forgery. But with the passage of the years it has become apparent that the older authorities were at least too impatient, and Mr. Holand's recent reexamination of the stone and everything connected with it has resulted in convincing many scholars of its genuineness. To me, as a student of archaeology, the most convincing point in its favor is the condition of the stone. This is a prosaic and mechanical consideration that would escape the notice of the philologist. But there are limitations, as we know, to "the gentle art of faking," and the Kensington Stone shows definite marks of weathering not only on the roughly smoothed surface which bears the inscription but *within the letters themselves*. As the stone was found under the roots of a good-sized tree in a part of the State that was not settled till the sixties of last century, it is impossible for us to account for this weathered condition on any other ground than that which assumes its exposure to the elements, letters and all, for generations or centuries.

11. Richard Hennig in *Terrae Incognitae*, III, 268-299, Leiden, 1938. In this chapter of his exhaustive three-volume history of the discovery of America, Professor Hennig presents a searching review of the evidence for and against the authenticity of the Kensington inscription. His presentation indicates a full acquaintance with all the literature dealing with this subject as well as familiarity with all the contributions to the study of the Norse discovery of America. He finds that there are several independent lines of evidence which prove the authenticity of the inscription. His only disagreement with the conclusions of the present writer is that he believes that the explorers came into the present state of Minnesota by way of the Great Lakes. In a later article he rejects this view in favor of the Hudson Bay route (see "Normannen des 11.

Jahrhunderts in der Hudson Bai und an den groszen Seen," printed in *Petermanns Geographischen Mitteilungen,* 1939, pp. 58-60).

12. Richard Hennig in "Rassische Ueberreste Mittelalterlicher Normannen bei Eingeborenen Nordamerikas" in *Zeitschrift für Rassenkunde* (1937), VI, 20-28, reviews and endorses the theory that the Mandans were racially and culturally influenced by intermarriage with the survivors of the Kensington expedition of 1362.

13. Richard Hennig in *Petermanns Geographischen Mitteilungen,* 1938, pp. 88-89, has an article "Zur Frage der Echtheit des Runensteins von Kensington" in which he discusses the views of certain European philologists, particularly those of Professor Hjalmar Lindroth (see no. 20) and Wolfgang Krause (see no. 18). Professor Hennig has also written a number of other articles on the Kensington Stone.

14. Halldor Hermannsson in *The Problem of Wineland* (1936), p. 50, mentions the Kensington Stone and, without presenting any arguments, contents himself with the sweeping statement that "whether we look at it from a runological, linguistic, historical or geographical point of view, it is perfectly clear that the inscription is a modern forgery."

15. William Hovgaard, author of *Voyages of the Northmen to America* (1914), has reviewed *The Kensington Stone* in *The American-Scandinavian Review* (1932), XX, 224-230, and in *Geographical Review* (1932), XXII, 507-509. He summarizes his findings in the following:

The book presents convincing argument in favor of the genuineness of the inscription. Although there are points which are difficult to explain satisfactorily, they are not of such a nature as to justify its condemnation, and some points which at first seemed obscure, have been unexpectedly cleared up by corroborative evidence. Most remarkable are the finds in the same region of medieval finds of Scandinavian origin.

It must be admitted that Mr. Holand's arguments for the

authenticity of the inscription are well supported. The theory of a forgery is contradicted by statements and affidavits from which there seems no escape, and the corroborative evidence is very convincing.

16. G. M. Gathorne-Hardy, Assistant Librarian of the House of Lords and author of *The Norse Discoverers of America* (Oxford, 1921). Mr. Gathorne-Hardy has a fourteen-page review of *The Kensington Stone* in the December, 1932, issue of *Antiquity* (England) and he also reviewed the book in the *English Historical Review* (1933), XLVIII, 155-156, *Geographical Journal*, LXXIX, 437-438, and *American-Scandinavian Review*, XX, 382-383. In these four reviews he has touched on almost every aspect of the investigation. He has also summarized his impressions in a letter to the present writer which is given below:

I have great pleasure in writing down my main reasons for being convinced by you of the genuineness of the Kensington inscription. I will make it as short as possible, but the effect of your argument is cumulative, and I cannot do justice to it in two or three sentences.

1. The modern Scandinavian population is exonerated by a conclusive alibi. You produce very strong reasons for believing the tree which covered the stone to have been 70 years old. To be on the safe side, beyond reasonable controversy, I halve that age arbitrarily and still find the alibi complete.

2. The theory of fabrication involves the presence of a runologist in Minnesota at a date when he must have been almost as striking a phenomenon as a fourteenth-century expedition. The opponents of the stone may reasonably be challenged to perform the easy task of identifying such a *rara avis*. They have not done so.

3. This point is reinforced by the singular eccentricity necessarily attributed to the hypothetical forger.

a. He is a scholar of considerable attainments. He can read Latin and is familiar with the rare work of Ole Worm in that language. He quotes correctly the mediaeval and not the modern version of the Lord's Prayer. He is a pioneer in the historical research leading to the association of Paul Knutson with American exploration. The date and admixture of Swedes and Norwegians are together beyond the chance of coincidence. He is also a bit of a geologist for he recognizes that the site of his inscription was once an island. . . .

b. Whether scholar or illiterate, he is evidently a silly ass. . . . He taxes his scholarship and his imagination to the limit to tell a long and circumstantial story, introducing figures— almost an unknown feature in runic inscriptions—and saying *prima facie* impossible things as that he is on an island 14 days from the sea. This all is not only superfluous, but increases with every word the chance of a fatal slip. Meantime he is spending at least two days carving the stone in a spot where it is most unlikely to be found, but where he is extremely likely to have his scalp removed at any moment. . . .

4. What is left on the other side? Merely the linguistic peculiarities—a two-edged weapon—for a modern scholar is more likely to write grammatically than a fourteenth-century Swedish sailor.

You have, besides, produced precedent for every point impugned and you argue with force that the irregularities criticized were probably much more common in colloquial usage. The alleged English words are, in particular, an obvious mare's-nest.

5. Finally, if we are still wavering, there are the battle axes, etc. They are mediaeval Scandinavian and apparently exclusively Scandinavian, in type. . . .

Well, I have been carried away into greater length than I intended or you desire, but if your case is not conclusive many men must be hanged annually on insufficient evidence.

17. *Journal of American History* (1932), XXVI, 120-145, contains a very detailed review of *The Kensington Stone* and concludes with the following words: "Mr. Holand has definitely overthrown all specific arguments against his contentions, and no authoritative answers have been made to the historical questions which he has raised, and the solution of which problems seems logically settled by his own deductions."

18. Wolfgang Krause, German runologist, has an article entitled "Runen in Amerika" in *Germanien* (1937), pp. 231-235, in which he attacks the authenticity of the Kensington inscription. He believes it was written by a man "whose daily speech was English, but who was much and thoroughly (eingehend) occupied with runes and the older Scandinavian language." He finds fault with the fact that the date on the stone is not accompanied by the medieval phrase equivalent to our Anno Domini. His solution to the problem is suggested by his question: "Who will maintain that the stone could not have been pushed in between the roots of the tree?"

These remarks show that Professor Krause is not familiar with the circumstances of the find, the weathered condition of the inscription, or the local history of the region where it was found. His objections are answered by Professor R. Hennig in *Terrae Incognitae* (1938), III, 289-290.

19. Lawrence M. Larson, historian, has an article entitled "The Kensington Rune Stone" in the March, 1936, issue of *Minnesota History*, pp. 20-37, which begins thus:

> With the publication of Hjalmar R. Holand's book, *The Kensington Stone*, many who had earlier been skeptical came to a reluctant conclusion that the discussion as to the authenticity of the Kensington inscription had been brought to a close. The author seemed to have met all the objections that hostile critics had been able to raise; he had built up an argument that seemed entirely plausible; and he had brought to the support of his contention an array of proofs that seemed incontrovertible and quite abundant. A few reviewers had the temerity still to condemn the book as a clever brief for an outrageous forgery, but these counted for little. Nearly all the reviews that came to the writer's attention seemed to concede that the author had proved his case.

But these acknowledgments by Professor Larson do not mean that he is satisfied that the inscription is authentic, for the rest of his article is devoted to the presentation of such arguments as he believes had not been answered. He concludes his article by advancing the opinion that the inscription is a forgery concocted in the early eighties by two men whose purpose was "to foist a new sort of hoax on credulous citizens for the enjoyment that the inevitable discussion would bring" (p. 36).

The article was answered by the present writer in the next issue of *Minnesota History* (17: 166-188).

20. Professor Hjalmar Lindroth, Swedish lexicographer. In a letter of January 11, 1938, to Professor Richard Hennig and printed by the latter in *Petermanns Geographischen Mitteilungen* (1938), pp. 89-90, Professor Lindroth states the attitude of modern scholarship toward the linguistic and runological aspects of the Kensington Stone in terms which the large majority of philologists familiar with this field will probably find acceptable. While his position is one of strict neutrality, he incidentally demolishes one of the chief linguistic arguments against the inscription (the objection based on the use of verbs in singular with subject in plural). Professor Lindroth's letter as given by Hennig reads as follows:

1. There exists a sharp conflict between the data which have reference to the find as such and those which concern the language. In the inscription are several linguistic forms that speak strongly against the possibility that the inscription was made in the fourteenth century. The runic characters also appear to be divergent from the types which we have assumed represented the fourteenth century. To be sure, the material available for comparison is somewhat scarce. On the other hand the reliableness of the testimony as regards the circumstances of the find seems to me to be very strong.

2. In my opinion therefore the obligation of presenting proof should not rest onesidedly on those who argue in favor of the authenticity. Especially should the runologist refrain from pressing the theory of a fraud until he is able to prove the origin of the runic alphabet of the inscription. If we have to do with a recent fraud, there should be no insuperable diffi-

culties to establish the proof. In fact, the question regarding the runes on the stone is a problem by itself which independently calls for an investigation.

3. The investigations which up to date have been made concerning the language of the inscription have been rather superficial in certain respects. If the forms *haþe*, *war*, *kom* (all in plural function)—instead of *hafdo*, *warom*, *komom*—are declared to be impossible for the latter half of the fourteenth century, it must nevertheless be conceded that *haþe* occurs in *Codex Oxenstj.* (end of same century), and singular verbs in plural function occur even earlier (in classic Old-Swedish) not so seldom (Noreen, *Altschwed, Gram.*, p. 475). We are here speaking of literary Swedish: In the colloquial speech such forms must have occurred much earlier and been far more common. The same applies presumably to forms like *war ok fiske* and *wore skip*. If the style may be described as of a decidedly nonliterary character (*cf.* Holand, p. 98), we certainly cannot demand that the writer of the inscription should have given the specification *Anno Domini*. To be sure, such considerations must in nowise keep us from emphasizing the forms which seem to be impossible, e.g., nonswedish (fråm, rise, þeþ, etc.).

4. Thus we find signs standing against signs. I doubt if the question concerning the authenticity of the Kensington Stone will ever be solved. In my opinion the last word has not yet been spoken.

21. Philip Ainsworth Means, historian, for the last three years has been occupied with a searching investigation of the Kensington Stone. The ramifications of this study have led him to the archives of Norway, Sweden, Denmark and Iceland. Coming thus from a scholar who has made such a thorough study of the inscription, the following tentative statement, from a new book on a related subject which will soon be issued by Mr. Means, is of great interest:

The Kensington Stone, dated 1362, is in my opinion indubitably an authentic inscribed stone as of that date. Some of my reasons for thus believing are:

1. The stone was found clasped in the roots of a tree in

1898. As the tree cannot have been less than 25 years old at that time—and it may have been a good deal older—the stone must have been in that spot since 1873 or longer. The formation of the roots which clasped the stone shows that the stone must have been there since the time when the tree began to grow. In 1873 or earlier the Scandinavian settlers in Minnesota were hard-working farmer folk who were struggling to earn their living under difficult conditions. If there was among them a man sufficiently erudite to be able to compose a runic inscription—which is most unlikely to have been the case—such a man would not have had the slightest shadow of motive for spending two or more days in cutting the inscription and for burying it in the ground in such a way that its discovery would be a very remote possibility. Nor could the thing, including the cutting of the inscription and the burying of the 200-lb. stone, have been done without attracting attention. For one thing, it would have been asked why the man was wasting his time in such impractical ways.

2. Creation of the inscription in 1873 or somewhat before that time being in the highest degree improbable, we can only conclude that the stone is far older, and that it was made in its date-year, 1362. It is possible to find proto-type runes of the fourteenth century or earlier, including the runic numerals of the inscription.

3. The oldest extant version of King Magnus's commission to Paul Knutsson (Powell Knudsson) dates only from about 1600, unfortunately. It is in the Royal Library, Copenhagen, MS. GL. kgl. sml. 2432, 4to, fol. 257, recto and verso. It is probably a copy made about 1600 from a much older original. At any rate, it proves that the Magnus document is not a recent fabrication. The text of the 1600 document accords with Mr. Holand's printing of King Magnus's commission on p. 75 of his 1932 book.

4. If it be objected that the inscriber of the stone, if working on it in the fourteenth century, ought to have dated it "in such and such year of the reign of King Magnus," or in some such form, I have two replies: (a) Such a form would have wasted much time by using more runic figures than necessary; it was much shorter to write the year; (b) The inscriber and his companions had been absent from Norway for years and

so could not know whether or not Magnus was still reigning; so, again, it was simpler to set down the year alone.

5. A modern forger, with books of reference, etc., handy, would almost certainly have sought to give a false air of antiquity to his work by using the antique form of dating. The ancient maker of the inscription, wishing to save time and labor in the dangerous circumstances under which he and his companions were, set down the date in the briefest possible way by writing the numerals of the year.

6. It seems to me that Mr. Holand is wrong with regard to the route taken by the expedition. I think that, having been to Greenland to look for the lost ones, they went to Vinland, between Cape Cod and the Hudson. A manuscript of the fourteenth century in Paris makes it look very probable that Vinland was then a secret colony of the King of Norway. From Vinland, as the inscription says, the expedition went west, possibly to some point near Duluth, where their ship or ships were left with ten men. The ship or ships may have been mere boats or even Indian canoes, built or acquired somewhere along the route. From near Duluth they could go overland in two weeks to some lake two days north of Kensington, from which lake they retreated doubtless to the place where the inscription was made.

22. Eilert Pastor, German historian, in *Wacht am Osten* (May, 1937), 4, 321-338, has an article entitled "Der Runenstein von Kensington" in which the merits of the problem are examined with keen insight and finesse. He writes:

Undoubtedly, we have reason to hope that the Kensington Stone, having told us so much already, will yet tell us more. No one can any longer doubt its genuineness and one must consider it as an important link in the history of the inhabitants of two continents and of the members of two races—a testimonial of unheard-of courage and tragic fate proudly borne and suffered—to speak with Holand—the most important runic inscription ever known to mankind.

23. Milo M. Quaife, historian, has an article entitled "The Myth of the Kensington Rune Stone" in *The New*

England Quarterly for December, 1934, in which he attempts to show that no valid arguments have been presented in favor of the stone. He concludes his presentation with the following summary (p. 638):

The laborious effort to demonstrate the validity of the runic record on historical grounds ends, therefore, in utter failure. The possibility remains that some future investigator, more competent than those who have labored hitherto to validate the runic inscription, may provide an historical basis for it worthy of serious attention. This has not yet been done, despite a quarter of a century of effort on the part of Mr. Holand and those who have accepted his view, and the runologists may continue their study of the inscription entirely free from any supposition that an historical presumption favoring its authenticity has been established.

A reply to Mr. Quaife's article was printed in *The New England Quarterly* of March, 1935, pp. 42-62.

24. A. A. Stomberg, Professor of Scandinavian Languages and Literature, University of Minnesota. Under the title "The Kensington Stone in Minnesota," Professor Stomberg has an article in *Allsvensk Samling* (Göteborg, Sweden, August 30, 1932) in which he reviews the arguments for and against the authenticity of the inscription in a clear and systematic manner. Being familiar with the local conditions of the finding place, he finds the circumstances to be such that they point inescapably to the conclusion that the inscription was not made after the region was settled by white men. He also finds the historical background of the fourteenth century to be in entire agreement with the assumption that the inscription is genuine. In his opinion the only question that has not yet been fully answered is whether or not the runes and linguistic forms of the inscription are justifiable in the light of fourteenth century usage. On this he ventures no opinion.

25. W. S. Wallace, University of Toronto Library. In a survey entitled "Literature Relating to the Norse Voy-

ages to America" in the *Canadian Historical Review*, March, 1939, Dr. Wallace writes:

His [Mr. Holand's] book is difficult to characterize. While using the language of impartial history, he is in reality a special pleader: he reminds one of the lawyer who seeks to squeeze out of the evidence every ounce of weight he can in favor of his client. . . . But it must be confessed that he builds up an impressive argument in favor of the authenticity of the Kensington Rune Stone itself. . . . Personally, I find it easier to believe that the Kensington Rune Stone is genuine than that it is a modern forgery.

26. James J. Walsh, author of *The Thirteenth, Greatest of Centuries*, has an article in *Columbia* of August, 1933, entitled "The First Prayer in America" in which he presents his views concerning the Kensington Stone. These are summarized in the following words:

More and more details of information are accumulating as the result of research that make any suspicion against the authenticity of the inscription untenable. Everything now, as was suggested in an article in *Science News Letter* some months ago—and *Science News Letter*, it must not be forgotten, is the organ of the National Scientific Research Council—points to the authenticity of the stone and the actual historicity of the details with regard to this expedition of Goths and Norwegians into the Northwest.

27. M. W. Williams, author of *Social Scandinavia in the Viking Age* and Professor of History, Goucher College, writes in the *Journal of American History* (1932), XXVI, 128-129:

By his book, *The Kensington Stone*, Hjalmar R. Holand has, I believe, established the authenticity of the inscription of that stone. He has added to our knowledge of American history the important fact that in 1362 a party of Swedes and Norwegians penetrated the American continent as far as the present state of Minnesota. In view of the evidence logically presented by Mr. Holand, it takes less credulity to accept this view than to persist in believing the inscription to be a fraud.

28. George Woodbine, Professor of History, Yale University. For a number of years Professor Woodbine has been using *The Kensington Stone* as a topic study in his seminar devoted to Methods of Historical Research. He has therefore had exceptional opportunities for weighing the evidence concerning the inscription. In a letter to the writer (publication permitted) he writes:

There is no historical subject outside of my own particular field that interests me more than that of the authenticity of the Kensington Stone. I am astonished at the number of teachers of American History who seem never to have heard of the stone; they neither believe its authenticity nor reject it; they know nothing about it. Something should be done to acquaint them with the facts of the case and to enable them intelligently to take sides in the controversy, and to have an opinion as to where, in their judgment, the weight of the evidence lies.

29. After proofreading of this book was completed, the author obtained a copy of the last published work on the discovery of America. This is Jörg Lechler's *Die Entdecker Amerikas vor Columbus*, Leipsig, 1939. Dr. Lechler's work is not so much a presentation of the facts of the discovery as it is a searching critical review of the findings of previous commentators, illustrated by a wealth of very helpful illustrations. On pages 51-57 he discusses the Kensington Stone which he calls of "auszerordentlichem historischem Wert." He says:

The inscription at first was naturally declared a fraud as it seemed out of the question that it could be true. With this fixed idea numerous examinations were made, for the purpose, under all circumstances, to prove that the inscription must be false. Any investigation inspired by the desire to impartially test the value of any linguistic or other objection to learn to what extent it militates against the authenticity of the inscription has not yet been made. At present we have only the excellent presentation of Mr. Holand to whose initiative we are indebted for the reopening of the investigation.

Dr. Lechler thereupon reviews the principal arguments against the Stone and fails to find that they have any importance.

INDEX

A (long) *and* Å, 291, 314
Æ *changed to* E, 298-299
AI *changed to* E, 298-299
Å, no rune for, 315
Å *and* O, 303, 314
Aarbøger for Nordisk Oldkyn-dighed, 46, 81 n., 238 n., 299 n.
Aasen, Ivar, 283
Aborigines of Minnesota, The, N. H. Winchell, 277, 282
Adam of Bremen, 3, 47, 48, 63, 70
Adams, James Truslow, *cited,* 318-319
Aftenblad (Bergen), 92 n.
Ager, W., editor of *Eau Claire Reform,* 132
Ahlquist, *cited,* 307 n.
Ako's obituary, 169 n.
Albany River, 71, 72, 142
Albrecht, Duke of Mecklenburg and King of Sweden, 135, 148, 292
Alexandria, Minn., 108, 121, 128, 207, 211, 212, 226
Alf, Bishop of Greenland, 143
Alfrædi Islenzk, 25 n.
Algorismus, 182
Algotsson, Benedikt, 135
Alliterative verse, 57
Allsvensk Samling, 331
Almanac or *calendarium perpet-uum,* 178, 179, 180. Cf. obituary
Almanak (1899), 310 n.
Alphabets, Greek, Latin, Runic, etc., 159
Altswedische Grammatik, Noreen, 291 n., 300, 302, 303, 306, 311 n., 312 n., 313, 314 n., 315 n., 316 n., 328
Altswedisches Lesebuch, Noreen, 290 n., 299 n., 305 n., 316 n.

Ameralik fjord (Lysufjord), 80
America, date of Leif's discovery, 28
"American and European Swords . . . U. S. National Museum," 236
American-Scandinavian Review, 323, 324
Amerika (Madison, Wis.), 105
Anchor stones, medieval, *see* Mooring stones
Annaler for Nordisk Oldkyn-dighed, 182 n., 307 n.
Annales Vetustissimi, 183 n.
Anderson, Rasmus B., 105 n., 219, 311
Andrew township, Minnesota, 234
Andrews, A. Leroy, 45
Angelic salutation, the, 183-184
Anteckningar till Vestgötalagen, 314
Antiquity (a magazine), 324
Apocopation, 302, 303, 304
Appalachian Mountains, 267, 268
Arabic numerals in northwestern Europe and Iceland, 181-182
Arctander township, Minnesota, 234
Ari Frodi, 190
Ari the Learned, 18, 61, 62
Ari Marson, 21
Arickaree Indians, 279 n.
Arkiv for Nordisk Filologi, 44, 82 n., 155 n., 289, 296 n., 300 n., 314 n.
Arndt, Wilhelm, 169
Arne, Bishop of Greenland, 80, 143, 146
Arnemagneanske Haandskrift, Det, 54 n.
Aslo, ancient name for Oslo, 314

INDEX

A CATALOGUE OF SELECTED DOVER BOOKS
IN ALL FIELDS OF INTEREST

A CATALOGUE OF SELECTED DOVER BOOKS
IN ALL FIELDS OF INTEREST

WHAT IS SCIENCE?, *N. Campbell*
The role of experiment and measurement, the function of mathematics, the nature of scientific laws, the difference between laws and theories, the limitations of science, and many similarly provocative topics are treated clearly and without technicalities by an eminent scientist. "Still an excellent introduction to scientific philosophy," H. Margenau in *Physics Today*. "A first-rate primer . . . deserves a wide audience," *Scientific American*. 192pp. 5⅜ x 8.
S43   Paperbound $1.25

THE NATURE OF LIGHT AND COLOUR IN THE OPEN AIR, *M. Minnaert*
Why are shadows sometimes blue, sometimes green, or other colors depending on the light and surroundings? What causes mirages? Why do multiple suns and moons appear in the sky? Professor Minnaert explains these unusual phenomena and hundreds of others in simple, easy-to-understand terms based on optical laws and the properties of light and color. No mathematics is required but artists, scientists, students, and everyone fascinated by these "tricks" of nature will find thousands of useful and amazing pieces of information. Hundreds of observational experiments are suggested which require no special equipment. 200 illustrations; 42 photos. xvi + 362pp. 5⅜ x 8.
T196   Paperbound $2.00

THE STRANGE STORY OF THE QUANTUM, AN ACCOUNT FOR THE GENERAL READER OF THE GROWTH OF IDEAS UNDERLYING OUR PRESENT ATOMIC KNOWLEDGE, *B. Hoffmann*
Presents lucidly and expertly, with barest amount of mathematics, the problems and theories which led to modern quantum physics. Dr. Hoffmann begins with the closing years of the 19th century, when certain trifling discrepancies were noticed, and with illuminating analogies and examples takes you through the brilliant concepts of Planck, Einstein, Pauli, Broglie, Bohr, Schroedinger, Heisenberg, Dirac, Sommerfeld, Feynman, etc. This edition includes a new, long postscript carrying the story through 1958. "Of the books attempting an account of the history and contents of our modern atomic physics which have come to my attention, this is the best," H. Margenau, Yale University, in *American Journal of Physics*. 32 tables and line illustrations. Index. 275pp. 5⅜ x 8.
T518   Paperbound $2.00

GREAT IDEAS OF MODERN MATHEMATICS: THEIR NATURE AND USE, *Jagjit Singh*
Reader with only high school math will understand main mathematical ideas of modern physics, astronomy, genetics, psychology, evolution, etc. better than many who use them as tools, but comprehend little of their basic structure. Author uses his wide knowledge of non-mathematical fields in brilliant exposition of differential equations, matrices, group theory, logic, statistics, problems of mathematical foundations, imaginary numbers, vectors, etc. Original publication. 2 appendixes. 2 indexes. 65 ills. 322pp. 5⅜ x 8.
T587   Paperbound $2.25

THE MUSIC OF THE SPHERES: THE MATERIAL UNIVERSE — FROM ATOM TO QUASAR, SIMPLY EXPLAINED, *Guy Murchie*
Vast compendium of fact, modern concept and theory, observed and calculated data, historical background guides intelligent layman through the material universe. Brilliant exposition of earth's construction, explanations for moon's craters, atmospheric components of Venus and Mars (with data from recent fly-by's), sun spots, sequences of star birth and death, neighboring galaxies, contributions of Galileo, Tycho Brahe, Kepler, etc.; and (Vol. 2) construction of the atom (describing newly discovered sigma and xi subatomic particles), theories of sound, color and light, space and time, including relativity theory, quantum theory, wave theory, probability theory, work of Newton, Maxwell, Faraday, Einstein, de Broglie, etc. "Best presentation yet offered to the intelligent general reader," *Saturday Review*. Revised (1967). Index. 319 illustrations by the author. Total of xx + 644pp. 5⅜ x 8½.
T1809, T1810 Two volume set, paperbound $4.00

FOUR LECTURES ON RELATIVITY AND SPACE, *Charles Proteus Steinmetz*
Lecture series, given by great mathematician and electrical engineer, generally considered one of the best popular-level expositions of special and general relativity theories and related questions. Steinmetz translates complex mathematical reasoning into language accessible to laymen through analogy, example and comparison. Among topics covered are relativity of motion, location, time; of mass; acceleration; 4-dimensional time-space; geometry of the gravitational field; curvature and bending of space; non-Euclidean geometry. Index. 40 illustrations. x + 142pp. 5⅜ x 8½.
S1771 Paperbound $1.35

HOW TO KNOW THE WILD FLOWERS, *Mrs. William Starr Dana*
Classic nature book that has introduced thousands to wonders of American wild flowers. Color-season principle of organization is easy to use, even by those with no botanical training, and the genial, refreshing discussions of history, folklore, uses of over 1,000 native and escape flowers, foliage plants are informative as well as fun to read. Over 170 full-page plates, collected from several editions, may be colored in to make permanent records of finds. Revised to conform with 1950 edition of Gray's Manual of Botany. xlii + 438pp. 5⅜ x 8½.
T332 Paperbound $2.25

MANUAL OF THE TREES OF NORTH AMERICA, *Charles Sprague Sargent*
Still unsurpassed as most comprehensive, reliable study of North American tree characteristics, precise locations and distribution. By dean of American dendrologists. Every tree native to U.S., Canada, Alaska; 185 genera, 717 species, described in detail—leaves, flowers, fruit, winterbuds, bark, wood, growth habits, etc. plus discussion of varieties and local variants, immaturity variations. Over 100 keys, including unusual 11-page analytical key to genera, aid in identification. 783 clear illustrations of flowers, fruit, leaves. An unmatched permanent reference work for all nature lovers. Second enlarged (1926) edition. Synopsis of families. Analytical key to genera. Glossary of technical terms. Index. 783 illustrations, 1 map. Total of 982pp. 5⅜ x 8.
T277, T278 Two volume set, paperbound $6.00

It's Fun to Make Things From Scrap Materials,
Evelyn Glantz Hershoff
What use are empty spools, tin cans, bottle tops? What can be made from rubber bands, clothes pins, paper clips, and buttons? This book provides simply worded instructions and large diagrams showing you how to make cookie cutters, toy trucks, paper turkeys, Halloween masks, telephone sets, aprons, linoleum block- and spatter prints — in all 399 projects! Many are easy enough for young children to figure out for themselves; some challenging enough to entertain adults; all are remarkably ingenious ways to make things from materials that cost pennies or less! Formerly "Scrap Fun for Everyone." Index. 214 illustrations. 373pp. 5⅜ x 8½.   T1251   Paperbound $1.75

Symbolic Logic and The Game of Logic, *Lewis Carroll*
"Symbolic Logic" is not concerned with modern symbolic logic, but is instead a collection of over 380 problems posed with charm and imagination, using the syllogism and a fascinating diagrammatic method of drawing conclusions. In "The Game of Logic" Carroll's whimsical imagination devises a logical game played with 2 diagrams and counters (included) to manipulate hundreds of tricky syllogisms. The final section, "Hit or Miss" is a lagniappe of 101 additional puzzles in the delightful Carroll manner. Until this reprint edition, both of these books were rarities costing up to $15 each. Symbolic Logic: Index. xxxi + 199pp. The Game of Logic: 96pp. 2 vols. bound as one. 5⅜ x 8.
                                         T492   Paperbound $2.00

Mathematical Puzzles of Sam Loyd, Part I
selected and edited by M. Gardner
Choice puzzles by the greatest American puzzle creator and innovator. Selected from his famous collection, "Cyclopedia of Puzzles," they retain the unique style and historical flavor of the originals. There are posers based on arithmetic, algebra, probability, game theory, route tracing, topology, counter and sliding block, operations research, geometrical dissection. Includes the famous "14-15" puzzle which was a national craze, and his "Horse of a Different Color" which sold millions of copies. 117 of his most ingenious puzzles in all. 120 line drawings and diagrams. Solutions. Selected references. xx + 167pp. 5⅜ x 8.
                                         T498   Paperbound $1.25

String Figures and How to Make Them, *Caroline Furness Jayne*
107 string figures plus variations selected from the best primitive and modern examples developed by Navajo, Apache, pygmies of Africa, Eskimo, in Europe, Australia, China, etc. The most readily understandable, easy-to-follow book in English on perennially popular recreation. Crystal-clear exposition; step-by-step diagrams. Everyone from kindergarten children to adults looking for unusual diversion will be endlessly amused. Index. Bibliography. Introduction by A. C. Haddon. 17 full-page plates, 960 illustrations. xxiii + 401pp. 5⅜ x 8½.
                                         T152   Paperbound $2.25

Paper Folding for Beginners, *W. D. Murray and F. J. Rigney*
A delightful introduction to the varied and entertaining Japanese art of origami (paper folding), with a full, crystal-clear text that anticipates every difficulty; over 275 clearly labeled diagrams of all important stages in creation. You get results at each stage, since complex figures are logically developed from simpler ones. 43 different pieces are explained: sailboats, frogs, roosters, etc. 6 photographic plates. 279 diagrams. 95pp. 5⅝ x 8⅜.
                                         T713   Paperbound $1.00

PRINCIPLES OF ART HISTORY,
H. Wölfflin
Analyzing such terms as "baroque," "classic," "neoclassic," "primitive," "picturesque," and 164 different works by artists like Botticelli, van Cleve, Dürer, Hobbema, Holbein, Hals, Rembrandt, Titian, Brueghel, Vermeer, and many others, the author establishes the classifications of art history and style on a firm, concrete basis. This classic of art criticism shows what really occurred between the 14th-century primitives and the sophistication of the 18th century in terms of basic attitudes and philosophies. "A remarkable lesson in the art of seeing," *Sat. Rev. of Literature*. Translated from the 7th German edition. 150 illustrations. 254pp. 6⅛ x 9¼. T276 Paperbound $2.00

PRIMITIVE ART,
Franz Boas
This authoritative and exhaustive work by a great American anthropologist covers the entire gamut of primitive art. Pottery, leatherwork, metal work, stone work, wood, basketry, are treated in detail. Theories of primitive art, historical depth in art history, technical virtuosity, unconscious levels of patterning, symbolism, styles, literature, music, dance, etc. A must book for the interested layman, the anthropologist, artist, handicrafter (hundreds of unusual motifs), and the historian. Over 900 illustrations (50 ceramic vessels, 12 totem poles, etc.). 376pp. 5⅜ x 8. T25 Paperbound $2.50

THE GENTLEMAN AND CABINET MAKER'S DIRECTOR,
Thomas Chippendale
A reprint of the 1762 catalogue of furniture designs that went on to influence generations of English and Colonial and Early Republic American furniture makers. The 200 plates, most of them full-page sized, show Chippendale's designs for French (Louis XV), Gothic, and Chinese-manner chairs, sofas, canopy and dome beds, cornices, chamber organs, cabinets, shaving tables, commodes, picture frames, frets, candle stands, chimney pieces, decorations, etc. The drawings are all elegant and highly detailed; many include construction diagrams and elevations. A supplement of 24 photographs shows surviving pieces of original and Chippendale-style pieces of furniture. Brief biography of Chippendale by N. I. Bienenstock, editor of *Furniture World*. Reproduced from the 1762 edition. 200 plates, plus 19 photographic plates. vi + 249pp. 9⅛ x 12¼. T1601 Paperbound $3.50

AMERICAN ANTIQUE FURNITURE: A BOOK FOR AMATEURS,
Edgar G. Miller, Jr.
Standard introduction and practical guide to identification of valuable American antique furniture. 2115 illustrations, mostly photographs taken by the author in 148 private homes, are arranged in chronological order in extensive chapters on chairs, sofas, chests, desks, bedsteads, mirrors, tables, clocks, and other articles. Focus is on furniture accessible to the collector, including simpler pieces and a larger than usual coverage of Empire style. Introductory chapters identify structural elements, characteristics of various styles, how to avoid fakes, etc. "We are frequently asked to name some book on American furniture that will meet the requirements of the novice collector, the beginning dealer, and . . . the general public. . . . We believe Mr. Miller's two volumes more completely satisfy this specification than any other work," *Antiques*. Appendix. Index. Total of vi + 1106pp. 7⅞ x 10¾. T1599, T1600 Two volume set, paperbound $7.50

THE BAD CHILD'S BOOK OF BEASTS, MORE BEASTS FOR WORSE CHILDREN, and A MORAL ALPHABET, *H. Belloc*
Hardly and anthology of humorous verse has appeared in the last 50 years without at least a couple of these famous nonsense verses. But one must see the entire volumes — with all the delightful original illustrations by Sir Basil Blackwood — to appreciate fully Belloc's charming and witty verses that play so subacidly on the platitudes of life and morals that beset his day — and ours. A great humor classic. Three books in one. Total of 157pp. 5⅜ x 8.
T749   Paperbound $1.00

THE DEVIL'S DICTIONARY, *Ambrose Bierce*
Sardonic and irreverent barbs puncturing the pomposities and absurdities of American politics, business, religion, literature, and arts, by the country's greatest satirist in the classic tradition. Epigrammatic as Shaw, piercing as Swift, American as Mark Twain, Will Rogers, and Fred Allen, Bierce will always remain the favorite of a small coterie of enthusiasts, and of writers and speakers whom he supplies with "some of the most gorgeous witticisms of the English language" (H. L. Mencken). Over 1000 entries in alphabetical order. 144pp. 5⅜ x 8.   T487   Paperbound $1.00

THE COMPLETE NONSENSE OF EDWARD LEAR.
This is the only complete edition of this master of gentle madness available at a popular price. *A Book of Nonsense, Nonsense Songs, More Nonsense Songs and Stories* in their entirety with all the old favorites that have delighted children and adults for years. The Dong With A Luminous Nose, The Jumblies, The Owl and the Pussycat, and hundreds of other bits of wonderful nonsense: 214 limericks, 3 sets of Nonsense Botany, 5 Nonsense Alphabets, 546 drawings by Lear himself, and much more. 320pp. 5⅜ x 8.   T167   Paperbound $1.75

THE WIT AND HUMOR OF OSCAR WILDE, *ed. by Alvin Redman*
Wilde at his most brilliant, in 1000 epigrams exposing weaknesses and hypocrisies of "civilized" society. Divided into 49 categories—sin, wealth, women, America, etc.—to aid writers, speakers. Includes excerpts from his trials, books, plays, criticism. Formerly "The Epigrams of Oscar Wilde." Introduction by Vyvyan Holland, Wilde's only living son. Introductory essay by editor. 260pp. 5⅜ x 8.   T602   Paperbound $1.50

A CHILD'S PRIMER OF NATURAL HISTORY, *Oliver Herford*
Scarcely an anthology of whimsy and humor has appeared in the last 50 years without a contribution from Oliver Herford. Yet the works from which these examples are drawn have been almost impossible to obtain! Here at last are Herford's improbable definitions of a menagerie of familiar and weird animals, each verse illustrated by the author's own drawings. 24 drawings in 2 colors; 24 additional drawings. vii + 95pp. 6½ x 6.   T1647   Paperbound $1.00

THE BROWNIES: THEIR BOOK, *Palmer Cox*
The book that made the Brownies a household word. Generations of readers have enjoyed the antics, predicaments and adventures of these jovial sprites, who emerge from the forest at night to play or to come to the aid of a deserving human. Delightful illustrations by the author decorate nearly every page. 24 short verse tales with 266 illustrations. 155pp. 6⅝ x 9¼.
T1265   Paperbound $1.50

THE PRINCIPLES OF PSYCHOLOGY,
William James

The full long-course, unabridged, of one of the great classics of Western literature and science. Wonderfully lucid descriptions of human mental activity, the stream of thought, consciousness, time perception, memory, imagination, emotions, reason, abnormal phenomena, and similar topics. Original contributions are integrated with the work of such men as Berkeley, Binet, Mills, Darwin, Hume, Kant, Royce, Schopenhauer, Spinoza, Locke, Descartes, Galton, Wundt, Lotze, Herbart, Fechner, and scores of others. All contrasting interpretations of mental phenomena are examined in detail—introspective analysis, philosophical interpretation, and experimental research. "A classic," *Journal of Consulting Psychology.* "The main lines are as valid as ever," *Psychoanalytical Quarterly.* "Standard reading . . . a classic of interpretation," *Psychiatric Quarterly.* 94 illustrations. 1408pp. 5⅜ x 8.

T381, T382   Two volume set, paperbound $6.00

VISUAL ILLUSIONS: THEIR CAUSES, CHARACTERISTICS AND APPLICATIONS,
M. Luckiesh

"Seeing is deceiving," asserts the author of this introduction to virtually every type of optical illusion known. The text both describes and explains the principles involved in color illusions, figure-ground, distance illusions, etc. 100 photographs, drawings and diagrams prove how easy it is to fool the sense: circles that aren't round, parallel lines that seem to bend, stationary figures that seem to move as you stare at them — illustration after illustration strains our credulity at what we see. Fascinating book from many points of view, from applications for artists, in camouflage, etc. to the psychology of vision. New introduction by William Ittleson, Dept. of Psychology, Queens College. Index. Bibliography. xxi + 252pp. 5⅜ x 8½.   T1530   Paperbound $1.50

FADS AND FALLACIES IN THE NAME OF SCIENCE,
Martin Gardner

This is the standard account of various cults, quack systems, and delusions which have masqueraded as science: hollow earth fanatics. Reich and orgone sex energy, dianetics, Atlantis, multiple moons, Forteanism, flying saucers, medical fallacies like iridiagnosis, zone therapy, etc. A new chapter has been added on Bridey Murphy, psionics, and other recent manifestations in this field. This is a fair, reasoned appraisal of eccentric theory which provides excellent inoculation against cleverly masked nonsense. "Should be read by everyone, scientist and non-scientist alike," R. T. Birge, Prof. Emeritus of Physics, Univ. of California; Former President, American Physical Society. Index. x + 365pp. 5⅜ x 8.   T394   Paperbound $2.00

ILLUSIONS AND DELUSIONS OF THE SUPERNATURAL AND THE OCCULT,
D. H. Rawcliffe

Holds up to rational examination hundreds of persistent delusions including crystal gazing, automatic writing, table turning, mediumistic trances, mental healing, stigmata, lycanthropy, live burial, the Indian Rope Trick, spiritualism, dowsing, telepathy, clairvoyance, ghosts, ESP, etc. The author explains and exposes the mental and physical deceptions involved, making this not only an exposé of supernatural phenomena, but a valuable exposition of characteristic types of abnormal psychology. Originally titled "The Psychology of the Occult." 14 illustrations. Index. 551pp. 5⅜ x 8. T503 Paperbound $2.75

FAIRY TALE COLLECTIONS, *edited by Andrew Lang*
Andrew Lang's fairy tale collections make up the richest shelf-full of traditional children's stories anywhere available. Lang supervised the translation of stories from all over the world—familiar European tales collected by Grimm, animal stories from Negro Africa, myths of primitive Australia, stories from Russia, Hungary, Iceland, Japan, and many other countries. Lang's selection of translations are unusually high; many authorities consider that the most familiar tales find their best versions in these volumes. All collections are richly decorated and illustrated by H. J. Ford and other artists.

THE BLUE FAIRY BOOK. 37 stories. 138 illustrations. ix + 390pp. 5⅜ x 8½.
T1437 Paperbound $1.95

THE GREEN FAIRY BOOK. 42 stories. 100 illustrations. xiii + 366pp. 5⅜ x 8½.
T1439 Paperbound $1.75

THE BROWN FAIRY BOOK. 32 stories. 50 illustrations, 8 in color. xii + 350pp. 5⅜ x 8½.
T1438 Paperbound $1.95

THE BEST TALES OF HOFFMANN, *edited by E. F. Bleiler*
10 stories by E. T. A. Hoffmann, one of the greatest of all writers of fantasy. The tales include "The Golden Flower Pot," "Automata," "A New Year's Eve Adventure," "Nutcracker and the King of Mice," "Sand-Man," and others. Vigorous characterizations of highly eccentric personalities, remarkably imaginative situations, and intensely fast pacing has made these tales popular all over the world for 150 years. Editor's introduction. 7 drawings by Hoffmann. xxxiii + 419pp. 5⅜ x 8½.
T1793 Paperbound $2.25

GHOST AND HORROR STORIES OF AMBROSE BIERCE, *edited by E. F. Bleiler*
Morbid, eerie, horrifying tales of possessed poets, shabby aristocrats, revived corpses, and haunted malefactors. Widely acknowledged as the best of their kind between Poe and the moderns, reflecting their author's inner torment and bitter view of life. Includes "Damned Thing," "The Middle Toe of the Right Foot," "The Eyes of the Panther," "Visions of the Night," "Moxon's Master," and over a dozen others. Editor's introduction. xxii + 199pp. 5⅜ x 8½.
T767 Paperbound $1.50

THREE GOTHIC NOVELS, *edited by E. F. Bleiler*
Originators of the still popular Gothic novel form, influential in ushering in early 19th-century Romanticism. Horace Walpole's *Castle of Otranto*, William Beckford's *Vathek*, John Polidori's *The Vampyre*, and a *Fragment* by Lord Byron are enjoyable as exciting reading or as documents in the history of English literature. Editor's introduction. xi + 291pp. 5⅜ x 8½.
T1232 Paperbound $2.00

BEST GHOST STORIES OF LEFANU, *edited by E. F. Bleiler*
Though admired by such critics as V. S. Pritchett, Charles Dickens and Henry James, ghost stories by the Irish novelist Joseph Sheridan LeFanu have never become as widely known as his detective fiction. About half of the 16 stories in this collection have never before been available in America. Collection includes "Carmilla" (perhaps the best vampire story ever written), "The Haunted Baronet," "The Fortunes of Sir Robert Ardagh," and the classic "Green Tea." Editor's introduction. 7 contemporary illustrations. Portrait of LeFanu. xii + 467pp. 5⅜ x 8.
T415 Paperbound $2.50

EASY-TO-DO ENTERTAINMENTS AND DIVERSIONS WITH COINS, CARDS, STRING, PAPER AND MATCHES, *R. M. Abraham*
Over 300 tricks, games and puzzles will provide young readers with absorbing fun. Sections on card games; paper-folding; tricks with coins, matches and pieces of string; games for the agile; toy-making from common household objects; mathematical recreations; and 50 miscellaneous pastimes. Anyone in charge of groups of youngsters, including hard-pressed parents, and in need of suggestions on how to keep children sensibly amused and quietly content will find this book indispensable. Clear, simple text, copious number of delightful line drawings and illustrative diagrams. Originally titled "Winter Nights' Entertainments." Introduction by Lord Baden Powell. 329 illustrations. v + 186pp. 5⅜ x 8½. T921 Paperbound $1.00

AN INTRODUCTION TO CHESS MOVES AND TACTICS SIMPLY EXPLAINED, *Leonard Barden*
Beginner's introduction to the royal game. Names, possible moves of the pieces, definitions of essential terms, how games are won, etc. explained in 30-odd pages. With this background you'll be able to sit right down and play. Balance of book teaches strategy — openings, middle game, typical endgame play, and suggestions for improving your game. A sample game is fully analyzed. True middle level introduction, teaching you all the essentials without oversimplifying or losing you in a maze of detail. 58 figures. 102pp. 5⅜ x 8½. T1210 Paperbound $1.25

LASKER'S MANUAL OF CHESS, *Dr. Emanuel Lasker*
Probably the greatest chess player of modern times, Dr. Emanuel Lasker held the world championship 28 years, independent of passing schools or fashions. This unmatched study of the game, chiefly for intermediate to skilled players, analyzes basic methods, combinations, position play, the aesthetics of chess, dozens of different openings, etc., with constant reference to great modern games. Contains a brilliant exposition of Steinitz's important theories. Introduction by Fred Reinfeld. Tables of Lasker's tournament record. 3 indices. 308 diagrams. 1 photograph. xxx + 349pp. 5⅜ x 8. T640 Paperbound $2.50

COMBINATIONS: THE HEART OF CHESS, *Irving Chernev*
Step-by-step from simple combinations to complex, this book, by a well-known chess writer, shows you the intricacies of pins, counter-pins, knight forks, and smothered mates. Other chapters show alternate lines of play to those taken in actual championship games; boomerang combinations; classic examples of brilliant combination play by Nimzovich, Rubinstein, Tarrasch, Botvinnik, Alekhine and Capablanca. Index. 356 diagrams. ix + 245pp. 5⅜ x 8½. T1744 Paperbound $2.00

HOW TO SOLVE CHESS PROBLEMS, *K. S. Howard*
Full of practical suggestions for the fan or the beginner — who knows only the moves of the chessmen. Contains preliminary section and 58 two-move, 46 three-move, and 8 four-move problems composed by 27 outstanding American problem creators in the last 30 years. Explanation of all terms and exhaustive index. "Just what is wanted for the student," Brian Harley. 112 problems, solutions. vi + 171pp. 5⅜ x 8. T748 Paperbound $1.35

SOCIAL THOUGHT FROM LORE TO SCIENCE,
H. E. Barnes and H. Becker
An immense survey of sociological thought and ways of viewing, studying, planning, and reforming society from earliest times to the present. Includes thought on society of preliterate peoples, ancient non-Western cultures, and every great movement in Europe, America, and modern Japan. Analyzes hundreds of great thinkers: Plato, Augustine, Bodin, Vico, Montesquieu, Herder, Comte, Marx, etc. Weighs the contributions of utopians, sophists, fascists and communists; economists, jurists,˙ philosophers, ecclesiastics, and every 19th and 20th century school of scientific sociology, anthropology, and social psychology throughout the world. Combines topical, chronological, and regional approaches, treating the evolution of social thought as a process rather than as a series of mere topics. "Impressive accuracy, competence, and discrimination . . . easily the best single survey," *Nation.* Thoroughly revised, with new material up to 1960. 2 indexes. Over 2200 bibliographical notes. Three volume set. Total of 1586pp. 5⅜ x 8.
T901, T902, T903   Three volume set, paperbound $9.00

A HISTORY OF HISTORICAL WRITING, *Harry Elmer Barnes*
Virtually the only adequate survey of the whole course of historical writing in a single volume. Surveys developments from the beginnings of historiography in the ancient Near East and the Classical World, up through the Cold War. Covers major historians in detail, shows interrelationship with cultural background, makes clear individual contributions, evaluates and estimates importance; also enormously rich upon minor authors and thinkers who are usually passed over. Packed with scholarship and learning, clear, easily written. Indispensable to every student of history. Revised and enlarged up to 1961. Index and bibliography. xv + 442pp. 5⅜ x 8½.
T104   Paperbound $2.50

JOHANN SEBASTIAN BACH, *Philipp Spitta*
The complete and unabridged text of the definitive study of Bach. Written some 70 years ago, it is still unsurpassed for its coverage of nearly all aspects of Bach's life and work. There could hardly be a finer non-technical introduction to Bach's music than the detailed, lucid analyses which Spitta provides for hundreds of individual pieces. 26 solid pages are devoted to the B minor mass, for example, and 30 pages to the glorious St. Matthew Passion. This monumental set also includes a major analysis of the music of the 18th century: Buxtehude, Pachelbel, etc. "Unchallenged as the last word on one of the supreme geniuses of music," John Barkham, *Saturday Review Syndicate.* Total of 1819pp. Heavy cloth binding. 5⅜ x 8.
T252   Two volume set, clothbound $15.00

BEETHOVEN AND HIS NINE SYMPHONIES, *George Grove*
In this modern middle-level classic of musicology Grove not only analyzes all nine of Beethoven's symphonies very thoroughly in terms of their musical structure, but also discusses the circumstances under which they were written, Beethoven's stylistic development, and much other background material. This is an extremely rich book, yet very easily followed; it is highly recommended to anyone seriously interested in music. Over 250 musical passages. Index. viii + 407pp. 5⅜ x 8.   T334   Paperbound $2.25

THREE SCIENCE FICTION NOVELS,
John Taine
Acknowledged by many as the best SF writer of the 1920's, Taine (under the name Eric Temple Bell) was also a Professor of Mathematics of considerable renown. Reprinted here are *The Time Stream*, generally considered Taine's best, *The Greatest Game*, a biological-fiction novel, and *The Purple Sapphire*, involving a supercivilization of the past. Taine's stories tie fantastic narratives to frameworks of original and logical scientific concepts. Speculation is often profound on such questions as the nature of time, concept of entropy, cyclical universes, etc. 4 contemporary illustrations. v + 532pp. 5⅜ x 8⅜.

T1180 Paperbound $2.00

SEVEN SCIENCE FICTION NOVELS,
H. G. Wells
Full unabridged texts of 7 science-fiction novels of the master. Ranging from biology, physics, chemistry, astronomy, to sociology and other studies, Mr. Wells extrapolates whole worlds of strange and intriguing character. "One will have to go far to match this for entertainment, excitement, and sheer pleasure . . ."*New York Times*. Contents: The Time Machine, The Island of Dr. Moreau, The First Men in the Moon, The Invisible Man, The War of the Worlds, The Food of the Gods, In The Days of the Comet. 1015pp. 5⅜ x 8.

T264 Clothbound $5.00

28 SCIENCE FICTION STORIES OF H. G. WELLS.
Two full, unabridged novels, *Men Like Gods* and *Star Begotten*, plus 26 short stories by the master science-fiction writer of all time! Stories of space, time, invention, exploration, futuristic adventure. Partial contents: *The Country of the Blind, In the Abyss, The Crystal Egg, The Man Who Could Work Miracles, A Story of Days to Come, The Empire of the Ants, The Magic Shop, The Valley of the Spiders, A Story of the Stone Age, Under the Knife, Sea Raiders*, etc. An indispensable collection for the library of anyone interested in science fiction adventure. 928pp. 5⅜ x 8.

T265 Clothbound $5.00

THREE MARTIAN NOVELS,
Edgar Rice Burroughs
Complete, unabridged reprinting, in one volume, of Thuvia, Maid of Mars; Chessmen of Mars; The Master Mind of Mars. Hours of science-fiction adventure by a modern master storyteller. Reset in large clear type for easy reading. 16 illustrations by J. Allen St. John. vi + 499pp. 5⅜ x 8½.

T39 Paperbound $2.50

AN INTELLECTUAL AND CULTURAL HISTORY OF THE WESTERN WORLD,
Harry Elmer Barnes
Monumental 3-volume survey of intellectual development of Europe from primitive cultures to the present day. Every significant product of human intellect traced through history: art, literature, mathematics, physical sciences, medicine, music, technology, social sciences, religions, jurisprudence, education, etc. Presentation is lucid and specific, analyzing in detail specific discoveries, theories, literary works, and so on. Revised (1965) by recognized scholars in specialized fields under the direction of Prof. Barnes. Revised bibliography. Indexes. 24 illustrations. Total of xxix + 1318pp.

T1275, T1276, T1277 Three volume set, paperbound $7.50

HEAR ME TALKIN' TO YA, *edited by Nat Shapiro and Nat Hentoff*
In their own words, Louis Armstrong, King Oliver, Fletcher Henderson, Bunk Johnson, Bix Beiderbecke, Billy Holiday, Fats Waller, Jelly Roll Morton, Duke Ellington, and many others comment on the origins of jazz in New Orleans and its growth in Chicago's South Side, Kansas City's jam sessions, Depression Harlem, and the modernism of the West Coast schools. Taken from taped conversations, letters, magazine articles, other first-hand sources. Editors' introduction. xvi + 429pp. 5⅜ x 8½. T1726 Paperbound $2.00

THE JOURNAL OF HENRY D. THOREAU
A 25-year record by the great American observer and critic, as complete a record of a great man's inner life as is anywhere available. Thoreau's Journals served him as raw material for his formal pieces, as a place where he could develop his ideas, as an outlet for his interests in wild life and plants, in writing as an art, in classics of literature, Walt Whitman and other contemporaries, in politics, slavery, individual's relation to the State, etc. The Journals present a portrait of a remarkable man, and are an observant social history. Unabridged republication of 1906 edition, Bradford Torrey and Francis H. Allen, editors. Illustrations. Total of 1888pp. 8⅜ x 12¼.
T312, T313 Two volume set, clothbound $25.00

A SHAKESPEARIAN GRAMMAR, *E. A. Abbott*
Basic reference to Shakespeare and his contemporaries, explaining through thousands of quotations from Shakespeare, Jonson, Beaumont and Fletcher, North's *Plutarch* and other sources the grammatical usage differing from the modern. First published in 1870 and written by a scholar who spent much of his life isolating principles of Elizabethan language, the book is unlikely ever to be superseded. Indexes. xxiv + 511pp. 5⅜ x 8½. T1582 Paperbound $2.75

FOLK-LORE OF SHAKESPEARE, *T. F. Thistelton Dyer*
Classic study, drawing from Shakespeare a large body of references to supernatural beliefs, terminology of falconry and hunting, games and sports, good luck charms, marriage customs, folk medicines, superstitions about plants, animals, birds, argot of the underworld, sexual slang of London, proverbs, drinking customs, weather lore, and much else. From full compilation comes a mirror of the 17th-century popular mind. Index. ix + 526pp. 5⅜ x 8½.
T1614 Paperbound $2.75

THE NEW VARIORUM SHAKESPEARE, *edited by H. H. Furness*
By far the richest editions of the plays ever produced in any country or language. Each volume contains complete text (usually First Folio) of the play, all variants in Quarto and other Folio texts, editorial changes by every major editor to Furness's own time (1900), footnotes to obscure references or language, extensive quotes from literature of Shakespearian criticism, essays on plot sources (often reprinting sources in full), and much more.

HAMLET, *edited by H. H. Furness*
Total of xxvi + 905pp. 5⅜ x 8½.
T1004, T1005 Two volume set, paperbound $5.25

TWELFTH NIGHT, *edited by H. H. Furness*
Index. xxii + 434pp. 5⅜ x 8½. T1189 Paperbound $2.75

LA BOHEME BY GIACOMO PUCCINI,
translated and introduced by Ellen H. Bleiler
Complete handbook for the operagoer, with everything needed for full enjoyment except the musical score itself. Complete Italian libretto, with new, modern English line-by-line translation—the only libretto printing all repeats; biography of Puccini; the librettists; background to the opera, Murger's La Boheme, etc.; circumstances of composition and performances; plot summary; and pictorial section of 73 illustrations showing Puccini, famous singers and performances, etc. Large clear type for easy reading. 124pp. 5⅜ x 8½.

T404 Paperbound $1.25

ANTONIO STRADIVARI: HIS LIFE AND WORK (1644-1737),
W. Henry Hill, Arthur F. Hill, and Alfred E. Hill
Still the only book that really delves into life and art of the incomparable Italian craftsman, maker of the finest musical instruments in the world today. The authors, expert violin-makers themselves, discuss Stradivari's ancestry, his construction and finishing techniques, distinguished characteristics of many of his instruments and their locations. Included, too, is story of introduction of his instruments into France, England, first revelation of their supreme merit, and information on his labels, number of instruments made, prices, mystery of ingredients of his varnish, tone of pre-1684 Stradivari violin and changes between 1684 and 1690. An extremely interesting, informative account for all music lovers, from craftsman to concert-goer. Republication of original (1902) edition. New introduction by Sydney Beck, Head of Rare Book and Manuscript Collections, Music Division, New York Public Library. Analytical index by Rembert Wurlitzer. Appendixes. 68 illustrations. 30 full-page plates. 4 in color. xxvi + 315pp. 5⅜ x 8½. T425 Paperbound $2.25

MUSICAL AUTOGRAPHS FROM MONTEVERDI TO HINDEMITH,
Emanuel Winternitz
For beauty, for intrinsic interest, for perspective on the composer's personality, for subtleties of phrasing, shading, emphasis indicated in the autograph but suppressed in the printed score, the mss. of musical composition are fascinating documents which repay close study in many different ways. This 2-volume work reprints facsimiles of mss. by virtually every major composer, and many minor figures—196 examples in all. A full text points out what can be learned from mss., analyzes each sample. Index. Bibliography. 18 figures. 196 plates. Total of 170pp. of text. 7⅞ x 10¾.

T1312, T1313 Two volume set, paperbound $5.00

J. S. BACH,
Albert Schweitzer
One of the few great full-length studies of Bach's life and work, and the study upon which Schweitzer's renown as a musicologist rests. On first appearance (1911), revolutionized Bach performance. The only writer on Bach to be musicologist, performing musician, and student of history, theology and philosophy, Schweitzer contributes particularly full sections on history of German Protestant church music, theories on motivic pictorial representations in vocal music, and practical suggestions for performance. Translated by Ernest Newman. Indexes. 5 illustrations. 650 musical examples. Total of xix + 928pp. 5⅜ x 8½. T1631, T1632 Two volume set, paperbound $4.50

THE METHODS OF ETHICS, *Henry Sidgwick*
Propounding no organized system of its own, study subjects every major methodological approach to ethics to rigorous, objective analysis. Study discusses and relates ethical thought of Plato, Aristotle, Bentham, Clarke, Butler, Hobbes, Hume, Mill, Spencer, Kant, and dozens of others. Sidgwick retains conclusions from each system which follow from ethical premises, rejecting the faulty. Considered by many in the field to be among the most important treatises on ethical philosophy. Appendix. Index. xlvii + 528pp. 5⅜ x 8½.
T1608 Paperbound $2.50

TEUTONIC MYTHOLOGY, *Jakob Grimm*
A milestone in Western culture; the work which established on a modern basis the study of history of religions and comparative religions. 4-volume work assembles and interprets everything available on religious and folk-loristic beliefs of Germanic people (including Scandinavians, Anglo-Saxons, etc.). Assembling material from such sources as Tacitus, surviving Old Norse and Icelandic texts, archeological remains, folktales, surviving superstitions, comparative traditions, linguistic analysis, etc. Grimm explores pagan deities, heroes, folklore of nature, religious practices, and every other area of pagan German belief. To this day, the unrivaled, definitive, exhaustive study. Translated by J. S. Stallybrass from 4th (1883) German edition. Indexes. Total of lxxvii + 1887pp. 5⅜ x 8½.
T1602, T1603, T1604, T1605 Four volume set, paperbound $11.00

THE I CHING, *translated by James Legge*
Called "The Book of Changes" in English, this is one of the Five Classics edited by Confucius, basic and central to Chinese thought. Explains perhaps the most complex system of divination known, founded on the theory that all things happening at any one time have characteristic features which can be isolated and related. Significant in Oriental studies, in history of religions and philosophy, and also to Jungian psychoanalysis and other areas of modern European thought. Index. Appendixes. 6 plates. xxi + 448pp. 5⅜ x 8½.
T1062 Paperbound $2.75

HISTORY OF ANCIENT PHILOSOPHY, *W. Windelband*
One of the clearest, most accurate comprehensive surveys of Greek and Roman philosophy. Discusses ancient philosophy in general, intellectual life in Greece in the 7th and 6th centuries B.C., Thales, Anaximander, Anaximenes, Heraclitus, the Eleatics, Empedocles, Anaxagoras, Leucippus, the Pythagoreans, the Sophists, Socrates, Democritus (20 pages), Plato (50 pages), Aristotle (70 pages), the Peripatetics, Stoics, Epicureans, Sceptics, Neo-platonists, Christian Apologists, etc. 2nd German edition translated by H. E. Cushman. xv + 393pp. 5⅜ x 8.
T357 Paperbound $2.25

THE PALACE OF PLEASURE, *William Painter*
Elizabethan versions of Italian and French novels from *The Decameron*, Cinthio, Straparola, Queen Margaret of Navarre, and other continental sources — the very work that provided Shakespeare and dozens of his contemporaries with many of their plots and sub-plots and, therefore, justly considered one of the most influential books in all English literature. It is also a book that any reader will still enjoy. Total of cviii + 1,224pp.
T1691, T1692, T1693 Three volume set, paperbound $6.75

THE WONDERFUL WIZARD OF OZ, *L. F. Baum*
All the original W. W. Denslow illustrations in full color—as much a part of "The Wizard" as Tenniel's drawings are of "Alice in Wonderland." "The Wizard" is still America's best-loved fairy tale, in which, as the author expresses it, "The wonderment and joy are retained and the heartaches and nightmares left out." Now today's young readers can enjoy every word and wonderful picture of the original book. New introduction by Martin Gardner. A Baum bibliography. 23 full-page color plates. viii + 268pp. 5⅜ x 8.
T691 Paperbound $1.75

THE MARVELOUS LAND OF OZ, *L. F. Baum*
This is the equally enchanting sequel to the "Wizard," continuing the adventures of the Scarecrow and the Tin Woodman. The hero this time is a little boy named Tip, and all the delightful Oz magic is still present. This is the Oz book with the Animated Saw-Horse, the Woggle-Bug, and Jack Pumpkinhead. All the original John R. Neill illustrations, 10 in full color. 287pp. 5⅜ x 8.
T692 Paperbound $1.75

ALICE'S ADVENTURES UNDER GROUND, *Lewis Carroll*
The original *Alice in Wonderland*, hand-lettered and illustrated by Carroll himself, and originally presented as a Christmas gift to a child-friend. Adults as well as children will enjoy this charming volume, reproduced faithfully in this Dover edition. While the story is essentially the same, there are slight changes, and Carroll's spritely drawings present an intriguing alternative to the famous Tenniel illustrations. One of the most popular books in Dover's catalogue. Introduction by Martin Gardner. 38 illustrations. 128pp. 5⅜ x 8½.
T1482 Paperbound $1.00

THE NURSERY "ALICE," *Lewis Carroll*
While most of us consider *Alice in Wonderland* a story for children of all ages, Carroll himself felt it was beyond younger children. He therefore provided this simplified version, illustrated with the famous Tenniel drawings enlarged and colored in delicate tints, for children aged "from Nought to Five." Dover's edition of this now rare classic is a faithful copy of the 1889 printing, including 20 illustrations by Tenniel, and front and back covers reproduced in full color. Introduction by Martin Gardner. xxiii + 67pp. 6⅛ x 9¼.
T1610 Paperbound $1.75

THE STORY OF KING ARTHUR AND HIS KNIGHTS, *Howard Pyle*
A fast-paced, exciting retelling of the best known Arthurian legends for young readers by one of America's best story tellers and illustrators. The sword Excalibur, wooing of Guinevere, Merlin and his downfall, adventures of Sir Pellias and Gawaine, and others. The pen and ink illustrations are vividly imagined and wonderfully drawn. 41 illustrations. xviii + 313pp. 6⅛ x 9¼.
T1445 Paperbound $1.75

Prices subject to change without notice.

Available at your book dealer or write for free catalogue to Dept. Adsci, Dover Publications, Inc., 180 Varick St., N.Y., N.Y. 10014. Dover publishes more than 150 books each year on science, elementary and advanced mathematics, biology, music, art, literary history, social sciences and other areas.